WITHDRAWN

To Print the News and Raise Hell!

Publication of this book was sponsored by the American Association for State and Local History, Nashville, Tennessee, under its continuing program to promote a better understanding of our national heritage at a local level. It is the recipient of the Association's Manuscript Award for 1967.

Wilbur F. Storey in 1868

"A Bacchus, A Satyr, A Minotaur, all in one."

Courtesy Chicago Historical Society

TO PRINT THE NEWS AND RAISE HELL!

A Biography of Wilbur F. Storey

by

JUSTIN E. WALSH

THE UNIVERSITY OF NORTH CAROLINA PRESS
Chapel Hill

Manufactured in the United States of America
Library of Congress Catalog Card Number 68-25913
Printed by The Seeman Printery, Durham, N. C.

FOR CY:

"Printing was the one art in which he excelled!"

Preface

THIS BOOK WAS WRITTEN BECAUSE PROFESSOR R. CARLYLE BULEY OF Indiana University directed my attention to Wilbur F. Storey in the spring of 1957. "You ought to look into Storey," Professor Buley advised. "Any man who cursed as colorfully and frequently, both in print and out, as Storey did, should be interesting."

I soon discovered that the only route to a biography of Storey was through the columns of the newspapers he left behind because none of his personal papers was preserved. This route involved several years of turning yellowed newspaper pages. Among the people and institutions who helped as the work progressed, first thanks are due to Brother Luke Azarius, F.S.C., and the staff of the Fitzgerald Library at St. Mary's College, Winona, Minnesota.

Mr. James M. Babcock, Chief of the Burton Historical Collection in the Detroit Public Library, Mr. Lewis Beeson, Executive Secretary of the Michigan Historical Commission in Lansing, and Mr. John Cumming, Director of the Clarke Historical Library, Mount Pleasant, Michigan, helped in uncovering materials on Storey's Michigan career.

Mrs. Mabel Stanfield, Curator, Northern Indiana Historical Museum, South Bend, recounted her memories of picnics at the old Chapin house where as a very young girl she heard talk about "that terrible man in Chicago" who was "related in some way to the Chapins." Her knowledge of South Bend newspapers was invaluable in unraveling a complicated family relationship.

Miss Margaret Flint, Assistant State Historian, Illinois State Historical Society, Springfield, and Mr. Biagino M. Marone, Director of the newspaper section of the State Historical Society of Wisconsin at Madison, sent microfilm files of the *Chicago Times* and *Detroit Free Press* on terms that made an exhaustive examination of each roll possible.

Miss Clara E. Follette, Librarian, Vermont Historical Society, Montpelier, saved me much time and expense in tracing the genealogy of the Storey family in America. Thanks also go to Mr. Archie Motley, Manuscript Librarian, and Mrs. Paul Rhymer, Curator of Prints, Chicago Historical Society, for their help in locating manuscripts and photographs dealing with Storey.

Brother J. Robert Lane, F.S.C., Chairman of the History Department at St. Mary's College, was a patient and understanding colleague. Professors Donald F. Carmony and Oscar O. Winther of Indiana University were both generous with advice and suggestions. Professors Frederick H. Schapsmeier and Robert J. Chaffin, colleagues at Wisconsin State University, Oshkosh, read the work in manuscript form and spotted many errors of commission and omission. Mrs. Judy Chaffin of Oshkosh merits special thanks for her careful typing of the final manuscript.

The greatest debt of all is due my wife, Mary Sue, who "lived" with Wilbur F. Storey for almost a decade, and as a dutiful "mistress" suffered deprivations without number, and almost without complaint. I join with my daughter Ramona in giving thanks that with her mother's constant help, "Daddy's Wilbur Fisk storybook" is finally finished.

In 1928, the late Professor Frederick Logan Paxson stated:

> A historian should work fully through the background material. That would be a prolonged task involving many weary hours of turning newspaper pages and exploring local and in-themselves unimportant political events. But without such a study it is impossible to prepare a biography of . . . historical importance.

It was in the spirit of Paxson's advice that this work was carried to completion. As a pioneer biography of a prominent man, the book undoubtedly contains lapses, gaps, and weaknesses of emphasis and interpretation. With no guidelines other than the newspapers Storey left behind, such shortcomings were unavoidable. My major focus is on the essential facts regarding the life and career of Wilbur F. Storey. No attempt is made to draw grand lessons of universal significance. An attempt has been made, however, to avoid distortion and serve truth. The man who emerges in what follows is the Wilbur F. Storey I found buried in the pages of the forgotten newspapers he published from 1838 to 1884.

This work grows out of the Midwestern Studies Program established at Indiana University by the late Professor Logan Esarey, as continued and expanded by Professors R. Carlyle Buley, John D. Barnhart and Donald F. Carmony. It has been my privilege to work with these last three men in the rich soil of the midwestern past. It is my hope that this book makes a contribution to the history of the area they know so well, while doing honor to the historical tradition they have served.

JUSTIN E. WALSH

Oshkosh, Wisconsin
December, 1967

Table of Contents

List of Illustrations

To Print the News and Raise Hell!

CHAPTER I

To Print the News and Raise Hell!

It is a newspaper's duty to print the news, and raise hell.

—Wilbur F. Storey, Statement of the aims of the *Chicago Times*, June, 1861.

AT 2:00 A.M. ON JUNE 3, 1863, THE STILLNESS OF NIGHT AT 74 Randolph Street in Chicago was broken only by the steady humming of a newspaper press "still working and throwing off the edition." Inside the two-story wooden frame building that housed the *Chicago Times* at that address, a white-maned editor whose full beard and wrinkled forehead belied his forty-four years, put the finishing touches on the day's lead editorial. "If the reader shall receive this paper," he noted, "it will have been printed before the arrival of the threatened military force."

At quarter-past three, a military company from nearby Fort Douglas surrounded the building, "and with fixed bayonets lined up and down the street on each side of the block." At exactly 5:00 A.M. the soldiers "burst in the rear door of the establishment and ordered the presses to be stopped." A large number of newspapers was seized and taken into the street where the officer in charge ordered his men to tear each into shreds. For the next thirty-seven hours, the *Chicago Times* was in the possession of the United States Army.[1]

This event, which highlighted a bizarre and raucous career in American journalism, was described by the editor as "one of the leading events in the history of this rebellion."[2] He spoke with some truth, for this suppression of a leading Democratic newspaper was one of the more noteworthy occurrences in Chicago during the Civil War. Today, the editor is mainly remembered as a "damned Copperhead" who published a "treason sheet."

Yet Wilbur Fisk Storey was certainly more than this. For almost half a century, from 1838 to 1884, he cut a swath through the untamed prairies of the Old Northwest, establishing newspapers that would, in his words, "print the news and raise hell!" From La Porte and Mishawaka in Indiana, through Jackson and Detroit in Michigan, to final notoriety and fame in Chicago, Storey created a brand of journalism calculated to bring him curses and infamy, money and circulation. At the same time his readers received news and sensation on a scale grander than the region had ever before known.

With the exception of his Civil War activities, Storey has been almost totally ignored by historians. The spokesman for Michigan Democracy, perhaps for the Democracy of the entire Northwest, for a decade before the war when he edited the *Detroit Free Press*, his Detroit career rarely receives more than a sentence indicating that he was a "successful" publisher before he moved to Chicago. Yet Storey witnessed the formalization of "black Republicanism" at Jackson, Michigan, on July 6, 1854. Storey dubbed this "fusion" party "the bastard offspring of illicit intercourse and the faulty amalgamation of incompatible genes."[3] He fought the good Democratic battle for the popular sovereignty scheme enunciated in the Kansas-Nebraska Act. He steadily defended Catholics and immigrants against "the outrages of Know-Nothingism." In Detroit, of course, the Irish and German immigrants habitually voted the Democratic ticket. He constantly blasted temperance reformers, "political preachers," and abolitionists in a way that the supposedly

1. *Chicago Times*, June 3 and June 6, 1863.
2. *Ibid.*, June 6, 1863.
3. *Detroit Free Press*, July 13, 1854.

more refined twentieth century would find outrageous. A pleader for "temperance in all things," he forgot the meaning of the word if anybody disagreed with Wilbur F. Storey.

That Storey was somewhat more than a "successful" publisher in Detroit is apparent from evidence in a few attempts made to examine, if only in a cursory fashion, his Detroit career. An early study stated that Storey "had a wider fame and fewer friends than any other newspaperman in Michigan."[4] In 1926 George Catlin described the editor as "a firebrand political advocate . . . adept in the use of a vast vocabulary of vituperation" who made a live newspaper with the support of an unthinking public "which enjoyed his savage diatribes as they would have enjoyed a dog-fight or the punishment of a fellow creature at the whipping post."[5] Clarence M. Burton went even further. "Under Storey's managership," Burton asserted, "the *Free Press* became one of the most profitable newspaper properties of the time and one of the strongest publications in the country."[6]

Although Storey's Detroit policy has never before been subjected to a detailed analysis, these evaluations are essentially correct. In the pages that follow, every facet of the *Free Press* under Storey's guidance is examined. From February 15, 1853, when "Wilbur F. Storey, Editor and Publisher" first appeared on the masthead, until June 4, 1861, the day on which Storey left Detroit for the more lucrative field of Chicago newspaperdom, he led a Democratic crusade against the abolitionist movement and the new Republican party. He promised in his *Free Press* prospectus to be "radically and thoroughly *democratic*." The story of the newspaper he sired in the keeping of this pledge constitutes an important chapter in the history of partisan journalism during the 1850s.

But over and above his politicking in Detroit, Storey was first a newspaper publisher who had to sell his product to survive. He believed, correctly judging by his Detroit success, that the public would buy that which it found interesting. Whatever else might be said of Storey's *Free Press*, it certainly was interesting. In its columns the story of the "Rochester rappings mania" (spiritualism) of the 1850s was preserved. American experiments in "Fourierism"

4. William Stocking, "Prominent Newspaper Men in Michigan," *Michigan Pioneer and Historical Collections*, XXXIX (Lansing, 1915), 156.

5. George B. Catlin, "Little Journeys in Journalism: Wilbur F. Storey," *Michigan History*, X (October, 1926), 522.

6. Clarence M. and Agnes Burton, *History of Wayne County and the City of Detroit, Michigan* (Detroit: S. J. Clarke & Co., 1930), I, 642.

were covered and ridiculed. An ardent Anglophobe, Storey covered the Crimean War in support of "Christian" Russia against English "hypocrites" allied with "heathen" Turks. It was also in the columns of the *Free Press* that Storey first experimented with the popular, sensationalized journalism that made the *Chicago Times* a widely read newspaper after the Civil War.

Most important of all, in the context of Storey's entire career, his excesses as a Copperhead firebrand are inexplicable unless his Detroit career is examined. Underneath all of his vitriol and vituperation lay a sincere patriotism, a radical Americanism as he understood Americanism, and a real, though certainly extreme, plea for justice in terms of Democracy (with a big D), the Constitution and sanity. He never considered the possibility that democracy might be realized, the Constitution upheld, or sanity prevail on terms other than those approved by Wilbur F. Storey. A passionate advocate of state rights, he viewed the election of Abraham Lincoln as a betrayal of everything he lived for and believed in. He was also an extreme Negrophobe, and his reaction to the Emancipation Proclamation was predictable in the light of his Detroit policy. When "Old Abe," the possessor of "whatsoever in human nature is false, treacherous, weak and cowardly," was elevated to the Presidency, Storey responded with the best weapons at his command: a poison pen and a penchant for invective which blackened him in the eyes of history.

The *Chicago Times* between 1861 and 1884 became a powerful newspaper. During the Civil War its coverage of the Army of the West under General Ulysses S. Grant was unequaled by any competitor, a fact frequently obscured because of Storey's sensational attack on Abraham Lincoln. In America's "Gilded Age" after the war, when "The World's Greatest Newspaper" (the *Tribune*) was not even the greatest in Chicago, the *Times* pioneered the modern Sunday newspaper. In competition with Joseph Medill, heretofore recognized as the leader in postwar Chicago journalism, Storey remained one step ahead of the *Tribune* for almost a quarter of a century. Although these things were true, and acknowledged by even his rivals when he died, Wilbur F. Storey has received little recognition for his accomplishments. When he is remembered at all, it is only to note that he said mean things about Abraham Lincoln and composed a headline in which he took the Lord's name in vain.

Storey deserves a more important niche in the history of nineteenth-century journalism, a niche that his forty-six years of influence and innovation justly earned him. It was Storey, the colorful but erratic newspaperman, who established a "female seminary" for typesetters in 1864, when he secretly hired and schooled forty lady typographers rather than succumb to the wage claims of the Chicago Typographical Union. In 1870 five members of the Lydia Thompson Burlesque Troupe horsewhipped "the dirty old scoundrel" while he strolled on Wabash Avenue. The ladies were upset by certain "aspersions" *Times* editorials cast on their virtue. While the caning and beating of newspapermen was "old hat" to nineteenth-century journalism, Storey was unique as the only editor publicly whipped by burlesque dancers.

If his life was unorthodox, so too was his journalism. Weary of the routine reporting of a killer's last-second repentance as the rope tightened around his neck, Storey's *Times* shocked the sensibilities of Chicagoans in 1875 with the bold, black, blasphemous announcement that the murderer was "JERKED TO JESUS!"[7] At the other extreme, when a revision of the New Testament appeared in 1881, the *Times* published the entire version in a single issue.[8]

The level of sensationalism Storey reached in the 1870s was not exceeded until Joseph Pulitzer and William Randolph Hearst became famous. It is doubtful if even these masters of muck would have outdistanced Storey had he enjoyed the technological advantages they commanded. The *Chicago Times* had no seminudes or blazing eight-column banners to dress up its pages and support its scandal-mongering. It made up for this with an excess of detail best described as half confession-magazine and half peep-show journalism. Divorce cases, murders, seductions and robberies were blazoned across the pages of Storey's newspapers under alliterative, epigrammatic headlines sure to catch the unthinking mob. The format and typography were always the most advanced that the technology of his day allowed. And legitimate news? As long as Storey lived the *Chicago Times* had no peer in the city for the widest coverage of up-to-date news from all over the world.

In July, 1853, Storey reviewed a medical journal published by the University of Michigan and observed that "quackery in physic, in politics, in temperance, and in religion" were all in one category. "We go for the Church of Jesus Christ, the Democratic

7. *Chicago Times*, November 27, 1875.
8. *Chicago Sunday Times*, May 22, 1881.

party, the Legitimate Practice of Medicine, and Temperance in All Things!" he asserted. "If men would adhere to these, they would live a healthy and happy life here, and be blessed hereafter."[9] Storey insisted that these four were the only things in life that good men should "go for." Ironically, in a career that spanned forty-six years, he ultimately adherred to none of them.

When Wilbur Storey spoke of the Church of Jesus Christ, he meant any church that remained apolitical while preaching the gospel as the editor felt it should be preached. With the exception of a two-year period immediately following his first marriage in 1847, he remained personally "unchurched" throughout his life. But this did not prevent him from maintaining a constant watch on religious developments while he delivered homilies on the real meaning of the Christian ethic. During the 1850s he penned a convincing series of essays on religious toleration to combat the excesses of the Know-Nothing movement. Then, after his mind began to crack in the late 1860s, he converted this interest in "the Christian churches" into a cynicism that approached blasphemy. Finally, with the editor's conversion to spiritualism after the death of his second wife in 1873, he made the *Chicago Times* the most prominent journalistic exponent of the spiritualist faith in the nation.

Storey's attachment to the Democratic party was deeper and more passionate than his adherence to any religious creed, but this too proved ephemeral, killed finally by the disaster visited upon that party by the Civil War. Storey began his newspaper career in 1838, when the Democratic party of La Porte County, Indiana, needed a sounding board for the Congressional election. For four years he championed the party's cause despite the fact that Democracy was an unprofitable undertaking in the Whig territory of northern Indiana. In the 1840s, Storey improved and perfected his ability as a partisan journalist with the *Jackson* (Michigan) *Patriot*. He proved so effective that the state party surrendered control of its official organ, the *Detroit Free Press*, to the thirty-four year old Jacksonite in 1853. For the next eight-and-one-half years Storey was bombastic in support of Stephen A. Douglas and popular sovereignty. When the Civil War erupted, he moved to Chicago and achieved lasting notoriety as the editorial leader of midwestern Copperheads. But once the war ended, Storey forsook his Democratic affiliation as he made the *Chicago*

9. *Detroit Free Press*, July 23, 1853.

Times an "independent" journal. He never returned to the party's fold, and died just six days before Grover Cleveland was elected President, the first Democrat since James Buchanan to hold that office.

Storey's interest in "the Legitimate Practice of Medicine" proved likewise evanescent. In the 1850s he regularly denounced the "Homeopathic" movement amongst doctors, but in 1873 he assaulted the medical profession when "spirits" informed him during a seance that a Chicago physican was directly responsible for his wife's death. The Chicago Board of Physicians denounced Storey as "being ignorant of medicine" because of his stand, and so he remained suspicious of doctors and drugs for the remainder of his life.

The most ironic tenet of all was Storey's plea for "Temperance in All Things." Both his personal life and his journalism proved that he did not understand the word. His newspapers, from the day he took over the *Detroit Free Press*, were blueprints of indiscretion. Nonetheless, Storey parlayed his original $3,000 investment in the *Free Press* into a million-dollar enterprise with the *Chicago Times* by 1875. The erraticism of his newspapers was mirrored in his private life. He was generally hated by almost everyone who had occasion to deal with him. He was married three times, but had no children. His propensity for private vice with abandoned women caused him to contract a syphilitic infection that led to slow insanity and total paralysis before his death. Through it all, Storey remained an innovator who set a new style for midwestern newspapers.

This man's story, as spectacular in achievement as it was repellent in many specific details, has never been told. And it should be, because Storey was the best-known editor in Chicago between 1861 and 1884. The pages that follow tell his story as it was culled from his newspapers, from the memoirs of various reporters and printers associated with him, and from pertinent public documents. The treatment is chronological, and throughout, those aspects of Storey's private life that touch upon his career as a journalist are incorporated into the narrative.

When Storey died, the Chicago *Arbeiter Zeitung*, organ of the radical socialists in the city, paid him respect. "Wilbur F. Storey was an exceptionally able journalist" who fought for his ideas "without regard for his life, his friends or his enemies." The tribute concluded with the ultimate compliment: "If he had been a socialist, instead of a capitalist, the coming revolution would be nearer upon us than it is now."[10] Storey would have sought no better eulogy than recognition by his enemies that "Wilbur F. Storey was an exceptionally able journalist."

10. Chicago *Arbeiter Zeitung*, as reprinted in the *Chicago Times*, October 30, 1884.

CHAPTER II

INDIANA:
An Editor Threatened!

Some basswood magistrate in La Porte, has threatened the Editor of the Herald with a personal chastisement, on account of some strictures in his columns upon his official conduct. Friend Storey, we have found a number of puppies who had the courage to *bark* at us, but none that ever dared to *bite*.

—*Goshen* (Indiana) *Democrat*,
December 5, 1839.

IN THE EARLY SPRING OF 1838, AN EIGHTEEN-YEAR-OLD "PRINTER'S devil" quit his bondage on the New York *Journal of Commerce* to join the Jacksonian migration then filling the empty reaches of the lower Great Lakes region of the Old Northwest. The financial panic made life precarious for aspiring printers on the eastern seaboard, and the call of the Golden West was more than this talented, supremely arrogant typesetter could resist. He was headed for South Bend, Indiana, and, on the surface, he was indistinguishable from thousands of others who made a like migration through the Erie Canal in the 1830s to build homes, establish fortunes, and create a civilization which in the next half-century would hold the political balance of the American Republic in its grasp.

Unlike many of the others, however, Wilbur Fisk Storey was destined, in the words of a contemporary, "to lead the spirit of enterprise as practically in the Northwest as if, with a thousand arms, he had cleared the forests with ten thousand hands and sowed the prairies." Before he died, he owned and edited the largest newspaper in the region, the *Chicago Times*, and he terrorized a great city of the West with his insanely vitriolic pen. Upon his death in 1884, a business and political rival noted quite accurately that Storey saw possibilities in the Northwest at a time when "its stillness was disturbed in vast areas only by the shrill cries of the creatures of the wood and rivers." More than any other newspaperman, Storey exploited latent opportunities as he secured correspondents "at every remote outpost" and sent "explorers for news" wherever needed in order to make the Northwest aware of its potential.

> In those days THE CHICAGO TIMES was the only newspaper known in a region where now stand majestic cities; if other newspapers are read in those cities today, they owe their fortune largely to following the example of Wilbur F. Storey in making a newspaper for people to read.[1]

Storey was born on a farm near Salisbury, Vermont, on December 18, 1819. He came from pioneer Vermont stock since his paternal grandfather, Solomon Storey, settled at Salisbury, "a wilderness at that time," in 1778. The first Storey to settle in America, William, was born at Norwich, Norfolk County, England, in 1614. William migrated to the Colonies in 1639, and is listed as an inhabitant of Chebaco Parish, Ipswich, Massachusetts, as early as 1641. Solomon, a fourth generation descendant of William, was born in Norwich, Connecticut, in 1726. "One of the original eight" who organized the Congregational Church at Salisbury, Solomon had four sons. The youngest, Jesse, born in Norwich in 1770, was the father of Wilbur F. Storey. When Solomon died at the age of ninety in 1816, Jesse took over the family farm, where he resided

1. Obituary of Wilbur F. Storey, *Chicago Herald*, October 28, 1884.

with his wife, Elizabeth Pierce, whom he had married on April 1, 1805.[2]

On the maternal side, the Pierces were originally from Holland, and family legend held that the Pierce women were especially noted as "housewives, dictators, and managers." Wilbur's grandfather, Samuel Pierce, a farmer, was born in Canaan, Connecticut, and moved to Salisbury in 1791. Wilbur was the fourth of six children born to Jesse and Elizabeth Pierce Storey. The others, in the order of their birth, were: Anson Lucien, Martha Emily, Mary Elizabeth, Marcus Aurelius and Henry Keeler. Only Anson and Mary survived at the time of Wilbur's death.[3]

The first ten years of Wilbur's life were passed on the family farm. Located three miles from town, "and within sight of the slopes and eternal skylines of the Green Mountains," it was an environment calculated to produce in the youngster the social aloofness that characterized his later life. His brother Anson, twelve years his senior, remembered Wilbur as a reserved, thoughtful youth, "very little given to play or association with other children." He was self-contained and self-reliant from earliest childhood, rather pale with deep, soft brown eyes, and he had "the air of a person many years his senior." Storey's reserve was regarded by other children as "an assumption on his part of a superiority in social and intellectual position" and he had no friends outside of the family circle.

When Wilbur was ten, his father sold the farm and moved the family to the village of Middlebury, where two years later, in 1831, the twelve-year-old boy entered a print shop for the first time when he was "bound out" to the office of the Middlebury *Free Press* as a journeyman printer. His formal schooling was limited to one term at the village academy. At the age of fifteen, "reserved in manner, indefatigable in work and study," he was remembered as "industrious, not looking for amusement, devoting all his spare time to reading."

Middlebury at that time had a public library, a college, and

2. For the genealogy of the Storey family see H. A. White, *A History of Rutland County, Vermont* (Montpelier: 1889), p. 762; and E. W. Salkeld, "The Story [*sic*] Family in Vermont" (MSS in the Vermont Historical Society Library, Montpelier).

3. For the genealogy of the Pierce family see obituary of Wilbur F. Storey, *Chicago Times,* October 28, 1884. The information on the family background and early childhood of Wilbur F. Storey in this obituary was provided by Anson L. Storey and Mary Storey Farrand.

"a cultivated population." The adolescent Storey enjoyed such advantages as could be acquired by contact with these things, and lacking formal education he, like so many other nineteenth-century editors of prominence, became self-made and self-educated. Years later, when he inquired of William M. Ferry regarding the educational background of Mort L. Hopkins, a *Chicago Times* associate, Ferry stated Hopkins' father "was a pioneer of our country. The extent of his library was the Bible, Rollin's Ancient History, Shakespere's [*sic*] Dramatic Works and the History of the United States." According to Ferry "Mr. Storey repeated the list and exclaimed, 'What more can a vigorous mind require?' "[4] The frequent references to the Bible, Shakespeare and the Founding Fathers in the columns of Storey's later newspapers would indicate that his own "course of education" must have been similar. That he had a vigorous mind, none would deny.

Storey stayed about five years in the *Free Press* shop, where he learned to set type under the supervision of the plant foreman. The paper was edited by Edward D. Barber, "a man whose main purpose at that time in the publication of a newspaper was opposition to Free Masonry." It is possible that Storey's lifelong opposition to the activities of secret societies, an opposition illustrated by his denunciations of the Know-Nothing movement while he edited the *Detroit Free Press* and his firm renunciation of the Knights of the Golden Circle during the Civil War, was acquired from the teachings of this paper. At any rate, he learned his trade rapidly and well and at seventeen he was sufficiently skillful and accurate to secure employment with the New York *Journal of Commerce*. He left Middlebury in 1836 with $17 in savings, a $10 gift from his mother, and "the blessing of both parents to make his way in the world." He never returned to Vermont, and he never saw his parents again.

The New York *Journal of Commerce* first exposed the young Vermonter to the Jacksonian political faith and a virulent racism, two tenets he held tenaciously until the end of the Civil War. Under the editorial direction of David Hale, it was for years one of New York's leading anti-abolition prints, and Hale himself impressed Story in a way no other editor ever succeeded in doing. Never one to praise any editor other than himself throughout his

4. William M. Ferry, "Ottawa's Old Settlers," *Michigan Pioneer and Historical Collections*, XXX (Lansing, 1906), 580-81.

career, Storey nevertheless saw fit to eulogize David Hale, when the latter died in 1849, as "a man of great moral worth" who "maintained a high character as a journalist and a citizen."[5] As editor of the *Detroit Free Press* in the 1850s Storey still considered the *Journal of Commerce* New York's most reliable newspaper and he lauded it as "an independent journal which has always maintained a correct position on the slavery question."[6]

Significant as was his ideological development, the tricks he learned about journalism in New York were even more important. In April, 1836, while Storey labored in the press room of the *Journal of Commerce*, James Gordon Bennett shored up his recently launched *Herald* by exploiting sex. Before either Joseph Pulitzer or William Randolph Hearst had been born, Bennett created that "sensational type of journalism which feeds upon sex, crime and scandal."

The occasion was the murder in a house of prostitution of a twenty-year-old streetwalker named Ellen Jewett. Bennett pulled all stops in his coverage of this "MOST ATROCIOUS MURDER." He treated readers to a "VISIT TO THE SCENE," with a detailed description of the house and corpse. "My God!" he wrote, "how like a statue! I can scarce believe that form to be a corpse." In the days that followed, *Herald* readers devoured a verbatim interview with the "madam" who discovered the body. For two months, the Ellen Jewett case kept New York buzzing while Bennett prospered as never before. And at the *Journal of Commerce* a young "typo" watched as thousands queued up daily at the *Herald* office, hungry for the latest salacious detail.[7]

Storey stayed only two years in New York, but long enough to "save a fund of $200" with which he set out for South Bend, Indiana. His older sister, Martha, had journeyed West in 1832 and settled in the village there where she taught school for three years. On December 24, 1835, she married Horatio Chapin. By 1838 when Wilbur joined them, the Chapins were well established as one of South Bend's leading pioneer families. An extended and tranquil visit, however, was probably impossible since Horatio Chapin, "a Whig, later a Republican, and an ardent Presbyterian,"

5. *Jackson Patriot*, January 30, 1849.
6. *Detroit Free Press*, January 12, 1854.
7. Oliver Carlson, *The Man Who Made News: James Gordon Bennett* (New York: Duell, Sloan and Pearce, 1942), see Chapter IX, "The Ellen Jewett Murder Case," pp. 143-57.

was not a man to tolerate the Jacksonian views of his upstart brother-in-law.[8]

Within a few weeks of his arrival in South Bend, Storey began publication of his first newspaper; in partnership with Edward Hannegan, register of the La Porte County land office, he founded the weekly *La Porte Herald.* Hannegan served in the United States House of Representatives from March 4, 1833, to March 3, 1837. He lost out in the 1836 race, however, and as a political plum the Van Buren administration named him to the La Porte post. In 1838 he was ready to try for Congress again, but La Porte lacked a Democratic newspaper for the aspirant to use as a sounding board. When young Storey showed up, anxious to "try his hand" as an editor, and with $200, the bargain was sealed. In March, 1838, the *Herald* was launched.[9]

A more colorful partnership than this short-lived joint enterprise between the eighteen-year-old Vermont apprentice and the flamboyant Hoosier Democrat would be difficult to imagine. In many respects as colorful and erratic a personality as Wilbur F. Storey, Edward Hannegan gained notoriety as Indiana's junior senator from 1843 to 1849 when he was known in Washington as the "cussinest and drinkinest Irishman in town." Deprived of renomination by Indiana Democrats in 1848, Hannegan wrangled an appointment as ambassador to Prussia out of the Zachary Taylor administration. In Berlin he became involved with a pert Potsdam courtesan, and in January, 1850, the Hohenzollern government declared him *persona non grata.* Disgraced, he returned to Indiana to practice law and declared his intention to run on the Democratic ticket for the presidency in 1852. He became addicted to dope instead, and died from the effects of addiction on February 25, 1859.[10]

With the La Porte newspaper Storey wrote the editorials, a most important function in the pioneer press, and the paper served to boost Hannegan in the 1838 campaign. But Hannegan lost the election, and when he subsequently quit the paper Storey was

8. George B. Catlin, "Little Journeys in Journalism: Wilbur F. Storey," *Michigan History*, X (October, 1926), 516; and John B. Stoll, *An Account of St. Joseph County from Its Organization*, Vol. III of *History of Indiana from Its Exploration to 1922*, Logan Esarey, ed. (3 vols., Dayton: Dayton Historical Publishing Co., 1923), pp. 224-25.

9. E.D. Daniels, *A Twentieth Century History and Biographical Record of La Porte County, Indiana* (Chicago: Lewis Publishing Co., 1904), p. 246.

10. Richard Banta, "Senator Edward Hannegan" (MSS in the Wabash College Library, Crawfordsville, Indiana).

forced to sell a half-interest to Joseph Lomax. There was trouble almost immediately, as Lomax had his own ideas about proper newspaper management. The new arrangement lasted until March, 1841, but it was a stormy partnership, with the two participants frequently denouncing one another as savagely as they did the "imbecile" Whigs.

There are no known extant samples of Storey's editorial style in his first months with the *Herald*. E. D. Daniels, writing in 1904, stated however that at the time Wilbur Storey began to edit the newspaper "he was severe and merciless [as a writer]. He dealt in the most bitter sarcasm, the most cutting satire, the harshest invective." He proved sharp and apt in controversy and Daniels concluded that "his expressions, though often more forceful than elegant, were well calculated to cut an opponent to the quick."[11]

The first known copy of a complete editorial by Wilbur F. Storey is a piece the *Herald* addressed to "Democrats of Laporte County" in October 1839. In it, Storey, but nineteen at the time, showed, in view of his age and inexperience, an amazing command of language and an admirable grasp of the Democratic political view:

> Will you quietly, passively let *Bank Aristocracy*, miscalled newfangled Whiggery, domineer over the denizens of this beautiful country? Surely not! Every consideration that can operate upon the mind and feelings of the true patriot, requires that you rise in the majority of your might and make noble display of your irresistible power. Although an incorporated, mercenary, partial partisan monopoly—leagued with the *wealth* of a *few* individuals in this country—have opposed themselves to you, and are making desperate efforts to crush the spirit of Democracy; yet if you will, you can defeat their most odious and blasting designs. You see, and feel, the oppression they are producing in our home commerce and trade. To a *few individuals* money is loaned with the greatest freedom. Those individuals are endeavoring to *monopolize the produce* of our country. They tell the farmers that they can have a stipulated price, and no more, for the hard earnings of their sweat and toil. In a few hours, a *few* speculators in this country can depress the price of wheat 25 percentum. How long will the people suffer those *few* to speculate upon the fruits of their labor, and *defraud* them out of a great portion of their substance? This question is

11. Daniels, p. 246.

> easily answered! Just so long as they tolerate an aristocratic system and monopoly.[12]

As early as December, 1839, Storey became "*An Editor Threatened*!" when he engaged in his first brawl with the judiciary, an occupation that became a lifelong habit and eventually resulted in his only prison sentence, a contempt of court conviction in 1875.[13] The only available particulars of the La Porte episode were those given by the *Goshen Democrat*, but these were enough to indicate that already in the second year of his career Wilbur F. Storey considered judges "fair game" for abuse. Subsequently, wherever he operated a newspaper, the cloak of "freedom of the press" made it open season on the judiciary, with the attack especially fierce and abandoned in the event an unfortunate judge or jury rendered a decision adverse to the interests of the editor.

In early 1840 another Storey trademark became apparent when the young editor undertook his first feud with an opposition publisher. With passions warming up for the upcoming national campaign, he decided that James S. Stuart, editor of the nearby Michigan City *Gazette*, a Whig organ, was "unworthy of a very serious notice." He therefore dismissed Stuart as "a degraded being, an abandoned reprobate, entirely reckless of truth, deceitful and treacherous, a filthy and loathesome blackguard, an object of pity and contempt rather than of ridicule."[14] Although only in his twentieth year, Wilbur F. Storey had arrived as a man "adept in the use of a vast vocabulary of vituperation."

The 1840 political campaign in La Porte was as wild as any northern Indiana witnessed that year. With an opposition sheet, the *La Porte Whig*, in operation, "the small shot flew thick and fast" as the two papers "fired at each other constantly." Before it was over, Joseph Lomax, apparently almost the equal of Storey in the fine art of political invective, found himself involved in a caning and knifing episode because of certain remarks the *Herald*

12. *La Porte Herald*, as reprinted in the *Goshen* (Indiana) *Democrat*, October 24, 1839.

13. When a Cook County Grand Jury indicted Storey on three charges of criminal libel in March, 1875, the editor was convicted of contempt of court for a series of ribald assaults on some members of the Grand Jury. He was given a ten day jail sentence by presiding judge Erastus S. Williams, but served only ten hours until the Illinois Supreme Court reversed the conviction. See Chapter IX, pp. 240-43.

14. *La Porte Herald*, February 22, 1840, as reprinted in Rollo B. Oglesbee and Albert Hale, *History of Michigan City, Indiana* (La Porte: Edward J. Widdell & Co., 1908), p. 163.

printed "reflecting on ladies of Whig persuasion." The *Whig* of June 17 took note of the "low, scurrilous abuse" of its Democratic counterpart and reprinted a *Herald* notice to subscribers to pay up with the notation "Does not the [*Herald*] editor know that under a statute of our State, debtors can avail themselves of the defense of *want of consideration*?" On June 24, the *Whig* counseled that "the editor of the Herald ought to be run through a *smut* mill." The *Herald*, of course, replied, but the replies "were often more emphatic than polite" and the historian of the campaign felt that "in any case they were such that they could not be quoted here with propriety."[15]

Thus it is certain that by 1840 Wilbur F. Storey had definitely acquired that penchant for the vile epithet that marked the rest of his career. In that year Storey saw his Whig opponents as "black-hearted falsifiers," "ignorant brawlers," "long-faced hypocrites," and "foul-mouthed slanderers." It is also certain that by this time Storey's detestation of abolitionism, always expressed in the most unequivocal prose, was firmly set. "Was [*sic*] ancient republican virtue, and the law abiding principles of the American people ever more grossly outraged," he asked, "than by the acceptance of such inhuman and insurrectionary principles, as those advocated by the abolitionists, by the Whigs of this country?"[16]

On March 7, 1840, in a long editorial headed simply "ABOLITIONISM," Storey aired his opposition to "these friends of the poor negro." His remarks were occasioned by an abolitionist meeting at the county court house that had been advertised in the *Herald*. Storey was incensed that Lomax had accepted the advertisement and noted that "when we published the Herald alone" such notices did not appear because "we believed the abolitionists to be no better than traitors to their country." Storey still felt this was the case as he emphasized that "if we published a paper, we would not wish to have a single abolition subscriber." He then depicted antislavery spokesmen as loafers, "too indolent to earn their bread honestly," who for money paid by the Anti-Slavery American Society "travel about the country . . . sponging wherever they go." He ended with a hope that if the county were again troubled by such loafers a citizens' committee request them to leave town. If

15. Jasper Packard, *History of La Porte County, Indiana* . . . (La Porte: S. E. Taylor & Co., 1876), pp. 461-62 and 209; and Daniels, pp. 246-47.
16. Packard, pp. 207-8.

after this they still remained, Storey felt that "coercive measures" were proper to make them "obey the will of the people."[17]

After the political campaign of 1840, the situation of the *Herald* deteriorated into a morass of bickering and mismanagement. Neither Storey nor Lomax was of a temperament to publish a newspaper on a co-operative basis, and also the subscribers were not always conscientious in remitting payment. The paper regularly ran a "Loafer's Department" that contained notices such as the following of September 8, 1840, "a mild specimen":

> The postmaster at Greensboro informed us that ABNER DICKERING refused to take the Herald from that office. He owes us $4.18. We have not heard from the *dishonest* rascal since.[18]

As the financial pinch of the *Herald* tightened by March, 1841, Joseph Lomax decided to play sharpie with his young partner and entered into secret negotiations with "a combination of Mishawaka people" to move the newspaper to the South Bend suburb for an annual consideration of $500. But Lomax sadly underestimated the resourcefulness of his adversary. One morning in March, as his plans were reaching fruition, Lomax came to town only to discover that Wilbur F. Storey "had become possessor of the office sometime in the night," loaded the press and equipment on wagons, and "was then half way across Terre Coupee prairie on his way to Mishawaka."[19] Storey got wind of Lomax's scheme and went to Mishawaka where he contracted to publish a newspaper for one year without any pay whatever.

Thus, three years to the month after it began, the first newspaper with "Wilbur F. Storey, Editor" on the masthead ended. For the next forty-three years only men who would limit their concern to the business and advertising aspects of publishing were considered as partners as Storey never again published any newspaper in which he did not retain absolute control of editorial policy. It is safe to conclude that he also never again published a newspaper "with a single abolition subscriber."

In the last week of April, 1841, the first number of the *Mishawaka Tocsin* appeared. *The South Bend Free Press and St. Joseph Advertiser* (hereafter cited as *Free Press and Advertiser*) remarked

17. *La Porte Herald*, March 7, 1840, as reprinted in Packard, p. 229.
18. Packard, p. 461.
19. Daniels, p. 246.

that "modern democracy is about to be established in the land" because "The Tocsin has sounded! The alarm bell has rung! The *Storey* is told and the faithful are called to arms." The South Bend weekly, struck by the blatant boastfulness of its new neighbor, resorted to Greek mythology for a parallel:

> Aesop relates that a mountain was taken with the pains of labor; the inhabitants in the neighborhood, astonished at the unusual noise and heavings, anxiously assembled, expecting that some horrible prodigy was about being introduced into the world. When in the midst of their alarm, out crept a mouse. Whether . . . Mishawaka . . . produces a "monster" or a "mouse" is for [the reader] to decide.[20]

After this inventive "welcome" the paper significantly added "the first paper appears very well," thereby acknowledging that at even this early stage typographical perfection was a hallmark of any newspaper produced by Wilbur F. Storey. While no known copies of the *La Porte Herald* or *Mishawaka Tocsin* exist, every copy of the *Jackson Patriot, Detroit Free Press* and *Chicago Times* examined by this writer corroborates the belief that throughout his career Storey conceived each issue of his paper as a typographical work of art that must be executed with the master strokes of a true artist. From that day at age twelve when he entered a print shop for the first time, he engaged in a lifelong passion for the possibilities of type. That he never quite lost his love for printing was indicated by the fact that in even his most prosperous years, as millionaire editor and publisher of the largest newspaper in the West, there were occasions when "he would take off his coat and work at the case." Franc B. Wilkie, his closest Chicago associate, further stated quite bluntly that "printing was the one art in which he excelled."[21]

The *Free Press and Advertiser* ended the word of welcome to its new Democratic neighbor with the observation "we have heard the editor is a gentlemanly and honorable man," and thus it wished "a good support to the Tocsin." The hope of a "gentlemanly and honorable" rivalry was to prove short-lived, since Storey opened shop in Mishawaka right in the midst of a special Congressional election to fill the Seventh District seat. It was true that the first

20. *South Bend Free Press and St. Joseph Advertiser*, April 30, 1841.
21. Franc B. Wilkie, *Personal Reminiscences of Thirty-five Years of Journalism* (Chicago: F. J. Schulte & Co., 1891), pp. 156 and 119.

campaign editorial was inoffensive enough, and undoubtedly one which might have prompted hopes of "gentlemanly and honorable" conduct. It was headed "TO THE POLLS!" and urged readers to support Democratic candidate James Bryce because he opposed a national bank, a high and oppressive tariff and the assumption of state debts by the Federal government. "Mr. Bryce is a veteran republican of the Jeffersonian school," Storey stated, and hence he deserved popular support.[22]

With the next issue, published two days before the election and dubbed *"the Storeyteller"* by the *Free Press and Advertiser*, the *Tocsin* rang more true to Wilbur F. Storey form. The front page contained the startling news of the "untimely" death of Henry S. Lane, by coincidence Whig candidate for Congress. Such "sad intelligence" undoubtedly meant the voters would "have no choice" but to elect Lane's Democratic opponent. No choice, that is, until the *Free Press* immediately got out a handbill "giving the lie to the report," circulated "by neighbor Storey for political effect." In his next issue, four days *after* Lane won anyway, Storey admitted "the rumor is without foundation, Mr. Lane being merely convalescent." He then launched into a long tirade against "contemptible British Whig editors" who stooped to "direct attack" upon partisan opponents.[23] Wilbur F. Storey, late of La Porte, had arrived in Mishawaka, and while his stay might not be marked by "gentlemanly and honorable" conduct, it would prove an interesting year, one in which Whigs would do well to keep constantly on their toes.

Much of the bickering in the following months was of the petty variety common in pioneer communities blessed with two newspapers of opposite political suasion. There were point by point refutations of the competitor's editorial stand, coupled with a vigorous assertion of what the participants deemed the principles of their respective parties. With Storey, however, in Mishawaka as later everywhere he published a newspaper, even the petty was seen in terms of universal, unchangeable truth. For example, when the Whigs of La Porte County accepted abolition support, Storey felt that "ancient republican virtue and the law abiding principles of the American people" were never "more grossly outraged." With such an outlook, "war" with the opposition was inevitable, especial-

22. *Mishawaka Tocsin,* as reprinted in *Free Press and Advertiser,* April 30, 1841.
23. This whole episode is recapped in the *Free Press and Advertiser,* June 4, 1841.

ly since a good feud was the surest way of boosting circulation in a hurry. Storey decried the battle "because we were not desirous of entering into a *personal* warfare with any paper," but he had no choice so long as the *Free Press* editors made "low slang and abuse the principal arguments in their productions." So long as "*truth* and *honor*" were the chief characteristics of Storey's "editorial effusions," the *Free Press* agreed that a personal quarrel should be avoided. But falsehood and error must be refuted and exposed. "Whenever we find neighbor Storey guilty of either," the *Free Press* concluded, "we shall fearlessly hold him up to the public gaze, regardless of his squirmings and writhings, or his monstrous horror of low slang and abuse."[24]

Wilbur F. Storey's twelve month stay in Mishawaka was a constantly trying time for him financially. His original $200 stake had long since been used up in the La Porte undertaking, and he had contracted to publish the *Tocsin* for one year without pay in order to deprive Joseph Lomax of a chance for a shady profit on what Storey considered his own La Porte investment. When his "squirmings and writhings" failed to boost circulation sufficiently, he became totally dependent on advertising revenues to keep his newspaper going, plus whatever profits he could realize from a "drug and stationer's shop" he opened in June, 1841. From early autumn the issues of the *Tocsin* became irregular,[25] but Storey, true to what he considered a solemn commitment to publish a newspaper for one year, stuck it out until March, 1842.

In December he tried to boost circulation with his first recorded plunge into the seamier side of journalism. In that month a certain Smith of Hudson, La Porte County, was murdered by a Mr. Egbert. The *Tocsin* gave it prominent play, with fulsome details on all particulars, including a verbal attack on the judge and jury who tried Egbert. The *Free Press* of January 7, 1842, felt it necessary to "call public attention to the scurrilous, malign and utterly disgusting statements" of the *Tocsin*, which were alike "an outrage to the sacred majesty of the law" and "an outrage to public decency."[26] Not even sensationalism could save the *Tocsin*, however, and as the deficit mounted in the first months of 1842 it became apparent that Mishawaka was not yet ready to support profitably a weekly newspaper of Democratic persuasion.

24. *Ibid.*, July 30, 1841.
25. *Ibid.*, October 8, 1841.
26. *Ibid.*, January 7, 1842.

When Wilbur F. Storey arrived in South Bend in the spring of 1838, he was eighteen years old. Exactly four years and two newspapers later, in March, 1842, he closed down the *Tocsin*, sold the press and effects for what they would bring, and at age twenty-two he left the Hoosier state for the greener pastures of Jackson, Michigan. He left no permanent imprint on the journalism of the area. The two newspapers he founded disappeared forever when he closed them down. He had gained valuable experience in the business of publishing a newspaper, however, experience that would be useful in his future endeavors. The four years in Indiana also saw the young Vermont native accepted as an equal by both partisan cohorts and the most bitter Whig opponents. Despite his extreme youth and almost complete lack of formal education, the opposition press of the area did not level one single attack on the editor because he was unlettered or a green upstart. This tribute of complete silence on the subject is not only mute testament to his maturity, but also convincing witness that he was in Indiana, as in childhood and throughout later life, a man "with the air of a person many years his senior." The Indiana years also witnessed the germination of the journalism that would make Wilbur F. Storey the terror of Michigan in the decade before the Civil War, a notorious Chicago Copperhead "traitor" during that conflict, and the creator of the first "sink hole" press in the Middle West in the not-so-sensitive seventies of the "Gilded Age."

CHAPTER III

JACKSON:
Be Temperate While Young!

If you wish to be happy when old be *temperate* while young!

—*Jackson Patriot*, May 18, 1847.

IF THERE WAS A TEMPERATE PERIOD IN THE LIFE OF WILBUR F. STOREY, it was between 1842 and 1853 when he resided in the village of Jackson, Michigan. There were several factors that helped to make these the years of relative calm in a life otherwise completely tempestuous. For one, the major circumstance in Storey's decision to settle there was the residence in that place of another sister, Mary Elizabeth, who had settled in Jackson about 1840 with her husband, Fairchild Farrand. Unlike Horatio Chapin in South Bend, Farrand was an ardent Democrat and a man of some influence in the politics of the community. Thus, if nothing else, Jackson definitely offered young Storey a more hospitable clime for family relations than northern Indiana afforded.[1]

1. For the relationship between Fairchild Farrand and Wilbur F. Storey, see the testimony of Alfred S. Trude, Storey's business attorney, in "The Storey Estate," *Chicago Times*, November 15, 1884.

In addition to this, Storey was in love in 1846, a condition that temporarily mellowed his otherwise completely cynical disposition. As a result, he not only got a wife but also, for two years and for the only time in his life, he was religious as he became, at the bidding of his bride, a prominent and active member of the local Congregational Church.

There were also professional successes. In 1844 he established the *Jackson Patriot*. Unlike his Indiana newspapers, it was a complete financial as well as political success. This newspaper's staying power is indicated by the fact that it has survived until the present as the Jackson *Citizen Patriot*. From 1845 to 1849 Storey enjoyed the good graces of the James K. Polk administration to the extent that he served as postmaster. From 1847 on, he owned and operated a highly successful drug and stationer's shop, "the finest in Jackson." Finally, in 1850, Storey so succeeded in winning over his neighbors that they elected him Jackson's delegate to the convention to revise Michigan's constitution. In short, during his Jackson sojourn, there was evidence of the taming and domestication of Wilbur F. Storey. But even during these "halcyon days," the "Storeyteller" of Mishawaka was never completely submerged.

When Storey arrived in Jackson in April, 1842, the village was in the first stages of boom. In 1838 the Michigan legislature commissioned the building of the state prison there and the residents looked forward to its completion "with great expectations in spite of the involuntary increase of undesirable population." The Michigan Central Railroad was completed to Jackson by the end of 1841 and thereafter construction rapidly pushed across the state. As for newspapers, Nicholas Sullivan started a Whig sheet, the *Jackson Sentinel*, in 1837 but it lasted only three years. It was succeeded in 1841 by the *Michigan State Gazette*, renamed the *Jackson American Citizen* in 1848. In 1838 George W. Raney and Ruben S. Chaney, with the financial "encouragement" of Fairchild Farrand, founded the *Michigan Democrat* but it died in their hands in 1841.[2] Thus by 1842, with a Whig newspaper in operation and the village showing every sign of a rapidly expanding prosperity, an ambitious twenty-two year old printer with four years of experience in Democratic journalism could hardly find a more promising locale in which to make a new start.

Storey waited until the national elections of 1844, however, be-

2. George B. Catlin, "Little Journeys in Journalism: Wilbur F. Storey," *Michigan History*, X (October, 1926), 516-19.

fore he plunged into the newspaper business again. For the first two years in Jackson he lived with the Farrands and "read law." He apparently intended at this time to become an attorney. The significance of this two year retreat from partisan strife for the sake of becoming conversant with law cannot be overstressed, for in the next twenty years Storey became a political theoretician of the first rank. In all of the bitter strife raised by the controversy over slavery and state rights prior to the Civil War, the northern view of the doctrine of state sovereignty had no more articulate or persistent champion than Wilbur F. Storey in the editorial columns of the *Detroit Free Press* and, later, the *Chicago Times*.

Any attraction that a career in law might have held for Storey was erased forever in 1844 when the necessity of getting the Democratic message to the voters of Jackson proved pressing enough to force him once again into the field of partisan journalism. Not only was it necessary to whoop loud and long for James K. Polk and the annexation of Oregon, but just as important, General Lewis Cass was running for the United States Senate. Throughout his Michigan career Storey indulged in few personal attachments, but until the day in 1857 when "black republican abolitionist" Zachariah Chandler finally succeeded in removing Cass from the Senate, the "Father" of Michigan had no more persistent booster than the editor who, in April 1844, brought out "Volume One, Number One" of the *Jackson Patriot*. With respect to this attachment to Cass, the only student of Storey's Michigan career stated: "For all other opinions rather than his own, with perhaps the sole exception of General Lewis Cass, for whom he had a real admiration, Mr. Storey seemed to have a supreme contempt."[3]

In beginning the *Jackson Patriot*, Storey entered into partnership with Ruben S. Chaney of the late, ill-fated *Michigan Democrat*. The venture was partially underwritten by brother-in-law Fairchild Farrand, an indebtedness that Storey never forgot until his mind failed him in the early 1880s. By the arrangement, Chaney supervised the business end of the paper while Storey presided over news and editorial matter. No copies of the paper prior to April 20, 1847, are extant so the tack pursued in the 1844 campaign can only be guessed. That it was convincing and successful there can be little doubt, however, since it resulted in the appointment in March, 1845, of Wilbur F. Storey as postmaster.

The Storey-Chaney partnership prospered from the beginning,

3. *Ibid.*, 521.

and within one year a small southern Michigan publishing empire, consisting of two newspapers and one magazine, flourished. The magazine, *The Michigan Farmer and Western Agriculturalist* was acquired in December, 1844. Popularly known as the *Michigan Farmer*, it was the foremost agricultural monthly in Michigan until its demise in the late 1850s. Storey retained control until he sold the magazine to his father-in-law, the Reverend Warren P. Isham, in December, 1847.[4]

The second newspaper, the *Ingham Democrat*, came into existance as the result of a foil that only Wilbur F. Storey could have perpetrated successfully. In March, 1845, the Michigan legislature passed an act that restored to the auditor-general, at that time Henry N. Walker, the entire control of the tax advertising of the state. It was a contract much sought by Michigan printers, but the 1845 act specified that the papers must be published in Ingham County. Upon hearing of the law, Chaney and Storey packed up a printing outfit and set out for Ingham County, where they found the field already occupied by another printer who had rushed in from Marshall. Storey proceeded to make up a form for a paper from the matter of the *Jackson Patriot* and named it the *Ingham Democrat*. Without type for the masthead of this pretense of a newspaper, the ever-resourceful Wilbur painted the name on with a brush and ink. Then he and his partner carried "three or four copies" to Henry Fiske, the Judge of Probate at Lansing, from whom they obtained certification that the papers had been printed in Ingham County. They then went to Detroit to show the papers and the certification to Walker. The upshot of this bit of enterprising journalism was that on April 1 the nonexistent *Ingham Democrat* was awarded the contract for advertising the tax sales of 1845.[5]

With the contract sewed up, Storey and Chaney arranged with a printer named Child to publish the *Ingham Democrat* for them at Mason, the county seat, until the term of the tax sale expired. Evidently there was some default on the part of Child, for Storey and Chaney replevined the printing plant. The press and equipment then disappeared, and the Jackson partners had to rush another stock of printing materials to Mason. Despite such difficulties, the *Ingham Democrat* continued for one year as by various

4. J. C. Holmes, "A Sketch of the Michigan Farmer," *Michigan Pioneer and Historical Collections*, VII (Lansing, 1886), 99-100; and Silas Farmer, *The History of Detroit and Michigan or the Metropolis Illustrated* . . . (Detroit: Silas Farmer & Co., 1889), I, 673-74.

5. Catlin, 519-20.

resorts Storey and Chaney managed to carry out their contract with the state.

In 1846 Wilbur F. Storey met Maria Parsons Isham, a lady of gentle character and refined background, who had attended the Reverend W. Fitch's female seminary in Detroit in 1842. Her father, the Reverend Warren P. Isham, was ordained a Congregational minister in Hudson, Ohio in 1830, where he edited and published the weekly *Western Religious Literary and Political Intelligencer.* In 1834 he sold the paper and moved to Michigan. The elder Isham settled first in Detroit, where in addition to his ministerial duties he "wrote articles for the daily press." In addition to carrying on his newspaper and church work, the Reverend Isham also wrote two books. One, *The Mud Cabin,* was later described by Storey as a work "giving a clear and faithful description of English working classes and properly setting forth the hypocrisy of English philanthropists in meddling with the institutions of this country." The other, *A Book of Travel in the Western States,* recounted family experiences in Ohio and Michigan in the 1830s. About 1844, the Reverend Isham moved with his wife and four children to Jackson.

Maria, born April 22, 1828, inherited much of her father's religiosity and some of his writing talent. In the late 1840s she was a regular contributor of filler "poetry" to the *Jackson Patriot,* and throughout the 1850s her travel and drama reviews frequently delighted readers of the *Detroit Free Press.* It was this young lady, whose temperament, background and inclinations were in every respect the antithesis of those of Wilbur Storey, who nevertheless married the Jackson editor in a Congregational Church ceremony read by the Reverend Gustavus L. Foster on June 22, 1847.[6]

The courtship and marriage had a temporarily soothing effect on Storey's character. One sign of this was the frequency with which maudlin poetry, which he always assiduously avoided printing in the columns of his newspapers, suddenly began to appear in a conspicuous corner of page one of the *Patriot.* Written by "Marie," the following was but one of dozens of examples of the sort that appeared around the date of the nuptials:

6. The Reverend W. Fitch, "Reminiscences of Detroit," *Michigan Pioneer and Historical Collections,* V (Lansing, 1904), 545; Homer Worthington Brainaird (compiler), *A Survey of the Ishams in England and America, Eight Hundred and Fifty Years of History and Genealogy* (Rutland, Vermont: The Tuttle Co., 1938), p. 319; obituary of Warren P. Isham, *Chicago Times,* September 24, 1863; and *Jackson Patriot,* June 22, 1847.

"Remembered Yet."

"Remembered Yet!" How much of happiness,
Of deep, soul-thrilling bliss, those words unfold!
Oh! how intense the joy, kindled by them
In the dark recesses of the soul, kindled,
Ne'r to be quenched again. How the slum'bring
Hopes of by-past time are wakened into
Life, by their magic influence,—and oh!
How thrillingly the music of those words
Doth steal o'er the wayward spirit, calming
Into tranquil rest, the troubled passions
of the breast.[7]

There were two more stanzas in a like vein, but these lines are enough to indicate that the spirit that composed such sentiments was not of a turn to cope successfully with that of her new husband.

There were at least two years of marital tranquility, however, years in which the *Patriot* for the most part was devoid of the more volatile type of personal abuse, and years in which Wilbur Storey made a serious attempt at conversion to the Congregational faith. In December, 1847, Wilbur became an officer of the Jackson Bible Society, organized under the aegis of the Reverend Gustavus L. Foster, and intended to promote the study of and respect for the "Holy Book" in the community.[8] During this same time, *Patriot* editorials suddenly emitted a religious fervor unknown before. One of these, an impassioned plea against capital punishment, was headed "To Hang or Not to Hang," and argued that no specious arguments in favor of "blood for blood" could outweigh the simple truth that "God, not man, holds the life of His creatures subject to His will." Executions were contrary to "the mild and benign" doctrines of the New Testament, Storey stated. He argued that life imprisonment was just as effective as execution because to the world the guilty one "is just as effectively cut off as though he had hung by the neck until dead, and his bones had been stripped of their flesh and wired and varnished by the anatomist." In conclusion, he said:

> No! No! Let God, not man, deal with the lives of His subjects. It is a horrible thing to force a man, unprepared, into the presence of his Maker.[9]

7. *Jackson Patriot*, April 27, 1847.
8. *Ibid.*, February 15, 1848.
9. *Ibid.*, February 13, 1849.

While the real Storey was not completely absent from these lines, containing as they did the rather unnecessary musings on "the anatomist's work," it is nonetheless difficult to believe that the author is the same man who almost thirty years later would also author the famous "JERKED TO JESUS!" head to give sensational emphasis to an unrestrained "yes" in reply to the query "To Hang or Not to Hang."

There were other evidences that Wilbur Storey was, during the late 1840s, a happily married man. Throughout his career, his newspapers were a graphic reflection of his inner mood to such an extent that his editorial pages were as valuable in determining his personal sentiments as would be a day-by-day diary for another person. Several instances can be cited to substantiate this. For example, in August, 1868, he began to suspect his second wife of an infidelity he could neither prove nor document, so the editorial pages of the *Chicago Times* for almost a month were given over to a series of essays on "the nefarious female" who goes "to the brink" in extramarital "flirtations."[10] Or in July and August 1873, when Storey became convinced that the malpractice of a Chicago physician was directly responsible for his second wife's death, the editorial pages of the *Times* bristled with personal essays denouncing "medical butchers," "dispensers of wild and unsafe drugs," and finally, the physician himself.[11] It was the same way in Jackson, although the subjects to be aired were of a happier tone. Thus, in February, 1848, he saluted "Young Ladies Who Read Newspapers":

> Young ladies who are accustomed to read newspapers, are always observed to possess winning ways, most amiable dispositions, invariably make good wives, and always select good husbands—a fact.[12]

Another aspect of Storey's talent that first came to the fore shortly after his marriage was his power and insight as an essayist on things in general. In a career that spanned more than forty years, he found occasion at one time or another to comment on most subjects of interest to mankind, and whether the topic be

10. *Chicago Times*, August 14, 1868; and Franc B. Wilkie, *Personal Reminiscences of Thirty-five Years of Journalism* (Chicago: F. J. Schulte & Co., 1891), pp. 144-45.

11. *Chicago Times*, July and August, 1873, *passim.*; Wilkie, pp. 205-7; see also Chapter IX, pp. 233-36.

12. *Jackson Patriot*, February 17, 1848.

"On Reading a Morning Newspaper," "A History of Political Campaigning in America," or "Free Love and Graham Crackers," his opinions constituted on the whole as entertaining and forceful a collection of insights as could be found among nineteenth-century American editors. On the importance of reading, for example, it was Wilbur Storey, with no need to apologize to Francis Bacon, who penned the following:

> No Time To Read.
>
> How often do you hear men excuse themselves from subscribing to a paper or periodical by saying they have "no time to read." When we hear a man thus excuse himself, we conclude that he has never found time to confer any substantial advantage either upon his family, his country, or himself. To hear a free man thus express himself, is truly humiliating; and we can form no other opinion than that such a man is of little importance to society. Such men generally have time to attend public barbecues, meetings, sales and other gatherings, but they have not "time to read." They frequently spend whole days in gossip, tippling and trading horses, but they lose a day in asking advice of their neighbors, sometimes a day in picking up news, the prices current, and the exchanges—but these men never have "any time to read." They have time to hunt, to fish, to fiddle, to drink, to "do nothing," but not time to read. Such men generally have uneducated children, unimproved farms and unhappy firesides. They have no energy, no spirit of improvement, no love of knowledge, they live "unknowing and unknown," and often die unwept and unregretted.[13]

In April, 1848, Maria Storey gave birth to a daughter, but the infant lived only three days. The effect of her death on the editor and his marriage seemed to be for the worse. It might have been the heat of the 1848 political campaign, but whatever the cause, the editorial page of the *Patriot* once again began to read more like what might be expected from a newspaper with "WILBUR F. STOREY, EDITOR" on the masthead. The cordial relationship with the Isham family also cooled, and in 1849 there was an open split between Storey and his father-in-law.

On June 15, 1847, the partnership between Chaney and Storey was dissolved. The official announcement stated "the business will hereafter be conducted by Ruben S. Chaney, to whom all debts

13. *Ibid.*, October 5, 1847.

of the establishment must be paid, and by whom all indebtedness of the firm will be discharged." This dissolution led commentators on the history of the *Jackson Patriot* to conclude that from this date Storey had no association with the newspaper. The very next sentence of the dissolution notice, however, read "the *editorial* conduct of the Patriot *will remain under the charge of W. F. Storey* [italics mine]." It was true that beginning with the June 27 issue the masthead read "JACKSON PATRIOT by Ruben S. Chaney." At the top of page two (the editorial page), column one, set in small caps, every subsequent issue carried the legend "WILBUR F. STOREY, EDITOR." Thus the proof is irrefutable that the *Jackson Patriot*, in its essentials, remained the brain child of Wilbur Storey until he moved to Detroit. The dissolution of the partnership was undertaken simply to free Storey of any indebtedness and give him, now that he had family obligations, the necessary capital to open "The Book Emporium, in Diamond's Block at the Post Office." This business venture was a success, carrying as it did "a splendid assortment of books, stationery, miscellany . . . the assortment is too complete and too varied to mention."[14]

Six months after Storey sold his interest in the *Patriot* to Chaney, he sold the *Michigan Farmer* to the Reverend Warren P. Isham, who conducted the magazine until 1857. The elder Isham seemed more than pleased with his new son-in-law, especially in view of Wilbur's successful business venture and active work in the Congregational Church. Then the Whigs won the 1848 presidential election, and as soon as Zachary Taylor took office, Storey was removed as postmaster. The loss of this patronage plum was unsettling. In addition to the reduced income, the "Book Emporium" was forced to move to No. 4 Empire Block, and with the loss of post office traffic, business lagged. Full column display ads, headed "BOOKS! BOOKS!" promised all sorts of wonders to prospective customers and ended with the invitation to "Come and See if These Things are not So!"[15] But the venture failed to revive. In June, 1849, proprietor Storey, caught in a conflict of conscience between Congregational ethics and business acumen, decided in favor of the latter.

In that month, while Storey "combined journalism with a drugstore and book shop," he engaged in a dispute with his father-in-law about the sale of alcohol from the drugstore. It is possible

14. *Ibid.*, June 15, June 27, July 6, and July 20, 1847.
15. *Ibid.*, January 16, 1849.

that relations had already begun to cool as the Mexican Cession renewed the agitation of the slavery question, since in 1842 the elder Isham had published an antislavery daily in Detroit for six months.[16] At any rate, the sale of alcohol by a church member was more than the temperance inclined Congregationalists of Jackson would tolerate. Storey's pastor, the Reverend G. L. Foster, approached his parishioner directly and requested him to stop. Foster had presided at the wedding of the editor in 1847, and in the following months had found him a dedicated, active missionary in the work of the Jackson Bible Society. But in 1849 the pastor's counsel went unheeded. When Warren Isham intervened on behalf of the church, Storey broke with both men. The upshot of the affair was that the editor "withdrew from the Congregational Church to which he belonged, and never again identified himself with any religious body."[17] He did put the "Book Emporium" back on a paying basis. The argument also provided the occasion for Storey's first attack on "meddling parsons" and "pharisaical priests" in the columns of the *Patriot*.

All accounts by persons acquainted with Maria Storey recount that she was, as her poetry indicated, a lady of personal warmth, great sensitivity, and amiable disposition. She was these things in addition to being a woman of indomitable religious faith who took seriously the Biblical injunction that "What God hath joined together, man shall not put asunder." Despite years of the harshest abuse and most insulting personal relationship, she remained married to Wilbur until his moral deterioration reached such a point that she was forced to admit her marriage, like the editor, was beyond redemption.

Franc B. Wilkie remembered Maria as "a petite, slender woman, with a sweet face." The marriage, said Wilkie, "was that of the Hawk and the Dove," and he was struck by how Maria remained with Wilbur as long as she did.[18] As early as 1853 it was noticed that Storey's "crabbiness reached even to his own fireside and in his Detroit days his wife . . . was treated very unhandsomely by him." He was so silent and morose in his private life that Detroit acquaintances could not recall Storey ever gave Maria a smile or spoke a pleasant word in her presence. People who saw the couple at dinner at the Michigan Exchange Hotel, where the Storeys lived,

16. William Stocking, "Prominent Newspaper Men in Michigan," *Michigan Pioneer and Historical Collections*, XXXIX (Lansing, 1915), 156.

17. Wilkie, p. 98.

18. *Ibid.*, p. 142.

declared "they often ate their meal without a word passing between them."[19]

Just when the marriage began to deteriorate is not certain. Throughout the eight years that Storey owned the *Detroit Free Press*, Maria was a frequent contributor. While the evidence suggests that the relationship was hardly amiable during this time, Mrs. Storey nonetheless moved to Chicago in 1861 and kept up at least the appearance of a marriage. The couple never lived together in Chicago, however, since Maria lived in a set of rooms at the Sherman House while Wilbur indulged in debauchery at the Portland Hotel. "For appearances, they met in parlors, dined together and . . . rarely exchanged words." It was not until the editor was already living with the woman who became his second wife that Maria finally consented to a divorce. This was in 1867, on grounds of "incompatability," with alimony set at $2000 a year.[20] Maria never remarried. In the 1870s she spent several years abroad traveling in Europe. In 1887 she put in a belated claim to Storey's estate that helped further complicate an entangled family squabble over the spoils. She was still alive in Detroit in 1896.[21]

While the marriage between Wilbur F. Storey and Maria Parsons Isham was foredoomed to failure, it was not, in the beginning, as unpromising a match as it turned out to be. The Ishams came from a journalistic and literary tradition, and one of the unexpected dividends of the union on the part of the editor was the acquisition of a newspaper reporter and drama critic of unusual imagination and talent who helped Storey make the *Detroit Free Press* the best known Democratic newspaper in the Middle West in the 1850s. Warren P. Isham (not to be confused with the Reverend Warren P. Isham), younger brother of Maria, joined the staff of the *Jackson Patriot* sometime in 1850, when he was but nineteen years old. A natural newspaperman, young Isham was one of the most prominent members of the Storey team until his death in 1863. His contributions to the success of the *Free Press* and his renown as a front-line correspondent during the Civil War are recounted below. Now it is sufficient to note that without the enterprising reporting of this brother-in-law, Storey's *Detroit Free Press* would have been a considerably duller newspaper with respect to its "local matter."

19. N. H. Bowen, "A Fighting Detroit Editor of Seventy-five Years Ago: The Career of Wilbur F. Storey Who Made the Free Press Famous," *Detroit Saturday Night*, May 5, 1928, Sec. 2, p. 1.
20. Wilkie, p. 142.
21. Catlin, 530.

It was in the fine art of journalistic politicking that the *Jackson Patriot* won most renown in the 1840s. Storey, always a chauvinist and expansionist, was a proud booster of James K. Polk and the Mexican War. He would have gone farther than Polk and annexed Mexico, convinced as he was that Providence intended that the American flag should wave from pole to pole. "The Mexican War is, perhaps, to be regretted as all wars are," Storey stated in one editorial. "But under the wisdom of Providence it may result in amassed good." The editor felt this was so because as the United States picked up additional territory there would be more room for "the downtrodden of Europe" to seek "an asylum of liberty" in this country. His musings on the destiny of the American Republic also hinted at his conviction of the superiority of the Anglo-Saxon race, a conviction that formed the basis of his rabid Negrophobia in the 1850s. As Americans conquered and inhabited the vast Southwest, Storey, from the vantage point of one comfortably ensconced in a thriving community in the Michigan interior, foresaw that "the imbecile Mexican nation will be lost in the progress of the Anglo-Saxon race," and this would be good.[22]

As early as August, 1847, when the rumor first appeared that the Whig party might nominate General Zachary Taylor as its candidate for the Presidency in 1848, Storey felt that the peculiarly prominent characteristic belonging to that party was "*blindness!*—inability to *see!*" He recounted the opposition's sad experience when Whig vice-president John Tyler succeeded William Henry Harrison in 1841 and promptly proceeded to veto all important Whig legislation. "They now seem willing to support a man of whose political views they know even less than they did of Tyler's," the *Patriot* observed. It would thus serve them right if they elected Taylor, secured a majority in Congress, and passed measures "for clearing out every frog-pond in the United States," only to have "Taylor play Tyler with them" by vetoing their internal improvement bills.[23]

With respect to local Congressional candidates, the *Patriot* supported Charles E. Stuart, Democrat, against James W. Gordon, Whig, with a sledge-hammer repetition of Stuart's virtues as opposed to Gordon's political vices. There was as yet none of the personal vituperation against political opponents which in the 1850s would make Storey the editorial scourge of Michigan Republicans

22. *Jackson Patriot*, August 24, 1847.
23. *Ibid.*, August 10, 1847.

and abolitionists. Rather, sentence by sentence, Storey hammered away on the theme that Stuart favored "good" things while Gordon was "feudal." Mr. Stuart "is in favor of voting men and money to prosecute the [Mexican] war to an honorable conclusion." Mr. Gordon "if we can judge by his speeches, is opposed to this policy." The Democrat "believes the war just on the part of the United States." The Whig "denounces the war as unrighteous and oppressive, and our brave soldiers as butchers and murderers." Stuart would "unshackle commerce, and make trade as free as the air we breathe, give scope to enterprise, and make the world one vast beehive." Gordon, on the other hand, believed in Feudalism and "would fetter commerce . . . [by] putting restrictions upon trade." In short, the Whig's "notions are all Federal, hence he is behind the age. Which of these men do you choose?"[24]

When the Whigs actually nominated Zachary Taylor in June, 1848, Storey published a scathing denounciation. The general, "a Louisiana slave holder and slave breeder" who "buys and sells negroes like cattle in the market," was the candidate of a party that sought to outlaw slavery in new territories of the Mexican Cession. This proved the opposition's hypocrisy, but Storey also wondered about the propriety of running a general, "a mere hero," for the Presidency. Taylor was "without an hour's experience in civil life," Storey observed, and was only nominated because "he successfully fought two or three battles in Mexico."[25]

During the campaign that followed Storey could not understand why "all sensible men" did not support Michigan Senator Lewis Cass, the Democratic nominee for President. Whigs were "rotten at heart." Their nomination of Taylor proved "their moral sensibilities are putrified."[26] For candidates of the third party Free Soil movement there was nothing but contempt. When Mark Littlejohn delivered a Free Soil speech at the Jackson courthouse before "a wondering and wonderful audience," the *Patriot* devoted a column to "Loose Dirt Run Mad" that offered a synoposis of the speech:

> [Littlejohn] touched casually upon Thomas Jefferson, the Declaration of Independence, our Fathers who fought and bled, the snow-capped hills of Maine, the highest peak of the Andes, the American eagle with extended beak, liberty,

24. *Ibid.*, October 19, 1847.
25. *Ibid.*, June 13, 1848.
26. *Ibid.*

equality, the footstool of the Deity, the ancient Romans, the serfs of Russia, foul leprosy, the Buffalo plant farm, the Rocky mountains. . . .[27]

In a long editorial prompted by the Free Soil movement Storey spelled out his position on the question of slavery in the territories. In it he referred to slaves as potentially "free men," an indication that he had not as yet become an advocate of white supremacy. He held, seven years before the passage of the Kansas-Nebraska Act led him to reverse himself completely, that Congress would never pass a law allowing the extension of slavery, and even if it did "the Supreme Court would undoubtedly pronounce it unconstitutional." Hence the Free Soil movement, by agitating the slavery question, engendered bad feelings between different sections of the Union that could well end in Civil War. A full thirteen years before the firing upon Fort Sumter, Storey stated his conviction that the national success of a sectional antislavery party would lead inevitably to "the dismemberment of the Union. [It] will destroy thus the fairest fabric the world ever saw." With this conviction, which he held tenaciously until the events of 1861 proved him correct, Storey would give no quarter to the abolitionist movement as it strengthened in the 1850s. "The UNION is above all price," he stated in Jackson, "and he who seeks to destroy it is worse than a traitor."[28]

While politics undoubtedly furnished the main motivation to Wilbur F. Storey for publishing a newspaper in Jackson, the extant copies of the *Patriot* prove that during these years, as later, Storey was conscious that a newspaper should serve a wider function than the mere "prating of a party line." He realized from the beginning that a newspaper without readers was an intolerable anomaly, and thus he took steps to insure the *Patriot* a steady patronage. Entertaining and informative feature matter, such as "A Geographical Memoir of Upper California" by John Charles Frémont, handsomely printed on page one, was routine.[29] "Filler" matter was intriguing, and even mundane matters were presented with a breezy flare intended as much to amuse as to inform Storey's loyal readers

"MARRIAGE," as recounted in the columns of the *Jackson Patriot*, illustrated the extent to which every item in a Storey-edited

27. *Ibid.*, September 26, 1848.
28. *Ibid.*, August 8, 1847.
29. *Ibid.*, January 16, 1849.

newspaper had to be read to appreciate precisely what "WILBUR F. STOREY, EDITOR" implied. When publishing marriage notices Storey was careful to point out whether or not he had received a remuneration. The usual format was:

> MARRIAGE. In Leoni, January 31, by the Rev. G. L. Foster, Mr. Ezra Sagendorph to Miss Anna Eliza Kaywood, both of Leoni. CAKE RECEIVED.[30]

In the unhappy event that an unfortunate couple overlooked the editor, the notice was still published, but in infinitesimally small type beneath the legend "REMUNERATION AWAITED." On some occasions Storey used nuptials as an excuse for a preliminary exercise in advice to the lovelorn. Thus

> MARRIAGE. . . . The fair bride has made us the happy recipient of a bountiful share of the wedding loaf. In this season of Valentines, it is pleasant to see "mate-choosing" begin to prevail. We are glad to know that *birds* are not the only creatures that fall under the sway of the Good Saint; but that our young friends have sought and found felicity, at "this season of the year," in the warm embrace of mounting, reciprocal love. It is good to
>
> "Go it while you're young,
> For when you get old, you can't."[31]

"Filler" matter not only entertained, it also propagated the Storey viewpoint. In the political campaign of 1848, *Patriot* readers could expect a steady diet such as the following:

> Take one letter from Taylor, and you have Tyler! —*Ohio Statesman.*
>
> Take one letter from Cass, and what sort of animal have you? —*Rough and Ready.*
>
> A whig editor to be sure; but in this case the animal would be of wood![32]

On January 25, 1848, Wilbur Storey greeted readers with a page one "Good morning" that announced the publication of the first number of the *Jackson Daily Patriot.* "A daily paper in Jackson?" Storey asked. "Will it pay? Can it be supported?" These were the questions which the editor explained he wanted answered.

30. *Ibid.*, February 6, 1849.
31. *Ibid.*, March 6, 1849.
32. *Ibid.*, August 8, 1848.

If the public wanted a daily newspaper then it should "step promptly forward, and subscribe, and pay. Yes pay, for we don't want a single subscriber unless he has the 'tin.' It is money that will make the mare go."[33]

In this fashion was issued the first daily newspaper in the city. The attempt proved premature, since Jackson was not yet large enough to support a daily either with sufficient subscribers or news matter. The *Daily Patriot*, which consisted of a single sheet, seven columns, printed on both sides, stumbled along for just two weeks. Then, on February 8, the editor announced a return to a weekly publication schedule. The editor of the Whig *Jackson Gazette*, "an imbecile" who advised Jacksonites to "do as little as possible to support the concern," was to blame according to Storey. Troubled by "green-eyed jealousy" because he published a paper "*only semi-occasionally*, and then [with] matter stale and unprofitable," the *Gazette* editor had convinced Jackson Whigs they "should support a foreign daily instead of one published in their own village."[34]

The loss of the Jackson postmastership in March, 1849, meant Storey would be dependent on local patronage to supplement his income. He was named inspector of the state prison later in 1849, but served less than six months.[35] Then, in the spring of 1850, he decided to run for election as a Jackson delegate to the convention called to revise the state constitution. His opponent was Austin Blair, later famous as Michigan's Civil War governor. The campaign, as might be expected, was heated but in this, his only try at elective office, Storey polled 1359 votes to edge the future governor by just over one hundred ballots. After this success Storey, in an editorial headed "Corruption Wins Not More Than Honesty," boasted of his win and accused Blair of trying to vitiate the public mind against the editor by a resort to an unfounded personal attack on his character and integrity. Blair replied that Storey had made use of whiskey on election day "in order to get men drunk first that they might more appropriately vote for him," and he ended by suggesting that if "corruption wins not more than honesty" Mr. Storey might then "try the honesty for once."[36]

The convention opened on June 4 and Storey received one of

33. *Jackson Daily Patriot*, January 25, 1848.
34. *Ibid.*, February 8, 1848.
35. Catlin, 522.
36. *Jackson American Citizen*, May 15 and May 22, 1850.

the ninety votes cast for president of the convention.[37] On June 19, after a morning debate on franking which included a long speech on how packages should be wrapped, Storey introduced his first resolution:

> *Whereas*, The amount of Buncombe that has been expended by the members of this Convention this morning, on the subject of postage, has cost the State more money than all the postage of members is likely to, therefore,
> *Resolved*, That the whole subject be dropped.[38]

The resolution "offered by Mr. Storey" was not adopted, and the convention passed on to the business of revising the constitution. In the proceedings of the next seven weeks, Storey conscientiously served the interests of his constituents while also looking after the welfare of "mechanics and laborers." Toward the close of the convention he became embroiled in a controversy with Governor John Barry that gained for the editor his first state-wide notoriety.

Among the dozen or so petitions introduced by Storey on behalf of interested constituents two were especially surprising. The first, presented for George F. Gardner and 150 other citizens of Jackson County on June 24, asked that "the franchise be extended to every male citizen of 21 years and that the word 'white' may be excluded from the Constitution, whenever and wheresoever the same may occur to the detriment of the colored citizens of Michigan." The second, presented on behalf of Mrs. Electa M. Sheldon and 157 other ladies of the village of Jackson, asked for a provision "prohibiting the manufacture, importation and sale of intoxicating liquors to be used as a beverage."[39]

Wilbur Storey's most significant contribution to the revised constitution of 1850 had to do with Article XVIII, Section Three, which dealt with convict labor at the state prison. This provision stated "No mechanical trade shall hereafter be taught the convicts at the State Prison of this state."[40] In the debate Storey vigorously and convincingly defended the rights of Michigan "mechanics and laborers" against what he considered unfair state competition if the prisoners were subsidized in trades. In arguing against a motion

37. *Report of the Proceedings and Debates of the Convention to Revise the Constitution of the State of Michigan, 1850* (Lansing: R. W. Ingalls, 1850), p. 2.

38. *Ibid.*, p. 150.

39. *Journal of the Constitutional Convention of the State of Michigan, 1850* (Lansing: R. W. Ingalls, 1850), pp. 115-16 and 287.

40. *Proceedings and Debates of the Convention, 1850*, p. 826.

to strike this section Storey asserted that subsidization of convict labor would offer the working class competition that "is unfair, unjust and ruinous." Further, if the provision did not stand as stated in the final draft of the constitution it would constitute discriminatory legislation against the most important single class of citizens in the state.

> What class of people do more to build your cities and villages? Who add more to the wealth and to the taxable property of your State than the mechanics? . . . [The mechanic] is indispensable. He is one of the great spokes of the wheel—aye, sir, he is one of the wheels itself—upon which we all roll to prosperity and greatness.[41]

The proponents of subsidizing mechanical trades for convicts argued that it was necessary if the state prison was to be self-supporting. Storey decried this position as "a dismal howl of 'expense, expense,' just as if it could be expected that a State Prison can go on the principle of a wind-mill." As Storey saw it, prisons had only two primary objects, the punishment of crime and the reformation of the criminal:

> But, in this State, these two objects seem to have been lost sight of. It seems no consideration with some that the State Prison is a public benefit, in so much as its walls form an effective barrier between the rogue, the highwayman, or the murderer, and the honest portion of the community.[42]

Storey's proletarian prose proved effective on this occasion because when the vote was taken his position prevailed thirty-five to twenty-five. The revised constitution of 1850 forbade the teaching of a mechanical trade to convicts. Storey had wanted the provision in the constitution, he said, because "every gentleman knows how desirable it is to avoid these collateral questions in politics." If left to the whim of the state legislature, he argued, the question would become political and he desired to "place the provision beyond the power of repeal through the efforts of interested contractors or other persons."[43]

So it was that the laboring man, "one of the wheels upon which we all roll to prosperity and greatness," found his most articulate champion at Lansing in 1850 in the person of Wilbur F. Storey.

41. *Ibid.*, p. 827.
42. *Ibid.*, p. 834.
43. *Ibid.*, p. 835.

Ironically, during the next thirty years, there was to be no more hated employer in the newspaper business than this same Wilbur F. Storey who until the day he died fought a bitter and successful campaign against the Typographical Union.[44]

On August 5, ten days before adjournment, Storey took the floor to introduce a resolution that led to the most bitter exchange recorded in the official convention debates. Democratic Governor John Barry had opposed Storey on the state prison issue, and despite the fact that the *Patriot* avidly supported Barry in his campaign for the governorship, Storey forgot partisan affinity as he asked:

> *Resolved*, That the Resolution adopted by this Convention on the 4th of June last, by which the Governor of the State was invited to take a seat within the bar of the Convention during its meetings, be and the same is hereby rescinded.

"I offer this resolution," Storey said, "for the single and significant reason that I am tired of seeing the Executive of the State . . . nosing about among the members of the Convention, logrolling with them upon questions which are to come up here for action." Further, Storey offered the resolution "in good faith" and because "the practice has become too palpable and too obnoxious to be longer overlooked."

The resolution was not adopted, but the reply of John S. Bagg of Wayne County would indicate that Storey's reputation for the sensational and unsavory was already well-established. "I am happy to think the resolution . . . came from the very source it did," said Bagg. "No other person of either party in the Convention, could have been stimulated by passion or otherwise, to have offered it." Since Storey was its source, Bagg concluded, "it not only falls harmless at the Governor's feet, but adds another laurel to his brow."[45]

After the convention closed, Storey returned to the journalistic wars in Jackson. For the next three years he stood sentinel over the Democracy, "guarding that party against all *isms* and preserving it in purity."[46] As the nation entered the final decade of crisis

44. See Chapter VI, pp. 119-20; and Chapter VIII, pp. 224-26.
45. *Proceedings and Debates of the Convention, 1850*, pp. 771-72.
46. *Jackson Patriot*, as reprinted in *Jackson American Citizen*, September 18, 1851.

over the slavery issue, Storey watched from his post in the *Patriot* office determined to quell all manifestations of northern antislavery sentiment. In September, 1850, Congress passed the harshest Fugitive Slave Law in the nation's history. Intended to quiet the slavery furor, the act had the opposite effect. Within a month northern antislavery elements were openly advocating civil disobedience in the name of a "higher law."

The reaction was noticeable especially among portions of the clergy who spoke against the law from their pulpits. In Jackson, the Whigs made adherence to the "higher law" a basic part of their political platform, and the clerical crusade was led by the Reverend G. L. Foster. Storey professed horror at the promulgation of such a doctrine by a political party. "Discord, social disorder, and unrestrained license, must be the result, if the new doctrine of the Higher Law should prevail."[47]

The fact that the Reverend Foster was particularly outspoken against the Fugitive Slave Law gave Storey added incentive. The dissident parishioner admitted his pastor had once enjoyed "our highest regard and confidence," but that was changed now that the minister was engaged in "warfare against the Union." As the conductor of a public press, Storey felt compelled to condemn and denounce Foster's "infamously atrocious doctrines." But mere condemnation did not suffice. Beginning in November, 1850, Storey undertook a campaign of vituperation against Foster clearly aimed at ruining the minister's good name in the community. For the first time in his career, Wilbur F. Storey used the columns of his newspaper to demolish the reputation of one who had incurred his enmity.

His campaign, "filled with the meanest and most contemptible species of abuse," was unrelenting. Reverend Foster "is not a right minded man" but one who "wears the sacred robes to cover a hypocrite and an intriguer." He was a preacher "descended from the sacred desk to wallow in the mire," a personification of "rebellion stalking at noon day in our streets." Or again, Foster was only "a pretended servant of the meek and lowly Jesus," a minister who stood "within the portals of the sanctuary of God, actuated by the most hellish passions." Foster stood helpless before this onslaught, and even counseled the Whig *American Citizen*

47. *Jackson Patriot*, as reprinted in *Jackson American Citizen*, November 27, 1850.

to ignore "Mr. Storey's observations" out of a sense of "Christian forebearance."[48]

The profession of journalism won over Storey irrevocably while he edited the *Jackson Patriot.* A genius in the art of typography from his earliest days in a print shop, the thrill of creating a weekly edition saturated with himself led him inevitably to seek out an opportunity to publish a daily edition. As the abolitionist movement renewed itself in the early 1850s, and Storey became "the self-constituted 'I AM' of the democracy of Jackson County,"[49] his desire to be at the forefront of the battle every day became overwhelming. When the official state organ of the Democratic party, the *Detroit Free Press*, ran into difficulty in January, 1853, party sachems offered Storey a half-interest for about $3,000. He accepted immediately, and within a year he made the *Free Press* the best known Democratic newspaper in the Old Northwest.

But it was not as a partisan journalist that Wilbur F. Storey is to be understood as a newspaperman. From the day he stepped into the *Free Press* office on February 15, 1853, he devoted his life to an unceasing effort to insure that each new edition outshone previous efforts. He became, in the words of a Detroit associate, "a fanatic in journalism." At least he had a fanatical streak, coupled with a burning desire to express his own convictions in print. This, with the addition of a sure instinct to ferret out and publish news, the more exciting the better, made Storey a spectacular newspaperman between 1853 and 1884. His success, achieved as a result of passionate attention to every detail in his newspapers, was attained only by constant, unremitting work that made of him a broken-down, burned-out old man before he was sixty.

Storey was thirty-four years old when he left Jackson. People who remembered him as a resident there said he was "reserved, a hearty hater, and one who in all matters in which he interested himself, was disposed to have his own way. He had a certain amount of popularity and is . . . remembered with respect."[50] The young apprentice from Vermont reached journalistic maturity with the *Jackson Patriot* between 1844 and 1853.

48. *Jackson Patriot,* as cited by *Jackson American Citizen,* November 27, 1850, March 12 and September 18, 1851.

49. *Jackson American Citizen,* September 18, 1851.

50. Obituary of Wilbur F. Storey, *Chicago Times,* October 28, 1884.

CHAPTER IV

DETROIT: Where's Mrs. Stowe!

Two young mulattoes have been lodged in the Litchfield, Conn., jail for an attempt to outrage the person of their mother. And among the free colored population of Connecticut? Where's Mrs. Stowe!
—*Detroit Free Press*, July 1, 1853.

JOSEPH CAMPAU AND JOHN R. WILLIAMS ISSUED THE FIRST NUMBER OF the weekly *Democratic Free Press and Michigan Intelligencer* on May 5, 1831, because a paper was "essential to the interests of the Democratic party." In June, 1835, it became a semiweekly, and three months later it became the *Daily Free Press*, "the first attempt of the kind in the State." The sheet was a folio, with a page about ten by seventeen inches. L. L. Morse and John S. Bagg purchased the paper on February 1, 1836, and enlarged it from four to six columns. A fire in January, 1837, destroyed the press, and publication was halted for six months. In 1846, the first power press in Michigan, and "the first west of Buffalo," was set up. The office at 50 Griswold Street was opened on September

22, 1850. Two years later Jacob Barnes and Company purchased the concern and installed Simeon M. Johnson as editor. On February 2, 1853, the Democratic party in Michigan convinced Jacob Barnes that it would be wise to sell the property to Wilbur F. Storey.[1]

With Franklin Pierce due to take office the following month, the party desired to revitalize its languishing state-wide daily, and Storey had proved his competence for the job through his nine years with the *Jackson Patriot.* According to the terms of the deal Storey received a half-interest in the *Free Press* while Ruben S. Chaney was guaranteed appointment as Jackson postmaster once Pierce took office.[2] A prominent Detroit Democrat, William Hale, retained the other half-interest until Storey bought him out in July, 1853.[3] From this date until he moved to Chicago, Storey retained full control and neither party, partiality, nor propriety dictated what he published in *his* newspaper.

When they announced the transfer of ownership Barnes and Johnson promised *Free Press* readers that the new editor "will discharge the duties of his responsible post with a single purpose to promote the interests of all."[4] They thereby released to Storey's control a limp Democratic sheet that showed every sign of an early expiration. It had changed hands three times since 1850, was short of circulation, short of cash, and for years had been short of capable editorial direction. Within a year, this picture changed. From a drab, seven-column party organ it was transformed into a typographically attractive eight-column Storey outlet, literally saturated with the political philosophy and personality of its energetic new custodian. The paper's first "enlargement," an additional column, occurred on February 17, only two days after Storey assumed control.[5] By October, Michigan had its first Sunday newspaper, initiated not to increase circulation but "so all the hands in our employ will be able to make the Sabbath 'a day of rest.' "[6] Besides establishing the first Sunday edition in Detroit, Storey also created a city news department "which didn't before exist,"[7]

1. Silas Farmer, *The History of Detroit and Michigan or the Metropolis Illustrated* . . . (Detroit: Silas Farmer & Co., 1889), I, 685-86.
2. *Detroit Free Press*, March 26, 1853.
3. *Ibid.*, July 15, 1853.
4. *Ibid.*, February 2, 1853.
5. *Ibid.*, February 17, 1853.
6. *Ibid.*, September 29, 1853.
7. William Stocking, "Prominent Newspaper Men in Michigan," *Michigan Pioneer and Historical Collections*, XXXIX (Lansing, 1915), 157.

and in the late 1850s William E. Quinby, later a principal owner of the *Free Press*, began to do legal reporting, "the first reportorial work of the kind on any Detroit newspaper."[8]

In 1853 Detroit was changing from a frontier trading post to a metropolis. By mid-century its population was 40,000, one-tenth the entire population of the state, and it was definitely a city on the move.[9] Editor Storey helped put the town "on the map" during the next eight years since a successful and outstanding newspaper was the best advertisement a city could have in the nineteenth century.

The general condition of partisan journalism, both nationally and in the Middle West, made the decade of the 1850s a particularly propitious time for a vigorous Democratic sheet, competently edited, to make its mark. The opponents of the Democracy, ably led by Horace Greeley and the *New York Tribune*, offered an aggressive and vital partisanship unmatched in Democratic ranks. The largest and most influential Democratic daily, and the only one that could pretend to a national influence approaching that of Greeley's *Tribune*, was James Gordon Bennett's *New York Herald*. But Bennett's partisanship at best was erratic, and in 1856 the *Herald* bolted James Buchanan to support Republican nominee John C. Frémont. The official "organ" of the party's national leadership, the Washington *Union*, remained without effective editorial management throughout the decade. In the South, Robert Barnwell Rhett's Charleston *Mercury* and Jefferson Davis' mouthpiece, the New Orleans *Delta*, propagated the "fire-eater's" gospel with such passion as to preclude any but a narrow sectional influence. On a national scale, then, in the 1850s, "Democratic journalism was in a sad state of confusion."[10]

This confusion was mirrored in the Middle West. The *Chicago Democrat*, effective Jacksonian voice since the late 1830s, apostatized in 1854 when its editor, John Wentworth, turned to the Free Soil cause rather than support Stephen A. Douglas' popular sovereignty. Douglas supporters countered by founding the *Chicago Times* in November, 1854, but the paper never caught on as an effective antidote to its chief rival, the abolitionist-inclined *Chicago*

8. Clarence M. and Agnes Burton, *History of Wayne County and the City of Detroit, Michigan* (Detroit: S. J. Clarke & Co., 1930), I, 642.

9. George B. Catlin, *The Story of Detroit* (Detroit: Detroit News Co., 1923), p. 505.

10. Roy Franklin Nichols, *The Disruption of American Democracy* (New York: Macmillan & Co., 1948), p. 58.

Tribune. In 1860 the *Times* supported John Breckinridge against both Douglas and Abraham Lincoln, and became noted chiefly for its strong support of southern secession in the months immediately following Lincoln's election. The oldest and strongest Democratic sheet in the Middle West, the *Ohio Statesman*, published at Columbus, also languished in the 1850s as its editor, Samuel Medary, grew weary after a quarter-century of partisan strife. In 1858 Medary abandoned journalism temporarily to take on duties as a territorial governor, first in Minnesota, then in Kansas. His exodus marked the end of the *Statesman's* influence beyond the borders of Ohio.

It was into this void that Wilbur F. Storey, with definite ideas concerning party dogma, stepped when he took over the *Detroit Free Press.* One of the chief ways in which the country at large subsequently heard of Detroit was through reprints of the spirited editorial thrusts Storey dealt his political, journalistic and other opponents. In the decade before the Civil War, Democrats throughout the region were exposed to Storey's counsel as practically every party newspaper in the Middle West reprinted the gospel as it appeared in his columns because it was the most vigorous articulation of the party's position to be found. It was thus that untold thousands knew of Detroit and Michigan only as they were written up in the *Free Press.*

Storey succeeded to the managership of the *Free Press* midway through a time of change for the American newspaper. The party press era of the Francis P. Blairs was ending, but not yet through. The popular press era of the James Gordon Bennetts and the Horace Greeleys was beginning, but had not yet matured. Partisan journalism did not die entirely until the Civil War nationalized politics. Popular journalism did not reach full bloom until the post-war "Gilded Age." In his guidance of the *Free Press* Storey succeeded to an amazing degree in combining both eras in his pages. He was consistently partisan, as the promise of his prospectus to be "radically and thoroughly *democratic*" indicated. At the same time he led in the change-over of the daily press from a dull record of routine affairs to a throbbing, often unhealthily seething cauldron of news, scandal and controversy. That he would do this was also indicated in his prospectus. He promised early, reliable and complete particulars on the commerce of the state and all leading points in the country. "The proprietor of the *Free Press* will spare no pains or expense," he concluded, in order that "a sheet will be furnished which shall be, not only in name, but in fact, a *newspaper*."[11]

Storey enlivened politics and considerably increased the space devoted to it while simultaneously he gave attention to local developments in society, theater, sports and "commercial intelligence." Under him the *Free Press* also pioneered in the Middle West with the publication of verbatim accounts of criminal court testimony, the bolder and dirtier the better, conspicuously displayed under screeching headlines intended to attract mob support. With leads written in a cynical, half-jocular vein, as if the courtroom grilling of a degraded half-wit was matter for a "Roman holiday," it did not make pleasant reading. Finally, although an apologist for Democratic men and issues, Storey refused the role of a party-line hack as he eschewed "Organism." Rather than organs, Storey called for an independent Democratic press "which will thunder its own sentiments and opinions on every occasion . . . instead of squealing the sentiments of this or that or other interest, or of this man, that man, or some other man."[12]

"A press which will thunder its own sentiments and opinions on every occasion" might serve well as the epitaph for the Storey years of the *Detroit Free Press*, because Storey did not write merely in support of those principles and parties in which he believed. More like an angry god, he thundered his bolts and epithets from the editorial columns, keeping constant watch that every item, from "City Intelligence" to "Fillers" supported his viewpoint or jabbed not so gently at his opponents. When he promised to be a "radical" Democrat, he never spoke with greater conviction. A man careful to warn abolition "fanatics" to beware of "excesses," he at no point stopped to follow his own advice. Thus, when forty subscribers quit his paper because of its views, Storey stated the *Free Press* "will not trim to suit the views of any man." He added that he "regards with contempt the man whose cry is 'Stop my paper!' " And then he closed with the solemn pronouncement that "he whose zeal runs away with his discretion is a poor discriminator of right and wrong."[13] On another occasion, when taking the *New York Day Book* to task because it was "extremely pro-slavery" he noted sagely that "there never was an extremist with a well-balanced mind."[14] Yet for Storey, without exception, the *Free Press* coun-

11. *Detroit Free Press*, February 15, 1853.
12. *Ibid.*, May 28, 1857.
13. *Ibid.*, March 22, 1853.
14. *Ibid.*, December 25, 1856.

seled constantly and zealously with apodictical certitude on all questions touching the commonweal. That opposing views might contain a shade of truth, or rationality, or even a right to public expression, was never considered.

What were the Democratic "values" upheld in Detroit by this "importation from Jackson, where the State prison is located?"[15] First, racism. Underlying all of Storey's other convictions was the certitude that the Anglo-Saxon race was ordained by the Almighty to spread the blessings of American liberty to all in the Western Hemisphere except Negroes. It was the former race that successfully carried out the American Revolution. It had then undertaken the subsequent peopling of the continent with patriots dedicated to a republican form of government. Its destiny was to see the American flag waving "from pole to pole," bringing the joys of freedom and self-government to all capable of such. In this connection, Storey did not consider the Negro even remotely worthy of consideration for freedom. At best, in his view, the Negro was a subhuman species who should preferably return to Africa, but under no circumstances was it possible for him to coinhabit the North American continent with white men in freedom.

This did not mean Storey was proslavery, a distinction he was always careful to make. Slavery was neither good nor evil in his view, was doomed to ultimate extinction, but until it died of "natural causes" it was the business of each state to settle the slavery issue to its advantage. Finally, there was absolutely no contingency under which the Federal government could have the slightest Constitutional authority to intervene in what was "obviously" a state concern.

Thus the second of Storey's Democratic "values" was the unquestioned supremacy of state governments vis-à-vis the central government. He foresaw, with fear, that if abolitionist sentiment should prevail state rights would perish. And with their death Storey felt American freedom would also be interred under the crushing weight of a central authority that would deny that people were capable of self-government in their local concerns. He considered himself a Jacksonian in this regard, in full sentiment with the principle "The World Is Governed Too Much!" that graced the

15. *Detroit Advertiser*, as reprinted in *ibid.*, January 15, 1857. This Republican newspaper so referred to Storey in protest to his "ridiculous libels" concerning Zachariah Chandler when Chandler replaced Lewis Cass as United States' Senator from Michigan. See Chapter V, pp. 103-5.

masthead of Francis P. Blair's *Washington Globe* during the Jackson years.

Storey was not an advocate of state rights, however, in the southern sense of that term. He denounced nullification and secession as damnable doctrines, and fought southern radicals as fiercely as he did any abolitionist. His views were based more upon a literal reading of the Constitution interpreted to mean that any right not explicitly granted the Federal government was of necessity reserved to the states. Any meddling by Congress with state concerns or any extension of Federal power beyond the narrow limits of strict construction were egregious usurpations destined to destroy self-government. Better to tolerate a local evil until the people themselves saw fit to eradicate it than risk an extension of Federal power with its concomitant lessening of local sovereignty.

These two tenets, racism and state rights, tenaciously held and constantly expounded, were at the heart of every political stand Storey took. Confident that they could be upheld only by the Democratic party, he was a Democrat. This meant that Democratic candidates on all levels would receive his support, while the opposition was assured of a steady stream of abuse and character assassinations rarely equaled. Abolitionists, "that class of men not satisfied to leave well enough alone,"[16] were in Storey's mind the most dangerous opposition while he lived in Detroit. Thus it was in the columns of the *Free Press*, against abolitionists and Michigan Republicans, that Storey perfected the techniques that shocked the nation when the same ammunition was turned on Abraham Lincoln.

The movement to abolish slavery, by force if necessary, had grown moribund in the late 1840s but was showing renewed vigor by 1853. Northern dissatisfaction with the Fugitive Slave Law of 1850, coupled with Harriet Beecher Stowe's classic reform tale that first appeared in book form in 1852, induced increasing thousands to conclude that slavery really was an intolerable evil that must be forcibly overthrown. No sooner was the Fugitive Slave Act enacted than the Reverend Theodore Parker, a New England Unitarian minister, enunciated the doctrine of a "higher law" above that of men. "When rulers have inverted their functions," Parker defined his explosive reasoning, "and enacted wickedness into a law which treads down the inalienable rights of man to such a degree as this, then I know no ruler but God, no law but

16. *Detroit Free Press*, March 17, 1853.

natural Justice."[17] By 1853, clergymen all over the North were expounding Parker's "higher law" as though it were the inspired word of God.

Besides clergyman, abolition publicists also renewed their efforts and found audiences ever more receptive to their pleas. *Uncle Tom's Cabin* was undoubtedly the most important factor in popularizing their ideas and broadening the base of their support. A special press consisting of thirty to forty newspapers, vigorously edited and widely quoted, circulated the message to the faithful by 1855.[18] Also by mid-decade powerful allies had been recruited among the daily press through such newspapers as Horace Greeley's *Tribune* in New York and Joseph Medill's *Tribune* in Chicago. While these latter two were not abolitionist in the sense that they preached an immediate crusade against the slave-holding states, they were adamantly against the further extension of slavery and they did not hesitate to adopt the "higher law" as their own to defend northern state Personal Liberty laws. When the Kansas-Nebraska Act passed Congress in 1854, and theoretically opened all territories of the United States to the possible extension of slavery, all elements of northern antislavery sentiment united in a hardened assault upon the institution itself. It was soon apparent that an irrepressible conflict was indeed in the making unless the Democratic party put its house in order and managed to maintain national ascendancy.

Wilbur Storey watched these developments with increasing concern. As early as 1839 he had predicted that the end result of abolitionism could only be the destruction of the Union. This conviction, coupled with an inordinate hatred of the Negro race, led him to conduct through the columns of the *Free Press* a one-man crusade against what he considered to be northern fanaticism. No other newspaper in the North was more persistent or violent in its condemnations of the "nigger worshippers." Storey understood that the form of extremism that burned the American flag and desecrated the Constitution of the United States might well result in bloodshed and civil war. And so he counterattacked, savagely and unremittingly, convinced that the best answer to both Massachusetts flag-burners and South Carolina fire-eaters was to

17. Reverend Theodore Parker, as quoted in Lawrence Lader, *The Bold Brahmins: New England's War Against Slavery, 1831-1863* (New York: E. P. Dutton & Co., 1961), p. 144.

18. Oscar Sherwin, *Prophet of Liberty, The Life and Times of Wendell Phillips* (New York: Bookman Associates, 1958), p. 102.

expose them as deranged. If this were done, all would be well with the body politic.

Throughout the 1850s, Storey saw both the slavery issue and abolitionist agitation as questions fundamentally involving state sovereignty. That the American Founding Fathers intended state supremacy with respect to the institution of slavery was in his mind an incontrovertible truth beyond the range of legitimate debate. When the Kansas-Nebraska Act brought the question to the fore, Storey decried the "Warfare Upon Popular Sovereignty" in an editorial that defined state rights and popular sovereignty as "synonymous terms. Destroy State sovereignty and the Union would be destroyed." Opposition to this view was "founded in the old instincts of federalism, which forever doubted and always will doubt, the capacity of the people for self-government." The power of the people resident in the area of a prospective state to decide their own institutions was "perfect, and the highest known to our institutions." The people of Nebraska, no less than the people of Michigan, might establish slavery at any time. "We should regret the introduction of slavery into Michigan, or into Nebraska. . . . But both have the right, and ten thousand acts of Congress cannot take it away."[19] Negro slavery, in this view, was not a consideration because "it is an issue of slavery or freedom for the white race, and not the black."[20]

This was the crux of the question as Storey saw it. "The white race is superior to the black . . . and the interests of twenty-five million of the former are paramount and ought not to be sacrificed to those of three or four million of the latter."[21] In an editorial headed "A Government of White Men" Storey stated unequivocally that the government of the United States was founded on a white basis, "made by white men, for the benefit of white men, to be administered by white men in such manner as they should determine." In his view, other races could have no part or lot in the American dream. "The Asiatic can never participate in it more than the negro," he maintained. "It is no oppression or proscription of either that he is excluded, because he has no right to be included." Both were inferior; neither could assimilate with Anglo-Saxons.[22]

19. *Detroit Free Press*, April 21, 1854.
20. *Ibid.*, September 23, 1854.
21. *Ibid.*, January 1, 1856.
22. *Ibid.*, July 27, 1858.

In October, 1855, "a look at the facts of history" with respect to attempts by Congress to regulate slavery through acts such as the Ordinance of 1787 and the Missouri Compromise of 1820 proved as "an incontrovertible fact that . . . these instruments [were] entirely powerless." That slavery did not exist in the Old Northwest "*is attributable solely to the doctrine of popular sovereignty*" Storey said. As proof he offered statistics showing that in spite of the Northwest Ordinance slavery was introduced into both Indiana and Illinois and continued to increase until the people themselves abolished it when they adopted state constitutions. By Storey's reckoning, under popular sovereignty the number of slaves in Indiana had been reduced from a high of 237 in 1810 to zero in 1850, while Illinois had gone from a high of 917 in 1820 to zero by the same year.[23]

Strident as Storey was in denying absolutely any power to the central government with respect to the issue of slavery, he remained in his own way a Federalist in upholding the ascendancy of Federal power in certain situations. At no point in his career, for instance, did he admit the right of secession and from the election of Abraham Lincoln to the outbreak of the Civil War he opposed the actions of the Confederacy. "The Federal government was constructed for all time, and is not a temporary expedient," he stated in November, 1860. If a state could secede at pleasure, he pointed out, then every state possessed the power to break up the government. "So weak a government was not contemplated by those who made it."[24]

So also with the doctrine of nullification. In Storey's eyes, the Fugitive Slave Law of 1850 was the unquestioned supreme law of the land, and state legislatures that decided otherwise by the passage of Personal Liberty laws would "destroy the stability of our Federal system of government." When the Supreme Court of Wisconsin, in the 1855 *Abelman* v. *Booth* decision, declared the Fugitive Slave Law unconstitutional and discharged from prison "convicts sentenced by it," Storey was incensed. Well might upright men exclaim "*O tempora! O mores!*" for the latter was debased, the former changed. Judges contaminated with the bacillus of nullification defiled the ermine. "Fanaticism sits upon the bench," Storey warned. "There is danger and reason for serious apprehension."[25]

23. *Ibid.*, October 9, 1855.
24. *Ibid.*, November 8, 1860.
25. *Ibid.*, February 10, 1855.

Storey never saw any inconsistency in the contradictory stands he occupied with respect to the Federal-state relationship. At heart, his outlook was determined by his hatred of the Negro, and although not a champion of slavery, he saw no merit in any attempts to alleviate the unfortunate situation of that race. The Negro was a savage, he felt, beyond the pale of civilizing influences. Those who held otherwise were demented, and their dementia endangered the future of the American Republic. Convinced that this was the case, he made the *Detroit Free Press* the most rabid Negrophobe sheet in the Middle West during the decade before the Civil War. Every trick of the journalist's trade was invoked in order that the Negro and his champion, the northern abolitionist, might be verbally slain.

Wilbur F. Storey was by no means alone among northerners in the racial attitudes he exhibited in the 1850s. The entire question of northern antipathy toward the Negro race during these years has to too great an extent been ignored. In the folklore of American history it is the racially liberal, benevolent and tolerant abolitionist who has emerged as the personification of the righteous, freedom-loving, typical northerner. According to the legend, when Civil War came, this northerner, halo in hand, went marching bravely off to battle in order to bring the blessings of democracy and liberty to his less fortunate black brethren in the South.[26] The fulminic pulpit of Theodore Parker or Henry Ward Beecher, the acrid pen of William Lloyd Garrison, or the impassioned oratory of Wendell Phillips have all been cited as proof that the vast majority of northerners accepted their common humanity with the Negro slave as justification for a war to insure Negro equality and freedom. Actually, instead of Negro equality, the exact opposite opinion—that the Negro was basically inferior to the white man—was more probably the prevalent view of most northerners of the Civil War generation.

At least there is strong evidence that, in spite of the favorable notices accorded prominent abolitionists because, as things turned out, they championed the "winning cause," in their own generation abolitionist fulminations did not dent the determination of a majority of northerners to preserve white supremacy. Even outside the ranks of the Democratic party northern commitment to racial

26. This is the line of argument used, for example, by Arthur Schlesinger, Jr., "The Causes of the Civil War: A Note on Historical Sentimentalism," *Partisan Review*, XVI (October, 1949), 968-81.

equality seems at best to have been vague. Certainly the concept of the innate superiority of the "white race" noticeably cut across party lines once Lincoln's Emancipation Proclamation brought the immediate possibility of racial equality to the fore. This northern antipathy was especially manifest in the Old Northwest, where "outrage over slavery and belief in white supremacy . . . were often harmonized in the antislavery intellect,"[27] and where, incidentally, Wilbur F. Storey's racial views enjoyed the widest circulation.

There can be no doubt that the Douglas wing of the Democratic party, with its strength centered in the very Northwest to which Storey spoke, generally agreed that while slavery was not morally right, the Negro nonetheless was an inferior person who could and should be denied social and political equality with the white man. The senator from Illinois spoke the consensus of his sectional followers when he stated at Ottawa, Illinois on August 21, 1858, in his first direct confrontation with Abraham Lincoln, that he was opposed to Negro citizenship in any and every form. "I do not hold that because the negro is our inferior that therefore he ought to be a slave," Douglas said. He pointed out that humanity and Christianity both required that every right, privilege and immunity "consistent with the safety of society" should be extended to the Negro. But, he insisted, this certainly could not mean equality with the white race. Stephen A. Douglas spoke for the entire Democratic party of the Northwest when he concluded that citizenship must be confined to white men, "men of European birth and descent."[28]

But conviction of the necessity to maintain white supremacy was by no means limited to Douglas Democrats in the Northwest. When circumstances forced Republicans of the region to face squarely the possibility that the end of the Civil War would bring racial equality as a major fruit, they did not hesitate to affirm their belief that equality between black and white on the North American continent was an impossibility. Some, such as Wisconsin Senator James R. Doolittle, insisted that emancipation be followed by colonization of "the unwanted race" in Africa because "the question of race is more troublesome than the question of condition."[29]

27. Jacque Voegeli, "The Northwest and the Race Issue, 1861-1862," *Mississippi Valley Historical Review*, L (September, 1963), 235.

28. Speech of the Hon. Stephen A. Douglas, Ottawa, August 21, 1858, in Robert W. Johannsen, ed., *The Lincoln-Douglas Debates of 1858* (New York: Oxford University Press, 1965), pp. 45-46.

29. Senator James R. Doolittle to Mary Doolittle, April 19, 1862, as cited in Voegeli, 243.

President Abraham Lincoln himself confessed his feeling that Negro freedom could not bring Negro equality because "the broad physical differences between the two races is disadvantageous to both." The President advocated postwar separation of the races, preferably by African colonization, because "on this broad continent" not a single Negro could be the equal of a single white man.[30]

Wilbur Storey, then, was speaking to a prevailing prejudice of his section when he preached his gospel of race hatred. His major significance in this regard lies not so much with the uniqueness of the things he said, but rather with the sheer nastiness with which he propagated his view. Daily, for eight and one-half years, the *Detroit Free Press* spoke as a piercing, unrelieved siren whose shrill cacaphony of racism resounded throughout the lower Great Lakes region where the newspaper was read, and listened to.

The first editorial that combined Storey's convictions with respect to Negroes and state rights appeared on March 17, 1853, when he saw fit to approve the action of the Illinois legislature in passing a law restricting Negro settlement in that state. "We do not propose to discuss the subject morally or politically," Storey began, though "we confess that we are inclined to favor these prohibitory laws." While granting it was "undoubtedly wrong" to pass a law that would "drive negroes or mulattoes, already settled, out of the State," Storey felt that since states might rightfully determine who may or may not be citizens it was "perfectly just and salutary" to prohibit Negro settlement. He concluded that abolitionists were the real culprits, driving the states to "the adoption of measures to prevent themselves from being run over by absconding negroes and migratory vagabonds enticed from their masters."[31]

Because Storey believed that the Negro could never attain social rank in the United States, the solution to the Negro question was African colonization. If he would return to Africa, his prospects would change. He would enjoy "to the fullest extent the blessings

30. "Address on Colonization to a Deputation of Negroes," August 14, 1862, in Roy P. Basler, ed., *The Collected Works of Abraham Lincoln* (9 vols., New Brunswick: Rutgers University Press, 1953), V, 371-72. Further evidence that belief in Negro equality was not the prevailing sentiment among northern white people of the Civil War generation may be found in C. Vann Woodward, "The Antislavery Myth," *American Scholar*, XXXI (Spring, 1962), 316; and Frank L. Klement, "Midwestern Opposition to Lincoln's Emancipation Policy," *Journal of Negro History*, XLIX (July, 1964), 169-83.

31. *Detroit Free Press*, March 17, 1853.

of life, liberty and property . . . and carry religion to thousands of his brethren . . . who know nothing of gospel truth."[32] Further, borrowing a page from the American Colonization Society, Storey held that transplanting the Negro to Africa, under the auspices of the Federal government, "is a work of *necessity*. It is a dictate of humanity."[33] By mid-April, 1853, American slavery was "a means employed by Infinite Wisdom to work out the regeneration of a benighted continent."[34] With "Gospel truth," "the dictate of humanity," and "Infinite Wisdom" all in accord, Storey was curious as to "what reasonable man can doubt" the necessity of African colonization?[35]

In airing such views, Storey was expressing the prevalent mid-century idea that Providence guided all nations to ruin or salvation. "Men and nations are alike instruments in His hands for the accomplishment of purposes vastly beyond the range of finite vision," the editor stated. African colonization was thus God's will because it would root out the evil of American slavery and restore the "Africans" to their divinely ordained home prepared to civilize the dark continent. The American Colonization Society, out of a sense of genuine concern to remedy the Negroes' lot, had been saying this since 1816.[36] In 1853 the view was echoed by the Detroit editor. It is impossible to believe that he was sincere, even temporarily, in this stand. Rather, the advocacy of colonization offered Storey a cloak of respectability to cover his rabid Negrophobia, and in addition, who could possibly argue with God as an ally?

As the possibility of colonization became more and more remote, and the strength of abolitionism more and more pronounced, Storey became more and more hysterical. While admitting slavery "is a great evil," it bore no comparison with the evils that would spring from any plan "of the manumitted slaves remaining in the country."[37] To those who argued that African colonization was an economic impossibility, Storey replied that universal emancipation would be far worse as it "would soon work the destruction of the African race in this country." In an editorial in May, 1853, he showed how "Abolitionism Is Inimicable to the Black Race" be-

32. *Ibid.*, March 31, 1853.
33. *Ibid.*, April 1, 1853.
34. *Ibid.*, April 14, 1853.
35. *Ibid.*, March 31, 1853.
36. P. J. Staudenraus, *The African Colonization Movement, 1816-1865* (New York: Columbia University Press, 1961), Preface, vii-viii.
37. *Detroit Free Press*, August 8, 1853.

cause God favored Negro extinction. "The free blacks, feeble in intellect, repulsive in person, and addicted to improvidence and vice," could not overcome the competition of whites. Extinction "seems like a melancholy fate" for the Negro, Storey concluded, "but we say let the work of the Almighty go on."[38]

As the decade progressed, and all schemes for African colonization failed, Storey asked "What Shall Be Done With Them?" After showing how the slave population in the United States had increased from 600,000 in 1790 to 3,200,000 in 1830, he voiced concern for 1950 when the number of Negroes "will have reached 52 millions." There was but one way of avoiding, in 1950, "a war of *castes*" between 50 million Negroes and 150 million whites. "That way is by colonization."[39] Abolition, which "would diffuse the negro population over the whole country," could only end in catastrophe. "Indeed," Storey asked, "what city would not diminish [its Negro population] if it could?" If the abolitionists persisted, Storey felt sure that "some violent remedy to the evils of a large black population" would be necessary.[40] Eventually, Negroes were no better than dogs in Storey's eyes. "Some . . . States have gone to work to establish negro citizenship within their boundaries. They have a perfect right to do this. They may, if they choose, make citizens of dogs."[41]

Storey considered not only the Negro, but all non-Causasians as inferor by nature to the white man. With respect to "The Chinese in California" there "probably does not exist on the face of the earth, a more cunning, thieving, and, where they possess power, turbulent and corrupt race than the inhabitants of the Celestial Empire."[42] In a call for the immediate annexation by the United States of the whole of Latin America, Storey discoursed on the "Hispanic-American Race" and called for extirpation in a manner resembling a twentieth-century advocate of genocide:

> Of all the nations of the world, laying claim to the description of civilized, the mixed Spanish, Indian and Negro people of Mexico, Central and South America are the worst. Devoid of the slightest spark of moral principle, devoted to the most debasing vices, and utterly destitute of industry or enterprise, they answer no purpose but to cumber the earth,

38. *Ibid.*, May 14, 1853.
39. *Ibid.*, May 6, 1854.
40. *Ibid.*, July 31, 1859.
41. *Ibid.*, June 14, 1857.
42. *Ibid.*, September 2, 1854.

> and to render worthless the territory upon which they have existence. . . . Wherever this race have sway, the country is withered beneath their rule as if by a blast of the deadly simoon; peace, virtue, and prosperity cease to exist, and anarchy and vice reign paramount. Such is the sad state of things at the present time, and so, we have no reason to doubt, it will ever continue to be until the places of the off-scourings of mankind are filled by another and better race. That time *must* come. A merciful and all-wise Providence never designed that any portion of His footstool should labor forever under a curse so disastruous [*sic*] in its effects as that which now impinges over a large portion of the Western Hemisphere. Deliverance must eventually be had. The rule of the effete Hispanic-American race must have an end. It is earnestly to be hoped that the hour of its dissolution may not much longer be protracted.[43]

With convictions such as these, it remained Storey's "humble opinion that the negro is not ready for freedom."[44] Besides, and most important to Storey, the Negro agitation distracted from the really serious problems confronting the country. No improvement of lasting significance could really be achieved, Storey felt, until Congress could turn its full attention to bettering communication and transportation with the Far West. One Sunday in 1858, dismayed that Congress was "in a state of continuous disruption" over the slavery issue, he stated that Negro inferiority "is the deliberately formed judgment of the entire civilized world." This was so because "there is not now, nor has there ever been, a nation, or kingdom, or tribe, nor so far as we are aware, a single individual of the negro race who has contributed anything to the vast store house of knowledge."[45]

It should be noted that one glaring inconsistency stood out in Storey's race attitudes. While repeatedly denying even the possibility of citizenship, civil rights, and such to the Negro, he just as consistently defended the rights of American Indians against the machinations of a government that to him abused and violated these "original Americans."[46] In a plea not to remove Indians forci-

43. *Ibid.*, April 19, 1854.
44. *Ibid.*, July 31, 1858.
45. *Ibid.*, December 5, 1858.
46. There is good evidence that Storey was not alone among northern Democrats in this inconsistency. See, for example, David Lindsey, "*Sunset*" *Cox: Irrepressible Democrat* (Detroit: Wayne State University Press, 1959), p. 263. Lindsey points out that Cox championed the cause of many minority

bly from Michigan, Storey noted that "to exile them beyond the confines of civilization would be inhuman, not less would it be cruel. . . . Let them have homes of their own," he added, "and let them realize that they are men and citizens, men with inalienable rights and immortal souls."[47]

Almost thirty years before Helen Hunt Jackson penned her famous plea for reform in Indian-white relations, Wilbur Storey insisted that the American government "has a moral obligation to secure the good of our fellow man," and this called for a complete change in Indian policy. In a very long editorial entitled "The True Governmental Policy Toward the Indian" Storey articulated a position that proved he was at least a generation ahead of his countrymen in the demand for a decent Indian policy. In it he pleaded with the Federal government to take the initiative in introducing a policy aimed at full citizenship for the Indians by teaching them agriculture and granting them individual land ownership from the public domain. Such regeneration could not be accomplished rapidly, the editor reasoned, but even though it took three or four generations "it would repay the most strenuous exertions." The Federal government possessed the power and means to help the Indian, and the safety and position of the Republic demanded that the effort be made. He resorted to elaborate proofs from history showing that man could be elevated, and asked "if the individual, why not the tribe, a large community, or nation?" He ended by noting that Americans were an energetic people renowned for "the peculiar facility with which they accomplish any undertaking in which they engage." Since the government partook of the energy of the individual and "it is the true province of this republic to improve mankind," efforts must begin at once "for the amelioration of the Indian race."[48]

Inexplicably, Storey maintained this concern for the Indian throughout his entire career. In the bloody Plains' wars of the late 1860s and 1870s, Storey's *Chicago Times* consistently sided with the red man. "We should, in all our dealings with them, be as scrupulously exact as if they were a nation of kings, instead

groups such as the Indians in the West, the newly arrived immigrants in eastern cities, the Irish insurgents in British jails, and Jews suffering under Russian pogroms. And he urged the United States government to prevent or remedy injustices to these groups. But for the injustices to the Negro, "Cox had a blind spot."

47. *Detroit Free Press*, January 26, 1856.

48. *Ibid.*, February 2, 1855.

of the palsied remnants of savage tribes."[49] According to the *Times* dishonest Indian agents and western white vagabonds were mostly to blame for Indian unrest, and at one point Storey went so far as to suggest that "Federal muskets be aimed" against "the deviltry of white men" instead of the Indians.[50]

With respect to the Negro, however, Storey's newspapers never changed. Both during and after the Civil War, the *Chicago Times* remained as rabid as the *Detroit Free Press* in the 1850s. Storey supported the anti-Negro stand of the *Free Press* by saturating its columns with a steady stream of abusive and sensational "news" items and "fillers" designed to heap ridicule and opprobrium upon the race. A favorite device was to report in fulsome detail court cases involving "cullud pussons." Another involved the regular exposé of occurrences in Detroit's Negro "dives." One of these stories was headed "ANOTHER NEGRO DEN BROKEN UP—WHITE WOMEN IN NEGRO DANCE HOUSE."[51] There were also reprints from southern newspapers, such as the account from the Marion, Mississippi, *Republican* of the fate of a Negro burned at the stake by a white mob for the murder of a white girl who resisted his "lustful advances."[52] The "filler," of course, had limitless possibilities. A sampling of the *Free Press*' daily articles might have included "A DARKEY RESTORED TO LIFE BY A DOG'S TAIL," "NIGGER WORSHIP IN MILWAUKEE," "A Disgusting Case—a White Girl Elopes With a Negro," or "Conjugal Infidelity Among the Darkies in Windsor."[53] The crudest, perhaps, was the following:

> Niggers . . . Niggers . . . Niggers.
>
> As to the eternal nigger question—nigger in the morning, nigger at noon, nigger in the evening, nigger sleeping or waking, seeing or smelling, in Congress or out—has not, really, the country had about enough of it?[54]

It is apparent that Storey's policy on the race question bordered on obsession. Even if considered in terms of the 1850s, it would be difficult to find another northern editor who so frequently and consistently reached so low to discredit the Negro. Even southern

49. *Chicago Times*, December 12, 1863.
50. *Ibid.*, June 19, 1867.
51. *Detroit Free Press*, June 10, 1858.
52. *Ibid.*, June 14, 1855.
53. *Ibid.*, July 21, 1855, April 13, 1856, January 4, 1859, and June 26, 1860.
54. *Ibid.*, February 10, 1856.

journals which defended slavery rarely engaged in such unremitting assaults upon the Negro as a human being. Yet the extremes to which Storey went on this question must be understood if his editorial policy as a whole is to make sense. Such a mentality could not be expected to engage in reasonable or responsible dialogue with respect to political issues. It was significant, for example, that Storey vociferously defended Abraham Lincoln and his conduct of the Civil War until the President declared the Emancipation Proclamation. Until the end of the Civil War, Storey's rank racism more than any other factor dictated his attitudes and policies.

Abolitionists received unceasing attention from Storey. Since he felt as he did about the Negro, it was beyond the editor's comprehension how any sane person could bother himself about the fate of those whom even the Constitution recognized as at best only three-fifths a citizen. The excesses of some of the better-known manumissionists furnished him with more than enough ammunition to supply his editorial arsenal. Since abolitionists were in total disagreement with Storey, they were demented. But dementia was not their worst sin. Far more malignant was the treason they preached with respect to the Federal government and the Constitution of the United States. Storey might have overlooked what he considered the harmless murmurings of idiots had they stopped there. But when they approved the sacrilege of Garrison's "Compact with Hell" and "prostituted Christian pulpits" with their "perverted" gospel, the limit was reached. Storey let loose, and in his attack he included under the general heading "abolitionists" such diverse elements as "spirit rappers," "socialists," "feminists," "atheists," and "free love" advocates.[55]

In Storey's first year with the *Free Press*, he concentrated on general denouncements of "Mrs. Stowe and her ilk." A frequently used tactic was to present abolitionists as money-grabbers devoid of any sincere interest in helping the Negro. When Dr. Gamaliel Bailey, editor and publisher of the *National Era*, a nationally circulated weekly newspaper, published a statement of condition in March, 1853, which showed an average circulation of 28,000 copies weekly at an annual cost of $25,000, the *Free Press* discoursed on "Being An Abolitionist to Some Purpose." It stated that Bailey lived in a $2,000 mansion, drove a carriage and pair "which no cabinet member can afford to do unless he has a private fortune,"

55. See "CONGLOMERATION," *ibid.*, June 7 and 10, 1853.

and dashed about the Capitol "like an Eastern nabob, giving parties to the tun, and making a big fuss generally." The paper concluded that Bailey's "investment in *negroism* is paying most usurious dividends" that enabled the doctor "to *stow* away a princely fortune."[56]

Harriet Beecher Stowe and her book held the limelight throughout 1853. In May, Storey delivered a long declamation on "The Practical Consequences" of the publication of *Uncle Tom's Cabin.* After establishing the necessity of censoring the reading of the young if morals were to be preserved he decried the tendency toward "amalgamated marriages, amalgamated elopments, and . . . amalgamated illicit intercourse" because Little Eva made many a young girl see "every Negro an Othello, and herself a Desdemona." He then cited specific examples. There was the young wife of a Brooklyn clergyman who, under "the very drippings of the sanctuary of HENRY WARD BEECHER," presented her husband with "a pair of woolly headed twins, for which the sooty coachman . . . was responsible." And several married and unmarried ladies, not satisfied with "kissing those whom the sun has fiercely kissed . . . exposed their shame by throwing themselves into the arms of some strapping negro." All of these things furnished "food for reflection" upon the propriety of allowing young girls to read *Uncle Tom's Cabin.* Storey ended by calling for the curtailment of the book's circulation lest "suitors who happen to be of the white species . . . have to adopt the prayer which Shakespeare puts into the mouth of the Moorish prince—'Mislike me not for my complexion.' "[57]

As abolitionist strength grew in the spring and summer of 1854, and the first steps were taken to form a new political party with abolition overtones, Storey decided a definition of the malady was in order. Under the heading "What It Is" the editor opined "Abolitionism is a rare institution" that embodies "more hypocrisy, more rascality, more irreligion in its ranks than any other institution which has ever existed."[58]

From this point on, there was no limit to the lengths to which Storey would go to discredit "these poor demented images of their Maker." They were "a niggardly set of fellows" and "false as hell itself."[59] To the question "What is Abolitionism?" he offered an answer in three words—"*fanaticism run mad.*" There were different degrees of the disorder, and fresh recruits betrayed "no such vio-

56. *Ibid.*, March 1, 1853.
57. *Ibid.*, May 6, 1853.
58. *Ibid.*, July 23, 1854.
59. *Ibid.*, June 10, 1855, January 1, 1856, and February 10, 1854.

lence as the old sinners." Rather, the malady was a sort of consumption that went on consuming "the common sense of a man until he is a crazy fanatic." The progression was regular and certain. The tendency was natural. The end was sure. From a decent citizen and a Christian, the abolitionist "descends to the condition of a valueless member of society and an infidel."[60]

The notion that the abolitionist movement represented "fanaticism run mad" was the key to understanding Wilbur F. Storey's attitude toward it. To attempt to abolish slavery within the procedural framework of the American political system was one thing. To advocate that slavery must be abolished at all costs and by any means was quite another. The latter position was fanatic, Storey felt, and since numerous abolition spokesmen took this position, he concluded that the entire movement was vitiated. In his view, the abolitionists intended not only to abolish slavery, but also to emancipate women from the fetters of family obligations. They spoke also for those who wanted marriage abolished so that man's natural instinct to mate could have full reign in the free love paradises they envisaged. Horace Greeley's speculations on the benefits of "passional attraction" proved this to the Detroit editor's satisfaction. Some abolitionists even looked forward eagerly to the day when man would be emancipated from the shackles of religion, and while Storey affiliated with no particular church or creed, he fancied himself a defender of the "Church of Jesus Christ" against those who would destroy it. Finally, Storey associated many abolitionists with the doctrines of socialism in one form or another, and he concluded they must be stopped before they brought about the ruination of the country.

In short, the moral righteousness of a crusade to abolish slavery was not a question in Storey's eyes. Over and above his racial attitudes which made any such crusade preposterous to begin with, Storey felt that the crusaders of the 1850s would ultimately abolish not only slavery, but the very foundations of civilized society as well—the family, religion and private property. They preached not social reform, but social revolution, and Storey would have none of it.

Whether or not he was correct in this evaluation, many of the pronouncements of abolitionist leaders tended to confirm the editor's suspicions. No one can read his newspapers without concluding that Storey was sincere in his efforts to expose abolitionists

60. *Ibid.*, June 10, 1855.

by every means at his command, and the man who damned fanaticism became in his own right a fanatic who pulled all stops in an effort to destroy the effectiveness of his opponents.

Storey seemed most upset by what he deemed the unnecessary interference in politics by Protestant clergymen who argued the antislavery cause. With respect to "Politics in the Churches" he stated that "a portion of the . . . clergy . . . are doing more effective work for the promotion and spread of infidelity than all the anti-religionists combined." How was it possible, Storey asked, "that a pulpit should be turned into a political rostrum without disgusting more or less of those who are accustomed to sit under it on every seventh day of the week?" Clergymen would be better to restrict themselves to the welfare of souls, Storey insisted, but instead ministers were attending political meetings and the bolder ones even "acted as orators thereat, thus directly joining a party organization." If churchmen continued such activities Storey was convinced they would destroy their churches as effective religious instruments.[61]

When a delegation of New England ministers petitioned the Senate of the United States, "in the name of God Almighty," to vote against the Kansas-Nebraska Act in March, 1854, Storey did not equivocate with respect to such "Clerical Assumption." The *Free Press* expressed doubt whether a more blasphemous document was ever spread before a public assembly in the United States. In addition to blasphemy, the offending ministers were also guilty of levity, and Storey especially wondered "how they know the will of God touching the Nebraska bill?" The assumption that Divinity counseled the defeat of the act "is not only shockingly wicked, but . . . is inadmissible in a human point of view."[62]

In the weeks that followed the introduction of the resolution, Storey delighted in exposing "One of the Signers" as an embezzler[63] and "Another of the Signers" as a seducer of innocent maidens.[64] Particular "political preachers" were favorite targets, and Henry Ward Beecher and Theodore Parker received a fair share of denunciation. Storey's jibes were not without humor. For instance, when it was reported that Beecher "says he means to vote against the Nebraska bill, though the ballot boxes be placed in the

61. *Ibid.*, March 24, 1854.
62. *Ibid.*, April 1, 1854.
63. *Ibid.*, May 7, 1854.
64. *Ibid.*, May 23, 1854.

jaws of hell," Storey added "well, every man has a right to vote in *his own precinct.*"[65]

In the last week of May, 1854, the nation received a vivid demonstration of the violence that Storey repeatedly warned would inevitably result from the "higher law" preaching of Reverend Theodore Parker and his followers. Shortly after six o'clock in the evening of May 24, a Negro named Anthony Burns was arrested in Boston on charges of theft and taken to the jury room of the Federal court house. Here, the Negro was confronted by Colonel Charles F. Scuttle of Richmond, Virginia, who claimed Burns as a runaway slave and demanded his return under the Fugitive Slave Act. Burns was detained overnight and it was arranged that the case would be heard the following morning.

Word of the arrest and detention got out the same evening, and Boston abolitionists swung into action. Inflamatory handbills were circulated on May 25 urging Bostonians to "Watch the Slave Pen!" lest a free citizen of Massachusetts be dragged into slavery. By Friday evening, May 26, the city was in a ferment, and a crowd gathered at Faneuil Hall to hear speeches by Theodore Parker and Wendell Phillips. Phillips got things off to a rousing start when he shouted "I am against squatter sovereignty in Nebraska, and I am against kidnapper sovereignty in Boston." He ended by urging the audience to see to it that the Negro did not leave the city of Boston and to prove that "Anthony Burns has no master but God."

Theodore Parker then came forward and delivered a wild, disjointed speech calling for "deeds for liberty as well as words." He proposed that the crowd meet at the court house at nine o'clock the following morning to free the incarcerated Negro. At that point someone in the crowd shouted "No, let's go tonight" and the Faneuil Hall meeting adjourned to Court House Square. The doors of the court house were stormed by the mob, bricks were thrown at the windows, and shouts of "Rescue him!" and "Bring him out!" resounded through the air. Just as the courthouse doors gave way a force of fifty police officers, armed with cutlasses, appeared to disperse the mob. Shots rang out and in the melee one of the policemen, James Batchelder, was shot and killed.[66]

When word of the Batchelder murder reached Detroit, Storey expressed a proper sense of outrage. In his sermon preceding the

65. *Ibid.*, June 17, 1854.

66. For the details of the Anthony Burns affair see Sherwin, pp. 323-29; and Lader, pp. 203-16.

shooting, Parker had advocated resistance to the Fugitive Slave Law, "the constitutional law of the land." He had cried "for white blood, denounced the government, and argued treason," said Storey, and to emphasize the point, the *Free Press* ran a half-column memorial to the slain officer, bordered in black:

NEGROPHOBIA
In memory of
JAMES BATCHELDER
aged 24 years,
who, on the 26th day of May, 1854
in the city of Boston,
in the very Temple of Law,
and in the performance of his duty as a policeman,
DEFENDING THE LAW AND ITS SANCTUARY
From illegal force and violence,
WAS MURDERED BY A MOB
Instigated to riot and bloodshed,
in the name of
HUMANITY AND FREEDOM,
by Theodore Parker,
a minister of the Gospel of Peace;
by Wendell Phillips,
a wealthy citizen of Boston,
and by other kindred spirits and advocates of
the "higher law."

It is true that the officer named above—a citizen and a white man—has been killed—murdered—at the instigation of a few fanatical abolitionists.[67]

When Parker and Phillips were indicted by a United States Circuit Court Grand Jury in Boston, in December, 1854, and charged with committing and inciting acts of violence, the *Free Press* found it "A Gratifying Indication." It registered dismay, however, when the charges were not pressed and throughout the rest of the 1850s Theodore Parker was consistently denounced as "the murderous parson."

As the activities of parsons in politics increased, Storey decided "the institutions of this country contemplate a complete separation of Church and State, in theory and fact." He favored such separation because "it is one of the best features of the Constitution." He added "it will be a taste of the millennium when priests

67. *Detroit Free Press*, June 4, 1854.

of all creeds and sects shall devote themselves singly to ghostly affairs, and leave temporal affairs to be managed by those educated to the business."[68]

Storey's attack on mixing religion with politics reached a climax when word reached him of the Kansas Emigrant Aid meeting at North Church, New Haven, where Henry Ward Beecher asked for rifles for Kansas. In an editorial headed "Religion and Rifles" the *Free Press* compared Beecher with Phineas T. Barnum. Each, "in his peculiar line," was a charlatan and a humbug. "Think of it!" the paper noted. "A meeting held in a church, conducted by ministers, assembled for the purpose of putting arms into the hands of men with which to shoot other men!" Rifles were not the weapons of the religion of Christ, Storey concluded, and the new dogma that the rifle was a greater civilizer than the Bible, a dogma propagated by "bloodthirsty and murderous priests," was not calculated to inspire peaceful nonbelievers with any love for the gospel.[69]

When logic failed, Storey resorted to satire. In June, 1856, the *Free Press* published an "intercepted, confidential correspondence" from the "Rev. Dr. Schreecher to His Friend and Brother, Horace Steeley." The letter came from the "Church of the Holy Rifles" where the Reverend Schreecher preached on the text "Go ye into the world and shoot the Gospel (from Sharp's rifles) at every creature." Under the new dispensation of "rifleism" Scripture could "be sent right directly home to the hearts of the people, and be inwardly digested by them."[70]

When many prominent clergymen gave public support to John C. Frémont, Republican candidate for President in the 1856 election, Storey published a long discourse on "The Hand of God as Discernible by Political Clergymen." He noted that just as they saw the hand of God in Frémont's nomination, so in 1840 "*the hand of God* elected [William Henry] Harrison." And such trouble for God's hand, to nominate and elect Harrison only to call him immediately to his everlasting home. "In these latter days [God] employs strange instrumentalities to accomplish His purpose," Storey noted on this occasion.[71]

"To what purposes are they devoting their churches?" This was the foremost question in Wilbur F. Storey's mind as he surveyed

68. *Ibid.*, April 18, 1855.
69. *Ibid.*, March 27, 1856.
70. *Ibid.*, June 14, 1856.
71. *Ibid.*, August 16, 1856.

religion and religious trends in the 1850s. To the extent that a church or minister preached orthodoxy and avoided controversial stands regarding moral questions with political implications, to that extent such a church or minister would have the unqualified support of the *Detroit Free Press.* Storey was absolutely consistent in this respect; and as a result, his newspaper was a prominent champion of religious orthodoxy among secular dailies in the Old Northwest. Utterly devoid of discernible attachment to any particular creed or sect, the editor could nonetheless wrap himself in the cloak of orthodoxy to score telling points against his opponents.

The heterodox views of some prominent antislavery spokesmen made defense of orthodoxy a natural ally of any antiabolitionist. Resolutions such as the one presented by Abby Kelley to the tenth anniversary meeting of the Massachusetts Antislavery Society—"that the sectarian organizations called Churches are combinations of thieves, robbers, adulterers, pirates and murderers"—helped convince respectable people of the basic irreligion of the manumissionists. Wendell Phillips' definition of the American church as "a synagogue of Satan" only served to make such a conviction firmer.[72]

In this view preachers who lent support to the antislavery movement were in reality lending their hand to the furtherance of infidelity. This concern of the pulpit with basic social and political evils was a new phenomenon in the American religious experience. Sharpened by the battles of the 1850s, it would expand into the "social gospel" school of religious thought in the post-Civil War period. And then, as earlier, opponents of such preaching would ground themselves in religious fundamentalism because refuge in "the old time religion" was so handy a garb to clothe indifference toward the basic inequities in American society. The "new" religion threatened the comfortable, easy existence by calling for basic social changes. So the respectable and solid citizens rejected its preachers, and it was to the respectable and solid portions of the community that Wilbur F. Storey, basically unregenerate as regards spiritual things, addressed his religious views.

Abolition publicists such as Gerrit Smith, the "mad" Horace Greeley and Wendell Phillips were of course not overlooked. They fostered miscegenation, Fourierism and treason. Extremes nurtured extremes, and "The Madness of Fanaticism" as expounded by the *New York Tribune* was met in kind. Storey cited a Greeley editorial that stated that "Congress should break up in wild disorder"

72. Sherwin, p. 154.

while Washington "blazed by the torch of the incendiary" if the Kansas-Nebraska Act became law. If the author of such sentiments "shall not be damned," Storey added, "then there is no justice in heaven."[73]

The first notice in the *Free Press* of Gerrit Smith occurred on January 28, 1854. Under the heading "A Modern Reformer" the newspaper noted the New Yorker's mental deficiencies. "A professor of the belief in land redistribution, SMITH is by far the largest landholder in the State of New York." Smith, according to the *Free Press*, also opposed war and thought the army should be abandoned and the navy dismantled, and hence "GERRIT SMITH is a harmless man."[74]

Harmless or not, Smith's career and ideas typified an erraticism noticeable in the activities of many prominent abolitionists. A man of unquestioned sincerity in his antislavery beliefs, Smith suffered from, in the words of a close associate, "a sort of pecuniary plethora" that moved him to donate at least $50,000 in cash to various antislavery groups. At the same time, he bestowed 120,000 acres of his estimated 750,000 acre estate as a gift to deserving freed colored men.[75] As an abolition philanthropist, then, Smith stood in the front rank of those who were willing to invest their fortunes as well as their time and ideas in the crusade for Negro freedom. But Smith also found time for other philanthropic endeavors aimed at improving society in the 1840s and 1850s, and his association with some of these movements furnished ammunition to people like Storey who opposed abolitionism per se.

For instance, Gerrit Smith was an early crusader for legislation prohibiting the manufacture and sale of liquor, "a man who screamed freedom while he would deny freedom of drink to the poor." One of the largest landowners in the country, he abhorred "land monopoly." A believer in women's suffrage, he coupled his feminism with a belief in the necessity for "free love." To cap the case against him, and incidentally to discredit his antislavery associates, Smith was also outspoken for "free religion" in which men entered into a directly personal relationship with the Creator. Thus, in Smith's view, all ministers and organized churches were superfluous, and he so stated.

By the time of the Kansas excitement in 1856, Smith changed

73. *Detroit Free Press*, May 13, 1854.
74. *Ibid.*, January 28, 1854.
75. Sherwin, p. 103.

his pacifism, and with the change Storey no longer considered him "harmless." The *Free Press* quoted Smith to the effect that "slavery must go out in blood. The time for abolishing it by the ballot box is gone by, never to return." Smith thus excited civil war to throw this "happy and prosperous country into . . . anarchy." The result would be "murder, rapine and desolation," and Storey prayed that "no considerable portion of the American people will render assistance to the realization of such terrible results."[76]

The meticulous care with which Wilbur F. Storey presided over every facet of his *Free Press* domain was indicated by the fact that from February 15, 1853, until June 4, 1861, there was only one occasion on which the newspaper published a completely favorable comment on any abolitionist. In November, 1855, Wendell Phillips delivered a lecture to the Detroit Young Men's Society, and the morning before the talk the *Free Press* announced the subject "will be some well selected literary topic, which will be ably handled by the speaker, and which will be highly interesting and instructive." Just how this favorable notice, which went on to describe the leading orator of abolitionism as one "who stands high as a man of literary tastes and attainments," slipped into Storey's columns was not explained. In September, 1855, however, the *Free Press* had announced "Positions open: Two news reporters for the city. Apply Free Press Office." One week after Phillips' lecture, the newspaper was again in need of two reporters, but now the announcement read "Positions open: Two *intelligent* news reporters for the city. Apply Free Press Office."[77]

Whatever the circumstance which allowed the original notice to appear, Storey undertook, beginning on November 16, a two week campaign against Phillips that more than made up for any misleading impression. Of the speech, the newspaper observed that Phillips made some desultory remarks that "he very truly observed . . . were hardly worthy to be called a lecture."[78] Then every day until November 29 the *Free Press* castigated Phillips with offerings that depicted him as "a moral traitor" who would be "guilty of treason in fact did not the Constitution make the offense consist in an overt act." Phillips was perhaps "afflicted with monomania or lunacy. It is charitable to suppose that he is." If he were of sound mind then his heart was black and he deserved

76. *Detroit Free Press*, September 12, 1856.

77. *Ibid.*, November 15, 1855, September 21, 1855, and November 22, 1855.

78. *Ibid.*, November 16, 1855.

to be "denounced, and execrated and spurned . . . instead of being received with listening ears."[79]

Of all antislavery spokesmen in the 1850s, Storey devoted the most attention to Horace Greeley of the *New York Tribune*. This was to be expected, since Greeley edited the most prominent daily newspaper on the antislavery side of the spectrum, and one that was second only to the *Chicago Tribune* in influence within the area of the circulation of the *Detroit Free Press*. Storey considered it his duty to provide midwestern readers with a strong antidote to Greeley's "rampant nonsense," and hence the *Free Press* paid careful attention to all utterances of "the bran bread philosopher."

And during the 1850s the Detroit editor could hardly have found a more suitable straight man than the New Yorker whose personal traits and editorial quirks so readily lent themselves as foil for ridicule and abuse. Storey noted Greeley's affinity for "Fourierism," phrenology, spiritualism and Graham crackers, and compared these ideas to "the abomination of Mormonism" but "a more fatal cancer than that which festers and maturates at Utah." He noted, accurately if acerbatingly, that the *New York Tribune* had championed "every attempt to 'reconstruct society'—and these attempts have been as often as annual," since 1842. The pretense of each attempt had been liberty, which in Storey's mind meant "anarchy, confusion, unrestrained license, polygamy, incest and the abasement of women." Horace Greeley had taught this liberty from the day of the establishment of his newspaper and Storey professed amazement that in spite of this "it is patronized more considerably than any other daily journal in the United States by clergymen."[80] Storey's antipathy for Greeley lasted until the latter died in 1872, and when the Democratic party nominated the "Fourierite candidate" for president in that year, Storey quit the party never to return to its fold again.[81]

When the *New York Tribune* became the advocate of the new doctrine of "passional attraction" in the autumn of 1855, the *Detroit Free Press* enjoyed a field day. No doctrine could have been more calculated to serve Storey's double purpose of discrediting "The Fruits of Socialism" while also serving his readers a generous potion of ribald sex. When the New York police raided a Broadway "Free Love Association," Storey admitted "the exposé is really

79. *Ibid.*, November 29, 1855.
80. *Ibid.*, May 2, 1857.
81. *Chicago Times*, May through November, 1872.

unfit to publish." He then proceeded to publish a full column describing "entertainments," "passional embraces" and "amusements." The headline read:

> Row Among the Free-Lovers—The Police Taken with an "Affinity" for "Passional Attraction" for the Harem.

"Greeley . . . and the rest may try to disguise the fact as much as they will," Storey added in a short editorial, "but it is plain that lust and sensuality are the main causes of the success of the 'Club.'" No talk of "social enjoyment," "individual sovereignty," or "other mystic themes intended to tickle the ears of silly women" could change the facts, Storey concluded. "It is only a brothel on a new plan."[82]

Under the headline "The Fruits of Greeleyism" the *Free Press* exposed the Cresco, Iowa, Free Love Union of "males and females who live according to the declared doctrines of their faith." The declared doctrines included, according to the *Free Press*, the principle that free love would bring the millennium; that fornication is "holy"; that bigamy is no crime; that the crime of adultery is fictitious and "what the law calls adultery is the highest and truest relation of which two persons are capable"; that bastards are "the most beautiful children in the world"; and finally that society "ought to be destroyed." The story ended by noting it "certainly does seem strange . . . that in the nineteenth century, in the midst of a civilized community, there are men and women who have [such] brazen hardihood."[83]

In the spring of 1854, Greeley's *Tribune* horrified the *Free Press* by publishing a series of articles "to ascertain the value of the Union to the people of the North in dollars and cents." In an editorial on "The Pecuniary Value of the Union" Storey acknowledged his humiliation to learn that there was an American citizen "so traitorous to the land of his birth . . . as to cooly sit down and calculate . . . the value of the Union to any particular section of it." There was no standard by which to measure the Union's value Storey said "except by comparison with every other country on earth."[84]

Greeley only appeared once in Detroit during the years that

82. *Detroit Free Press*, October 20, 1855.
83. *Ibid.*, August 31, 1855.
84. *Ibid.*, May 4, 1854.

Storey operated the *Free Press.* That was on March 29, 1854, while Greeley was "itinerating through the West," and the *Free Press* coverage of his lecture was not nearly as abandoned as might have been expected:

> The philosopher stands low in stature, with a bend indicating plainly enough his notorious characteristics—a living witness to the truth of phrenology. We did not get close enough to hear the subject of the discourse [but?] a phillipic the lecture might have been against tobacco, tea, coffee, or white bread—bran being the favorite esculent of the lecturer. . . . Whatever it was, it was listened to by a large auditory, a flattering thing to a speaker, no matter what his reputation.[85]

When Greeley returned to New York, however, he published some observations on Michigan that raised Storey's ire. The *Tribune* editor observed that Michigan had been passed by in the general rush westward because "her prairies are wet and sour, and she has too many of those shallow reservoirs of mud and water which try to be ponds." In addition to the political and ideological differences that separated the New York and Detroit editors, this report struck Storey in a most tender spot as he always championed the cause of the localities in which he published a newspaper. "We have always regarded GREELEY as humbug," Storey noted on this occasion.[86]

So went the battle of Wilbur F. Storey against the most widely read antislavery editor in the country. In addition to the editorial and news attacks, Greeley also received regular attention in the "fillers." Typical were two lines that appeared in September, 1856:

> An abolitionist thinks it would be a "God-send" if H. G. could be "got on board the ship of state." It would be a blessing to get him on any ship that was outward bound.[87]

From the "Fiery Immolation" on July 4, 1854, when William Lloyd Garrison desecrated the American flag and burned a copy of the Constitution of the United States, to "The Bloody First Act of the 'Irrepressible Conflict' Drama"—John Brown's raid on Harper's Ferry in October, 1859—Storey watched the progression of abolitionist fanaticism with sincere alarm. Each manifestation of

85. *Ibid.*, March 30, 1854.
86. *Ibid.*, April 11, 1854.
87. *Ibid.*, September 27, 1856.

extremism in "Bleeding Kansas," the heated debates in Congress that caused Preston A. Brooks to assault Charles Sumner, and finally the "martyrdom of Old Brown" all served to convince Storey of the correctness of his position. To his credit, he denounced the southern extreme as vociferously, if not as frequently, as he did abolitionists. The handling of the Kansas crisis by both the Pierce and Buchanan administrations was also denounced fiercely, as Storey attempted to be the voice of moderation, immoderately pleading his cause. His was not the only voice saying these things in the 1850s, but the *Detroit Free Press* under his direction said them more stridently and consistently than any other newspaper in the Middle West. He articulated, in an extreme way, the sentiment of the many northern Democrats who formed the backbone of what became the Copperhead movement during the Civil War, a conflict that Storey repeatedly predicted was inevitable if abolitionism were not stopped.

Storey was not completely opposed to reform. "New brooms are desirable articles," he stated, "for the same reason that new mayors of our larger cities are occasionally desirable—they sweep clean. . . . But we suspect there is such a thing as sweeping the carpet too clean . . . so harshly as to damage it."[88] It was in the light of "sweeping the carpet too clean" that he viewed most abolitonist agitation. In a long editorial headed "Reformers" Storey spelled out his position. A reformer, one who removed an evil and replaced it with a good, was esteemed by honest men everywhere. He stood in vivid contrast to "the petty bigots and small brained fanatics" who passed for reformers in the 1850s. Jesus Christ was Storey's favorite reformer because rather than condemn and revile His enemies, He used reason. "No bigotry, no intolerance, no bitter words, no imprecations upon opponents," but rather "gentleness and love" had marked the work of this "Primal Reformer" of the world. The effective reformer was the one who now followed in the Master's footsteps, and Storey felt he was not to be found in the America of 1854. Instead the country was filled with "knaves, scoundrels, and cut-throats." Impious men, these, only pretended followers of Christ but actually "exact copies of Satan, the first hypocrite, and in their base deceptions, they almost outdo their great original."[89]

Actually, it was not so much that abolitionists were less than

88. *Ibid.*, April 13, 1855.
89. *Ibid.*, June 15, 1854.

Jesus Christ that most disturbed Storey. Rather it was his conviction that they would "incite to disunion, sedition and civil war" in order to implement their schemes, and in this they must be stopped. In the course of his daily campaign against "Mrs. Stowe and her ilk," the editor said many wise and prudent things. For example, in "Questions to be Pondered" in June, 1855, he noted "we must look at things as they are, and not as we would have them."[90] On another occasion, he said with much wisdom that zealotry never addressed the intelligence of man "but, whether in religion, morals or politics, seeks to bring men's necks to the blocks, and release or behead them as they subscribe to or reject the fiery creed that is thrust before them."[91]

Storey understood these things to be true, yet he was no less the zealot with the *Detroit Free Press.* A man who recognized the futility of looking at things "as we would have them, instead of as they are," he still proceeded to ignore completely the very real fact that a significant proportion of northerners believed the enslavement of human beings because of an accident of color to be an intolerable evil. A man who preached the necessity of an appeal to the intellect if men were to be won over to truth, he nonetheless strove incessantly to produce a newspaper that specialized in the gratification of the baser instincts of the mob who built his city circulation to the highest in Detroit. Wise enough to see that only fanaticism "seeks to bring men to the block as they subscribe to or reject a fiery creed," every number of the *Free Press* issued by Storey sought no less than the verbal "beheading" of all who rejected his creed.

Had he been a man of more moderate temperament; had he stopped to follow the good advice he so frequently doled out in his editorial columns; had "no bigotry, no intolerance, no bitter words, no imprecations upon opponents" really been the guiding principles of his editorial policy, he might have enjoyed posterity's recognition that he was the greatest journalist in Michigan in the decade before the Civil War. But then, he would not have been Wilbur F. Storey.

90. *Ibid.*, June 13, 1855.
91. *Ibid.*, November 1, 1855.

CHAPTER V

DETROIT: Radically and Thoroughly Democratic!

In politics, the *Free Press* will be radically and thoroughly *democratic*—not in name merely, but in the advocacy of those great principles of popular liberty which have always been the cardinal doctrines of the republican party in this country, and which are the supporting pillars of the National Union.

—*Detroit Free Press*, Prospectus of Wilbur F. Storey, February 15, 1853.

WILBUR F. STOREY SECURED CONTROL OF THE DETROIT FREE PRESS because Michigan Democrats felt he could spearhead the drive against their political opponents better than any other newspaperman in the state. They did not realize that Storey's notion of what constituted proper Democracy encompassed all sorts of things extraneous to the interests of the party. The range of his Democratic beliefs was indicated by a "Statement of Religious and Political Faith" in June, 1853, when he noted "a natural aversion to all sorts of humbugs and isms" whether they be temperance laws, spiritual manifestations, Uncle Toms, or whatnots. "Our readers know that we are not extremely fastidious in denouncing and holding up to ridicule all those things which are calculated to pervert or lead astray the public mind," Storey said. By the editor's reasoning, the church was "the great and all-sufficient instrument" by which the world was to be morally regenerated and the Democratic party was "a like lever by which the earth is to be politically regenerated." If men got outside of these two instruments they would be "running after strange gods, and evil and not good will come of it."[1]

All of the elements in this statement were as essential to the cause of Democracy in Storey's eyes as was the verbal annihilation of Republican politicians. Democrats who had views other than these were read out of the party, because in the mind of Wilbur Storey his convictions on all questions were synonymous with the true principles of the party. Those who questioned this were either ignorant, hopelessly imbecile, or "black republican" traitors.

Storey succeeded to the editorial direction of the *Free Press* just three weeks before Franklin Pierce was inaugurated. After four years of Whig drought, sanity and economy would be restored to the national government. The *Free Press* marked the occasion properly with a series of florid panegyrics that oozed with sloppy sentimentality. Four days before the inauguration Pierce was lauded because he would rid Washington of "official and semi-official cormorants whose dreams are of pillage, and whose scent in their waking hours is close upon the flesh-pots of Egypt."[2] When Whig newspapers protested the Democratic scramble for spoils, the *Free Press* reminded readers of an even more "Melancholy Spectacle" in 1841 and 1849 when "ravenous wolves" exhibited such greed that they killed two presidents. "It is remembered with sorrow that the office seekers killed old GENERAL HARRISON in a month, and that even that hearty old soldier GENERAL TAYLOR lasted but a year."[3]

Actually, in the first six weeks that Storey edited the *Free Press*

1. *Detroit Free Press,* June 20, 1853.
2. *Ibid.,* February 28, 1853.
3. *Ibid.,* March 25, 1853.

he had little time to devote serious attention to the new administration in Washington. He arrived in Detroit just three weeks before the municipal election of 1853. In the campaign the city was embroiled in a bitter debate over the church-state relationship to public education. In January some Catholic priests, "a few only" the *Free Press* insisted, demanded that a portion of the city tax revenues for public schools be allocated to help sustain the parochial system. The Wayne County Democratic convention ignored the priests, but nominated several Irish Catholics for city offices. Detroit Whigs then accused the Democrats of a sellout "to Romish priests," and early in February dissident Democrats fielded a ticket of "Independent candidates" pledged against any diversion of tax revenues to sectarian purposes.

In addition to this, Joseph Warren, editor of the Whig-leaning *Detroit Tribune*, launched a bitter attack against the Catholic Church. Since the Irish Catholic vote was essential to a Democratic victory, and since the Democratic party was split into the "Independent" faction which declared against parochial use of tax funds and the "Regular" slate which refused to so declare itself, a Whig victory seemed assured. It was into the midst of this local brawl that Wilbur F. Storey stepped when he took over the *Free Press.*

In this situation, Storey had to tread carefully lest he further aggravate party harmony. "We have been a resident of Detroit about ten days," he stated on February 19, "and however much we might be inclined . . . to take one side or the other of a question which is purely local in character, we should deem it the part of modesty, at least, that we gain a residence in the city before foisting our opinions upon the community."[4] One week later, "lest silence lead to misapprehension," Storey defined the position of the *Free Press*: "The democratic ticket we understand to have been regularly and fairly nominated. . . . This fact is all that we desire to know. The Free Press will faithfully sustain the democratic ticket."[5]

Storey gave this degree of support to the "Regular" slate against the "Independents" right up to election day. At the same time, however, he deemed it his duty to defend Detroit Catholics against the vituperative attacks of Warren and the *Tribune.* During the campaign, Warren printed a "sermon" by a certain Kirkland, a

4. *Ibid.*, February 19, 1853.
5. *Ibid.*, February 23, 1853.

Protestant street preacher, that stated "every Catholic wife is a whore, every daughter a prostitute, every born Catholic a bastard, and every Catholic orphan asylum a mere refuge for the bastard children of priests, nuns and unmarried women of the Catholic Church."[6]

With respect to the specific school issue, the *Tribune's* policy was indicated by an editorial headed "THE WAR UPON EDUCATION" that accused the Catholic clergy of plotting the destruction of the entire public school system in the United States. "The Romish priesthood" was doing this because in America, as all over the world, "it opposed the cultivation of the intellect [and] the improvement of the mind." Fortunately, Warren concluded, the Papists in Detroit "reveal the cloven foot at almost every step," and hence the community had been warned in time.[7]

Storey witnessed this campaign, and remained silent. "We have never had the reputation of concealing our opinions," he stated, but propriety, and any chance for a Democratic victory, dictated silence until after the election. In defense of the "Regular" nominees the *Free Press* noted "it is not enough that a candidate be *suspected* of holding adverse views. . . . Suspicions should be reduced to certitudes." With respect to the Common School system, it "must be preserved" because it was "grand in inception," "most munificent in its object," "a noble Structure," "the sheet anchor of free institutions" and "the pride and hope of the republic." Should elected Democrats try to change this, "we would be the first to denounce them, and to insist that the undoubted prevailing wishes of the people should be faithfully observed."[8]

On election day, the *Free Press* asked "an avoidance of excitement and intemperance" because "nothing can bring greater reproach upon the good name of a city than disorderly and riotous conduct at the elections." As was inevitable, the Democrats sustained an overwhelming defeat, although "there was no disturbance at the polls."[9] The day after the canvass, Storey noted how right it was that Americans were jealous of religious interference in governmental affairs. The entire separation of church and state and perfect toleration of all religious opinion were the most prominent features of the American system. But, in the city election, "a large

6. *Detroit Daily Tribune*, as reprinted in *Detroit Free Press*, May 3, 1853.
7. *Detroit Daily Tribune*, March 12, 1853.
8. *Detroit Free Press*, February 25 and March 1, 1853.
9. *Ibid.*, March 7 and March 8, 1853.

portion of the people have believed that the preservation intact of some of their public institutions was at stake. *Hence the results*!"[10]

In the weeks that followed, Storey spelled out his conviction that there must be a complete separation of church and state. On March 10 he stated that every public school in the nation must be kept "entirely and thoroughly free" from all sectarian influences. There was no "half-way mark" in this regard, Storey felt, and if the schools could not be so preserved then he suggested dividing the funds among all sects to be used by each in its own way. It was his preference, however, to "exclude everything bearing upon religion . . . even the Bible," because school was not the place where children should learn their religion. "Leave this duty not to the school teacher, but to the parent and pastor."[11] When the *New York Tribune* declared in favor of the Common School system Storey found himself in the unusual position of agreeing with Horace Greeley. "It is not often that we find anything that we can commend" in the *Tribune*, Storey stated. "But for once the Tribune's views are just, patriotic and right."[12]

The uproar in Detroit in the spring of 1853 over the use of Common School funds by parochial schools was a local manifestation of what threatened to become a national issue. It was touched off in the autumn of 1852 when Bishop John Hughes of New York allowed the publication of a series of articles in his diocesan newspaper, the *Freeman's Journal*, urging Catholics everywhere to unite in demanding public money for the support of their own schools. Hughes was the best-known and most respected Catholic prelate in the United States at this time, and since his official organ had originated the proposal, his fellow clerics throughout the nation interpreted it as a command to act. By the following spring, the issue was of major importance in every state that boasted a sizable Catholic population.[13]

In most of these states, the issue was hottest in the urban areas where the Irish and German elements, rabidly Catholic, clustered together in their immigrant "patches" and provided the vital backbone to the northern city vote that went to the Democratic party on election day. When Protestants reacted, immediately and vio-

10. *Ibid.*, March 8, 1853.
11. *Ibid.*, March 10, 1853.
12. *Ibid.*, March 21, 1853.
13. Ray Allen Billington, *The Protestant Crusade, 1800-1860: A Study of the Origins of American Nativism* (New York: Rhinehart & Co., 1952), pp. 292-93.

lently, the school issue inevitably became intertwined with Democratic politics in these cities. In Detroit, Wilbur F. Storey's first move was to separate the school question from the platform of his party. "Any attempt to foist upon the democratic party issues which are foreign to the principles and policy of party organization," he stated, "should be promptly met and decidedly rebuked."[14]

But in declaring against parochial school use of tax funds, Storey was very careful not to divorce his newspaper from a solid defense of the Catholic Church against a rising tide of Protestant attack. Such a defense was natural to the editor for several reasons. For one, the Irish in Detroit did vote a straight Democratic ticket and were being subjected to a daily assault by the leading Whig newspaper in town. For another, the official position of the Catholic Church on the slavery issue came closer to one that Storey could approve than the position of any other major denomination in the United States. As one leading diocesan weekly put it: "As a general rule wherever you find a free-soiler, you find an anti-hanging man, woman's rights man, an infidel frequently, bigoted Protestant always, a socialist, a red republican, a fanatical teetotaller, a believer in . . . every devil but the one who will catch him."[15] Storey's *Free Press* could not have put the case against abolitionism more succinctly.

A similar point of view was evident in the Catholic press throughout the country, and the Catholic hierarchy consistently cited Scripture and Church tradition to prove that slavery was compatible with the practice of religion. Human bondage, according to the argument, was not morally wrong so long as the theological conditions for "just servitude" were met. Regularly throughout the 1850s Storey was able to cite extensive extracts from the preachments of the Catholic bishops that proved that slavery was not wrong per se and that churchmen had no business interfering in political questions. A pastoral letter issued by the American bishops after they convened in Baltimore in the spring of 1858 so coincided with Storey's position that he published it in its entirety. He gave special emphasis to the concluding paragraph that exhorted the Catholic clergy to

14. *Detroit Free Press*, April 2, 1853.

15. *The Pilot* (Boston), as cited in Oscar Sherwin, *Prophet of Liberty, The Life and Times of Wendell Phillips* (New York: Bookman Associates, 1958), p. 130.

"leave to worldlings the cares and anxieties of political partisanship" and "study only to win to truth the deluded children of error . . . so that becoming all to all, you may gain all to Christ."[16]

But neither sympathy with the position of the Catholic Church on slavery nor the desire to placate Irish sentiments for the polling booth stopped Storey from castigating both Catholics and Protestants with perceptive candor when their arguments over the school question became "A Source of Alarm." He felt free to say that the conduct of many Protestants was "illiberal, intolerant and indefensible," but at the same time the attitude of some Catholic clerics and newspapers was "outrageous and anti-republican, not to say in some respects intolerable." He rebuked Catholic spokesmen for their intemperate and unmeasured denunciation of the Common School system and stated that the allocution of Pope Pius IX describing civil marriages as concubinage was "disgraceful and damnable." But while Catholics bore the primary responsibility "for the recent upheavings" over the school question, the *Free Press* was careful to add that the "unceasing goadings of Catholics and Catholicism" by American Protestants probably furnished "a sufficient apology for complaint and perhaps retaliation." Storey ended his comments with a pledge that "we intend to speak fearlessly and plainly on these subjects. It is time the press should do so."[17]

The religious discord caused by the Common School controversy in 1853 was but a preliminary to the renewal of an all-out attack upon Catholicism and foreign immigration later in the decade. Throughout the uproar, Storey defended immigrants and pleaded for religious toleration. After the advent of the Know-Nothing movement, he openly championed the cause of religious freedom for Catholics.

At first, however, he limited himself to pleas for tolerance. In late 1853 and early 1854, a defrocked Catholic priest from Italy, Father Alessandro Gavazzi, made a sensational tour of the country during which he exposed "the secrets and abominations of the

16. *Detroit Free Press*, June 1, 1858. The best analysis of the attitude of the Catholic Church toward the slavery controversy is found in Madeleine H. Rice, *American Catholic Opinion in the Slavery Controversy* (New York: Columbia University Press, 1944). According to Miss Rice, two currents were especially noticeable among northern Catholics. One, there was almost unanimous agreement that the principles and ideals of abolitionism threatened the safety of the country and conflicted with Catholic ethics. Two, the existence of slavery was compatible with the tenets of the Catholic faith.

17. *Detroit Free Press*, May 3, 1853.

Romish church." Gavazzi was "a commanding personality"—six feet tall, beardless, but with long black hair and compelling eyes, uniformed in monkish garb with a blazing cross interwoven over his breast. Disenchanted with Rome because of the papal failure to support the Italian revolutionary movement after 1848, Gavazzi fled to England and in March, 1853 was imported to the United States by the American and Foreign Christian Union. He preached "Destruction to Popery" in a series of speeches in northern cities in the summer and autumn of 1853.[18] Gavazzi attracted large audiences. In Buffalo and Cincinnati his incendiary harrangues provoked riots and bloodshed.

Before he arrived in Detroit Gavazzi's "Farewell Lecture" was announced, and Storey "heartily rejoiced" at the news in an editorial that spelled out the editor's position with great precision. Storey confessed he had no argument with the former priest or the Catholic Church and admitted Gavazzi's right to speak out. But unfortunately, the lectures had promoted hate instead of brotherly love, riot and bloodshed instead of true religion. In the United States, "where the largest liberty of thought and action is accorded to every individual," Storey reminded readers that "we cannot be too liberal in exercising the heaven-born virtue of charity."[19] Religious intolerance refused to heed the voice of moderation, however, particularly if the voice so speaking was that of Wilbur F. Storey.

In June, 1854, "An Old Enemy in New Habilliments" appeared in Detroit when Michigan Know-Nothings organized. Storey, who condoned Negro slavery and believed all non-Caucasians incapable of civilized life, was nonetheless prompt to damn this resurrection of the Native American movement because it "proscribed men *for the accident of their birth* [emphasis added] and denied the rights of conscience." The *Free Press* pledged an unremitting campaign against "everything of this sort . . . and we call upon the community to reprobate [Nativists] and their infamous purposes."[20]

During the next three years, the newspaper used every means to keep its pledge, but the righteousness of its crusade was tainted by political opportunism. In every election after the formation of the new Republican party all opposition candidates were tied-in with native, white, Protestant supremacists. Thus, on the one hand

18. Billington, pp. 301-2.
19. *Detroit Free Press*, January 6, 1854.
20. *Ibid.*, June 6, 1854.

Storey made a sincere effort to expose the dangers that a secret political organization posed for the American political system. On the other hand, there was no doubt that he made use of the Know-Nothing furor to discredit Republicans who had no connection or sympathy with the movement. There were enough Native American adherents who also supported the new Republican party in the Detroit area, however, to lend credence to some of the editor's charges.

In an early denunciation Storey stated that the new Nativist movement was vastly objectionable because "it is a *secret organization*; and of all political machinery, secret associations . . . are the most dangerous and the most to be dreaded." This was so because no man knew who would be the victim of persecution. He concluded with a denunciation of the movement's organizers as "charlatans and bigots—political adventurers and cut-throats,—enemies of good order—disturbers of the public quiet."[21]

Storey felt, however, that he must "go into the contest with clean hands." Before launching his attack on the Know-Nothings, therefore, he stated "it is impossible to close our eyes to the fact that foreign born citizens" bear a good deal of blame "for the proscriptive spirit abroad in the land." These immigrants had not sufficiently "cast off their nationality and regarded themselves as American citizens." Instead, they had formed "into separate societies or clans" and refused to integrate with American life. Until they changed this, some Americans would inevitably regard them with suspicion.[22]

This said, Storey proceeded to lash out unmercifully at the Nativists. In "The Eight Inquiries" he asked eight questions that any citizen who had to face his God, his conscience, or George Washington and Thomas Jefferson, should answer. He then noted "it will be a very sorry day for free government, when in America, men shall be proscribed on account of their religion or their nativity." He pointed out that if one religion could be proscribed then there was no safety for any. Then, shifting directly to the Catholic issue, Storey reminded his readers that Catholics were "among the earliest settlers of American soil, and among the sternest and purest patriots of the American revolution. Their blood flowed as freely as that of protestants."[23]

21. *Ibid.*
22. *Ibid.*, June 17, 1854.
23. *Ibid.*, June 13, 1854.

Throughout the summer and fall of 1854 Storey kept up the attack. In July he drew a parallel between "The Jacobins of France and the Know-Nothings of America" in which he warned that "the voice of experience enunciates a warning so solemn," with respect to secret societies "that it must not be disregarded."[24] When E. C. Z. Judson, "with a sobriquet of Ned Buntline," was revealed as the founder of the movement, Storey offered *Free Press* readers a character sketch: Buntline is "a graduate of the penitentiary—a pimp of vice and debauchery—a low-lived, black hearted scoundrel—a brothel bully."[25]

Storey's characterization of Buntline, who is best remembered as the creator of the dime novel after the Civil War, was not without justification. In August and September of 1854 Buntline was touring the country with a crackpot who styled himself the "Angel Gabriel." The two specialized in anti-Catholic agitation, and in late September Buntline's second wife, Lovanche Swart, had her husband imprisoned on bigamy charges when he married an actress named Josie Juda before the formality of obtaining a divorce. Buntline had also served a year in the New York penitentiary on Blackwell's Island in 1849-50, on conviction of inciting to riot. He is also remembered as the genius who convinced William Cody to change his name to Buffalo Bill, thereby starting an American legend.[26]

On October 11, 1854, the *Detroit Free Press* published a five and one-half column exposé of the new Nativists on page one under the headline:

Know-Nothingism Exposed in
All its Naked Deformity,
with the Names of the
Prominent Actors.[27]

As the fall elections drew near, Storey moved to identify Republican candidates with the Know-Nothings. In "Let Proscription Be Proscribed" he solicited the defeat of Silas M. Holmes, Republican candidate for State Treasurer, on the grounds that Holmes was "a second-degree Know-Nothing." On election eve, Storey styled the canvass as "A Contest for Religious Freedom"

24. *Ibid.*, July 11, 1854.
25. *Ibid.*, October 5, 1854.
26. See Jay Monaghan, *The Great Rascal, The Life and Adventures of Ned Buntline* (Boston: Little, Brown & Co., 1952).
27. *Detroit Free Press*, October 11, 1854.

and asked that only Democrats be elected. "We do not mean to say that *all* men who do not belong to the democratic party are know-nothings," he clarified. "There are undoubtedly exceptions; but those who are exceptions are in bad company."[28]

Throughout the remainder of his Detroit career, Storey defended the Catholic Church in his columns. When the *Tribune* campaigned against the sale of some city property to the Detroit diocese, Storey upheld the transaction. In September, 1855, he earned the personal thanks of the diocesan newspaper, the *Catholic Vindicator*, for a series of editorials defending Catholics' right to vote. When Massachusetts Know-Nothings desecrated a Catholic convent at Roxbury in April, 1855, the *Free Press* expressed a proper sense of outrage.[29] In fact, until the editor's mind began to crack in the years following the Chicago fire in 1871, Storey's newspapers consistently defended Catholic citizens against manifestations of anti-Catholic bigotry. The reason for this position, over and above what appeared to be Storey's sincere conviction that Roman Catholics offered no real threat to American institutions, was the fact that in Detroit, as later in Chicago, the Irish Catholic immigrants formed the essential core of Democratic strength at the polls. Thus Irish sensitivities must be placated by the local Democratic newspaper, and Storey did this with full coverage of St. Patrick's Day festivities and Finnian picnics, coupled with ribald denunciations of the British Empire and a consistent defense of Catholicism.

The *Detroit Free Press* also defended foreign immigrants in its columns. A full year before the revival of the Know-Nothing movement, the newspaper denounced the Whig party because it "always discouraged every measure calculated to induce foreign immigration to our shores."[30] In April, 1855, Storey stated that if there was any danger to American institutions from foreign influences "it comes not from the sturdy and industrious immigrants who dig our canals, make our railroads, people our cities, and subdue our forests." Rather, with aspirations for liberty, and seeking homes for themselves and their posterity, they "wed liberty with that eagerness which arises from life-long deprivation of its exercise."[31] In September, 1858, Storey returned to the theme of immigration and

28. *Ibid.*, October 25 and November 3, 1854.
29. *Ibid.*, March 13, September 9, and April 17, 1855.
30. *Ibid.*, August 11, 1853.
31. *Ibid.*, April 1, 1855.

stated "the idea that this country should be an asylum of the oppressed of all nations [came] of the American revolution."[32]

The solid, consistent and liberal defense of American Catholics and foreign immigrants proved that Wilbur F. Storey could not be conveniently fitted into the reactionary niche so frequently reserved by historians for advocates of state rights and white supremacy. In fact, his intellectual processes and political stands were simply beyond facile categorization or easy summary. In many respects devoid of consistency, but blessed with incisive logic whenever he put his pen to a pet project of apologetics, Storey could in one breath denounce the Negro in the crudest and most vulgar terms, while in the next he would plead compassionately that the Founding Fathers intended that the United States "should be an asylum of the oppressed of all nations." Fanatically intolerant of all who disagreed with his political opinions, Storey at the same time penned a convincing set of essays on religious toleration. Almost completely lacking in formal education, the editor could nonetheless roam the entire span of world history and English literature to seek out parallels in support of his arguments. Absolutely consistent within his own frames of reference, he simultaneously defended the Indian while reviling Negroes and Asiatics; a champion of the absolute sovereignty of state governments, he was appalled that states refused to enforce the Federal Fugitive Slave law; a defender of Christianity against atheists, agnostics, socialists and heretics, he assiduously avoided affiliation or contact with any particular creed or sect.

In short, whatever opinion Wilbur F. Storey happened to entertain with respect to a given issue was the only true opinion. Since it was the true opinion, it was also the Democratic opinion, and this meant in the 1850s that true Democrats had to reprobate prohibition laws, uphold sound currency against wildcat banks, abjure spiritualism while they censured the Mormons, and insist upon American expansion in the Western Hemisphere while upholding Yankee dignity abroad. If any Democrat questioned the necessity of incorporating all of these things into the party platform, he was anathematized despite the fact that Storey felt faction should "not be permitted to raise its head from the dust, and extreme counsels [should] be disregarded from public favor."[33]

When outstate Democrats in Michigan questioned the prudence

32. *Ibid.*, September 28, 1858.
33. *Ibid.*, June 4, 1853.

of making opposition to prohibition a test of party loyalty in 1853, Storey uttered "A Few Words Plainly Spoken" in which he promised that upon the liquor law as upon every other question of public interest "we shall speak *boldly, unequivocally,* and *independently,* advocating what we believe to be *right,* and mercilessly exposing *wrong,* wherever we know, or have good reason to suspect, it exists."[34] Then Storey proceeded to expose as corrupt and unworthy all Michigan Democrats who took exception to *Free Press* editorial policy. Inevitably, the outstate papers ("whelping dogs") united in protest against the fact that outside of Michigan the *Free Press* was quoted as speaking the sentiments of the state party "whereas at home it is well-known to speak only the views of W. F. Storey and Co., (a very small company at that)." The *Hillsdale Democratic Gazette* asked editorially "don't you know that Storey can't be controlled or even advised by anyone—that he is one of the most self-willed and stubborn men in Michigan? [In addition he] is almost always wrong." The *Coldwater Sentinel* joined the protest when it refused to make opposition to spiritualism "a test of democracy." Storey noted such attacks with chagrin. Not only did they disrupt party unity, but he also felt that editors "within the democratic fold" who desired to express differences of opinion with Democratic contemporaries, should "employ a civil tongue and courteous language—instead of indulging in denunciation and vituperation."[35]

At the end of Franklin Pierce's first year in office Storey took "a fair, just and enlightened" view of the President's work and concluded "every candid mind must concede that there is very much in it to commend, and very little indeed to condemn."[36] Then, in March, 1855, Pierce vetoed an internal improvements bill that included appropriations for the improvement of Michigan's St. Clair Flats and St. Mary's River. If this was not a national improvement (the only type Storey would admit the Federal government should finance), then there was nothing national. Directly involved, Storey felt, was "full one-half of the whole population of the Union." Rather than allow the President to "palsy our arms and the arms of faithful Democrats all over the Northwest" Storey threatened that Pierce "must abandon this ground, or [we] will abandon him."[37] The following year Pierce vetoed a second bill

34. *Ibid.*, June 27, 1853.
35. *Ibid.*, July 17, July 22, and August 5, 1855.
36. *Ibid.*, January 20, 1854.
37. *Ibid.*, March 10, 1855.

on the same subject, and this when added to "mistaken policy in Kansas" led Storey to "thank God that President PIERCE's term of office is drawing to a close."[38] The *Free Press* never again uttered a kind word for Franklin Pierce.

"Men's appetites cannot be controlled by legal enactments; and it is an inherent desire in the human heart to seek that which is forbidden—a never to be forgotten example of which . . . is the fall of our first Mother."[39] With these words the *Detroit Free Press* touched off its holy crusade against the enactment of a prohibitory liquor law in Michigan. Storey, "knowing many . . . have the fullest faith" that a liquor law would "prove a thorough and radical cure of a disease which is destroying so many immortal souls," felt reluctant to discourage its approval. Admittedly "ardent spirits" injured "both mind and body" while they "blunt the moral sensibilities, benumb the social affections and make of a man a beast."[40] All of these things about liquor were true, and sad, and regrettable, Storey felt, but a coercive prohibition law was not the remedy for the evil.

With the same passion he displayed against abolitionists and Know-Nothings, Storey spelled out "The Consequences" if Michigan adopted prohibition. He cited statistics showing that in Detroit alone not less than $100,000 was invested in breweries that produced 80,000 barrels of beer and ale annually. If, as the "pestiferous vagabond lecturers" advocated, this manufacturing were outlawed the economic consequences for the community would be vast. And there was no reason or sense in a crusade against beer and ale. "They are luxuries that a large portion of our people must and will . . . enjoy." Law would not deprive men of their drink, and those who thought it could were

> irresponsible and worthless, bankrupt in reputation as they are in purse—for the most part "reformed drunkards," who have been drawn from the mire only to relapse deeper into the gutter—men depraved and debauched in their instincts as they are lazy and indolent in their habits.[41]

The law passed the legislature in 1853 anyway, and proved unenforceable. Storey pointed out its unenforceability and asked

38. *Ibid.*, May 21, 1856.
39. *Ibid.*, April 13, 1853.
40. *Ibid.*, April 6, 1853.
41. *Ibid.*, April 16, 1853.

"What Next?"[42] The *Free Press* remained opposed to legal prohibition but stressed "*It is the regularly enacted constitutional law of the State*, and must be obeyed." While the law obliged obedience it remained the right of every citizen to question its propriety and constitutionality. "This is a right we intend to exercise," Storey concluded.[43] And exercise his right Storey did, and until the day he left Detroit. All of the usual techniques of "filler" ridicule and slanted reporting of cases involving drunks were employed to discredit a law that was but "one phase more of black republican fanaticism in 1855."[44]

The extent to which the *Detroit Free Press* kept the editor's promise to be "thoroughly" Democratic was proved by the newspaper's handling of obituaries. When a death was announced, it made all the difference in the world whether the departed one had belonged to the Democratic party in life. When Mrs. Millard Fillmore and Mrs. Lewis Cass died within two days of one another in 1853, this was illustrated strikingly. At the time the former first lady's demise was announced the *Free Press* noted quite simply "the telegraph brings the mournful news of the death of Mrs. Fillmore, wife of the ex-President. She was a very estimable woman." Two days later the paper again printed mournful news: "Mrs. Lewis Cass expired Thursday night about 11 o'clock. Thus the golden bowl is broken; a pure spirit has flown to paradise."[45]

When prominent Detroit Democrat Isaac Crary died in May, 1854, he rated two full columns on the editorial page that ended with the rhetorical flourish reserved for the party faithful. The paper decided it was unnecessary to "dwell upon his private virtues" since "the avenues of his heart were ever open to the claims of benevolence, of religion, and of public improvement." The obituary concluded that he was snatched away in the prime of life, when his ripe experience had prepared him for scenes of still greater public usefulness. "But he has gone, and, with hundreds of others who were honored by his friendship, we can but drop a tear to his memory."[46] In the eight and one-half years that Wilbur F. Storey published a newspaper in Detroit, judged by the evidence of the *Free Press* columns, not one prominent Detroiter of Whig or Republican affiliation died.

42. *Ibid.*, February 19, 1854.
43. *Ibid.*, May 3, 1855.
44. *Ibid.*, May 29, 1859.
45. *Ibid.*, March 31 and April 2, 1853.
46. *Ibid.*, May 9, 1854.

"Gatherings," a potpourri of tidbits from all over the world, also brought Democratic tidings:

> Joseph Bassett, a revolutionary pensioner, age 93 years, died at Hyannis on the 7th. He was an honest man, a sound democrat, and the father of 24 children.[47]

The proper recognition of "American Chivalry Abroad" was also an essential part of a "thoroughly" Democratic outlook. Thus when the young son of the United States Ambassador to Spain, Pierre Soulé, fought successful duels with the French Ambassador and a Spanish grandee, the youngster's conduct was "very highly extolled" by the *Free Press* because it was about time the Spanish nobility "had a little touch with American quality." According to the *Free Press* account, young Soulé challenged a Spaniard who spoke slightingly of Mrs. Soulé, and in the subsequent match the Spaniard was shot in the knee. "They are beginning to find out on the other side that Americans are considerable pumpkins," Storey gloated. "All right!"[48]

With respect to hemispheric expansion, Democracy dictated that "Cuba naturally belongs to us. We trust Gen. PIERCE's administration will not end without its acquisition."[49] But Cuba was small, and Democracy must realize that what could be accomplished there in a single stroke would never succeed in Mexico because the Union was not ready to absorb all of that country yet. Further, it was not desirable "that we should ever swallow her at a single bolt. We should take her as a man eats his dinner—in mouthfuls." California and New Mexico were fair installments, Storey felt, but now that they were digested it was time to detach "another slice—say the Mesilla valley." That done, Storey hoped the United States might wait awhile "before having another of the entertainment act before us. We must civilize as we go. We must occupy as we annex."[50]

The most serious threat to the Democratic party in the 1850s lay with what Storey considered the politization of the abolitionist movement with the birth of the Republican party. In Storey's eyes this new party never represented anything else but rampant abolitionist fanaticism, and hence it must be struck down. This was

47. *Ibid.*, July 15, 1855.
48. *Ibid.*, January 13, 1854.
49. *Ibid.*, March 16, 1854.
50. *Ibid.*, May 26, 1854.

especially true in Michigan, he felt, where, from the first formalization of the Republican movement the opposition to Democracy became the majority party in state politics. From the first ominous rumblings of a new party movement, Storey was uncompromising, and overall, brilliant, in his warnings of the disastrous possibilities inherent in a sectional party dedicated to the forcible settlement of the slavery issue. As early as April, 1853, the *Free Press* expressed fear that "the hydra of abolitionism, fanaticism, and disunion" would "rear itself" as the dominant opposition party in the country. "This monster of frightful mien—this party made up of white abolitionists, black abolitionists, and fugitives from slavery—this rabble of discord and destruction," was organizing, Storey said, "for a desperate assault upon the democratic party and . . . the Constitution."[51]

An apparently harmless piece entitled "New Territories," which told of how the Committee on Territories in the United States Senate reported a bill for the organization of Nebraska and Kansas, appeared in the *Free Press* in the first week of 1854. In taking note of this intelligence, Storey commented "it is no part of the business of Congress to legislate for these territories." All Congress could do with such embryo states was set the machinery of their governments in motion. The people inhabiting them would then do the rest. "If they want slavery, they shall have it, and *vice versa*," Storey proclaimed.[52]

With these words Storey stated concisely what was to be his unalterable position on the Kansas-Nebraska Act. Through all of the torrent of emotion and politics that this act loosed in the following months and years, he remained a consistent champion of Stephen A. Douglas' popular sovereignty. The consequences of the Kansas-Nebraska legislation were little foreseen in 1854. The "little civil war" that would make Kansas a warm-up battleground for 1861; the emergence of the Republican party as an effective political instrument for abolitionist sentiment; the disruption of the Federal Union and the turning of brother against brother in four years of bloody civil strife—none of these was foreseen or intended. But Wilbur F. Storey was wary of these possibilities from the beginning.[53]

From the first appearance of the report of the Douglas Com-

51. *Ibid.*, April 22, 1853.
52. *Ibid.*, January 6, 1854.
53. *Ibid.*

mittee in January, until the final passage of the Act in the House in May, 1854, Storey reiterated his stand on popular sovereignty. Day after day after day, full columns were devoted to the subject under headlines such as "Popular Sovereignty," "The Present Crisis," "No Extension of Slavery," or "The Responsibility of the Northern Democracy." Generally these editorials contained the same themes —only the people actually settled in Kansas had the constitutional right to decide the slavery issue in that territory; slavery could not subsist as far north as Kansas, so it was needless to agitate the question; those who did agitate it anyway were scoundrels, or worse. Occasionally, buried in the midst of the verbiage, Storey uttered thoughts that read as prophecy in the light of the events of 1861. For example, on February 28, in a full column of print appeared this one sentence:

> Should the day ever come when the whole Northern people, or the great body of them, should combine in enforcing [the forcible abolishment of slavery] that day would witness the irruption of the States . . . as one by one they withdraw . . . from the Confederacy.[54]

Storey's insistence that civil war would come inevitably of abolition politics, a theme he had articulated repeatedly since his first days in journalism with the *La Porte Herald*, was heeded by almost no one. The very extremism with which he propagated his views tended to discredit his opinions even with responsible elements of his own political party. Even when he hammered away daily on the inevitability of civil war in the months immediately following Abraham Lincoln's election, few Democrats and no Republicans listened. As the unfolding of events proved him prescient, he still earned only the derision and reprobation of his contemporaries.

The preliminary skirmishing of Michigan's antislavery forces in the months following the introduction of Douglas' bill, skirmishing that eventuated in the July meeting at Jackson that settled on the name Republican for the new party movement, was duly noted in the *Free Press*. The first "anti-Nebraska" meeting in Detroit was held in February with future Senator Zachariah Chandler as the featured speaker. The meeting was "dull and spiritless" according to the *Free Press*. The list of prominent people who attended consisted of "many unknown to our oldest and extensively

54. *Ibid.*, February 28, 1854.

acquainted citizens" and was most probably copied from tombstones, an allegation "we do not positively assert, but. . . ."[55]

May 24, 1854, was a very special day for the *Detroit Free Press*, so much so that the news had to be treated in a very special way. The lead editorial rated page one, with a full column dressed as follows:

LATEST NEWS.

GLORIOUS NEWS FROM WASHINGTON!

This was followed by a six-inch deep wood carving of the American Eagle, head proudly erect, with a neck shawl flowing in the breeze bearing the legend "Democracy Triumphant." Then

THE NEBRASKA BILL–
PASSED ! ! ! !

Passage of the Nebraska Bill Through the House — — — Triumph of Popular Sovereignty.

The editorial, following a long dissertation devoted to the triumph of popular rights over Federal dictation, concluded with the observation that

> The chief excellence of the measure is that it established a *principle*, which, if faithfully observed in the future,—as it will be, as it *must* be,—will still the angry waters of sectional strife. It will withdraw from the halls of Congress the firebrand which has so long threatened conflagration to the fabric of the Union. It will remove the only apple of discord between the North and the South.

The festivities ended with a four-inch deep woodcut of a booming cannon, superimposed upon the Stars and Stripes. When the occasion demanded, newspapers "by W. F. Storey and Co." always made the most imaginative and advanced use of the devices that mid-century typographical technology made possible.

"The firebrand of slavery" refused to leave the halls of Congress with the passage of the Kansas-Nebraska Act. Instead, a call went out within a month announcing an "independent" convention to meet at Jackson on July 6. Storey read the call and foresaw dissolution of the Union if the "independents" fulfilled

55. *Ibid.*, February 19 and February 21, 1854.

his suspicions. He pointed out that "calm and patriotic people in all parts of the country" desired that slavery should be removed as a national issue. There could be no further agitation of the subject in Congress "unless thrust there by just such agitation" as that proposed by the Jackson meeting.

> Do these men *want* agitation? Have they become *Abolitionists*? Are they prepared for the *denouement* of the schemes that have for some time been hatching away among the disunionists . . . of whom they are acting as adjuncts?

It was Storey's opinion that the Jackson "independents" were entirely heedless of the ultimate consequences of their actions. And so he emphasized his insistence that the only possible result of an attempt to renew the slavery controversy was "the UNION or DISSOLUTION—that is the complexion that must speedily come."[56]

Two days after the July 6 meeting Storey took note of "the odor of negroism" filtering forth from Jackson. His man on the scene at the historic meeting was a nineteen-year-old ex-student named J. Sterling Morton who had been expelled from the University of Michigan the previous May after he aired his grievances against the University administration in the columns of the *Free Press*.[57] Morton's reports, published on July 8 and 9, were properly derisive of "the fusion ticket," "cullud pussons," and the counsel of the *New York Tribune* "which was prevalent." It was not until July 11 that editorial notice was given to the new party. Every day thereafter for the balance of the summer the *Free Press* was livid against sectional parties. The Jackson platform mentioned Washington and Jefferson, a desecration that Storey felt should cause the author to blush with shame. "But once man has fallen, it is in his nature to know no shame," he observed. "His ruthlessness respects not the character of the living or the memory of the dead."[58]

The state leaders of the new movement were special objects of Storey's scorn. They had set upon a strange cruise among the rocks and shoals of abolitionism in quest of personal political preferment. "We have known of many cases of mental hallucination

56. *Ibid.*, June 28, 1854.

57. James C. Olson, *J. Sterling Morton* (Lincoln, Nebraska: University of Nebraska Press, 1942), p. 26. For the relationship between Storey and Morton and the *Free Press* campaign against President Henry J. Tappan of the University of Michigan, see Chapter VI, pp. 130-32.

58. *Detroit Free Press*, July 11, 1854.

in politicians," Storey said, "but never one to equal this. It caps the climax of modern absurdities."[59] As the fall elections approached Storey was disturbed by "The Tendency to Sectionalism." He cited the plank in the Jackson platform that stated "no more slave states shall be admitted to the Union" and said "let that party have a majority in Congress . . . and disunion will ensue."[60] By October, "Union or Disunion" was the only question of consequence for Michigan. Democrat David Stuart, First District Representative in Congress, "MUST BE SUSTAINED. . . . It would be a disgrace to send an abolitionist to Congress." As Republican strength grew toward election day, Storey warned Democrats "no greater calamity could befall the State than the success of the fusion party."[61]

Against Republican candidates a steady stream of accusations flowed. Candidate for Congress William A. Howard's "tastes, habits, methods of thought and general proclivities" fitted him perfectly for Know-Nothingism. Notice, he was not a Know-Nothing, but "narrow and bigoted in his views, he is just the man to embrace all of the proscriptive tenets of the order, as well to satisfy the morbid prejudices of his soul, as to subserve his own selfish purposes."[62] Both Howard and gubernatorial candidate Kingsley S. Bingham were wildcat bankers according to the *Free Press*, and Bingham especially was unsafe and "likely to enlist in speculations to plunder the State."[63] Silas M. Holmes, running for state treasurer, was castigated in a manner illustrative of *Free Press* opinion on all Republicans. Holmes belonged to a class of men

> who preach what they do not practice—who would impose rules of conduct upon others which they do not observe themselves—hypocrites, in short—praying, psalm-singing hypocrites—men with long, solemn faces and garb of Puritan cut, but under and behind which corruption stinks—moral and religious Oily Gammons—whited sepulchres . . . for whom we confess we have no kindlier feeling than contempt, repugnance and scorn.[64]

Storey's abuse of Republican politicians in 1854 represented a new departure for the editor. Prior to this, to be sure, he had

59. *Ibid.*, July 13, 1854.
60. *Ibid.*, October 25, 1854.
61. *Ibid.*, September 19 and October 24, 1854.
62. *Ibid.*, October 25, 1854.
63. *Ibid.*, November 1, 1854.
64. *Ibid.*, September 18, 1854.

never been reticent in denouncing men so imbecile that they did not belong to or support the Democratic party. But his denunciations had never before quite reached such a level of personal malice, the clear indication that he was writing from the vantage point of almost soul-consuming hate. From this point on, however, personal hate became a trademark of Storey editorials against political opponents, and later against all people he disagreed with for any reason whatsoever. He was perhaps unequaled in the history of nineteenth-century American journalism in this respect. Certainly no one, not even the elder James Gordon Bennett, surpassed the Detroit Democrat.

William L. Bancroft, a dissident Democrat who supported the Republican ticket in 1854, was one of the first to notice the change. In a letter that Storey published in the *Free Press* Bancroft ended a reply to Storey's charges with the comment "you . . . charge against me with a greedy haste, indicative of personal animosity rather than of cool judgment or the common courtesy of gentlemanly intercourse."[65] Bancroft's observation was one that would hold true until the day in August, 1884, when Wilbur F. Storey was finally adjudged to be of unsound mind.

Almost all of the charges against Republican candidates in the 1854 election were based on gross innuendo. Less than in any other electoral campaign did Storey have any personal issues with which to flay the opposition. And when election day came, his efforts had been to no avail. The first six columns of his paper on Wednesday, November 8, were given over to a speech by Lewis Cass. Buried in column seven was the comment: "A complete fusion, know-nothing victory is indicated. . . . We doubt whether any democrat . . . is elected."[66] A calamity had befallen the state of Michigan.

The remainder of Storey's Detroit career was an unhappy time for him politically on the local and state level. The new Republican party retained control of the state government right up to the Civil War. In the city races, it was touch and go, with the Republicans controlling the mayor's chair on all but one occasion. None of this served to dampen Storey's conviction, however, that only a "radically and thoroughly *democratic*" sheet could best sell his party to a majority of Michigan voters.

Throughout 1855 every action of the legislature at Lansing was

65. See letter of William L. Bancroft in *ibid.*, October 26, 1854.
66. *Detroit Free Press*, November 8, 1854.

ridiculed as "con*fusion* confounded." It was "a mongrel legislature," palpable, bold, ruthless, and unblushing in its violations of the state and Federal constitutions, reckless in its violations of personal liberties, and extravagant in its misuse of state funds. In short, the entire work of the first year of Republican government was "abominable and disgraceful."[67]

In the news accounts of Republican doings, the *Free Press* bristled with such interpretive accounts as the report of that party's state convention of 1855:

> THE GRAND "REPUBLICAN" FIZZLE — — — CHOPFALLEN DEMAGOGUES—SWEARING AT THE STATE COMMITTEE—IMPOSITION UPON THE CITIZENS OF KALAMAZOO—WILL THE FUSIONISTS ACT LIKE HONEST MEN?

One and three-quarters columns of satire and invective ended on this note: "O fusion! fusion! what a poor, decrepit, despised thing thou art, deserted by friends, despised by all honest men, your time has come, your days are numbered, you're a dying skunk; dig a hole and bury thy useless and offensive carcass."[68]

Despite the verbal excesses of the *Detroit Free Press* when dealing with Republican policies and politicians, the newspaper's editor was quick to condemn "the filthy journalistic practices" of the Republican press generally. With righteous self-assurance, Storey castigated opposition newspapers because they were "illiberal and querulous towards everything." Their main business, said the *Free Press*, was "agitation—their main weapons detraction and calumny." Furthermore, their columns were "foul-mouthed and teemed [with] the grossest billingsgate." In a burst of indignation against what he termed "the Seward organs," Storey even went so far as to state that newspapers that deliberately misled unsuspecting readers should not be allowed to publish without legal reprimand.[69]

But when Wilbur F. Storey was dealing with particular Republican politicians, such rules did not apply. When Mayor Benjamin M. Hyde won re-election in February, 1856, he proposed convening a public meeting to "discuss the propriety of establishing a police force for the city." On the evidence of the *Free Press* columns since the day Storey took over, no proposal should have

67. *Ibid.*, December 12, 1855.
68. *Ibid.*, September 15, 1855.
69. *Ibid.*, March 10, 1853.

made more sense. Not a day passed when "City Intelligence" did not report full and intimate details of robberies, rapes, homicides, brawls and the doings of Detroit's "Magdalens." Mayor Hyde estimated his proposed force would cost about $18,000. After giving the matter "reflection," Storey decided "this would be a very heavy outlay for a very small benefit." Besides, it was a Republican proposal, and "only those with a vested interest in a police force, a prospective chief and officers, favor its creation."[70]

From 1854 on, Storey seemed incapable of political opposition on a level above the most base. His attacks on Mayor Hyde illustrated this well. By June, 1857, "there probably is not in the city a person who would aspire to the office of mayor so unfit for it as the present incumbent." After this observation, the *Free Press* described how Hyde's weekly reports to the city council disclosed the extent of the Mayor's education. "It obviously has not been that of the commonest school." In addition Hyde's habits of business were of the loosest character and it was well known that he pandered to any interest, "however vile," that could serve him. Hyde exercised no beneficial influence upon city affairs because he was "constitutionally and by habit incapable of exercising any." Commanding respect from no quarter, Hyde at best was "a demoralizing and pestilent" influence.[71] Two days later the *Free Press* had an exclusive revelation respecting Hyde:

> A keeper of one of "those" houses was arrested on Friday, and who does the reader suppose is her bail for appearance in court? We tell him who! *the Mayor himself*! And the Mayor has a pecuniary interest in the premises upon which she carried her trade.
>
> Very few of the people of Detroit are fully aware, we apprehend, of the sort of Mayor we have among us.[72]

But Benjamin Hyde was small game compared to the calamitous possibilities when the Republican party ran a ticket in a national election. In the year 1856, when Storey was a delegate to the Cincinnati convention that nominated James Buchanan for President, two objectives were uppermost in the editor's mind. First, the country must be saved from civil war by the election of the Democratic ticket nationally. Second, control of the state apparatus must be won in Michigan lest Lewis Cass lose his seat in the

70. *Ibid.*, March 7, 1856.
71. *Ibid.*, June 27, 1857.
72. *Ibid.*, June 29, 1857.

Senate to a "black republican abolitionist." To achieve both, Storey entered the campaign with relish. Special weekly editions were printed, spreading the Democratic gospel state-wide. Nationally, "Free niggers, Free Shooting and Frémont" were denounced.[73] On the state level, "the Nigger government at Lansing, which cost Michigan $1,000,000" must be retired.[74]

As early as January, 1856, Storey turned his guns on Cass' probable successor should the Republicans prevail:

> Mr. ZACHARIAH CHANDLER is a demagogue, with political aspirations far above his intellectual capacity. He wants exceedingly to go to the United States' Senate, a position he would simply burlesque. He is naturally, and by force of habit, a buffoon. . . .[75]

This notice of Chandler was the first of a continuous series of assaults on one of Michigan's foremost Republicans. The personal malice inherent in many of Storey's anti-Chandler diatribes reminds one of his later attacks upon the country's first Republican President. Incapable of legitimate political opposition, Storey viewed all Republicans as personal enemies who must be verbally slain.

When Detroit Republicans met to ratify the nomination of John Frémont for the presidency in June, 1856, the *Free Press* reported:

> Zach Chandler was the first speaker. He said he was a bogus delegate to the Philadelphia convention. . . . He went and asked some senators what kind of man Frémont was. They told him Frémont was right,—that he was opposed to slavery aggrandizement; and so the Michigan delegation, with these assurances, voted for him, and John-no, James-no, John C. Frémont was the candidate chosen. Chandler said every little fellow who came to market knew who Frémont was. He was the *first* man that ever explored the Rocky mountains! that he had distinguished himself in our army and navy! and that he ran away with Tom Benton's daughter! [Frémont was married to Jessie Benton, daughter of Missouri Senator Thomas Hart Benton.] He thought that was enough. Buchanan was a black bear; Frémont was a grizzly bear. Buchanan was a bachelor and Frémont had run away with a girl. He then said something about weak

73. *Ibid.*, August 28, 1856.
74. *Ibid.*, January 16, 1858.
75. *Ibid.*, January 25, 1856.

> knees, curved spine, & c.—very appropriate in the speaker—and left the stand.[76]

After the Republicans carried Michigan in 1856 and sent Chandler to the Senate, Storey mused about the Republican proclivity to bring to the surface men who were, almost without exception, "intellectual dwarfs":

> . . . and we have to count Michigan as having added to the list of weak men brought to the surface by the "republican movement." We must count her indeed as having added the weakest man to the link of weak men sent to the Senate. . . . We must do more; we must count her as having sent to the Senate the weakest man that ever took a seat in that body from any State. This is her glory. . . .
>
> But this is not perhaps the worse of it. Were Chandler only weak, did he know just enough to keep his mouth shut, the humiliation of the State might escape observation at Washington, but there is no hope in this respect. The difficulty is that the man is not aware that he is a loafer, and an ass, and comparatively speaking, an idiot. He is apparently not aware of this, but on the contrary, like most preposterous ignoramuses he has a settled conviction . . . that he has lacked only the opportunity to acquire greatness. This is his conviction, and deeming the Senate his true theater, we may be sure that when he gets there he will continually be opening his mouth, instead of keeping it perpetually closed; and we may be equally sure that as often as he does this, just so often will Michigan have occasion to be ashamed of herself—just so often will Michigan be the object of broad grins and sarcastic leers. . . .[77]

The Republican newspapers in Detroit responded to Storey's ravings against Chandler. The *Daily Advertiser* suggested the *Free Press* publisher should return to his natural habitat at Jackson in the vicinity of the state prison. The *Tribune* articulated what must have been the sentiment of all Republicans, and not a few Democrats, when it observed Storey's remarks transcended all ordinary bounds of party rancor. "It is unctuous of the slimy rottenness which shapes it into set phrases." Decent people were amazed as they would be at "the blasphemies of a drunken prostitute, or the profane ravings of a fish-woman." The *Free Press,* rejoicing in filth

76. *Ibid.*, June 24, 1856.
77. *Ibid.*, January 13, 1857.

and fondling nastiness, "stations itself on its dirty eminence" to fling debris at decent passers-by.[78]

Opposition censure, as usual, had no effect upon Storey as there was no let-up in his offensive against Chandler. The paper was partially sympathetic when Chandler was seriously burned in a fire in his home in August, 1858. The *Free Press* reported the particulars of the event and remarked "the occurrence is a sad one. We trust no permanent injury may ensue."[79] Nevertheless, in the bitter days that followed during the 1860 campaign and the secession crisis thereafter, Chandler remained, in his political functions, an idiot who called for "a little bloodletting" to settle the slavery issue.

Storey saw the 1856 campaign as a contest between a national party and a sectional party "which would madly employ force to abolish slavery."[80] He heaped ridicule on John C. Frémont and was one of the prime movers in circulating the false rumor that Frémont was secretly a member of the Roman Catholic Church, a strategem that gained wide circulation in the Democratic press of the Middle West in the hope that it would deprive the Republican nominee of Know-Nothing support.[81] But most of Storey's editorial space was devoted to boosting the fortunes of James Buchanan. Apparently Storey realized Frémont could not win nationally, and hence he concentrated his fire against local Republicans.

First District Congressman William Howard had no chance for re-election. He had "Gone Up the Missouri River" when he joined a Congressional team in an on-the-spot investigation of the Kansas difficulties. "Mr. Howard's constituents might have reason to say

78. *Detroit Weekly Tribune*, January 20, 1857. The reaction of the opposition press to Storey generally, plus the series of feuds and libel cases in which he was involved while in Detroit, are treated in Chapter VI, pp. 121-30.

79. *Detroit Free Press*, August 3, 1858.

80. *Ibid.*, March 21, 1856.

81. See *Detroit Free Press*, July and August, 1856, *passim*. Storey went to elaborate lengths to prove that Frémont was a Catholic who had forsaken the church "in whose bosom he was baptized and nurtured." The editor cited witnesses who had seen the Republican nominee "cross himself with holy water," genuflect, confess his sins, and such. The *Free Press* published an interview "with the Jesuit priest [unnamed] who married Frémont in the Catholic rite," and the paper gave wide circulation to the story of an unnamed Detroiter who had served with Frémont in the army and found him so devout that the Detroiter converted from Protestantism to Catholicism. This ploy, repeated by Democratic newspapers throughout the country, caused great embarrassment to the Republican party as it attempted to refute the tales while not appearing to take an anti-Catholic position akin to Know-Nothingism.

'well done' had he remained at his post," Storey said. "But since he has deserted . . . and gone on a ridiculous partisan errand" the constituents said instead "thou wicked and slothful servant."[82] When Kingsley S. Bingham was renominated for governor "The Impudence of Black Republicanism" was more than the editor, "in our brief experience with politics," had ever witnessed.[83]

The Republican party's national ticket was defeated in 1856, as Storey had hoped. But the solace derived from the election of James Buchanan was small indeed since the opposition made a clean sweep in Michigan. And once Buchanan took office, Storey became more and more enamored of Stephen A. Douglas for 1860. It was apparent that Douglas would have been his personal choice in 1856, and once the Thirty-fifth Congress met in December, 1857, "amidst an unheralded conjunction of tensions" which would "draw its bewildered members into a whirling vortex,"[84] the editor immediately sensed Buchanan's inadequacies.

The Lecompton fiasco, in the course of which the President "betrayed" popular sovereignty, was the signal for the *Free Press* to lessen its support of the administration. At first Storey gave Buchanan credit for sincerity despite the fact that "Mr. Buchanan's stand is certainly not the view of the Democratic party."[85] As Buchanan persisted, the *Free Press* broke with him completely and began a vigorous fight to avoid the split that sounded the death knell for the Democratic party and, more important, the Federal Union. In fact, the only bright spot on Storey's political horizon during Buchanan's administration was in November, 1857, when Mayor Benjamin Hyde, his "hide on the fence," was "most effectually skinned" by Democrat Charles Patton in the municipal election.[86]

By March, 1858, it was clear to Storey that "there is no danger to the Union but [by] the disruption of the democratic party."[87] Since Storey saw this as true, he begged the Buchanan administration to abandon its Lecompton policy and resume "a just and democratic Kansas policy." If the President refused he would "behold his Administration broken down and powerless in the second year

82. *Ibid.*, April 11, 1856.
83. *Ibid.*, July 10, 1856.
84. Roy Franklin Nichols, *The Disruption of American Democracy* (New York: Macmillan & Co., 1948), p. 132.
85. *Detroit Free Press*, December 11, 1857.
86. *Ibid.*, November 4, 1857.
87. *Ibid.*, March 16, 1858.

of its life, and the party which bore him to power . . . split into fragments."[88] When Buchanan refused to back down on the question of admitting Kansas with a slave constitution, Storey switched openly to an advocacy of the Douglas brand of Democracy because "it is eliminating slavery slowly but safely." The Republican party, on the other hand, was "in the death throes"; its state Personal Liberty laws prohibiting slavery "would have sent even George Washington to prison"; and the Democratic party must "bury its differences" and go on to victory with Douglas in 1860.[89]

The issues and importance of the 1860 national election were stated clearly in March, 1860, before either party held its nominating convention. In a long editorial headed "THE COMING ISSUE," Storey traced the origins of the 1860 crisis back to William Lloyd Garrison's earliest activities in the 1830s. It had grown bigger during the opposition to the admission of Texas and the pendency of the Wilmot Proviso and Compromise of 1850. The Kansas-Nebraska Act, followed by the "excitement" in Kansas, had strengthened antislavery radicalism which reached full development with William A. Seward's "irrepressible conflict" speech in 1858. Now the issue must be met face to face. "Union or disunion, peace or irrepressible conflict?" Storey asked. This was the issue facing the American electorate in 1860 as seen by the *Detroit Free Press*.[90]

The convention of the Democratic party at Charleston, S. C., in April was the first since "the convention which formed the Federal constitution . . . upon whose action so much seemed to depend." If that convention "shall nominate Stephen A. Douglas HE CAN BE ELECTED." If it nominated any other "the event of the contest, at best, will be doubtful."[91]

Storey was slightly disheartened when "a few Southern hotheads" sabotaged the Douglas nomination at Charleston. When Douglas received the Baltimore convention's nomination in June, the editor spoke of the Democratic party as "the only living national party, . . . AND ITS CANDIDATES MUST BE ELECTED AS THE ONLY SURE WAY OF PRESERVING THE NATIONAL UNION."[92] As the summer progressed, and it became apparent that the Demo-

88. *Ibid.*, April 8, 1858.
89. *Ibid.*, September 25 and September 28, 1858, March 4, 1859 and May 28, 1859.
90. *Ibid.*, March 2, 1860.
91. *Ibid.*, April 8, 1860.
92. *Ibid.*, June 24, 1860.

cratic split was a mortal blow that would deliver the national government into the hands of "black republicans," Storey became frightened. A sincere lover of the Federal Union, he realized the most impassioned pleas were helpless to elect Stephen A. Douglas and he foresaw with bitterness that Abraham Lincoln's victory would be disastrous.

If ever a man seemed trapped by the excesses of his own rhetoric, that man was Wilbur F. Storey in the summer of 1860. So extreme, so wild, so totally without ballast had been his counsel since he had taken over the *Detroit Free Press* that no one, not even the members of his own political party, believed him sincere in this hour of political crisis. Storey ceased publishing the more outrageous attacks upon Republicanism, but to no avail. Sometimes, he attempted to overlook the import of Lincoln's victory with fanciful musings regarding the 1862 and 1864 elections. One item on October 18 was all but a concession of victory to the Republican ticket. In it Storey, without hope for 1860, predicted "the democracy will sweep all the northern States . . . and nearly all, if not all, the southern States" in the 1862 elections. "And in the same connection we predict that Stephen A. Douglas will be elected President in 1864 by larger popular and electoral majorities than have ever been given to any one for the Presidency."[93]

One week before election day, an amazingly temperate analysis of the situation facing the country appeared in the *Free Press*, amazing for its clear-sighted reasoning and for the absence of the vituperation for which Storey was most noted:

IS DISSOLUTION IMMINENT?

We have no desire to magnify the threatening danger. We seek only to keep the people of Michigan informed of the true state of the impending crisis. . . .

We ourselves say that the election of LINCOLN will not be cause for dissolution. But we cannot close our eyes and ears to the possibility, the almost certainty, that dissolution will be the immediate consequence of his election.

If it shall not be the immediate consequence the calamity will have been averted by the character of the House, which will be determined on the day of the Presidential election.

If the House shall contain a majority of conservative men, that fact may possibly have a tranquilizing effect upon the Southern mind. Certainly that fact will furnish South-

93. *Ibid.*, October 18, 1860.

ern Union men with a powerful weapon for the battle for the Union which they must fight if LINCOLN shall be elected.

Does not the whole conservative North—do not even conservative republicans who may vote for LINCOLN—owe something to the Union men of the South? . . .

We are not alarmists. We would not, if we could, excite groundless fears. We only wish to do our duty as journalists in representing things *as they are.*[94]

The 1860 election results marked the temporary eclipse of Wilbur F. Storey. A man passionately devoted to the principles of the Democratic party as expounded by Stephen A. Douglas; a man who throughout his career fought abolitionist sentiment and Republican politics furiously and without compromise; a man who foresaw as few others in the Middle West the dreadful consequences that Abraham Lincoln's election portended for his beloved country, Storey could not quite recover from the shock of having his most dreadful premonitions realized. His political party and the political structure he so strenuously defended were to be no more.

In this situation, there was only the *Detroit Free Press* for consolation. On November 7, 1860, the day after Abraham Lincoln was elected President of the United States, Wilbur F. Storey was "GLAD." Under this heading he proclaimed his relief that the election was over because politics could now be confined "within reasonably narrow limits" while Storey concentrated on filling his columns "with matter much more acceptable" to the general reader. "We intend to make the *Free Press* the best news and commercial journal in the Northwest," he concluded.[95] With all else lost, Storey's journalism would come to the fore and he would concentrate on making his newspaper "the best in the Northwest." But the force of events was to dictate otherwise.

As the situation reached crisis proportions immediately after Lincoln's victory, Storey turned with hatred against James Buchanan. The President was guilty of high treason against the Democratic party because of his "criminal schemes and simple madness." The election of Lincoln was "upon Buchanan's head," Storey said. "If the Union shall be severed, that, too, will be upon his head."[96] The alleged right of secession, "A Monstrous Fallacy,"

94. *Ibid.*, October 28, 1860.
95. *Ibid.*, November 7, 1860.
96. *Ibid.*, November 9, 1860.

was also damned by the *Free Press.*[97] At the close of 1860, when Buchanan spoke of reliance on Divine Providence to see the country through the crisis, Storey accused the President of seeking refuge in the Deity because "Mr. Buchanan deems it his duty not to do his duty because any attempt to do it would be resisted."[98]

In February, 1861, when Republican radicals in Congress moved to sabotage measures intended to avoid civil war, Storey, in a widely quoted editorial which first gained him national prominence, promised "A Fire in the Rear" if an antislavery war commenced. As usual, he spoke from firm conviction, but "the fire in the rear" that Storey was to ignite against the Lincoln administration was not to be fanned in the city of Detroit. As Fort Sumter came and the first troops mobilized, Storey supported the early attempts to crush secession. The old verve, however, was missing from his pages during these unhappy days. It was as if events had gotten completely out of hand as fanaticism and passion buried rational settlement.

In addition to his country and the Democratic party, Wilbur Storey also had an abiding love for the region of the United States in which he lived. He saw the Old Northwest come to maturity in the quarter-century before 1860, and he realized that Detroit no longer afforded the pulse for the region's further growth and expansion. His prognostications of future growth were noted in March, 1858. He pointed out it had been but a few years since Ohio, Indiana, Michigan and Illinois were the Far West into which the great streams of emigration flowed. While these states still offered "splendid and unsurpassed inducements to settlement," they were no longer the Far West. Emigration now poured through and beyond them across the Mississippi into Kansas, Nebraska, Iowa and Minnesota. Beyond these were New Mexico, Arizona, Utah, Washington and Oregon, "containing in themselves the element of a vast empire." The day was not distant, Storey noted, when the Mississippi river would be "the grand dividing line" between East and West. "When that day comes, . . . the center of capital and commerce . . . will have followed the star of empire, and shifted toward the geographic center of the continent."[99]

So it was that as Civil War came, and his marriage to Maria Isham was in the final stages of disruption, Storey cast about for new journalistic fields to conquer. In May, 1861, Cyrus McCor-

97. *Ibid.*, November 16, 1860.
98. *Ibid.*, December 22, 1860.
99. *Ibid.*, March 30, 1858.

mick, of reaper fame, decided to sell the *Daily Chicago Times*, a weak Douglas sheet with a circulation of less than 1,000. Storey, convinced that it was Chicago more than any other city in the region that most truly "followed the star of empire toward the geographic center of the continent," decided to buy. Detroit's "radical and thorough" Democrat, with Civil War raging, took on a new challenge in Chicago, a challenge destined to bring him notoriety, fame and a fortune of several million dollars. He was also to secure a deserved niche in Civil War history for reasons that had little to do with his genius as a journalist.

The editorial policy of Wilbur Storey with the *Detroit Free Press* has never before been subjected to a detailed analysis. His Civil War policy of "treason" in Chicago so overshadowed everything he did before or after that conflict that historians who have bothered with him at all have concluded that he was only a "successful" publisher in Detroit before he moved to Chicago.[100]

Yet he was surely more than this. The sensational content of his editorials, which made such "good copy," assured him a wide readership far beyond the circulation area of the *Free Press*. The impact of his attitudes on the Middle West in the decade before the Civil War cannot be measured with exact precision. But it is impossible to read his newspapers for these years and not conclude that above all else, Storey was sincere in the stands he took. George E. Catlin, the only student of Storey's prewar attitudes, corroborated the intensity of the editor's sincerity:

> Whatever the Whigs or Republicans of those days thought of his partisanship or zeal, no one can read his editorials now without giving him credit for sincerity. . . . He evidently really believed that the cause of the Republicans and Free Soilers was calculated to disrupt and ruin the country.[101]

More important than sincerity, however, is the proof which the *Detroit Free Press* under Wilbur F. Storey gave that the editor

100. See, for example, George F. Milton, *Abraham Lincoln and the Fifth Column* (New York: The Vanguard Press, 1942); Frank L. Klement, *The Copperheads in the Middle West* (Chicago: University of Chicago Press, 1960); Donald B. Sanger, "The Chicago *Times* and the Civil War," *Mississippi Valley Historical Review*, XVII (March, 1931), 557-80; and L. E. Ellis, "The Chicago *Times* During the Civil War," *Illinois State Historical Society Transactions for the Year 1932*, XXXIX (Springfield, 1933), 136-81.

101. Wilbur F. Storey folder (George B. Catlin papers, Burton Historical Collection, Detroit Public Library).

foresaw the outbreak of the Civil War. Mort L. Hopkins, who joined the *Free Press* staff about 1859 and moved to Chicago with Storey in 1861, said "the sagacity of Storey in judging of the times and the probable course of events was strikingly displayed in the Fall and Winter of 1860-61." After the election of Lincoln, the *Free Press* predicted the secession of the southern states, and published almost daily accounts of the speeches and utterances of southern leaders. "At that time," Hopkins added, "it was generally estimated to be a badly distorted judgment." Whatever may have been Storey's purpose in such a course of action, Hopkins with great truth concluded that "time was swift in approving his skill as a prophet."[102]

Because Storey really did believe that disruption and ruin would inevitably follow the triumph of Republican policies, he saw the election of Abraham Lincoln as a stunning personal defeat. The derision with which his warnings of impending catastrophe were met, even while daily events proved him correct, led him to seek a more hospitable clime for his views. As a champion of Stephen A. Douglas he could find no more promising enterprise than the revitalization of the almost defunct Douglas organ in Chicago. He decided to move and rally the feuding factions of the Illinois Democracy around "the Little Giant" preparatory to a glorious victory for Douglas in 1864.

The mood in which Storey left Detroit after more than eight years as editor of the *Free Press* was one of confusion and profound sorrow. The confusion was engendered by the outbreak of Civil War. "There will be no bounds to the astonishment of future generations," Storey had written, "that troubles involving such calamities to the human race, which could have been settled by concessions so slight on either side . . . should have produced war and the overthrow of the Republic."[103]

And then, on June 4, when the last number of the *Free Press* under Storey's direction appeared, there was sorrow. It was the supreme personal irony of the editor's career that the last editorial he penned for the *Detroit Free Press* announced the death of Stephen A. Douglas. With this final tribute, in which Storey saw fit to speculate on the mysteries of death as well as pay respects to his favorite statesman, Wilbur F. Storey said farewell to Detroit:

102. Mort L. Hopkins, "Reminiscences of Story [*sic*] and the Chicago *Times*," *Proceedings of the Michigan Press Association* (22nd Annual Meeting, Grand Rapids, July 9-11, 1889), p. 41.

103. *Detroit Free Press*, April 7, 1861.

DOUGLAS.

A great calamity is upon the nation. STEPHEN A. DOUGLAS is dead. The silence of death enters our heart as we write these lines,—for who shall fill his place? We admired, loved him, as we admired and loved no other great man of our generation. A large party clustered round his giant intellect as their brain and their heart. He was opposed as no other American statesman has been opposed—he was sustained with an intensity of confidence and devotion none other awakened save CLAY. His name, his acts, are now before the world forever. The inexorable destiny of genius is now his. Civilized man will forever gaze upon and criticize him. No recall, no expedients, no new fields—all is past for him. He lives forever as he died. We have no fears as to the result. The great rebellion which distracts the country evinces that he knew American institutions as no other statesman has ever known them, and above all, it has united the testimony of the nation to his devoted patriotism. We mourn for the country, not for him. The excitement of such a life as his makes even three [*sic*] score years and ten drift to the past with terrible rapidity. He lived long enough to be glorious—not long enough for the nation. Yet we are proud, and feel it is one of the bonds which will strengthen the patriotic unity of the people that even his political opponents mourn his death, and, in this hour of national convulsion, weep as bitterly over his grave as they would over the best of one of their own.

We confess that there is something terrible in the idea that he is gone, that his massive frame, his iron will, were not powerful to defy even death. The common lot of man seems more certain now that it is his lot—the King of Terrors more resistless since his departure. So great was the man—so marked by all the intense energies of life and will—that his end will fall upon every ear as a wonder—a violation of nature.

"We shall ne'er see his like again."[104]

104. *Ibid.*, June 4, 1861.

CHAPTER VI

DETROIT: For the Benefit of Those Who Have a Taste for Such Things!

For the benefit of those who have a taste for such things, we append the closing scene of an execution which recently took place in New York. The name of the subject was Clark. He had been convicted of killing a policeman.

—*Detroit Free Press*, February 18, 1853.

WHEN WILBUR F. STOREY DIED IN 1884, HIS CONTEMPORARIES IN THE newspaper profession recognized him as a great journalist. The recognition was widespread, and was not motivated by any feeling that no unkindness should be uttered over the remains of a deceased fellow craftsman. Even opponents joined the chorus because they, more than anyone else, had reason to know that Storey's

Chicago Times had been a newspaper of a new type in the Middle West. This was especially true for the two decades following the Civil War when Storey, in the words of the *Chicago Herald*, "pioneered in making a newspaper for people to read."

The groundwork for the greatness of the *Chicago Times* between 1865 and 1884 was laid in the columns of the *Detroit Free Press* in the prewar decade, for in Detroit as later in Chicago, Storey sought primarily to "make a newspaper for people to read." To accomplish this goal, the editor poured his entire self into a project that consumed fourteen to sixteen hours a day, six days a week. The result of his massive effort was that a property he purchased for $3,000 in February, 1853, brought $30,000 eight and one-half years later.

Wilbur F. Storey had many qualifications for a great newspaperman that he sharpened and perfected with the *Free Press*. In addition to a sure command of language, he was a genius in the art of typography. Literally no aspect of the print shop escaped his attention. One *Free Press* printer remembered him as a man "of a somewhat mechanical turn who used to go frequently into the press room and oil up the machinery and help get it into good running order."[1] James A. Tiller, another *Free Press* compositor in the 1850s, remembered his employer as a man particularly watchful of headline form and arrangement. Headlines were marked by the editor in the type desired, as "pica lf," "cond pica," or "lt face cond." "The general result," said Tiller, "showed good taste and judgment, and rarely had to be changed."[2]

As a regular ritual, between 11:00 P.M. and midnight, Storey went to the composing room to supervise the make-up of the editorial page. Not a word was spoken during this procedure as the foreman "had the matter laid out in galleys on the stone." Storey pointed to the article he desired to go first, then to the second, and so on, "the matter being lifted into its place as he designated until the principal articles were disposed of." This done, Storey

1. John Drew, "Reminiscences," in *Detroit News-Tribune*, November 7, 1897 (in Clarence M. Burton Scrapbook, Vol. 5, Burton Historical Collection, Detroit Public Library, p. 168). Drew added that one day Storey visited the press room, oiled the machinery, and then "unconsciously slipped the can into the tail pocket of a very fine coat, where it dripped all over his back and ruined his other garments."

2. James A. Tiller, "More About Storey," *Detroit News-Tribune*, September 23, 1900 (in Friend Palmer Scrapbook, Vol. 17, Burton Historical Collection, Detroit Public Library, p. 164).

"put on his hat, turned off the gas, and went home, usually between 12 and 1 o'clock."[3]

Franc B. Wilkie, Storey's closest associate on the *Chicago Times*, substantiated the claims of Detroit witnesses to Storey's excellence as a printer. As Wilkie recalled, Storey made a special study of type for display heads, and each headline "according to the importance of the article, must have so many lines of such a kind and size—a disposition which he perfected after a long and exhaustive study of possible type effects." This mastery of type enabled Storey to spread "great, staring headlines through his columns, which were black, numerous and full of promise of startling information." To make sure the desired effect was achieved, Storey placed each article "in the columns according to its news value," Wilkie said. "It must 'break over' the top of the column (i.e. it must be divided at a certain part), so as to show a certain amount in one column and a certain amount in the next."[4]

Wilbur Storey was also endowed with an extraordinary capacity to judge men. He surrounded himself with an able staff in Detroit, a staff so good that he moved it almost intact when he left for Chicago in 1861. For the first five years, only five men were responsible for the entire news and editorial work connected with the *Free Press*. In addition to Storey himself, there were Harry M. Scovel, Warren P. Isham, Thomas B. Cook and Moses M. Ham. James E. Scripps, who began a half-century career in Detroit journalism with the *Daily Advertiser* in 1859, was so impressed by the talent this group exhibited that he remarked this little staff "was as remarkable a combination of journalistic ability as perhaps ever existed on any American newspaper."[5] Even a cursory perusal of the *Free Press* between 1853 and 1858 would suffice to convince the skeptical that Scripps did not greatly exaggerate in this evaluation.

Harry Scovel was copy editor when Storey purchased the concern. He was the only editorial employee the new proprietor retained, and his competence was proved by the fact that Storey took Scovel along to Chicago in 1861. In Detroit, Scovel "acted

3. Moses Ham, *Recollections*, as cited in James E. Scripps, "Wilbur F. Storey—Detroit's First Great Journalist—Some Recollections of a Very Remarkable Man," *Detroit News-Tribune*, September 16, 1900 (in Palmer Scrapbook, Vol. 17, p. 155).

4. Franc B. Wilkie, *Personal Reminiscences of Thirty-five Years of Journalism* (Chicago: F. J. Schulte & Co., 1891), pp. 114-19.

5. Scripps, "Wilbur F. Storey," Palmer Scrapbook, p. 155.

as proof-reader, exchange editor and telegraph editor all in one." James E. Scripps, who knew Scovel as a personal friend, remembered him as "a good-natured, plodding individual, with no interest outside the office." Scovel had the same capacity for total dedication to his work that Storey himself exhibited, and this led to a quarter-century association between the two men. Franc B. Wilkie also noted Scovel's talented efficiency. "He could go through 100 newspaper exchanges, apparently only glancing at them," said Wilkie, "and yet [he] would never miss an item of the smallest consequence."[6] It was this man, on the job daily, who was Wilbur Storey's chief assistant in making each edition of the *Free Press* a model reproduction of the typographer's art.

The "City Intelligence" page contributed more than any other factor toward making the *Free Press* the foremost newspaper in Detroit. Coverage of the local scene increased from barely a half-column in 1853 to a full page by 1860. The mastermind behind this feat was Warren P. Isham, city editor, and brother-in-law to Storey. A polished and imaginative writer, Isham even dabbled in drama. In 1859 his play about "a white girl who married the negro employee of her father" had a short run at the Metropolitan theater, "the only theater in Detroit at that time." Thomas M. Cook, "bold and reckless," was Isham's chief partner on the city side, and Scripps testified "it would be hard to say which possessed the greatest inventive faculty."

In the 1850s Detroit was a dull, dead sort of place that frequently "did not furnish the material for one local paragraph." Often a whole day's trudging about on foot would uncover nothing beyond a few convictions in the police court for drunkenness and disorderly conduct. Invention was thus an integral part of the necessary equipment for any reporter who intended to remain long in the employ of Wilbur F. Storey. And invention was the chief stock in trade of both Warren P. Isham and Thomas M. Cook.

Early in the evening Isham and Cook would take their seats on opposite sides of the reporter's table. Each would sharpen his pencil, and then Isham would write on a slip of paper "What have you got, Tom?" Cook would read the communiqué, append "Not a damned thing," and return the slip to his associate. The city editor would then prepare a list somewhat as follows:

A Child Eaten by a Bear in Hamtramack
Death of a Child in a Huckster's Wagon

6. *Ibid.*; Wilkie, p. 123.

Narrow Escape from Drowning in Windsor
Suspected Murder of a Woman on Croghan Street
Remarkable Intelligence of a Dog on Gratiot Street
Singular Accident to a Cow in Springwells
Child Choked with a Button on the River Road

Cook would scan the list, check the items he would write, and Isham took the rest. Then, "quietly, right under the eyes of the severe 'old man' [Storey], the sharpened pencils would run to and fro until late in the evening."[7] The next morning's edition sparkled with startling news, graphically portrayed. The other Detroit dailies, with reporters who confined themselves mostly to facts, could not match such enterprise and the majority of the people took the *Free Press* because it was the most interesting newspaper in town.

The only other member of the staff until 1858 was Moses M. Ham, commercial reporter who occasionally also wrote an editorial. He was also the only Detroit associate of Storey who saw fit to pen an extensive memoir of the editor. According to Ham, Storey was about five feet ten inches in height and weighed around 160 pounds. He wore a full black beard, with shaggy eyebrows, and his dark, glossy hair was always brushed with scrupulous care. "He was also scrupulously neat in his attire," said Ham, "and was probably one of the best dressed men in town." He had dark grey or hazel eyes coupled with brusk manners that gave him an air of fierceness and made him generally dreaded and disliked. The personal toll that the years of toil in Detroit exacted on Storey was indicated by the fact that by 1861 both his hair and beard had turned snow white. When he arrived in Chicago, he was immediately dubbed "the white maned evangel of treason" by his opponents.[8]

Of Storey's manner of conducting business, Ham said "in all his goings and comings Storey was one of the most regular men I ever saw." He arrived at the office at 9:00 A.M., usually first visited the counting room where he looked over the business of the day before and determined any matters that might be referred to him. He then sorted the morning mail, taking eight to a dozen papers that he wished to look over, and went to his room. Here he worked until about four o'clock when his copy was ready and the hardest part of his day's work done. Then, when the weather

7. Scripps, "Wilbur F. Storey," Palmer Scrapbook, p. 155.
8. Ham, *Recollections*, as cited in *ibid.*, p. 154; Wilkie, p. 114.

was good, "he took a ride for a couple of hours behind a little white horse that he used to drive." He returned to the office again shortly after nine in the evening, and worked in the room with his assistants, where he had a table and chair like the others. As a rule he wrote little or nothing in the evening, confining his efforts to looking over the exchanges, examining proofs and supervising the work of others. "As some of the men were writing," Ham concluded, "it was understood there was to be no conversation and the whole office ran along as quietly as a well-ordered school."[9]

Storey's late afternoon rides appear to be the only relaxation he allowed himself during the eight years he lived in Detroit. Otherwise, he was at his post in the *Free Press* building at 50 Griswold Street "just across the alley south of the Newberry building." The editor's desk faced the street from the end of a store-shaped first-floor editorial room, "a position from whence he could see everyone who came in and overlook all his assistants." The atmosphere was "as solemn as a church. . . . Even conversation was in whispers," Scripps noted.[10]

Storey's employees either adjusted to this situation or sought employment elsewhere. Many of them seem to have admired him for his energy, efficiency and ability, even his courage; but he certainly inspired nothing like affection among his co-workers. Quite the contrary; almost all accounts by reporters and printers who were at one time in his employ recalled the fear and trepidation he inspired in the office. Moses Ham said Storey was very particular about little things. "No words were to begin with a capital letter except the few allowed by universal practice . . . and his own copy was to be set exactly as it was written."[11] Ham's remarks lend credence to one story that made the rounds of press rooms concerning a young *Free Press* printer who ran into trouble with capitalization. Storey, according to the tale, yelled "Haven't I told you that there are only two words in the English language which *have* to be capitalized—Jesus Christ and Wilbur F. Storey—and if you are short of capitals be sure to capitalize Wilbur F. Storey."[12]

William E. Quinby, who joined the staff as a legal reporter in

9. Ham, as cited in Scripps, "Wilbur F. Storey," Palmer Scrapbook, p. 154.
10. *Ibid.*, p. 155.
11. *Ibid.*, p. 154.
12. R. Carlyle Buley, *The Old Northwest, Pioneer Period, 1815-1840* (Bloomington: Indiana University Press, 1950), II, 507, footnote.

1858 and became sole owner of the newspaper in the 1870s, recalled that under Storey "style and make-up were as inflexible as the laws of the Medes and Persians, unchangeable." The editor gave few directions, expecting all to be familiar with his methods and carry them out. "If at the end of years one who had done faithful work all that time made a solitary mistake, he was censured no less vigorously than one who erred every day of the week."[13]

Moses Ham seconded Quinby's observations. Once a printer who had the audacity to change Storey's punctuation on an article the editor wrote was discharged on the spot. Ham stated further that Storey frequently went for weeks without addressing a word to his associates. But if a man failed in any way "he heard very quickly from it . . . in a way to make the hair stand up straight." Wilbur F. Storey "could say meaner things in fewer words than any person I ever saw," Ham concluded. "The goodly feeling of fellowship between man and man was left out when he was made."[14]

Reporters associated with Storey after he left Detroit indicated that he never changed. Franc Wilkie, who joined the *Chicago Times* in 1863 and stayed until after Storey's death, wrote "Storey never seemed willing to admit that a man had done a good thing." He had office spies, who received special favors, and while "the treatment was killing" Wilkie admitted "it produced incessant efforts to advance." Mort Hopkins, *Times* city editor, was impressed with how the wastebasket "was not only the receptacle of rejected manuscript, but the narrator of the feeling of Storey when reading an article." If copy was torn but once in two, it expressed a mild dissent; twice, a decided disapprobation. Every succeeding mutilation represented "a corresponding intensity of repugnance" and sometimes the pieces were no larger than a dime. "This was evidence [Storey] was profane inwardly at the time of the tearing, and would have been so audibly had there been an auditor present."[15]

It was impossible to suspect the extent of Storey's hostility to

13. William E. Quinby, "Reminiscences of Michigan Journalism," *Michigan Pioneer and Historical Collections,* XXX (Lansing, 1906), 508.

14. Ham, as cited in Scripps, "Wilbur F. Storey," Palmer Scrapbook, p. 155.

15. Wilkie, p. 149; Mort L. Hopkins, "Reminiscences of Story [*sic*] and the Chicago *Times," Proceedings of the Michigan Press Association* (22nd Annual Meeting, Grand Rapids, July 9-11, 1889), p. 45.

employees on the evidence of his public utterances. As a delegate to the Michigan constitutional convention of 1850 he championed the cause of "mechanics and laborers," and under his direction both the *Free Press* and the *Chicago Times* avowed the right to strike and defended the eight-hour day.

With his own typographers, however, Storey carried on a war that did not end until his death. John H. Seitz, founder of the Detroit Typographical Union, recalled in 1902 that the Detroit Union was founded because of dissatisfaction with hours and conditions when Storey inaugurated a Sunday edition. The printers "got together" and drew up a list of grievances and suggestions. When "the boys" presented their case to their employer, "Mr. Storey told them to 'go to hell,' or something like that." He hired outside printers, and the Union made no headway at the *Free Press* during Storey's tenure.[16]

In justice to Storey, it should be noted that the most outspoken of his former employees in Detroit, Moses Ham, tempered his remarks with the observation that "he did know how to get up a newspaper, and the man in his employ who attended to his business was sure of good treatment."[17] Compositor James A. Tiller added still "another thing in Storey's favor" as an employer. "Storey paid wages in full on Saturday night."[18] Tiller's assertion substantiated a boast Storey himself made in 1857 when replying to charges of financial mismanagement leveled by the opposition press against the *Free Press*. "The employees of the establishment exceed forty and . . . not a person employed fails to receive his dues weekly, or oftener if he desires them."[19] This was no idle boast on Storey's part, for hard taskmaster that he was, he was nonetheless consistently fair in insuring that all employees were remunerated on time according to the agreed upon terms.

Storey was a resident of Detroit exactly three months before he became involved in his first libel action. The suit was brought in Wayne County Circuit Court by Joseph Warren, editor of the *Detroit Tribune*, and was the first of a series of libel cases involving the two editors. The battle originated in February, 1853,

16. John H. Seitz, "Interesting Story of An Early Strike: The Peculiarities of An Old Time Editor," *Detroit Journal*, March 10, 1902 (in Burton Scrapbook, Vol. 7, p. 96). For the battle of the *Chicago Times* against the Union shop, see Chapter VIII, pp. 224-26.

17. Ham, as cited in Scripps, "Wilbur F. Storey," Palmer Scrapbook, p. 155.

18. Tiller, Palmer Scrapbook, p. 164.

19. *Detroit Free Press*, January 18, 1857.

one week after Storey took over the *Free Press.* Warren at that time indulged himself in a daily attack against the Roman Catholic Church. Within three weeks, Storey took to defending his Irish Catholic readers, although it was not until May 25 that the *Free Press* took out after Warren by name. This was a few days after Warren had named Storey as an impotent man whose deficiencies led him to seek gratification as a denizen of dens of debauchery.

There was a touch of irony in the fact that Storey's first feud in Detroit involved him in a brawl with an opposition editor, because the last paragraph of his *Free Press* prospectus in February stated an intention "to cultivate relations of the utmost courtesy [with our] contemporaries of the press." Although editors of political journals might disagree, Storey asserted that "there is yet nothing in their position that should allow them for a moment to forget that they are, or, at least, ought to be—gentlemen."[20]

Storey was not completely insincere in this statement, for at no point in his career prior to February, 1853, had he attacked an opposition editor on other than political or journalistic grounds. But then, Storey had never before encountered an adversary quite like Joseph Warren. Warren became editor of the *Tribune* in 1852, and was by political conviction first a Whig, and later a Republican. An anti-Catholic bigot, he also dabbled in Know-Nothingism for awhile in 1854-55. He was remembered by contemporary journalists as a bold, fearless, completely indiscrete writer.[21]

On May 3, 1853, Warren loosed his first attack upon his new neighbor when he described Storey as "depraved, corrupt, rotten at heart, and . . . incapable of right thoughts or right actions." Any man who defended southern slavery, said Warren, deserved himself to be a slave. The life and conduct of "the *Free Press* Caliban" proved he was completely void of everything "good, and liberal, and human and generous. Such a man was designed by nature for a highwayman or a pickpocket;—she only failed to give him the courage and skill to fulfill his mission."[22]

Similar attacks followed in the next three weeks. Around May 25 the piece attacking Storey's sexual prowess appeared. Up to this point, Storey had confined himself to general condemnations

20. *Ibid.*, February 15, 1853.

21. James E. Scripps, "Some Other Old Time Journalists," *Detroit News-Tribune*, September 23, 1900 (in Palmer Scrapbook, p. 157); William Stocking, "Prominent Newspaper Men in Michigan," *Michigan Pioneer and Historical Collections*, XXXIX (Lansing, 1915), 156.

22. *Detroit Weekly Tribune*, May 3, 1853.

of "our Whig contemporary," "religious bigots," and the like. Of course, he was perfectly capable of replying in kind, and beginning on May 25, he did. But in his reply, not even Storey stooped to the level of questioning Warren's marital relations or sexual irregularities. In fact, at no time in his career did Storey ever publish an *editorial* attack that violated the sanctity of this particular area of human relationships. Even during the Civil War, when every issue of the *Chicago Times* seethed with malice against the "crude, illiterate bar-room witling" in the White House, the sanctity of Abraham Lincoln's hearthstone was never crossed. But it was an attack of just this nature that Joseph Warren printed in the *Tribune* against Storey.

Even such a dispassionate and removed witness as James E. Scripps agreed that Warren "grossly libeled Wilbur Storey and a criminal suit followed. . . . There was no defense possible and conviction was inevitable."[23] The *Grand Rapids Enquirer*, which took both editors to task for an exhibition "disgusting to the readers and disgraceful to the parties," also partially exonerated Storey. It wrote that since Storey's connection with the *Free Press* Warren had "assailed him with slander and abuse, even to invading the sanctity of his domestic hearth, which no man except lost to every sense of shame would have done."[24]

Storey had his own thoughts on the matter. "When we are attacked, basely and cowardly, in the tenderest relations of life, we most certainly will retaliate."[25] Storey then observed that the *Tribune* "vegetated under the nursing care" of a fugitive from the criminal authorities of the state of New York.[26] The charge that Warren was a fugitive from a New York penitentiary led the *Tribune* editor to begin libel proceedings on May 27. Warren, who "is himself a libel upon humanity," sought $5,000 for defamation of character.

Storey professed astonishment when presented with the summons. "Libel! We have yet to learn that is it possible to libel a wretch who is the walking personification of falsehood and detraction . . . a living, moving gangrene in the eyes of the community—a stench in the nostrils of decency." Warming to his subject, Storey went on to establish that Warren libeled every object upon which

23. Scripps, "Other Old Time Journalists," Palmer Scrapbook, p. 157.

24. *Grand Rapids Enquirer*, as reprinted in *Detroit Free Press*, June 14, 1853.

25. *Detroit Free Press*, June 14, 1853.

26. *Ibid.*, May 25 and 26, 1853.

he placed his hands or eyes. Further, Warren was a libel upon himself, for he gave lie to the human shape. "Libel, indeed!" Storey concluded, as he promised to expose Warren to "public execration as a vile, grovelling, crime-stained wretch, who, if he had just deserts would have been on the chain gang long ago."[27]

Besides letting loose a tirade against Warren, Storey also instigated his own suit for damages. In the following three years the battle was continuous, with Storey in court on at least three separate occasions to answer charges of libel brought by Warren. Storey contented himself with just the one case against Warren, but it was a sure winner that promised the assessment of a heavy fine and imprisonment until politics intervened to deprive Storey of a major victory.

The settlement of the various cases was not arrived at until the autumn of 1855. During their pendency, both editors fired at one another. In August, 1853, Storey defended a resort to violence against "editors of a certain sort" when Warren was badly beaten in a tavern brawl with an Irish Democrat. The *Free Press* admitted that the provocation must be great and the case extreme before violence would be justified. "Yet we scarcely know what less an editor of a newspaper can expect, who applies opprobrius epithets to private individuals and daily assaults private character." There were times, Storey warned, when forebearance was not a virtue because "there are men who can only be taught good manners and a proper respect for the common courtesies and decencies of life by the infliction of a personal chastisement."[28] Warren reprinted Storey's remarks on this occasion and branded the *Free Press* editor a malicious, premeditated liar who would crawl under the steps of his neighbor's door to avoid a physical encounter with a man of his own strength. "Out [with] . . . such a sneaking, mob-inciting poltroon," Warren concluded. "He is too contemptible to be kicked."[29]

After this exchange, the editors remained silent for the next six months as the first litigation in the libel cases was heard. Then, in February, 1854, Warren renewed his onslaught against Catholicism as the municipal elections approached. Inevitably, Storey was once again dragged in, and in an editorial headed "Personal" he reviewed his side of the controversy. He recalled, truthfully, how

27. *Ibid.*, May 27, 1853.
28. *Ibid.*, August 6, 1853.
29. *Detroit Weekly Tribune*, August 9, 1853.

during his first five months in Detroit the *Tribune* had made almost daily assaults upon him. Then, Storey noted, Warren "one day ventured to open the private door of our domestic sanctuary and thrust his villainous face therein." At that point, the *Free Press* stripped Warren of his borrowed plumage and applied the lash to his naked back.

> Since that period this editor—this licentious vagabond—this tippling hypocrite—this literary thief . . .—this pimp whose sheet is a sluice way of calumny—this traducer of private character and vampire of personal reputation—has left *us* pretty much alone.

But what was bred in the bone could not easily be plucked from the system, and now the *Tribune* had resumed a personal assault upon Storey. "The end of the rope has been reached," Storey proclaimed. He promised to so excoriate Warren "that he will not forget it for the next dozen years, should God in His singular providence so long inflict society with such a blotch as he upon its surface."[30]

As political passions were fired by the excitement over the Kansas-Nebraska Act and the subsequent formation of the Republican party, Storey carried out this threat. Warren replied in kind, and on occasion struck a note very close to the truth in evaluating the mentality of Wilbur F. Storey. When Storey was heatedly denouncing the sectionalism of the Republican party and castigating Protestant preachers who involved themselves in politics, Warren noted that Storey "has no adequate estimate of the importance in a free country of the freedom of opinion, of the unfettered right of every man to canvass public matters." Rather, said Warren, Storey pretended to wield the lightening of excommunication "as if he had authority from the Almighty to say to men 'Ye shall not think, but if you do, you must think just as I.' "[31]

In the autumn of 1854, the first of the two cases Warren had pending against Storey was decided. The jury found Storey liable to the extent of $50 for damage to his adversary's reputation. Warren had sued for $5,000, so Storey was not unduly perturbed. "The jury," Storey reasoned, "went into an elaborate estimate of the value of the plaintiff's character, and by a very nice mathe-

30. *Detroit Free Press*, February 24, 1854.
31. *Detroit Weekly Tribune*, August 8, 1854.

matical calculation arrived at the conclusion that it (the plaintiff's character) was worth the precise sum of fifty dollars."[32]

As the municipal elections approached in March 1855, Warren returned to his favorite pastime of attacking Catholics. In February, the *Tribune* noted that "the enviable notoriety of being the meanest, vilest and worst man in the State, out of the penitentiary, must be conceded to" Storey. To which the *Free Press* shot back "With those who know [Warren] best he has the unenviable reputation of being the meanest, vilest and worse man in the State, out of the penitentiary, *or in it*."[33]

On April 5, the jury in the second case decided "*that the plaintiff has sustained damages to the amount of six cents*; or to translate the verdict literally, the jury determined that [Warren's] character is susceptible to damage to the amount of six cents." Since Michigan law provided that in libel cases involving a settlement of less than $50 the plaintiff "shall recover no more costs than damages," Storey, upon the rendition of the verdict, immediately paid twelve cents to the clerk of the court. The payment was made so promptly, Storey explained, because otherwise he feared the manager of the hotel where Warren formerly lived might garnishee the damages to pay partially "a back indebtedness for board."[34]

Joseph Warren, of course, saw triumph in both verdicts. Not only had he proved the baselessness of Storey's charge that he was an escaped New York convict, but the trials had also established that Wilbur F. Storey was insane. Storey's defense counsel had argued that the *Free Press* editor had been impelled to publish the charge against Warren because of the frenzy into which he was thrown by Warren's attacks. "In other words, his defense was *insanity* or *folly*; and on that ground the jury has let him off with nominal damages. If in this he can find consolation, we confess ourselves happy to have furnished it," Warren concluded. In the same issue of his paper, Warren admitted he was sued for an overdue rent bill, but it was an unjust debt, and he had lost because the case was heard before an Irish Justice of the Peace. Since his rent difficulties were not just matter for public examination, Warren also threatened to initiate another libel suit against Storey.[35]

During the course of all this litigation, Storey bided his time

32. *Detroit Free Press*, September 19 and 20, 1854.
33. *Ibid.*, February 7, 1855.
34. *Ibid.*, April 5, 1855.
35. *Detroit Weekly Tribune*, April 10, 1855.

in anticipation of the final settlement of his own libel case against Joseph Warren. The day of triumph arrived on June 26, 1855, when a Wayne County Circuit Court jury found the *Tribune* editor guilty of criminal libel which resulted in a six-month jail sentence. On June 28, the lead editorial in the *Free Press* was headed "A Convict." In it Storey supposed "that no one will now question the fact that the embodiment of vile instincts and beastly vulgarity" who edited the *Tribune* "is a convict."[36] Warren charged he lost "because the jury were six Catholics, and we don't know how many were locofoco partisans."[37] He appealed the verdict, but was denied a retrial. Then, on August 20, Kingsley S. Bingham, Governor of Michigan, granted executive clemency and pardoned Warren.

The exact motivation for Bingham's action was unclear. Warren had supported Bingham in the 1854 election, but there did not appear to be an intimate or even particularly warm relationship between the two men. Certainly, Bingham was nowhere near Warren on the Catholic question. On the other hand, since the day of his nomination by the Republican party, Bingham had suffered the constant barbs and shafts of Storey at his vitriolic best. The pardon of Warren undoubtedly offered the Governor the only direct opportunity he enjoyed to exact telling revenge against the Detroit Democrat. Whatever Bingham's motivation, Storey stood aghast before such a pride-crippling blow. "Henceforth let no man feel that the law is his shield," he moaned.[38] Storey kept after Bingham every day from August 21 through September 21. On the latter date he concluded the argument with the observation that the Warren pardon finally "reveals to the people of Michigan the heart and mind of the man, who, in an evil hour, they elected to the Chief Magistracy."[39]

Throughout the episodic battle between Joseph Warren and Wilbur F. Storey most Michigan newspapers condemned the conduct of both men. Depending upon party affiliation, they might sympathize slightly with one or the other, but generally there was agreement that such deportment was a disgrace to the newspaper profession. One exception was the *Detroit Daily Advertiser*, a morning Republican newspaper that unabashedly aligned itself with Warren. The *Advertiser* had stood by, of course, through the campaign of Storey against abolitionists, political preachers, and

36. *Detroit Free Press*, June 28, 1855.
37. *Detroit Tribune*, as reprinted in *ibid.*, June 27, 1855.
38. *Detroit Free Press*, August 21, 1855.
39. *Ibid.*, September 21, 1855.

"black republicans." It had been an eyewitness to the daily abuse of Negroes, Michigan politicians who were not Democrats, and all Detroit citizens who differed with Storey on any subject ranging from spiritualism to the proper disposal of strong liquor. In view of this, even though the *Advertiser* was not empathetic with the Know-Nothing tendencies of Warren and the *Tribune*, it could feel no sympathy or respect for Storey.[40]

The *Advertiser* commenced its attack in the summer of 1855. For the remainder of Storey's stay in Detroit, the two papers remained adversaries. Unlike the *Tribune-Free Press* brawl, however, the latter battle remained out of the courts as the two editors confined their differences to verbal blasts from their respective editorial columns. The strategic chieftain of the *Advertiser* during the fray was Rufus Hosmer, a man with physical drawbacks that Storey was quick to twist to his advantage. According to James E. Scripps, "Hosmer was one of the most corpulent men who ever made Detroit his home." Apparently he was so obese that forty years later Scripps still remembered the chair Hosmer occupied in the *Advertiser* office. "It must have been made on purpose for him."[41]

Such obesity gave Storey a natural opening, but Hosmer always replied in kind. In July, 1855, Hosmer published a series of notices warning Detroiters to "Beware the Dog." The animal belonged to General Cass and "is kept chained up, on Griswold street, is regularly aired, and led to his meals."[42] For his part, Storey discoursed on "Anti-Metastasis" with the pointed observation that "there is no remedy for grossness. . . . It cannot be transferred . . . it is a disease, habit . . . its indices are a peculiarly animal contour of the face, eyes which keep you in expectation of a grunt."[43] In "Scarcely A Simile" Storey hesitated to say Hosmer "wears his wits in his belly and his guts in his head" because if such were the fact Hosmer's "wit would be inexhaustible."[44] Or again, the *Advertiser* editor "is a counterfeit presentment of a man—the embodiment of grossness—the living statue of vulgar, perverted humanity."[45]

Hosmer retaliated with even more vile stuff on Storey. The

40. *Detroit Daily Advertiser*, August 22, 1855.
41. Scripps, "Other Old Time Journalists," Palmer Scrapbook, p. 156.
42. *Detroit Daily Advertiser*, July 10, 1855.
43. *Detroit Free Press*, July 12, 1855.
44. *Ibid.*, August 16, 1855.
45. *Ibid.*, July 13, 1855.

Free Press proprietor, "a canting, pharasaical professor of religion" was "spewed" out of the church to which he belonged and "left a rotting nuisance in the nostrils of the world." Storey had remained a church member long enough "to exemplify one of Christianity's leading doctrines—total depravity," and then left "having done his share toward the substantiation of revealed religion." Lest he be accused of ill will in these remarks, and also out of a sense of justice to Mr. Storey, Hosmer felt obliged to add the opinion of Storey's friends:

> They say . . . that he is insufferably egotistical, arrogant, self-sufficient, conceited, overbearing, and dictatorial. That he is without refinement, cultivation, tact, delicacy, good sense or sound judgment. That he is oblivious of his word, wrong-headed to a degree, obtuse and tyrannical. But with these slight qualifications, he is quite considerable of a fellow.[46]

The wild abandon with which Storey propagated his political and personal viewpoints inevitably spilled over into his private feuds and invited exact retaliation. In Joseph Warren and Rufus Hosmer he met two men capable of exactly this. Hosmer perhaps reached the lowest with the following, extracted from a full column "Biography" of Storey that had no foundation in fact:

> A short time back [Storey] procured from Cincinnati a comely prostitute whom he brought to reside in Detroit. He established her in a house on Russell street . . . [and] bestowed upon her much of his time, especially of nights. . . . But clouds will darken the brightest sunlight. Storey's Cincinnati Aspasia was detected by a policeman . . . and this drew attention to the house . . . which from being well and comfortably warm, became too hot to hold its occupants.[47]

Such antics as these enraged many in Michigan, and brought reprobation from outstate newspapers. The *Coldwater Sentinel* decried "the filthy personalities which the editors . . . have . . . been flinging at each other." The *Ann Arbor Argus* admonished the Grand Jury of Wayne County "to present both for a violation of the statute against obscene publications."[48] But neither heeded

46. *Detroit Daily Advertiser*, September 21, 1855.
47. *Ibid.*, September 24, 1855.
48. *Coldwater Sentinel* and *Ann Arbor Argus*, as reprinted in *Detroit Free Press*, October 14, 1855.

such censure as both editors continued the game until the day Storey moved to Chicago.

The man who owned and edited the *Detroit Free Press* in the 1850s was governed by an insatiable appetite for sensation and meanness. True, he pontificated piously about proper newspaper ethics. He damned the cheap and the tawdry, that class of newspapers that "pander to a morbid or vitiated public sentiment." He decried newspapers that stooped to language intended "to shock tender sensibilities." He asserted no "record as will gratify prurient tastes" should be published. Above all, he expressed concern over newspapers that were "oblivious of all sense of decency and propriety [and that] ruthlessly assail private character, and seek to damage personal and official reputation."[49]

But these were meaningless words from the pen of Storey who in his restless and reckless way always needed something going in his columns, some individual to castigate as an object of public contempt. When politics or personal enmity were not sufficient, Storey was likely to turn on almost anyone. No rhyme or reason was detectable in his choices for character assassination other than a morbid desire to subject victims to verbal crucifixion just "for the hell of it." Not even academic personnel were safe once Storey determined his course, as his attack on Dr. Henry P. Tappan, President of the University of Michigan, proved.

The editor selected Christmas Eve, 1853, to begin his attack against Tappan. It was occasioned by the publication of the President's annual letter to the Board of Regents. Storey proposed "to poke around amongst the rubbish" of the report. He found it "not creditable to any undergraduate . . . as a literary performance." Tappan's affectation in using the title "Chancellor" instead of "President" was another source of consternation. "Our advice to you, Mr. Tappan, is that you . . . let go of that title, just as you would let go of a hot potato. It will burn if you don't." Storey also cautioned against Tappan's leaning towards "the Prussian system," because the President had visited Germany in the summer of 1853, and hired a German astronomy professor named Brunow. "Do not forget that Michigan is not Prussia, and Ann Arbor is not Berlin."[50]

49. For two of the best specimens of Storey on the ethics of journalism, see "Suggestive Reflections" in *Detroit Free Press*, July 20, 1853, and "On Crime Reporting," in *ibid.*, September 6, 1854.

50. *Detroit Free Press*, December 24, 25, and 28, 1853. For a detailed analysis of Storey's campaign against Dr. Tappan see Charles M. Perry, "The

Soon President Tappan was *"a thorough and unmitigated ass."* Storey questioned the method by which Tappan had secured the presidency and charged he had deceived the Regents. The editor accused the academician of favoritism because the latter discharged an elected member of the Board to replace him with a friend named Palmer. Storey even hinted that Tappan took commissions on purchases made for the University.[51] By the spring of 1854, a goodly number of the Democratic newspapers in the state, following Storey's cue, joined in the fun.

Even recalcitrant students were allowed their say in the *Free Press* "Letters" column, and the case of one young man was particularly noteworthy in view of his future prominence and later association with Storey. J. Sterling Morton, future governor of Nebraska and Secretary of Agriculture in the second administration of Grover Cleveland, enrolled at Ann Arbor in September, 1853, shortly after his family moved to Detroit. But Morton was more prankster than student and "did not spend much time worrying about the problem of academic honors." He was in and out of mischief throughout the school year, and finally in late April, 1854, University officials threatened him with expulsion. Young Morton did not take kindly to such a threat, and addressed his case to Storey in a series of ribald letters signed "M" which ran in mid-May. When Dr. J. Adams Allen, "an eclectic in medicine," was dismissed as head of the University medical department, Morton complained "the rottenness in Denmark is beginning to smell in the nostrils of the people. Is it not a shame that the University . . . should sink so low?" In another letter, "M" described "Mr. Tappan and his toadying pimps and advisors" as unfit for their high positions. Even in an age of educational permissiveness such abuse of university administration by a student would not be taken lightly. In 1854, it was not taken at all as J. Sterling Morton was promptly and unceremoniously dumped from the student roll.[52]

Morton returned to Detroit and secured a job as a reporter for the *Free Press.* His first assignment was the meeting of "Independents" at Jackson in July. In October, Morton moved to Nebraska, and became one of the founding fathers of that state. Throughout the 1860s and 70s he was a frequent contributor of "Political In-

---

Newspaper Attack on Dr. Tappan," *Michigan History*, X (October, 1926), 495-514.

51. *Detroit Free Press*, January 25 and 31, 1854.

52. James C. Olson, *J. Sterling Morton* (Lincoln: University of Nebraska Press, 1942), pp. 26-35; *Detroit Free Press*, May 16 and June 30, 1854.

telligence" to the *Chicago Times*, and in 1884 only the objections of Wilbur Storey's widow prevented Morton from being named as administrator of Storey's estate.

Toward spring, 1855, peace was restored between Storey and the University. In late January he boasted editorially "President Tappan . . . has . . . dropped the title of 'Chancellor,' a fact which augurs returning sense, indicates respect for public opinion, excites in us symptoms of esteem . . . and animates a hope that we shall be able to make something of the man yet."[53] During his remaining years in Detroit, Storey seemed satisfied with the University and its administration.

The only occurrence that threatened to renew his ire was an 1858 proposal that women be admitted as students. The whole "Feminist" movement of the 1850s was deprecated by the *Free Press* as part of "abolitionist-socialist madness" destined to destroy the family and debase morality. If women were admitted at Ann Arbor, Storey did not hesitate to state "we predict for the university downfall and ruin."[54] When the Board of Regents in October, 1858, "put a quietus upon the question," Storey was ecstatic. He congratulated the Board for preserving the institution "from degeneracy . . . if not, in fact, total destruction." Had women been admitted Storey felt sure "it would have been but a short time before [the University] would have sunk to a level with Oberlin . . . and other bastard, one-horse institutions."[55]

Almost from the moment Storey took over the *Free Press* its circulation climbed steadily.[56] In addition to the fare already indicated, the newspaper also printed the juiciest and spiciest accounts of mayhem and scandal, local, foreign and imaginary. As readership increased, so did advertising revenue. With the additional income, Storey's scruples intensified: "We are not sure that newspapers, in lending themselves to quack advertisements, do not make themselves party to the fraud; we seriously think of refusing all such advertisements at any price." And so he proceeded to be very particular before admitting an ad; so particular indeed that, with all of his acidic opposition to abolitionism, he did not

53. *Detroit Free Press*, January 27, 1855.
54. *Ibid.*, July 4, 1858.
55. *Ibid.*, October 3, 1858.
56. Exact circulation figures were not found by this writer, but Scripps and Ham testify that the *Free Press* outsold city rivals by five to six hundred copies daily. Storey's own figures, as published on September 20, 1856, were 2,420 daily, 1,008 semi-weekly, and 14,672 weekly for an aggregate of 18,100 copies.

flinch at taking revenue from its proponents. When Foster's Panorama of Uncle Tom's Cabin, "Enlarged and Improved: embracing 1,000 HUMAN FIGURES," appeared at Firemen's Hall "for six nights only!" six advertisements for the Panorama appeared in the *Detroit Free Press*.[57]

By far the most intriguing and constant companion of *Free Press* readers from February 21, 1853, to December 5, 1854, was a certain DR. LISPENARD who gazed knowingly from the black depths of a half-column display ad that proclaimed:

> MOST EXTRAORDINARY WORK!
> SHOULD BE READ BY EVERYONE!
>
> DR. LISPENARD'S POCKET COMPANION, OR MARRIAGE GUIDE, beautifully illustrated, 12½¢. 5 for 50¢
>
> This little work is introduced as a private instructor for married people, and more particularly those about to marry. —There is nothing that married people can require or wish to know but what is fully explained in this Marriage Guide. It is beyond all comparison the most bewitching and interesting little work ever published.

This was followed by a two-inch deep woodcut of the distinguished Doctor, and the advertisement ended with the solemn assurance that the book could be "sent to any part of the world, securely packed from observation and so as to defy the inspection of the most curious."

Almost every biographer who has undertaken a pioneer account of any prominent figure in nineteenth-century American journalism ends by assigning to his subject the distinction, or infamy, of creating "yellow" journalism. The honor has been claimed for both the senior and junior James Gordon Bennett; Horace Greeley has his votaries; "Marse" Henry Watterson, Joseph Medill, even Henry Raymond along with a host of less significant figures receive occasional mention. About the only point of agreement to emerge from this plethora of claim and counterclaim is that William Randolph Hearst and Joseph Pulitzer were definitely not the first publishers to discover that sex and violence, prominently displayed, sell newspapers. The reader may judge for himself where Wilbur Fisk Storey fits in this spectrum of the shoddy, spectacular and sensational. It may be said without qualification that the post-Civil War *Chicago Times* stood second to no newspaper of its time as

57. *Detroit Free Press*, July 27 through August 2, 1853.

a daily carnival of filth replete with graphic portrayals best described as a riot of the raucous and repugnant. This was especially true as Storey went progressively insane in the late 1870s, and his newspaper became progressively more unsavory. The genesis of the sensationalism was apparent in the *Free Press* of the 1850s. It was tame, perhaps, when compared with the later *Times*, but this said, it remains true that between 1853 and 1861 few editors so consistently defiled their columns as did Storey.

Murder. Rape. Seduction. Prostitution. From all over the United States the accounts were gathered, sifted, condensed and fitted in under headlines such as "SHOCKING DEPRAVITY," "HOW TO GET RID OF A FAITHLESS WIFE," "SUICIDE BY SWALLOWING A RED-HOT POKER," "FOUNTAIN OF BLOOD IN A CAVERN," "HORRORS OF OPIUM SMOKING," "SAVED BY HIS WIFE'S CORPSE," or "A LITTLE BOY WITH DELIRIUM TREMENS."[58] Frequently the "STARTLING INTELLIGENCE" under such heads occupied no more than three or four lines:

> A woman arrived in Chicago a few days ago with the body of her husband, which she was taking east for burial. On the route, she fell in love with a young man, and, on the arrival of the cars at Chicago, they went off together, leaving the body in the depot.[59]

"Gatherings" invariably consisted of whole pages of such, with the monotony broken by spicy, pointed tidbits such as the following:

> A late Illinois paper contains the announcement of the marriage of R. W. Wolf to Mary I. Lamb. "The wolf and the lamb shall lie down together, and a little child shall lead them"—after awhile.[60]

> In a late speech, Lucy Stone [prominent feminist] said "We know there is cotton in the ears of men. Let us look for hope in the bosom of women." She probably meant to say "Better look for hope in the eyes of men, for we know there is cotton in the bosom of women."[61]

58. *Ibid.*, February 6, 1856, February 21, 1856, January 29, 1856, April 3, 1857, March 20, 1857, December 11, 1855, and October 21, 1855.
59. *Ibid.*, December 4, 1855.
60. *Ibid.*, April 15, 1856.
61. *Ibid.*, December 11, 1855.

Particularly "good" items from other newspapers sometimes rated a full column. Thus "DEATH IN THE BRIDAL BED," in Baltimore, offered full details on the death of a sixty-year-old groom who died from "organic disease of the heart" one hour after retiring with his seventeen-year-old bride. "ROMANTIC HOMICIDE" in New Orleans chronicled the sad demise of William Taylor, "stabbed in nine places by Agnes Anderson, with whom he had lived in illicit intercourse." By far the favorite with Storey was "SCAFFOLD SCOURINGS," a daily feature that highlighted executions. Typical was the account of the hanging of William Darkey in Buffalo for wife-killing:

> When the cap was pulled over his face, he somewhat rallied, and his groans and cries . . . were harrowing to hear. An instant and he was moved forward onto the trap, feelling [*sic*] wildly about with his hands. . . . An instant more, and he stood alone, grasping convulsively at the air [and so on for a full column].[62]

The biggest play, however, was reserved for Detroit scandal, spilled all over "City Intelligence" on page three. Prostitution, rape and "HORRID MURDER" furnished the raw material for vivid portrayals that left nothing to the reader's imagination. "Mother Dolsen's House," No. 99 Croghan Street, "kept on the plan of an assignation house," received the treatment on June 9, 1857. Sometimes the doings of local "Magdalens" served as the basis for some homespun philosophizing. Thus, when "Indian Sue" was murdered, the *Free Press* observed:

> One more unfortunate gone to the grave and to judgment. A life of sin and degradation—of which the sink holes of Detroit have seen a large share—is ended appropriately by a violent death, in a wretched hovel, unwept and dishonored. So goes the world.[63]

Local sensations occasionally even succeeded in edging politics off page one. The case of "Grandpa Willard Daniels," a "HORRID TALE OF CRIME," did this in February, 1857. It covered two full columns, the gist of which related how Grandpa Daniels was taking his granddaughter to Detroit when "he commenced the most improper importunities." The relationship blossomed into a two-month affair that ended in an abortion mill. The details of each

62. *Ibid.*, January 30, 1855, May 14, 1853, and December 3, 1854.
63. *Ibid.*, August 12, 1857.

stage were furnished complete, and the story ended with a prayer for the mother's grief:

> God strengthen the poor mother's heart . . . when she learns that her father has ruined her idolized daughter. We are told that her parting injunctions to the old man were: "Father, be careful of my daughter; watch over her for she is young and inexperienced, and is going to a large city where there are many temptations." How cruelly has he disregarded his daughter's injunctions.[64]

It was "HORRIBLE" in 1855 when Ellen Murphy and her husband spent one Sabbath "on a drunken spree." It apparently was also cold, since Mrs. Murphy passed out in a stupor on her doorstep, and froze to death. Her husband dragged the body into the house, where he left it on the hallway floor. When police asked him next morning why he had not put the corpse on the bed, Murphy replied "I'll be d——d if I was going to sleep with a dead woman."[65]

On August 17, 1858, the *Detroit Free Press* celebrated the successful completion of the Atlantic telegraph, "one of the most important events of history," by completely revamping the paper's format. It was enlarged by a column, headlines became more elaborate, stories were better spaced, and the size of type increased to afford much easier reading. From this improvement until the outbreak of the Civil War, the newspaper moved continuously in the direction that the *Chicago Times* took after the war. A comparison of the *Free Press* before and after 1858 proved its indiscretions were now more blatant, more frequent, and much more handsomely served.

About this same time the staff was increased. William E. Quinby began to cover the courts, and in 1860 he was dispatched to Washington as the paper's personal political correspondent, a move that made Wilbur F. Storey the first editor in Michigan with his own man in the nation's capital.[66] Austin L. Patterson became business manager in 1859, and he remained business manager of Storey's newspapers until the editor's death. J. Logan Chipman also joined the staff in 1859 as a reporter, and in the same year

64. *Ibid.*, February 3, 1857.
65. *Ibid.*, February 18, 1855.
66. Clarence M. and Agnes Burton, *History of Wayne County and the City of Detroit, Michigan* (Detroit: S. J. Clarke & Co., 1930), I, 642.

Mort L. Hopkins began his long association with Storey as a reporter and editorial writer.

The major difference that these changes made from a typographical standpoint rested in the fact that headlines now became multi-decked. Each deck was set in boldface, and a complete headline frequently ran five to eight inches deep in a column. A typical front page after August 17, 1858, would feature one long story with a headline similar to the one of July 1, 1859:

HORRIBLE MURDER!

A Man Shoots at his Wife and Blows out the Brains of a Little Daughter and Breaks his Gun over his Wife's Head after the Murder.

The inventive touch of Warren P. Isham and Thomas Cook was apparent in much of the sensational local stuff printed in the *Free Press.* The newspaper regularly ran sordid and gruesome accounts of local suicides, murders, and such without ever mentioning names, addresses or other specifics of the principals involved. The stories were eagerly devoured by the nearly 4,000 daily subscribers that the paper served by 1861.

As early as 1840, the editor of the *La Porte Whig* observed that the first newspaper of Wilbur F. Storey read as if the editor "had been run through a smut mill." The remark was undoubtedly prompted by party differences, for the *La Porte Herald* at its worst was no more than a passionately partisan journal. It was likewise in Jackson, where the *Patriot* was a typographically attractive, solidly Democratic, and interesting weekly newspaper. It represented clean, crisp journalism at its best for that era, for the most part minus the sordid, the tawdry, the distasteful. Once Storey set foot inside the office of the *Detroit Free Press*, however, his journalism changed.

He did not inherit a scandal sheet, for the paper before his time was a dull, spiritless montage of scissors and paste enterprise. Overnight it became certainly the dirtiest newspaper in Michigan, and in all probability, the dirtiest in the Middle West. Not only the editor, but most of his staff seemed habitually to "run through a smut mill" before they put pen to paper. But throughout his Detroit years, there was another side to Storey the editor, a side that existed continuous with and contiguous to the political ravings, character depravations, and dirt.

First and foremost, Wilbur F. Storey was a newspaperman. In this capacity he was ahead of most of his contemporaries. His advanced notions of what the *news* in newspapers meant did not reach full fruition until the postwar years with the *Chicago Times*. But just as the genesis of Storey journalism at its worst was clearly present in the *Detroit Free Press*, so also was the genesis of Storey journalism at its best. And its best was very good indeed! A history of the newspaper under his direction would be neither complete nor just without an examination of some of the good things Storey did as a Detroit newsman from 1853 to 1861.

First, it was with the *Detroit Free Press* that Storey pioneered the Sunday newspaper. For years prior to 1853, Mondays had been the dullest day of the week for daily newspapers. Until after the Civil War, with improved rapid communication, the Sabbath quiet just did not furnish enough matter, political, social or otherwise, to get up a good Monday morning edition. Storey saw this, and within his first year in Detroit he eliminated the Monday issue when on October 2, 1853, the *Free Press* went on a Tuesday through Sunday publication schedule. The religious community protested at first, but since in those days the edition was always put together the night before, Storey replied that the change enabled the *Free Press* family to join the rest of mankind in "keeping holy" the Lord's day. For almost eight years thereafter, the *Free Press* was the only Sunday newspaper available in the state of Michigan.

But it was not just the introduction of a Sunday edition that made Storey a pioneer of Sunday journalism. From the beginning he was cognizant that the increased leisure his readership enjoyed "every seventh day" called for a different kind of newspaper than the regular daily edition. The predominantly "feature touch" for Sunday, which became an actuality with the *Chicago Sunday Times* in 1866, was present in embryo with the *Free Press* after 1853.

For example, a review of the week's market appeared Sundays on page one under the headline "COMMERCIAL INTELLIGENCE." The front-page on the Sabbath also might feature such area studies as "BURY'S HOUSE AT GROSSE ILE," or "A VISIT TO ST. MARY'S HOSPITAL." The latter recounted a visit to a Catholic hospital run by the Sisters of Charity. The story ended with a prayer that "if ever we find ourselves alone, friendless, destitute and sick . . .

we may fall into the hands of the Sisters of Charity."[67] Despite the usual fare that marked the *Detroit Free Press*, such features were not uncommon.

Or again, there might appear on Sunday morning a long exposition on "Billiards," which explained the how and why of the game, along with short personality sketches of prominent masters. The continuously running feature for the Sunday edition was also hit upon by Storey in 1858 when the Free Press ran a series on "THE PUBLIC CHARITIES OF DETROIT." The Sisters of Charity were first, followed by the Marine Hospital, St. Vincent's Orphan Asylum, the Ladies Orphan Association, and the Presbyterian Waifs. These all appeared on page one, and ran from six-and-one-half to eight colunms in length.[68]

When Storey put his mind and his newspaper behind a special promotion, he did it right. In 1854 the first passenger train over the Great Western Railway, connecting Detroit and Niagara, was due on Tuesday, January 17. Storey considered the occasion momentous, and began a steady build-up that reached a crescendo of civic promotion to mark the event. He started with a "SUGGESTION," prominently played on page one, that "Business concert [to close] all the stores and shops on the principal avenues and streets." This would enable "our people to turn out *en masse*" to mark "the most important and interesting event that ever occurred in our city." This was followed by lavish appeals to civic pride, promises of spectacular parades, bands, and excitement. When the day arrived, Storey published "AN EXHORTATION!" The next day he turned all of page one over to "THE EVENT!" The date, it must be remembered, was 1854. There were no typewriters, no telephones, no instant communication. Each word had to be handwritten, corrected and edited, and then hand-set. Only fifteen hours after the arrival of Detroit's first passenger train, the *Detroit Free Press*, in the face of these obstacles, had three-and-one-half columns of solid minion covering the background, the parade, the arrival, the banquet, the appointments of the dining hall. The menu was reproduced in full, and the account ended with a summary of every speech and toast offered for the occasion.[69] It was a job that would have done credit to any newspaper thirty years later.

Detroit. Michigan. The Old Northwest. Storey plugged them

67. *Detroit Free Press*, July 7, 1855, and September 29, 1857.
68. *Ibid.*, July 25 through August 29, 1858.
69. *Ibid.*, January 14, 17, and 18, 1854.

as a matter of policy. In "Reciprocal Trade and Free Navigation" he dreamed a dream that became reality 100 years later. In April, 1854, he called for a treaty between Great Britain and the United States for free navigation of the St. Lawrence and co-operation in building a canal "around the falls of Niagara." If this were accomplished, Detroit and all other lake cities "would be ocean ports, between which and the whole world a trade as direct and profitable could be carried on as though situated on the sea-coast."[70]

In the summer of 1854, when a cholera epidemic struck, the *Free Press* led the way in demanding the establishment of a city Board of Health.[71] Humanitarian crusades were also undertaken. When Dorothea Dix launched her plea for reform in mental institutions, the *Free Press* backed her without equivocation. None of the rancor against "silly and nosey old women" appeared in a series of editorials one of which noted that the insane "must not be cruelly treated."[72] In the midst of the Panic of 1857, the unemployed and hungry received attention. "To search out and assist . . . whomsoever is hungry and ill-clad [is] no less a pleasure than a duty," one editorial stated.[73]

But the charity that Wilbur F. Storey preached was to be carried out under private auspices. "The doctrine that it is the duty of the government to furnish land to the landless . . . bread to the hungry, clothes to the destitute, and labor to the idle . . . is the most demoralizing and pernicious doctrine of any age," Storey stated. "We know of no surer way of vagabonding individuals and communities."[74]

Storey could also put his spleen and rancor aside on occasion to indulge in light essays. As a New Year's gift in 1858, he informed *Free Press* readers

> On the Glories of A Little Woman.
>
> All men have their taste in regard to women and their characteristics. Some affect the blonde, others the brunette; some incline to the short, others again to the tall. Some prefer the plump and rosy, some the fat and lazy; and yet more, some even fancy the lean and cadaverous. Let her be what she will, maid, young or old matron, comely or hideous, she finds her admirers among one of the many classes of

70. *Ibid.*, April 13, 1854.
71. *Ibid.*, July 22, 1854.
72. *Ibid.*, April 28, 1854.
73. *Ibid.*, November 6, 1857.
74. *Ibid.*, March 14, 1858.

masculinity. For our part we like what we always did and always shall like—a little woman.

Standing on the corner of Jefferson avenue the other day, there came tripping along the prettiest little specimen of the kind—one who captivated our fancy, and originated the above reflections. A perfect little woman in every respect she was, not even excepting hoops, and as she passed on with an air that said "Valuable goods come in small packages, if you please sir," we reflected, and reflecting thought how happy is he who has just such a one stowed away in some snug nest, exclusively for his own benefit.

There is beauty in the diminutiveness of a small woman. Your large ones are in the way, and are too dignified—your fat ones are lazy, and as for embracing them, it is an impossibility (unless you adopt the ruse of the Iowa lad who loved a fat damsel. Taking a piece of chalk in each hand, and embracing as far around as he could, he made a mark on each side, and then went around and embraced the rest). Your tall ones are fully up to your own mark, which isn't agreeable as, if you happen to be short, she has to get down on her knees to lay her head on your bosom; and your lean ones are invariably old maids, which we always detested, believing that the Creator never intended any such result from his handiwork. . . . But your little woman, well she is petite, pert, pretty and piquant; she is quick and lively, and the chances a thousand to one she has the "devil" in her, bigger than a woodchuck. Of dignity she hasn't the slightest, neither is she prim and precise. She is full of fun. If you want a right-down frolic, she is always ready, and he is a lucky man who engages in such and does not get his hair pulled half a dozen times where he desires it once. She is agreeable, always laughing, talking and singing. She is spunky. You may be afraid to trust her overflowing spirits while you go downtown on business; and think you can shut her up in a bandbox on her good behavior, but you are mistaken, for she has grit enough to fill a body four times as big, which will not brook any such slight. She is tenacious of her rights. Perhaps you think, when you are playfully inclined, that you can toss her up to the ceiling and catch her as she comes down, just for amusement. The misguided individual who attempts it does so at the risk of having his eyes scratched out. She is neat, a miniature volume of poetry printed in diamond type, on gilt-edged paper and bound in gold and morocco. Last of all, she is affectionate, and when you come home at night, she will climb into your lap, lay a soft cheek to yours, and with a pair of arms which will just reach around your neck, she will make you think yourself the happiest man alive.[75]

The outbreak of the Civil War brought Storey's genius for getting the news and publishing it to the fore. His campaign against Abraham Lincoln tended to obscure the fact, but three of the most prominent correspondents that the war produced, Warren P. Isham, Franc B. Wilkie and Sylvannus Cadwallader sent dispatches that were the exclusive property of the *Chicago Times*. Storey was on top of the possibilities as soon as hostilities began. On April 13, the *Free Press* announced afternoon editions would be published daily at 2:00 and 6:00 P.M., "giving the latest news by Magnetic telegraph." Four days after Sumter was fired upon, the paper was printing dispatches direct from Dixie by Warren P. Isham, who toured southern capitals and sent back a series of "Impressions." Few, if any, other midwestern newspapers were so quick in getting eyewitness accounts from the southern heartland.

If the *Detroit Free Press* from 1853 to 1861 was schizophrenic, it was so because journalism's foremost schizoid had ironclad control of the establishment. Storey as yet did not suffer from mental imbalance, but his personality defects, so graphically reflected in both his personal life and his newspaper, clearly indicated alternating delusions of persecution and omnipotence. In no other way can the dichotomies of logic in both the man and the newspaper during these years be explained. Based upon the evidence, Wilbur F. Storey proved at Detroit that he was the original Jekyll and Hyde of American journalism.

On June 4, 1861, Henry N. Walker purchased the *Free Press* for $30,000.[76] The deal had been in the making for about three weeks, as Storey agreed on May 20 to pay Cyrus H. McCormick $23,000 for the *Daily Chicago Times* as soon as the *Free Press* interests could be sold.[77] Storey's formal farewell consisted of a brusque, fifteen line announcement at the top of his editorial page

75. *Ibid.*, January 3, 1858.

76. For the details of this transaction see Memorandum of Agreement between Henry N. Walker, Charles H. Taylor and Jacob Barnes (in Henry N. Walker papers, Free Press material, Burton Historical Collection, Detroit Public Library).

77. William T. Hutchinson, *Cyrus Hall McCormick* (New York: Appleton, Century Co., 1935), II, 54.

on June 4 that he was leaving Detroit (he did not specify for where) with the assurance that the *Free Press* remained in capable hands. The *Tribune*, despite almost a decade of bitter rivalry, wished him well and paid tribute to the ability and energy Storey displayed in newspaper management. "We wish him success in his new enterprise, where his capacity for newspaper conduct will have a still wider field."[78] Rufus Hosmer, filled with hatred to the end, waited five days to print a cryptic, two-sentence notice of

> AN IMPROVEMENT.
>
> We have neglected to notice the fact that Henry N. Walker . . . has become the editor and proprietor of the Detroit Free Press. Mr. Walker has character and reputation, and the community will consequently be gainers by the change.[79]

So ended the Detroit career of Wilbur F. Storey. Amazingly, no evidence has been uncovered that he was assaulted, shot at, or whipped despite his barbed pen. In fact, with the exception of the Warren libel cases, he apparently was not even brought to court. For some reason, his Detroit victims "laid off," no matter how they may have felt. Things like horse-whippings, assassination attempts, libel suits, even a short term of imprisonment, would occur often once Wilbur established himself in Chicago.

In retrospect then, what did it all mean, these eight and one-half years in Detroit? In many ways inspired and magnificent as a newspaperman, Storey nonetheless incurred only contempt among the vast majority of his Michigan contemporaries. The official voice of the Democratic party in his state, his extreme counsel helped insure that his party would win no major statewide election after the formation of the Republican party. A specialist in pandering to the baser instincts of mankind in order to build circulation, Storey's real contributions to broadening and improving the scope of the daily newspaper in the Middle West would be overlooked by a posterity that remembered only the stench. James E. Scripps, looking back forty years later, after Storey made millions with the *Chicago Times* only to end as an insane, dissipated, and totally helpless wreck, recalled that it was

> . . . sad to look back on the utter fruitlessness of so earnest a life as Mr. Storey's. He left no children, made a fortune

78. *Detroit Daily Tribune*, June 5, 1861.
79. *Detroit Daily Advertiser*, June 8, 1861.

but lived to see it vanish, and built up a great newspaper which ceased as soon as his master hand was withdrawn. His most lasting achievement was the impulse he gave to journalism in Detroit during the short period of eight years during which he managed the fortunes of the Free Press.[80]

80. Scripps, "Wilbur F. Storey," Palmer Scrapbook, p. 155.

CHAPTER VII

CHICAGO: A Fire in the Rear!

> The fanaticism which will have dissolved the Union will not . . . be allowed to convulse the continent with Civil War. Never! It must be stopped. . . . Public opinion commands it to stop, and . . . if it shall attempt war then it will be assailed with a fire in the rear which will compel it to stop.
>
> —*Detroit Free Press*, February 6, 1861.

THE ONLY NOTICE WILBUR F. STOREY HAS RECEIVED AT THE HANDS OF American historians deals with a period of less than four years in a journalistic career that spanned forty-five years. From June 8, 1861, until April 17, 1865, the *Chicago Times* under Storey's direction led the opposition of midwestern Democrats to the administration of Abraham Lincoln. The personal vendetta Storey organized against the sixteenth President resulted in the suppression of his paper at one point. The lengths to which he carried his attack would haunt him after Lincoln's martyrdom. Storey's war policy put him squarely before one of the most effective epithets ever hurled in American politics—COPPERHEAD. The *Times* did not support Abraham Lincoln. Its editor was a blackguard, a traitor. It is this that history books record.

The verdict is unanimous. Scholars as well as popularizers speak with one voice in condemnation of the editor who audaciously, and as the war progressed, with increasing distastefulness, assailed the "mean, wily, illiterate, brutal, unprincipled, and utterly vulgar creature" whose fate it was to direct the United States of America through the nation's greatest ordeal. The utter viciousness of Storey's crusade against Lincoln proved that the editor justly earned much of the opprobrium that has been heaped upon him. But denunciation without qualification, frequently offered as the sole explanation of the policy of the *Chicago Times* during the Civil War, does violence to the truth and an injustice to the editor.

The wartime excesses of Storey can properly be understood and evaluated only in the context of the man's entire life. The Lincoln cult, which emerged immediately after the tragic events of April 15, 1865, to be nurtured and cultivated without surcease during the century since, makes such an evaluation difficult. This is so because, as frequently transpires in cases of assassination, the victim became sacrosanct. The infamy justly merited by the assassin never sufficed as some of it transferred to those who were the victim's detractors before his death.

Still, a dispassionate assessment of the role played by the northern wing of the Democratic party during the Civil War must be attempted if truth is to be served. That party's role was one of political opposition, always heated and oftentimes vile. Partisan opposition, when coupled with fanatical devotion to his own political precepts, thrust Storey to the forefront in the battle against Lincoln. While much of what he did was distasteful, the more so when viewed in retrospect after the President's assassination, it would nonetheless be incautious to brand the editor's opposition as treasonous.[1] To say this does not detract from the true greatness of Abraham Lincoln as an American statesman. On the contrary, such an admission adds to Lincoln's stature for it is no misstatement of

1. The most widely read biographer of Lincoln, Carl Sandburg, suggested that Storey helped pull the trigger of John Wilkes Booth's pistol on the night of April 15, 1865. "Had Booth merely permitted himself to be led by such newspapers as the . . . *Chicago Times* then he would have felt himself correct and justified to go forth with a brass pocket pistol . . . [to send] a merciless bullet through [Lincoln's] head." *Abraham Lincoln, The War Years* (New York: Harcourt, Brace & Co., 1939), IV, 340.

fact to say that Abraham Lincoln was the most opposed President in the nation's history. Yet in the face of overwhelming odds which included "the fire in the rear" promised by Storey and his ilk, Lincoln succeeded, at the eventual cost of his life, in preventing a perpetual fragmentation of the American experiment in federalism. Had secession prevailed, it would have spelled the end for the Union that both the President and the editor, each in his own way, loved.

It must be remembered that Abraham Lincoln was elected as a sectional candidate by only 39% of the total popular vote cast in 1860. Thus, from the beginning, he was assured of complete rejection by that area of the country that attempted to form the Confederacy and where the institution of Negro slavery was legalized and an integral part of the social structure. This opposition alone was enough to ensure Civil War once Lincoln was inaugurated.

But southern opposition was only one of the forces Lincoln had to meet and overcome. In his own strongholds, the North and the West, he also met bitter denunciation from the beginning. During the first eighteen months of his administration members of his own Republican party castigated him unmercifully in word and manner not unlike that which made Wilbur F. Storey infamous.[2] Lincoln's most publicized northern opposition, of course, came from the ranks of Democratic partisans engaged in the eternal American struggle for control of the nation's political machinery. Politics, contrary to popular belief, did not cease during the Civil War, and Democrats throughout the North spent much of their energy in an attempt to turn the populace against the party in power so that a Democratic administration might set things right once again.

Republicans raised the shibboleth of "treason" at each manifestation of Democratic opposition, and the picture of Copperheads as traitorous wretches of blank intellect moved by a satanic determination to overthrow the American government in the hour of its gravest crisis has prevailed. Such caricature remained good Republican strategy until the twentieth century, but it is not history. It is simply too facile an explanation to dismiss all northern Democrats who opposed the Republican party and Abraham Lincoln as "traitors." Rather, in the absence of clear proof of co-opera-

2. The most comprehensive treatment of Republican opposition to Lincoln is found in T. Harry Williams, *Lincoln and the Radicals* (Madison: University of Wisconsin Press, 1941).

tion with plots for armed insurrection against the Lincoln government which the majority of free-state Democrats considered legally, if accidentally, elected, would it not be more accurate to accept Lincoln's partisan opponents simply as American citizens who were of Democratic persuasion? It was true that many Democrats were frequently swept beyond the bounds of rational opposition by the emotions and pressures that the war loosed, but not more frequently than radical Republicans when they found reason to oppose the policy of their chosen leader. It was also true that Democratic pronouncements against Lincoln frequently crossed the bounds of good taste. So did Republican statements, and given the rough and tumble of mid-century politics, the Democratic behavior was that expected on the part of partisans out of power. Unless the propaganda of the Republican party be accepted at face value, however, the blandishments that northern Democrats directed against Abraham Lincoln cannot be defined as treason if the constitutional guarantee of free speech remains valid in war.[3]

In the case of Storey it must be noted that at no point did he equivocate with respect to his views. Once secession and rebellion became facts, he gave unhesitating support to the Federal government. Of course, he had not supported Abraham Lincoln for the presidency, but once Lincoln was inaugurated Storey's newspapers moved to support the President and the war. In fact, until Sep-

3. A precise definition of the term "Copperhead" is impossible. Republicans of the Civil War era defined all northern non-Republicans who opposed the policies of the Republican party as Copperheads, and equated the term with treason. Historians have reached no agreement on a proper definition. Secret societies, peace Democrats, conservatives, and outright Confederate sympathizers have all been lumped together at one time or another as Copperheads. George Fort Milton placed all northern Democrats in Copperhead ranks, and called them "the fifth-column of the Civil War." Wood Gray was not quite so harsh, but he cautioned that the Copperhead mentality would have "necessitated vigilance in any period." James D. Horan saw Copperheads as a conspiratorial apparatus that specialized in "nightly terror, violence and fanaticism. The true scope of the Copperheads will probably never be known." A recent student of the movement, Frank L. Klement, said "it was complex and nearly intangible from the start." Klement concluded that, far from being guilty of treason, Copperheads were "actually watchdogs of civil liberties." It is into this maze of charge and counter-charge, frequently devoid of substantiating evidence, that Wilbur F. Storey has been indiscriminately cast by almost every historian who has studied his Civil War career. See George F. Milton, *Abraham Lincoln and the Fifth Column* (New York: The Vanguard Press, 1942), p. 117; Wood Gray, *The Hidden Civil War: The Story of the Copperheads* (New York: The Viking Press, 1942), p. 224; James D. Horan, *Confederate Agent, A Discovery in History* (New York: Crown Publishers, 1954), p. 16; and Frank L. Klement, *The Copperheads in the Middle West* (Chicago: University of Chicago Press, 1960), pp. 36-37.

tember, 1862, first in the *Detroit Free Press* and then in the *Chicago Times*, Storey defended Lincoln vociferously against the almost daily assaults of the President's own partisans.

Once Lincoln made it apparent that he would free the Negro, however, this support was replaced by unrelenting vituperation. It is the latter part of Storey's policy alone that has been associated lastingly with his name. Like the editor's contemporary Republican opponents, historians have seen everything from Confederate sympathy to participation in a plot to remove the Northwest from the Union in the activities of Storey and the *Times* during the years that Abraham Lincoln was President. But such an appraisal is not accurate, for Storey fanatically loved his country. It was precisely because his attachment to the Union was fanatical that he became the leading anti-Lincoln fanatic once the President converted the war into what the editor felt was an "unconstitutional crusade to free four millions of negro barbarians." Storey may be censured legitimately for vileness. His war conduct most certainly manifested a complete lack of decorum or prudence. A strong argument perhaps can even be made that, given the exigencies produced by the Civil War, the government would have been justified in abrogating his right to publish. But absolutely no evidence has been uncovered that Wilbur F. Storey betrayed the United States of America.

As early as February, 1854, Storey cast a covetous eye at the Chicago newspaper field. The defection of John Wentworth and his *Chicago Democrat* when the Kansas-Nebraska bill was first introduced left "A GOOD OPENING" in Storey's mind:

> We think the city of Chicago must be a capital opening for a Democratic newspaper. There seems to be none of that stamp now, all those claiming to be such having a villainous odor of abolitionism.[4]

There was no doubt that Wentworth's defection left a serious journalistic gap for the Democracy in the largest city of Stephen A. Douglas' home state. One of the pioneers of Chicago journalism, Wentworth commenced a quarter-century association with the *Democrat* in November, 1836, and in July, 1837, he purchased full control of the Jacksonian sheet. Until 1854, Wentworth's *Democrat* was the leading party daily in Chicago. In that year Wentworth refused to support the Kansas-Nebraska Act, however, and he con-

4. *Detroit Free Press*, February 10, 1854.

verted the *Democrat* into a Free Soil paper that by 1860 supported the Republican party and Abraham Lincoln.[5]

But 1854 was too early for the Detroit editor to fill the void, as in June of that year Illinois supporters of Stephen A. Douglas brought out the first issue of the *Chicago Times*.[6] During the next seven years the troubles that plagued the Democratic party also plagued the *Times*. After Cyrus H. McCormick bought control of the paper in June, 1860, it openly defended the right of secession by the South should Lincoln be elected. After the outbreak of war, it continued this policy as circulation and revenue fell. It was in this situation that Storey purchased the concern. The taint that the *Times* was a pro-Confederate sheet could not be easily removed, and identification as a "Jeff Davis organ" proved the greatest drawback the new resident from Detroit had to overcome during his first six months in Chicago.

There were also technical difficulties that added to the heavy odds against success. The presses and type were worn out from years of neglect, and Storey was forced into heavy indebtedness to refurbish the newspaper in every branch. He brought less than $7,000 in cash with him from Detroit, since the sale of the *Free Press* was a time payment deal not completed until December,

5. See Don E. Fehrenbacher, *Chicago Giant, A Biography of "Long John" Wentworth* (Madison, Wisconsin: The State Historical Society Press, 1957).

6. The *Chicago Times* developed from a small, nonpartisan daily, the *Chicago Courant*, first issued in November, 1853, and owned by William D. Wilson and A. C. Cameron. In June, 1854, Isaac Cook, Daniel Cameron and J. W. Patterson purchased the paper and changed the name to the *Chicago Times*. In August, 1854, James W. Sheahan of Washington, D. C., a close personal friend of Stephen A. Douglas, became editor. In 1855, Sheahan became proprietor. In 1858, William Price was taken in as a partner and the name was changed to the *Daily Chicago Times*. In the spring of 1860, the two partners split over the question of whether to support Douglas or John C. Breckinridge as the Democratic presidential nominee. Circulation fell, and in June the paper was sold to Cyrus H. McCormick who merged it with the pro-Buchanan *Chicago Herald* that he already owned. E. W. McComas, a Virginia state rights Democrat, was hired as editor and the paper followed a policy sympathetic to southern secession in the months following Abraham Lincoln's election. Its circulation and advertising fell noticeably, and in May, 1861, McCormick decided to unload a losing property. He found a willing purchaser in Wilbur F. Storey, and on June 8, 1861, the first copy of the *Daily Chicago Times* under Storey's direction appeared. See L. E. Ellis, "The Chicago *Times* During the Civil War," *Illinois State Historical Society Transactions for the Year 1932*, XXXIX (Springfield, 1933), 136-37; Alfred T. Andreas, *History of Chicago From the Earliest Period to the Present Time* (Chicago: A. T. Andreas & Co., 1886), II, 495; and William T. Hutchinson, *Cyrus Hall McCormick* (New York: Appleton, Century Co., 1935), II, 46-47.

1866.[7] In addition to financial difficulties, Storey also faced the most prominent Republican daily in the West, the *Chicago Tribune*. With unlimited capital at the disposal of its editor, Horace A. White, the *Tribune* reigned supreme in the Chicago newspaper field. Thus it was that Storey made his Chicago debut as a stranger loaded with debt who published a newspaper of limited circulation because in the popular mind it was identified with southern sympathies.

Storey had no illusions about the task ahead. His *Times* prospectus of June 9, unlike the *Free Press* statement of eight years earlier, was devoid of boasts or claims of superiority. Just as "the proof of the pudding is in the eating," Storey noted, so "the proof of a newspaper is not in promises but in performances." Therefore, the new publisher of the *Times* "will not hope for public approval of the paper further nor faster than it has been earned."[8] This short statement, plus the observation that the "facilities of the establishment are not now sufficient to supply the demand which it is believed the paper will have" constituted the extent of Storey's declaration of intent. Beginning with a plea for public indulgence until "a four-cylinder Hoe press, capable of printing ten thousand sheets per hour" was received, Storey undertook an enterprise that he would parlay into a multimillion dollar business before his death twenty-four years later. But on June 8, 1861, this was all in the postwar future. First there was the business of the Civil War to be concluded.

When the Republican party nominated Abraham Lincoln in May, 1860, Storey saw him as "the man DOUGLAS beat two years ago. That is all the reputation he has." The Republican platform, "a very latitudinous creed," started off with the Declaration of Independence and, "after touching upon a little of everything, winds up by inviting everyone, no matter whether he agrees with it or not, to co-operate with the party."[9] Storey soon felt that Lincoln's nomination was "STILL-BORN," according to the heading of an editorial in the *Free Press* that pointed out:

> Lincoln is not a statesman; he has not been a soldier; he is not an orator; he has performed no distinguished service of any sort; he has never betrayed administrative abilities—the

7. See Free Press material (in Henry A. Walker papers, Burton Historical Collection, Detroit Public Library).

8. *Daily Chicago Times*, June 9, 1861, as reprinted in *Detroit Free Press*, June 12, 1861.

9. *Detroit Free Press*, May 19, 1860.

nomination of this description of man for the Presidency is never fit to be made.[10]

Throughout the campaign, Storey viewed Lincoln as a political nonentity, accidentally nominated, who in the movement of circumstances would most likely be elected President of the United States. There was at no point any extensive indication of the abusive vituperation to be loosed against Lincoln in the heat of the Civil War.

In the rapid march of events following election day, Storey was quick to support the Federal administration and condemn secession. On November 8, the *Free Press* stated that no one state or any number of states could secede. "The Federal government was constructed for all time, and is not a temporary expedient," Storey proclaimed.[11] As the crisis developed secession became "a monstrous fallacy,"[12] and as 1860 drew to a close Storey gave a pledge of support to Lincoln. "We will strengthen his hand and the hand of any other which is raised to defend the Union of our Fathers."[13]

"The Constitution and the Union" was the key phrase in evaluating Storey's whole attitude toward the Civil War in general and Abraham Lincoln in particular. As long as it remained a war to preserve the Union and uphold the Constitution, the war would have his support. As long as Lincoln took no step outside of the narrow limits Storey established for the President, the publisher would "strengthen his hand." But really, the whole business was tragically needless. Storey had warned repeatedly where abolition fanaticism would lead. As radical Republicans moved in early 1861 to sabotage compromise measures, Storey printed his famous "A Fire in the Rear" editorial. He took pleasure in noting how congressional abolitionists "wince awfully" under the threat of such a fire. Determined to press the issues separating North and South "to a bloody termination," they found it a distasteful prospect to do some fighting in the North before making a descent upon the South. "The apparition of any army of Northern men, forbidding an anti-slavery war, is not a pleasant sight to see," he concluded. "Nevertheless, it is a sight that they will be compelled to look upon."[14]

10. *Ibid.*, May 22, 1860.
11. *Ibid.*, November 8, 1860.
12. *Ibid.*, November 16, 1860.
13. *Ibid.*, December 11, 1860.
14. *Ibid.*, February 6, 1861.

Thus the stage was set and the terms decreed. "The break-up of the Union is the greatest calamity that the world will have known for a century, if not, indeed, the greatest calamity that has ever befallen mankind."[15] The tragedy was caused by fanatics on both sides, Storey felt, and he would have no dealings with any war to abolish slavery. Secession must be stopped, however, and so long as the war were waged by *constitutional* means to preserve the Union, it was the duty of every loyal American to support the administration.

In late February, 1861, the decisive question was "INTO WHOSE HANDS WILL HE FALL?" If what Storey termed the Seward-Wood-Cameron faction of the Republican party controlled Lincoln after he assumed office, "we shall have hope in the future." If the President-elect were won over by abolitionists, however, all hope was gone.[16]

Within a week of the outbreak of hostilities, Storey pledged "Democrats and all conservative men will do their duty in the present dreadful emergency." He added that Democrats would not forget that abolitionists had caused the war. But the South labored under delusion if it thought the North would be divided. The free states stood solidly united and would press on to victory. Westerners, above all, were loyal. "They will stand true to the constitution, and are willing to die, if need be, to maintain the Union against all foes, foreign and domestic."[17]

Storey gave this support because he saw no reason to doubt that "the preservation of the Union under the constitution" was the animating principle of Lincoln's conduct. But the people must understand this too, and feel it, and act upon it. "If the war lasts a century it must be transmitted from father to son, from army to army, from ruler to ruler, that the object of this war is the preservation of the freedom of the people, and not the subjugation of a section."[18]

Before Lincoln's policy became clear, the *Free Press* frequently foretokened how Storey would treat Lincoln if the object of the war became other than the preservation of the Union. During "THE HEGIRA OF LINCOLN" to Washington for the inauguration, the President-elect's speeches showed he was "all a muddle." After Lincoln took the oath of office Storey stated "the President

15. *Ibid.*
16. *Ibid.*, February 21, 1861.
17. *Ibid.*, April 16, April 25 and May 1, 1861.
18. *Ibid.*, June 1, 1861.

evinces his appetite for blood" though "his oath was registered in heaven." Storey pointed out that "Jeff Davis has taken a like oath . . . but Mr. Lincoln says it is not registered where his is, and that seems to make, in his opinion, all the difference in the world."[19] Once the war began, such notices ceased and they did not reappear until after the issuance of the preliminary Emancipation Proclamation in September, 1862.

For the first fourteen months that Wilbur F. Storey lived in Chicago, his newspaper never wavered in its consistent, at times even vigorous and impassioned support of the President. The political fortunes of the Democratic party were forgotten as Storey hewed literally to the dying advice of the man whose political fortunes he had moved to Chicago to help repair. The last political statement of Stephen A. Douglas to his fellow Democrats had been a plea to "forget party—all—remember your country. The shortest road to peace is the most tremendous preparation for war." The editorial policy of the *Chicago Times* from June 8, 1861, until the first rumor that Lincoln contemplated a policy of emancipation proved that Storey, to his credit, did precisely what Douglas advised.

Frederick F. Cook, who was employed by Storey as a reporter for more than twenty years, stated that "had Douglas lived, it is more than probable that the course of the *Times* would have been quite different [during the war]." Cook based this estimate "upon the authority of one who came with Mr. Storey from Detroit." According to Cook's informant Storey purchased the *Times* "with the idea of making it the organ of the Douglas Democracy; and fate decreed that the first number under his direction should chronicle the Senator's funeral."[20] In view of what followed once emancipation passed from rumor to fact, Storey's support of Lincoln must be examined in detail.

First, his columns during these months did not cease a continuous villification of the Negro. The abolitionist wing of the Republican party was also castigated, but not from the point of view of political partisanship. In fact, politicking ceased for Storey as the *Times* urged national unity to put down the rebellion. During these same fourteen months the Republican press harped on the President constantly, and in Chicago the *Tribune* was espe-

19. *Ibid.*, February 26 and March 10, 1861.

20. Frederick F. Cook, *Bygone Days in Chicago: Recollections of the "Garden City" of the Sixties* (Chicago: A. C. McClurg & Co., 1910), p. 331.

cially forceful in its denunciation as Lincoln showed no sign he would emancipate the slaves. But Storey maintained his moratorium on politics and defended Lincoln. The editor pointed out "we are under no obligation to defend Mr. Lincoln's administration . . . but it is our duty to maintain such a position before the people as will inspire them with confidence."[21] When some Democrats asked why the *Times* supported the war policy of the government "with so much cordiality" the editor replied with a long editorial which told

WHY WE DO IT.

. . . .

> It is the duty of every citizen to serve his country in the manner which his conscience directs. . . . Insurrection exists in the land. The laws of the Union are set to defiance. . . .
>
> The alternatives are government or no government. . . . Mr. Lincoln is the head of the government, and upon him, as such, devolves the duty of meeting the insurrection and suppressing it if he can. If he hesitated to do this he would live forever a man of infamy, an imbecility. He has no option. It is his duty to his country, to democrats as well as republicans, to North as well as South, to all parties, all sections, to all ages of time. He stands in the breach and must defend it. He cannot, he must not let the light of American liberty stand in the darkness. If then it is his duty to defend the government, it is our duty to sustain him in all proper efforts to that end. It is true that tomorrow we could not vote for him if he was a candidate for the Presidency,—that we deem the party he belongs to mischievous in their principles, and that we will, whenever he exceeds his powers . . . hang about him and attack him with all the power God has given us. But our duty to our government, to American institutions, is above all jealousies and party advantages.[22]

This statement, published just eighteen days after Storey took over the *Times*, was his guideline for action. He did not promise more than he expected to deliver. He would sustain Lincoln out of a sense of patriotic duty *unless*, and as events were to prove, it was a very important unless, the President exceeded his power. "There is no higher duty in this war than to give a generous support to the President so long as it is manifest that he is striving

21. *Chicago Times*, June 16, 1861.
22. *Ibid.*, June 22, 1861.

honestly to discharge the awful responsibilities weighing upon him."[23] Exactly one year after Lincoln's election, Storey went so far as to say "we feel sorry for the President [for] if we believed most of the papers which urged his election, we should be justified in assailing him everyday."[24]

Storey chose to assail abolitionists instead. This group, "a minority within the President's party," did not abandon their policy even "in the darkest peril of the Union." For a quarter-century, Storey stated, they had proposed to destroy the Constitution and divide and conquer the country. "We are justified in saying they are disloyal in this," Storey said, because if they achieved their conquest it would "not be over rebels, but over the liberties, the prosperity, the very existence of this great country"[25]

Since Lincoln showed no sign that he heeded abolition counsel, Storey defended him against the assaults of the radical newspapers. The *Chicago Tribune* was "shameful, willful and malicious," although it was not as bad as William Lloyd Garrison's *Liberator* which referred to the President as "the slave-hound of Illinois." In December, 1861, Storey boasted with truth that his *Times* was the only newspaper in Chicago that supported the President. At one point, the *Times* even asked for the suppression of the "incendiary" papers. "Why are they allowed to spawn their treason among the people and the army . . . and permitted to carry on their conspiracy to destroy the popular confidence in the President?"[26]

Storey tempered his support slightly when Lincoln delivered his message to Congress in December, 1861, and did not propose a specific policy on the proper disposition of the slavery issue. The message "is not so clear and explicit as it ought to be" Storey felt. But the editor's fears on this occasion proved groundless, as he himself asserted two days later when Lincoln was reported to have struck out a paragraph calling for abolition from a report of Secretary of War Simon Cameron. "Old Abe has been faithful and true," the *Times* rejoiced, and he deserved "the most heartfelt thanks" of all loyal people.[27]

The various war measures pursued by Lincoln in 1861 were also upheld by the *Times*. "The battle must be fought and the

23. *Ibid.*, September 19, 1861.
24. *Ibid.*, November 9, 1861.
25. *Ibid.*, November 13, 1861.
26. *Ibid.*, September 17, October 19, and December 7, 1861.
27. *Ibid.*, December 5 and December 6, 1861.

victory won," Storey stated. To accomplish victory he supported the draft and the suspension of habeas corpus. He also denounced proposals for a peace convention. "The sword is . . . the only possible arbiter," the editor proclaimed. There was "no doubt" of the power of the government "under the constitution" to draft men for public service. With respect to habeas corpus the *Times* felt "there was a necessity for severe and vigorous measures to save the Union." In taking this stand, Storey was careful to add "it is only just to the prisoners that they shall be confronted with a jury of their countrymen" and not held for months without trial.[28]

Through the first eight months of 1862 the *Times* wavered in its support of Lincoln and the war to the exact proportion that its editor felt abolition influence was increasing or waning in the highest Republican councils. Early in January, when Edwin M. Stanton replaced Simon Cameron in the War Department, Storey said "we breathe freer."[29] Since Cameron had suggested the use of Negro troops in the Union army, Storey was thankful he would no longer be in Lincoln's "inner circle." But Storey demanded absolute consistency on Lincoln's part, and any hint the President might depart from the editor's line of approved conduct was quickly noted.

When General David Hunter, in mid-May, 1862, proclaimed "at the single stroke of the pen" the emancipation of all slaves in South Carolina, Georgia, and Florida, Storey saw it as a "STARTLING EVENT." If Hunter proceeded on orders from Washington, Storey did not hesitate to state that "the hitherto professions of Abraham Lincoln, President of the United States, have been false as hell itself." Even Lincoln's revocation of Hunter's order did not satisfy Storey, for in his revocation statement Lincoln claimed that the power of emancipation was a power reserved to the President alone, acting in his capacity as Commander-in-Chief. "We protest that the President can do nothing as Commander-in-Chief that he cannot do as President," Storey stated. The Constitution made no provision for emancipation, and when the President "overrides the constitution he becomes himself a rebel engaged in the destruction of the government."[30]

Inconsistencies on the part of Lincoln and hints that he might take action that Storey considered unconstitutional, served to lessen

28. *Ibid.*, September 13, October 14, and November 2, 1861.
29. *Ibid.*, January 14, 1862.
30. *Ibid.*, May 17, May 19, and May 21, 1862,

the *Times* support as the war entered the summer of 1862. But these inconsistencies did not alter Storey's conviction that Democrats must continue to support the war. Success by the southern rebels would be infinitely worse than anything the Republicans might do for "there will be no cure for it, whereas any measure which the party in power might adopt will be susceptible to some degree of remedy." Therefore, Democrats must not, "under any probable prospective circumstances," withhold support from the war.[31]

When the abolitionist demand for immediate emancipation became heated in August, 1862, and Lincoln "refused to succumb to their most radical and fanatical demands," Storey wrote of "THE DUTY OF STANDING BY THE PRESIDENT." On August 26, Lincoln's famous letter to Horace Greeley which stated the only purpose of the war was to save the Union was published in the *Times*. The President told the New York editor "My paramount objective is to save the Union, and not either to destroy or save slavery." Storey read the letter and in a fit of ecstasy announced "these be letters of gold" for which "we thank the President from the bottom of our heart."[32]

Ironically, Storey's joyous binge on this occasion constituted the last favorable comment the *Times* would publish with respect to the President until after the cessation of hostilities. In approving the stand, Storey overlooked the full import of the last sentence of the Greeley letter: "If I could save the Union without freeing any slaves, I would do it; if I could save it by freeing all the slaves, I would do it; if I could save it by freeing some and leaving others alone, I would do that." The fact that Lincoln clearly stated it might be necessary to free all the slaves to save the Union was not understood by Storey.[33]

The evidence in the columns of the *Detroit Free Press* and the *Chicago Times* until September, 1862, proved beyond question that Wilbur F. Storey gave constant support to Abraham Lincoln in his conduct of the Civil War during the first seventeen months of that conflict. Every action taken by the Chief Executive during that time was subjected to the closest possible scrutiny by the editor, but on balance there was no question that he approved Lincoln's course. The onus of pro-southern sympathy that the

31. *Ibid.*, July 16, 1862.
32. *Ibid.*, August 26, 1862.
33. *Ibid.*, August 30, 1862.

Times displayed prior to June, 1861, cannot be assigned to Storey because in his last months with the *Free Press* he showed the same support for Lincoln that he continued upon moving to Chicago. The truth of these facts, however, did not deter Storey's Republican opponents from branding him with the charge of treason. They did it repeatedly, and some of their charges have been used since to substantiate claims that Storey always was a pro-Confederate wretch.

Storey himself best answered these charges at the end of his first year in Chicago. In an editorial headed "DOWN WITH THE SECESSIONISTS" he noted it was time that this cry, "learned by rote and parroted against the democracy," should lose its terror. He pointed out that no more disgraceful epithet could be applied to any man than that of "traitor." And yet Republicans, for partisan purposes, had implied that all Democrats were traitors. This despite the fact that since "the first gun from Sumter" Democrats had sprung to arms in defense of the government. Storey ended by warning Republicans that if they continued to use the appellation "traitor" then sooner or later it would come home "like the chickens to roost, on those from whom it emanated."[34]

Most of the things noted in this editorial were true of the conduct of Storey and his Republican opponents prior to September, 1862. Little evidence can be found in his newspapers that he was antiwar, pro-Confederate, disloyal, or inciting violence. On the other hand, there was plenty of evidence that prominent Republican politicians and newspapers were refusing support to Lincoln and counseling violence against Democrats.

From the day Storey set foot in Chicago, the Republican *Tribune* denounced the man and his newspaper for "overt secesh sympathies." Its motive, Storey explained with justification, was "to create prejudices against it [the *Times*] amongst people who do not see it." At the same time the *Tribune* leveled disloyalty charges against Storey, it castigated Lincoln in no uncertain terms for the President's refusal to emancipate immediately. Pleas from Storey that the *Tribune* join "as we do in sustaining honest Old Abe in his patriotic efforts to save the Union" fell on deaf ears. In July, 1862, at a time when Storey every day counseled Democrats that they must support the war, the *Tribune* called upon "the government, citizens and people of Illinois" to "suppress the *Times*, hang its editor, burn its equipment and annihilate all white men con-

34. *Ibid.*, June 25, 1862.

nected with it."[35] Such excess was completely unjustified at that time, and undoubtedly influenced Storey's own conduct once Lincoln adopted emancipation as official policy.

The battle between Storey and the *Chicago Tribune* continued until the day Storey died. Shortly after he arrived in Chicago he laid down an absolute rule that the *Tribune* should always be referred to as "the poor old morning abolition newspaper concern of this city." Mort L. Hopkins noted that "the frequency with which the Tribune was thus characterized stung the usually dignified Horace White, and on one occasion he made a formal protest against such a christening of his newspaper." White's protest occurred in February, 1864, and Storey obliged the *Tribune* editor at that time with a detailed justification of the appellation:

> The poor old morning abolition newspaper concern of this city excepts to being called the poor old morning abolition newspaper concern of this city. . . . We style it the poor old morning abolition newspaper concern of this city because it is "wanting in good, valuable or desirable properties," and is "not good, excellent or proper" as a newspaper. For these reasons it comes squarely within the definition of our first adjective appellative. Old is a relative term. It claims to be the oldest newspaper established in Chicago. It is issued in the morning, and is devoted to abolitionism. It is a concern because it is "an establishment or firm for the transaction of business." Our definitions are taken from standard authorities, and, with the facts, not only justify, but we think, commend the appropriateness of our nomenclature. If it is objected that the title is cumbersome and inelegant, we can only reply that our habits as democratic journalists, as well as the rule of our party, compel us to sacrifice all other considerations to accurate and truthful statement.[36]

"The poor old morning abolition newspaper concern" was not alone in the castigation of Storey during the "loyal" months. In a letter dated August 7, 1862, Illinois' Republican Governor Richard Yates called the attention of Secretary of War Edwin M. Stanton "to the urgent and almost unanimous demand from loyal citizens that the Chicago Times should be immediately suppressed." Yates based his request upon the fact that the policy of the *Times*

35. *Ibid.*, September 19, and December 24, 1861, and July 24, 1862.

36. See Mort L. Hopkins, "Reminiscences of Story [*sic*] and the Chicago Times," *Proceedings of the Michigan Press Association* (22nd Annual Meeting, Grand Rapids, July 9-11, 1889), p. 43; and *Chicago Times*, February 10, 1864.

encouraged citizens to avoid the draft.[37] Yates made this charge despite the fact that not one word against the draft had been published yet in the *Chicago Times.* Rather, immediately after Lincoln issued a call for 300,000 additional men in July, Storey said "we will throw all the influence this journal can exercise in aid of a prompt response to the call of the President."[38] Only two days before Yates asked for the newspaper's suppression on grounds it discouraged support of the draft, the lead editorial in the *Times* was headed "300,000 MORE" and expressed pleasure that the administration has "at last awakened to something like realizing the magnitude of the rebellion." In fact, said Storey, if 300,000 would not prove "crushing, the administration are criminal in not calling for . . . whatever number would constitute an overwhelmingly crushing force."[39] Far from discouraging co-operation with the draft call, Wilbur F. Storey feared 300,000 men would not suffice and he begged the administration to ask for more, "a million if necessary."

Yates' next door neighbor, Governor Oliver P. Morton, of Indiana, added his voice against Storey in a letter to the War Department dated June 25, 1862, that noted "the insidious and vituperative attacks of the Chicago Times, among others." Morton, who was notorious for seeing Knights of the Golden Circle hiding behind every bush in Indianapolis during the summer of 1862, felt the *Times*, the *Indiana Daily Sentinel*, and the *Dayton Empire* should all be suppressed because by "their continued apologies for Confederate crimes" they fostered sedition in his state.[40]

In addition to attacks by Republican newspapers and governors, the *Times* was also under constant fire from Republican controlled civic organizations. The Chicago Home Guard, a Civil War municipal military organization which specialized in "playing soldier," threatened to attack the *Times* and "clean it out good." It didn't, even when Storey labeled its members as "insignificant and cowardly barking dogs."[41]

37. Richard Yates to E. M. Stanton, August 7, 1862, in *The War of the Rebellion: A Compilation of the Official Records of the Union and Confederate Armies* (128 vols., Washington: Government Printing Office, 1880-1901), Ser. 3, II, 316. Hereafter *The War of the Rebellion* will be cited as *Official Records.*

38. *Chicago Times*, July 10, 1862.

39. *Ibid.*, August 5, 1862.

40. Oliver P. Morton to Hon. Edwin M. Stanton, June 25, 1862, in *Official Records*, Ser. 3, II, 176.

41. *Chicago Times*, August 7, 1862.

By September, 1862, the *Chicago Times* was firmly established as a competitive Chicago newspaper. On November 5, 1861, it had moved from the cramped, decrepit shop at 78 Dearborn Street to a new building at 74 Randolph Street, between Dearborn and State. A new four-cylinder Hoe press with a capacity of 10,000 sides per hour was installed before the move; new type was purchased to enliven and beautify the paper's appearance; and a job printing department, "serving customers in a style that will secure their continued patronage," was opened. The building that now housed the *Times* was three stories in height, with dimensions of 60 by 100 feet. To help finance these necessary improvements, Storey sold a half-partnership in the business to Ananias Worden, and boasted "the progress of THE TIMES . . . is something unprecedented in the history of western journalism."[42]

This boast, an exaggeration in November, 1861, was not without some foundation. With a new press and type the paper took on the technical excellence that had characterized Storey's *Detroit Free Press.* The news features that had served so well in Detroit also began to appear. War news overshadowed all, including the editorial page. Within four months of Storey's arrival in the city, the latest news, handsomely served, was most extensively available in Chicago through the columns of the *Times.* Beginning December 18, 1861, a night edition, with "intelligence several hours later than that published . . . in the afternoon," was begun. By July, 1862, "The City" began to resemble "City Intelligence" of Detroit days as the first sensational headline appeared in a Chicago newspaper owned by Wilbur F. Storey:

ATTEMPT TO COMMIT RAPE.
Alleged Use of Chloroform to Stupify
the Victim.
Synopsis of the Case—Domestic In-
tercourse of the Parties—An
Erring Widow.[43]

By September, 1862, Storey could truly boast "EVERYBODY who wants the news reads THE TIMES. . . . Our enterprise is without parallel in Chicago."[44]

It was at this point, with the paper well established on its

42. *Ibid.*, June 20, July 7, October 21, and November 5, 1861.
43. *Ibid.*, July 17, 1862.
44. *Ibid.*, September 25, 1862.

merits as a news and commercial journal, that Abraham Lincoln announced his intention to emancipate the slaves. A hint of what might be expected should Lincoln do this appeared in the *Times* as early as June, 1861. "Mr. Lincoln will not make this an anti-slavery war," Storey noted. "So long as he does this, a united nation will strengthen his arms." But, Storey warned, the instant Lincoln abandoned "this high position" he would break "the spell of patriotism which has, so far, saved the republic."[45]

It must be emphasized that the government response to the slavery issue was the major factor in determining Storey's attitudes during the Civil War. With a deep-seated hatred of the Negro race and an irrational certitude that Anglo-Saxon superiority was ordained by the Almighty, Storey supported Lincoln so long as the President took no step to free the slaves. The extent of Storey's Negrophobia was proved with the *Detroit Free Press*, but for uninitiated Chicagoans the *Times* was not slow to make its position clear.

On June 15, 1861, an editorial headed "The War" counseled the government to treat southern slaves as it would "Confederate oxen, asses, provisions and machinery [or] horses and cavalry equipment."[46] One week later, Storey reminded his readers that "the war has no relation to slavery. What becomes of the negro is of no importance."[47] The depth of his anti-Negro sentiment was apparent when the Chicago Board of Education suggested "amalgamation" of the races in the public schools. The Board's action represented a serious injury to public educational institutions Storey felt because "there is in the great mass of people a natural and proper loathing of the negro which forbids contact with him as with a leper. . . . This feeling is entirely defensible and ought to be encouraged."[48]

As abolitionists became loud in their insistence for a policy of emancipation, Storey became shrill. "He who would proclaim emancipation . . . is a madman," he asserted. As a body Negroes are "incapable of taking care of themselves . . . and as a population they would be the worse infliction that has ever befallen any country."[49] On another occasion the *Times* compared freed slaves to "locusts" and predicted if emancipation were tried the white race,

45. *Ibid.*, June 22, 1861.
46. *Ibid.*, June 15, 1861.
47. *Ibid.*, June 26, 1861.
48. *Ibid.*, August 2, 1861.
49. *Ibid.*, October 8, 1861.

"impelled by the first law of nature," would be forced to exterminate them altogether.[50]

When the second call for a national draft came in 1862, Storey hoped the government would not include Negroes in the conscription. Since the South did not put guns in the hands of Negroes, Storey pleaded that the North "not descend lower in the scale of civilization" by doing so. He noted an approval of the employment of Negroes to build fortifications and dig entrenchments, "but do not force white soldiers into an unnatural and repugnant association."[51]

In case the editorial page did not get Storey's message across, the *Times* "news" stories did. Typical was "ANOTHER CASE OF NEGRO EQUALITY":

> A large, uncouth negro followed two white ladies on Clark, between Monroe and Adams, last evening at dusk. When one woman's husband asked him why he followed so close, the black replied "none of your d—–d business." A scuffle followed until two soldiers restored order. At that point a negro sympathizer intervened by saying "the negro has more right to be on the street than soldiers." This disgraceful expression of sympathy so encouraged the darkey that he declared with insolent bravado "I can whip any d—–d son of a b—–h who wears Uncle Sam's clothes." The soldiers proceeded to administer the black wretch such a castigation as he richly deserved.[52]

On September 17, 1862, just five days before Abraham Lincoln issued his preliminary Emancipation Proclamation, Wilbur F. Storey penned a short editorial on radical newspapers and character assassination. The editorial was intended for abolitionist consumption and castigated the abolition press for its refusal to grant that antiabolitionists were sincere in their opinions. "Instead of meeting argument with argument, and manfully attacking a theory or a policy which is believed to be erroneous, the radical [abolitionist] attacks the man who upholds the opposing theory, denouncing him as a criminal, and attempts to destroy the force of his arguments by destroying him or his reputation."[53] Beginning on September 25 Storey, by his own definition, became the most radical newspaper editor in the Middle West.

50. *Ibid.*, November 25, 1861.
51. *Ibid.*, July 12, 1862.
52. *Ibid.*, July 23, 1862.
53. *Ibid.*, September 17, 1862.

The campaign of vituperation and radical denunciation began slowly. On September 23, the *Times* noted Lincoln's statement of intention and commented "the President has no constitutional authority to issue this proclamation, none whatever." It added the hope that the proclamation would "serve to shorten the war." The very next day, however, the President was guilty of "a monstrous usurpation, a criminal wrong, and an act of national suicide." Democrats must still support the war, the *Times* maintained, but "not to preserve the government, for that is subverted. [Democrats must fight] to maintain *a government*." On September 25, Storey indicated genuine hurt at the President's act. He pointed out that never before in the history of the country had a President been "more cordially sustained by political opponents" than was Lincoln by the Democrats. "He has been defended by the party which opposed his election against the attacks of the party which sought and procured it."[54]

As the force of the proclamation sank in, the *Times* harnessed all of its energy to stir up a campaign of ridicule against "Czar Abraham." The timing of the proclamation, just six weeks before the 1862 Congressional elections, convinced Storey that bipartisanship was dead, "buried by the President's own hand." And so Storey swung into action—against Lincoln, against Republicans, against Negroes, especially against Negroes.

On September 27, the *Times* ran a front-page "interview" with a soldier named Jonathan. It was headed "WHAT ARE YOU FIGHTING FOR?" and ended:

> Wouldst thou fight for a Union with Negro slavery in it? There is no other Union to fight for. Why not fight for a new Union? Because the old Union had liberty in it as well as slavery, and the new Union may not have liberty at all.[55]

In October the *Times* revealed "A STARTLING PLOT" on the part of Republican governors to withhold troops from the Union army until emancipation became official. As for Lincoln, "the country is beginning to understand that he is weak, and that he is surrounded by imbeciles, fanatics and conspirators." With respect to the Negro, Storey's shrieks became one long, unrelieved howl. He asked "SHALL ILLINOIS BE AFRICANIZED?" and warned the people they "must set their faces against [Negro]

54. *Ibid.*, September 23, 24, and 25, 1862.
55. *Ibid.*, September 27, 1862.

immigration if they would preserve the State to the uses of their children." As election day approached Storey asked "SHALL THE NEGRO VISITATION BE REVIVED?" He answered "yes" if the people voted Republican; "no" if Democracy were sustained.[56]

On election day, 1862, the *Times* published the following parody of the popular "We Are Coming Father Abraham" march:

Song of the Democracy
Selected for the Chicago Times

We are coming Father Abraham, Three Hundred Thousand Strong.
To save you from the clutches of the abolition throng.
You've heard from Pennsylvania and from Indiana, too,
And Ohio has been speaking through her ballot box to you!
The sturdy men of iron, from the Furnace and the Mine,
With the Hoosiers and the Buckeye boys are swinging into line!
They are marching to the music of the Union as of yore,
And Illinois is coming after them, Three Hundred Thousand more.

We are marching Father Abraham, to that familiar tune
With which, so often, in former years we've reared the same old coon!
Once more from hill and valley, it rings forth with cheering sound,
To gladden every household where a loyal heart is found.
See! Every star is blazoned with the banner we unfold;
For the Union that our Jackson saved, our SHERMAN will uphold!
To scatter all the nation's foes—the Union to restore.
We're coming Father Abraham, Three Hundred Thousand more.

We are coming Father Abraham, and as we march along,
We'll relieve you of the "pressure" of the abolition throng!
You told them that you couldn't make a pig's leg of its tail,
And that against the comet papal bulls would not avail.
They wouldn't heed your anecdotes or listen to your pleas,
They swore that white men should be slaves and niggers should be free.

56. *Ibid.*, September 25, October 22, 10, and 27, 1862.

But you need not mind their ravings now, nor trouble at their roar,
For we're coming Father Abraham, Three Hundred Thousand more.

We are coming Father Abraham, to cast away your fears,
Tis the democratic "slogan" that is ringing in your ears!
They pretend to call us traitors! But we point you to the blood
That soaks into Virginia's soil, or—that dyes Potomac's flood—
That stains the hills of Maryland, the Plains of Tennessee—
Such "traitors," Father Abraham, the Union loves to see.
It's a growing "traitor" army that is thundering at your door,
And Illinois'll swell the columns by Three Hundred Thousand more.

We are coming Father Abraham, to vindicate the laws,
To hold the Starry Banner up—to guard the Nation's cause;
Our motto is "The White Man's Rights"—For this we've battled long—
For this we'll fight with sinewy arms, with earnest hearts and strong—
For this we'll burst Fort Warren's bars, and crumble Lafayette—
For we'll crush the Nation's foes and save the Union yet.
Thus speaks the North! Oh, Abraham, you'll heed its mighty roar,
When Illinois shall swell the chorus by Three Hundred Thousand more.[57]

When the Democrats won impressive gains in the election, Storey was convinced that he now spoke for a majority of northerners. His efforts redoubled, especially as Lincoln gave no sign that he would not make emancipation official on January 1, 1863. The President was "a creature of pity and contempt; an irresolute, vacillating imbecile . . . [who] has yielded to the Satanic influences surrounding him." When a Chicago preacher suggested the war was a visitation from heaven for some great national sin, Storey said "it is our theory that the great national sin for which heaven is punishing the American people is the election of Lincoln to the Presidency. We confess it is a sin for which the American people ought to be punished."[58]

57. *Ibid.*, November 4, 1862.
58. *Ibid.*, November 15, 1862.

In the month before emancipation became official, Storey began to tread on ever more questionable ground. Stories of "SHOCKING BARBARISM" and "OUTRAGES BY FEDERAL SOLDIERS" began to swell the *Times* columns as the newspaper moved against the entire war effort. After the massacre at Fredricksburg Storey stood "apalled at the magnitude of the disaster." He had some valid points, as 13,000 Union casualties testified. "And all this human life sacrificed to no purpose whatsoever," the editor lamented. He exonerated General Ambrose Burnside of guilt and pointed directly to the administration, "men whose hands are dripping with gore," as the authors of the butchery, "the most stupendous homicide of modern times." Soon Lincoln and his cohorts were accused of mass murder. "We repeat it, murder [as repayment] for the generous devotion of the people."[59]

On December 4, Storey demanded a peace convention to end the senseless slaughter. In the last week of 1862 Storey warned Lincoln, "a President entered upon an office for which he has not a single qualification," that the threatened manifesto "will make it a war to liberate four millions of semisavage negroes." This fact insured the loss of Democratic support.[60] On the last day of 1862, convinced the President would "proceed deliberately and maliciously to divide the North," Storey called upon the Northwest "to prepare to take her destiny into her own hands."

On New Year's Day, 1863, Abraham Lincoln committed a deed "that will be known in all history as the most wicked, atrocious and revolting deed in the annals of civilization." Storey's diatribe against the issuance of the Emancipation Proclamation, headed simply "THE DEED," stated:

> The deed is done—the deed which unites the people of the South forever in their rebellion; which converts the war from a constitutional contest for the integrity of the Union to an unconstitutional crusade for the liberation of three millions of negro barbarians; which destroys the last hope of the preservation of the old government and inaugurates a future dark, uncertain and dreary—the deed is done.[61]

In the days that followed, Storey turned his editorial guns on the entire war effort. The war became "a John Brown raid on an extended scale" led by a "lank, nerveless, almost brainless and

59. *Ibid.*, December 2, 19, and 20, 1862.
60. *Ibid.*, December 4 and 22, 1862.
61. *Ibid.*, January 3, 1865.

vacillating old man" whose "judgment (always weak) was paralyzed." The "news" stories from Washington became hysterical, screaming in black, boldface:

FROM WASHINGTON.
THE INAUGURATION OF THE REIGN OF RAPINE AND MURDER.
THE FAITH AND HONOR OF THE NATION VIOLATED BY THE PRESIDENT.

The story following this head began "Mr. Lincoln has now deliberately cut loose from all restraint, and has sold himself body and soul (a precious little modicum of the latter he has) and his country so far as he can, to the abolitionists."[62]

No invective was too severe for the President in the first month after Emancipation. "It is difficult to believe that so foolish an old joker can be President," one editorial concluded. The terrible example of Abraham Lincoln was a "visitation from Providence" that ought to warn the world for a thousand years to come. At the end of January, the *Times* discoursed on "THE AWFUL CALAMITY OF ABRAHAM LINCOLN" and said that one would search history in vain for a parallel to the experiences of the people of the loyal states since Lincoln's election. Vast armies had been wasted, vast resources consumed and a huge debt contracted, "and all in vain, and a thousand times worse than vain." A "piratical crew" had seized the American government, "an argosy freighted with so many of the best hopes of mankind," and in their madness and hate "consigned all to hopeless wreck."[63]

But the vituperation against Lincoln was as a song of love when compared to the symphony of hate now loosed in the *Times* against Negroes. One story detailed the activities of a minister who impregnated several female members of his congregation. It was headed

NEGRO CIVILIZATION.
Its Beastiality and Degradation—Incompetency of the Negro Race to Observe the Laws of Society.[64]

62. *Ibid.*, January 12, 26, and 7, 1863.
63. *Ibid.*, January 12, 14, and 27, 1863.
64. *Ibid.*, January 8, 1863.

The treatment in this story was typical of *Times* policy until after the Civil War.

The *Times* reports from the battlefield now echoed Storey's views. "VOICES FROM THE ARMY" told how Negroes rode in ambulances while white soldiers walked after the battle of Vicksburg. "FROM MURFREESBORO" the Army of the Cumberland was "floundering in the mud" and the soldiers were "heartily tired of the war."[65] In addition to diatribes against the President and Negroes, and slanted news stories which at best could produce only disquiet on the home front and suspicion among the troops in the field, the *Times* also reiterated that the time was perhaps not far distant when the states of the Northwest "will take their destiny into their own hands, and determine it according to their own interests and inclinations and desires."[66]

As the *Times* became more abusive, demands that it be quieted became more frequent. At first, complaints were limited to the editorial columns of the *Chicago Tribune*, which called the *Times* "malignant" and editor Storey "a fiendish skunk."[67] In January, 1863, the Chicago Board of Trade banned the paper from its reading room and the *Times* reporter from the building. The same month, the Galena and Chicago Union Railroad forbade the sale of the *Times* on its trains. On February 12, General Stephen A. Hurlbut forbade its further circulation in his Department of the Tennessee.

Storey was not silent about such attacks. He promised the *Tribune* that if any action were taken against the *Times* "not a stone of the *Tribune* will be left."[68] When word of General Hurlbut's action reached Chicago, Storey let loose with a savage attack. "General Hurlbut and Governor Yates are boon companions; they get drunk together and have the *delirium tremens* together," Storey said. It was in their drunken carousals and the frenzy of their delirious excesses that Yates and Hurlbut "do acts affecting the lives and fortunes of thousands." The attack ended by noting "the festering corruption" that "holds saturnalia in the public service everywhere."[69]

Northern resentment against the Lincoln administration reached its height in the spring of 1863. The war was not going well, and

65. *Ibid.*, February 10 and 26, 1863.
66. *Ibid.*, January 28, 1863.
67. *Chicago Tribune*, as reprinted in *Chicago Times*, February 3, 1863.
68. *Chicago Times*, February 23, 1863.
69. *Ibid.*, February 12, 1863.

with the added impetus given by the Emancipation, there was a widespread movement among Democrats to reach an accommodation with the Confederacy. Slavery, of course, had never been a legitimate issue in Democratic eyes. As they moved to support Lincoln in the early efforts to suppress the rebellion, their slogan read "the Union as it was, the constitution as it is." Every act of the administration, every event of the war itself, was judged in light of this slogan. When the force of events made this position untenable, many Democrats turned to personal abuse against the President and refused further support of the war effort. Very few re-examined their basic premises in light of reality.

The opposition was especially pronounced in Ohio, Indiana and Illinois. Here, Samuel Medary, a Columbus, Ohio, newspaper editor, and Clement L. Vallandigham, a Dayton, Ohio, politician of exceptional charm and wit who articulated Democratic sentiments from the stump, joined hands with Storey to mobilize public opinion against any war to free slaves.

Samuel Medary founded *The Crisis*, a weekly newspaper, on January 31, 1861. Only the month before he had resigned as territorial governor in Kansas. Long active in Ohio politics and journalism, he was known for years before the war as the "Old Wheelhorse of the Democracy." A political theoretician of the first rank, Medary used his *Crisis* forum as a sounding board for the theoretical justification of Copperheadism. When he died on November 7, 1864, a Republican opponent stated unequivocally that "Old Sam" was "one of the vilest scoundrels that ever lived. When Sam Medary died one of the devil's own children went home to his father's house." A close associate on *The Crisis*, however, took a different and more accurate view when he eulogized "his greatest anxiety seemed to arise from the fear of outliving constitutional liberty."[70]

In his own way, Medary was as consistent as Storey in demanding that no war be fought to free the slaves. He was not as generous as his Chicago counterpart in supporting Lincoln prior to September, 1862, but he also was not quite so vile after Emancipation became a fact. More a theoretician than political activist, Medary used *The Crisis* to prove that the states antedated the

70. A good, brief analysis of Medary in the Civil War appears in "The Nature of the American Civil War: The Verdict of Three Kansas Democrats," in James C. Malin, *On the Nature of History: Essays About History and Dissidence* (Ann Arbor, Michigan: J. W. Edwards, Inc., 1954), pp. 207-26.

Federal government, and hence were superior to it. When emancipation was first proposed, Medary stated such an exercise of power by the President "would be absolute, unconditional and irreparable destruction of the Union."[71] From this point on Medary advocated peace, even if it meant surrender to the South. He asserted the right of Union soldiers to desert the cause of those who "would betray white civilization" and his Columbus newspaper office was the scene of several riots and disturbances provoked by those who considered his utterances treasonable.

Clement L. Vallandigham first secured national attention in July, 1861,when he delivered an impassioned speech in the House of Representatives calling for a cessation of hostilities and peace. Republican pundits immediately denounced him for treason, and demanded that he be deprived of the means for uttering such "foul and damnable" sentiments. Such attacks drove Vallandigham to consider himself a martyr to free speech, and he forthrightly became even more impassioned in his demands for peace.[72]

It is as part of this vortex of political passion, all in the midst of a bloody Civil War, that the editorial policy of the *Chicago Times* in the spring and early summer of 1863 must be judged. Storey was not alone in the things he said, but he said them more consistently, more frequently and to a wider audience than any other man in the Middle West. Untold thousands were inflamed by the incendiary excesses of Storey and though the editor did not cross the thin line to overt treason, his conduct proved he lacked the capacity for both prudence and patriotism which should mark a man with his potential to influence opinion for good or ill in the midst of the greatest crisis his country had faced.

In March, 1863, General Ambrose E. Burnside, "a man with faith in force and the threat of force," was assigned as Commander of the Department of the Ohio (covering Ohio, northern Kentucky, Indiana and Illinois). In April, Burnside issued General Order Number Thirty-eight which provided "those who commit acts for the benefit of our enemies will be tried as traitors and spies," and "the habit of declaring sympathy for the enemy will no longer be tolerated." The order concluded that arrested individuals would be subject to military procedure.

71. *The Crisis*, Columbus, Ohio, July 15, 1862.

72. David Lindsey, "Clement L. Vallandigham: Traitor or Martyr?" *Tradition, The Magazine of America's Past*, III (November, 1960), 46-57. For a detailed and dispassionate analysis of the Copperhead movement in the Middle West, see Klement, *Copperheads in the Middle West*.

Midwestern Democrats raised a storm of protest against the suspension of the Bill of Rights, the overthrow of the Constitution, and other evils, real and imagined, that they read into Burnside's order. Vallandigham was especially indignant. He had been gerrymandered out of his Dayton area congressional seat by the Republican-controlled Ohio legislature, and in March he returned home to conduct a one man crusade for "free speech and peace." When Burnside's order was propagated Vallandigham declared himself loyal only to "General Order Number One, the Constitution of the United States." His incendiary pronouncements led to several civic disorders in Dayton, and as he became more outspoken, General Burnside decided to move.

At 2:00 A.M. on May 4 Vallandigham was aroused from his sleep and arrested by 150 troops acting under General Order Thirty-eight. The next day there was a riot, and Burnside instituted martial law in Montgomery County to maintain an uneasy peace. The spectre of military despotism aroused Democrats throughout the Midwest, and the subsequent trial and banishment of the Ohioan to the Confederacy on a charge of treason did little to allay fears that American liberty was at an end.

Storey, of course, had not been silent through the whole gathering storm. He took note of each imprisonment, each incursion of civil liberties by the "Washington Dictatorship." An editorial headed "THE CRUSADE AGAINST THE FREEDOM OF SPEECH" stated "the attempt to fetter the press of this country is as visionary and impracticable as would be an attempt to fetter thought."[73] By March, Storey felt all who were really loyal to the Union must "wash their hands of all part in the war" because "the war is the most terrible engine for the destruction of the Union which Beelzebub himself could have invented."[74]

When Vallandigham was arrested Storey scored "the worst case of illegal and arbitrary proceeding against an individual" in the nation's history. "Our own views have not always been in perfect accord with all those of Mr. Vallandigham," Storey explained, "but we do not believe a more loyal citizen lives than he." The editor concluded that the only safe course for Democrats was "to keep quiet."[75]

By the end of May, Storey hoped Vallandigham could reach

73. *Chicago Times*, February 2, 1863.
74. *Ibid.*, May 7, 1863.
75. *Ibid.*

the "free State of New York" where Democratic Governor Horatio Seymour, "obedient to the obligations of his oath," secured citizens against "the executioners of usurpation. We thank heaven that there is a State of New York, where military lawlessness does not raise its hideous crest." In the last week of May, Storey printed a final comment on the Vallandigham episode. "If a terrible retribution does not fall upon the perpetrators of this foul wrong, then is not God just."[76]

That did it. From his headquarters at Cincinnati General Burnside notified the commander at Camp Douglas to take possession of the *Times*. In the early hours of June 3, the order was carried out. For the next two days, Chicago witnessed its wildest episode of the Civil War. Chicago was a Democratic city at the time. It had a Democratic mayor and City Council. If that were not enough, the *Times* was the municipality's official organ. It was soon evident that no matter what the justification, the thin-skinned Burnside had committed a diplomatic error.

The troops took possession of the office at 5:00 A.M. Shortly after sunrise a crowd began to gather about the Randolph Street entrance to the building. By evening the thoroughfare from State Street to Dearborn Street was "a solid pack of humanity." A mass meeting was called for the north side of Court House Square in the evening. When the time came, and a thousand cries of "Storey! Storey!" met no response, the crowd moved two blocks west to the Square, where by eight o'clock almost 20,000 people were gathered. There was real danger that Chicago might undergo a "civil war" within the Civil War, particularly if a Copperhead demagogue should inflame the passions of the mob with an incendiary harangue. A riot was avoided, but not until Wirt Dexter, a prominent Republican attorney whom Storey had shrewdly hired for his defense, assured the crowd that Burnside's action did not have the sympathy of local Republicans.[77]

Dexter spoke the truth. Already in the morning of June 3 Judge Van H. Higgins, a *Tribune* stockholder, brought representatives of both sides together to petition Lincoln to revoke the order. Re-

76. *Ibid.*, May 23 and 27, 1863.

77. Cook, pp. 53-54; *Chicago Times*, June 3 and 5, 1863. See also "The Suppression of the Chicago Times," (Chicago: The Chicago Times, 1863) 32 pp. of "pertinent material" from the columns of the *Times* in the Chicago Historical Society; and "General Burnside's Order No. 84, Suppressing the Chicago Times, And Its History," (Chicago: The Chicago Times, 1864), 8 pp. in the Chicago Historical Society.

publican Senator Lyman Trumbull joined in the communiqué that noted that "the peace of this City and State, if not the general welfare of the country, are likely to be promoted by the suspension or rescinding of the recent order of General Burnside." The Higgins group, "a meeting of citizens of all parties," respectfully asked the President to take immediate action.[78]

Lincoln acted on June 4 when he informed Secretary Stanton that "I have received dispatches which induce me to believe we should revoke or suspend the order suspending the Chicago Times." The diary of Gideon Welles suggested the entire cabinet regretted Burnside's action because it gave "bad men the right of questions, an advantage of which they avail themselves. Good men, who wish to support the Administration, find it difficult to defend these [Burnside's] acts." In any event, Stanton wired Burnside the same day: "In conformity with the views of the President, you will revoke the order. . . ." In the evening Burnside notified Camp Douglas: "By order of the President of the United States, the order suppressing the publication of the Chicago Times is hereby revoked."[79] On the morning of June 5, a small issue of Storey's newpaper reappeared.

Frederick Cook, a *Times* reporter at this time, recalled later that "the one personality least concerned in this crisis was the owner and editor of the Times, Wilbur F. Storey." With his usual sagacity, Storey saw the order would not stand. Meantime, his paper gained nation-wide publicity. Another staffer, Franc B. Wilkie, said "the attempt at suppressing the Times was an immeasurable benefit to the financial interests of the journal." It became one of the nation's widely-read papers, and its circulation "bounded upward in unprecedented fashion."[80]

It was true, as Wilkie noted, that the circulation of the *Chicago Times* "bounded upwards" as a result of the suppression. But long before the action of General Burnside in June, 1863, the newspaper was the most widely circulated of any west of the Appalachian Mountains. Sylvannus Cadwallader, exclusive *Times* corre-

78. Senator Lyman Trumbull to Hon. Abraham Lincoln, President, June 3, 1863, in *Official Records*, Ser. 1, XXIII, Part 2, 385.

79. John T. Morse, ed., *Diary of Gideon Welles,* I, 321 as cited in Milton, p. 172; Edwin M. Stanton to Major General Burnside, June 4, 1863, in *Official Records*, Ser. 3, III, 252; A. H. McLean, by command of Major General Burnside, to Commandant, Fort Douglas, June 4, 1863, in *Official Records*, Ser. 1, XXIII, Part 2, 386.

80. Cook, p. 51; Franc B. Wilkie, *Personal Reminiscences of Thirty-five Years in Journalism* (Chicago: F. J. Schulte & Co., 1891), p. 101.

spondent with General Ulysses S. Grant, noted that as early as February, 1863, "the Times had acquired a wonderful circulation throughout the U. S.—the largest by far, to that date, ever secured by any paper outside the Atlantic cities. Its news from the western armies was early, complete, and greatly superior to that of any competitor."[81] Even rival editors recognized the news value of Storey's paper, as the comment of the Republican Cincinnati *Daily Commercial* attested: "We read the Chicago Times. It is the best of a bad class of newspapers in the West."[82]

The Civil War, of course, was of decisive importance in developing techniques of modern war correspondence because it was during that conflict that transmission of news by telegraph first occurred on a large scale. According to the conclusion of the most meticulous scholar of the subject, the campaigns in the East received the best coverage.[83] But in the West, the *Chicago Times* left all rivals far behind in its coverage of events in Missouri, Tennessee, and along the lower Mississippi. In the spring of 1863, it was noted that "the whole country has been dependent on the Chicago Times for news of Grant's campaign." This was so because Storey's man with Grant, Sylvannus Cadwallader, had so ingratiated himself with the General that he availed himself of Grant's official couriers.[84]

It was no accident that Storey's paper achieved such precedence for news. From the opening of hostilities, he was on top of the possibilities with special evening editions. Before the war was underway a week, the editor's brother-in-law, Warren P. Isham, was sending on-the-scene reports from the South. No expense was spared in order that Storey's readers get the news quicker and in greater detail than patrons of rival newspapers. According to Franc Wilkie, western correspondent for the *New York Times* until Storey stole him in September, 1863, his instructions upon joining the *Chicago Times* read: "Telegraph fully all the news, and when there is no news, send rumors."[85]

81. Benjamin P. Thomas, ed., *Three Years With Grant As Recalled by War Correspondent Sylvannus Cadwallader* (New York: Alfred A. Knopf & Co., 1955), pp. 56-57.

82. *Cincinnati Daily Commercial*, July 1, 1863, as cited in J. Cutler Andrews, *The North Reports the Civil War* (Pittsburgh: University of Pittsburgh Press, 1955), p. 659, note 78.

83. Andrews, *passim*.

84. Louis M. Starr, *Bohemian Brigade, Civil War Newsmen in Action* (New York: Collier Press, 1954), p. 282.

85. Wilkie, *Reminiscences*, p. 114.

As Wilkie's instructions indicated, expense was no consideration with Storey where news was concerned. But if things were slow, if solid news were lacking, rumor served as well. Once the editor established himself in Chicago, Warren P. Isham settled down in Memphis, Tennessee, to follow the fortunes of Union forces in that theater. By 1862 dispatches from Memphis over the signature "W.P.I." won for Isham a reputation as the most imaginative and enterprising correspondent among western reporters. His capacity for invention had been perfected by eight years of practice at the city desk of the *Detroit Free Press*, and whenever things were slow on the battlefield in the Department of the Tennessee, the soldiers in the ranks waited breathlessly for the *Times* to see what mischief Isham had dreamed their Generals into.

In April, 1862, Isham received his first threat of court martial for a dispatch that described how a Union General availed himself of "favors" in a bordello on the outskirts of Memphis. As the Brigadier reached "an advanced stage of undress," a party of Confederate officers arrived. It was not clear, according to Isham, whether the rebels were looking for the Yankee or merely renewing "an acquaintance with the ladies of the establishment." At any rate, their arrival was most untimely for the Union man who, "clad only in underdrawers," was forced to beat his retreat through a rear window. When the unfortunate scamp returned to headquarters, he told a "harrowing tale of escape from spies and robbers," but Isham guessed the truth, went to the ladies for the straight dope, and published it in the *Times*.[86]

Isham's impudence knew no bounds. On May 20, 1862, the *Times* recounted how "Our Memphis Correspondent" was treated one morning when he encountered a mounted party of Union soldiers, and was stopped by the officer in charge:

> "Where are you going?"
> "Nowhere in particular."
> "What is your business?"
> "Nothing in particular."
> "Who are you?"
> "The correspondent of the Chicago Times."
> "You are, hey? By God, I'll see about that. What in hell brought you here?"

86. Emmet Crozier, *Yankee Reporters, 1861-65* (New York: Oxford University Press, 1956), p. 319.

"Anybody with ordinary common sense would suppose I came here in pursuit of my legitimate business."

"Hell and damnation. Do you know who I am?"

"It is easy enough to recognize you. Your little peculiarities are in everybody's mouth. You are General Wood [Brigadier General Thomas J. Wood, one of Major General Henry W. Halleck's division commanders]. Glad to find you so amiable."

"By God, sir, I'll show you how to ride by my quarters on the gallop. I put you under arrest. There is an order against any damned civilian coming into the lines."

"Never heard of it."

"Everybody knows it. You knew it."

"That is rather complimentary to your officers. I have been in their company three weeks, and I am very certain they did not know it."

"You are under arrest. I'll show you there's a God in Israel."

Isham was then hauled to the guardhouse and not released until he received a personal reprimand from General Halleck himself.[87] Tales such as these won Isham the disfavor of General Grant who warned the *Times* correspondent to "stop your cock-and-bull yarns from Memphis." But Isham was heedless of such counsel, and on August 8, 1862, the *Chicago Times* published the last Memphis dispatch from "W.P.I." It was a startling story about a formidable fleet of rebel ironclads holed up at Pensacola waiting to advance northward. It was pure fabrication, and so incensed Grant that he sent a copy of the article to General William T. Sherman, commander at Memphis, along with a letter that stated that since Isham's piece "is both false in fact and mischievous in character, you will have the author arrested and sent to the Alton Penitentiary . . . for confinement until the close of the war, unless sooner discharged by competent authority."[88] Grant provided the "competent authority" himself when three months later, on November 12, he released Isham from prison.

The most startling aspect of the arrest and imprisonment of Warren P. Isham was the reaction of his brother-in-law, Wilbur F. Storey. Here was a case tailor-made to become a *cause célèbre*. Isham had been arrested without specific charge, imprisoned without trial, and for three months denied legal counsel. He was the

87. *Chicago Times*, May 20, 1862.
88. Thomas, p. 3.

most prominent newspaper man with the western armies. He was the youngest brother of Mrs. Wilbur F. Storey. For thirteen years he had been closely and intimately associated with his brother-in-law on the *Jackson Patriot*, the *Detroit Free Press*, and the *Chicago Times.* Since the outbreak of the rebellion he had been conscientious and regular in furnishing Storey with eyewitness copy from the front. And yet not one word of the arrest and imprisonment of Warren P. Isham appeared in the *Chicago Times* until *after* he was released. Then Storey limited himself to a reprint of "A PRISONER RELEASED" story from the *Springfield* [Illinois] *Register* followed by two short sentences that stated:

> It is literally true that Mr. Isham and his friends have not been able to ascertain the reason of his arrest and imprisonment. No charges were preferred against him at Memphis, and none at Alton, and none could be made against him anywhere with the slightest foundation in fact.[89]

Storey's only concern seemed to be with the loss of a Memphis correspondent. He remedied this in mid-October when he hired Sylvannus Cadwallader, city editor of the *Milwaukee Daily News*, to replace Isham. It proved a fortuitous choice for Storey, because "the man Storey sent to replace Isham, cultivated a friendship with Grant unmatched in the annals of the Bohemian Brigade." He soon outdistanced the best of the correspondents in the Department of the Tennessee.[90]

Isham returned to Chicago after his release, where Storey proceeded "to make his life a sheol." In August, 1863, he embarked on the steamer "Sunbeam" to visit relatives in Ontonagon, Michigan. The second morning out a storm struck and sunk the vessel. There were no survivors. Storey waited one full month before he published the following obituary:

> In the midst of war, when thousands are falling daily, it is not much that *one* should have sunk in the waves of Lake Superior, and through them into the dark and illimitable ocean which "rolls all around the world." But there is here a desk claiming his presence, on which he communicated daily with thousands. Some of these thousands, at least, were moved by his gentle humor to rejoice with him when he did rejoice, and some have felt their hearts beat faster as he struck answering chords of sympathy. To them this

89. *Chicago Times*, November 14, 1862.
90. Thomas, p. 5; Starr, p. 280.

> slight and imperfect tribute to his merits and memory, even in the midst of events "big with the fate of nations," and of columns crowded with their rehearsal, will not be without interest.[91]

The exact reason why Storey treated Warren P. Isham so hatefully was difficult to understand. Sylvannus Cadwallader recalled that when Storey hired him to replace his brother-in-law the editor appeared completely unconcerned over Isham's plight. Franc Wilkie, who knew both the editor and the reporter on an intimate basis, believed Storey was actually pleased when Isham was accidentally killed. "It relieved him of a brother-in-law he appears to have profoundly hated," Wilkie noted.[92] The only plausible explanation of Storey's conduct, in view of Isham's long and spectacular service to Storey newspapers, rested in the fact that the editor's marriage to Maria Isham had reached a stage of deterioration beyond repair by the summer of 1862. The formality of a divorce did not occur until 1867, but the couple had not lived together as man and wife since at least June, 1861. The treatment of Isham was not the only example of Storey's blanket excoriation of everyone in any way connected with a matter the editor found personally displeasing. The pattern would be repeated several times in the years after the Civil War when the *Times* rolled to its greatest heights.

It would be difficult to imagine a more unlikely specimen for front line duty as a correspondent than Sylvannus Cadwallader. Franc Wilkie was *New York Times* correspondent in the Department of the Tennessee in late October, 1862, when Cadwallader made his debut among western reporters. "He was a slender man with dark, mysterious eyes, a swarthy complexion . . . [a man who] moved about in a nervous, uneasy manner," Wilkie recalled. He arrived in camp wearing a round-tipped coon skinned cap, slouched on his head to make him an object of incredulity. "He was not at all disposed to be companionable with other newsmen or anybody else," Wilkie said, and his fellow reporters gave odds that he would last less than six weeks.[93] How completely they misjudged the newcomer was apparent within six months as Cadwallader established himself as the best news correspondent in the West.

91. Wilkie, *Reminiscences*, pp. 94-96; *Chicago Times*, September 24, 1863.
92. Thomas, p. 5; Wilkie, *Reminiscences*, p. 96.
93. Franc B. Wilkie, *Pen and Powder* (Boston: Little, Brown & Co., 1888), p. 203.

Cadwallader's first scoop occurred in December, 1862. While the reporter "galloped at full speed" through rebel-held country south of Memphis with exclusive news of Confederate General Earl Van Dorn's raid that destroyed the Federal depot at Holly Springs, he was captured by a Confederate force. Cadwallader had foreseen such an eventuality, and came well provisioned to bribe his way to freedom. A few fresh cigars discriminately distributed, when coupled with a swig from his canteen which he had foresightedly filled with good "rectified" whiskey, did the trick. Not only did the *Times* get an exclusive account of Van Dorn's raid, but also the added embellishments of the dangers attendant upon capture by the hated rebs.

After the initial repulse of General U. S. Grant at Vicksburg, Cadwallader bribed three Negroes to steal a skiff and took turns rowing with them seventy-five miles downstream to Eagle's Bend, where they arrived just before the mail boat left. As a result, the *Times* had a two day exclusive on the early fighting in the Vicksburg campaign.[94]

Early in 1863 Cadwallader succeeded in establishing an "in" with Ulysses S. Grant which proved immediately beneficial to the *Times*, and made the reporter the most reliable source from Grant's army for the remainder of the war. One night in January, "about midnight," Cadwallader and Colonel William Duff were engaged in "conversation" when General Grant happened by in search of a drink. Duff poured a generous serving into an army cup and gave it to the General, who seemed surprised and chagrined when he saw Cadwallader was present. He took the drink, and said nothing. Grant's reputation as a heavy drinker was well-established before the Civil War, of course, and rumors were rife that he was more drunk than sober as he led the western armies. Any mention by Cadwallader of this event, and the *Times* could have an exclusive that confirmed many people's worst suspicions. Not a word about the episode was penned by Cadwallader, however, and from this time on the representative of the *Chicago Times* enjoyed exclusive access to the important sources for news among the Army of the West.

As early as mid-February Grant repaid part of the debt to Cadwallader when he personally countermanded General Stephen Hurlbut's order of suppression against the *Times* in the Department of the Tennessee. "I dislike the general tenor of the *Times* as

94. Starr, p. 280.

much as any officer in the Department," Grant said, "but anyone has the right to pay for it and read it."[95]

In addition to Isham and Cadwallader, Storey also had Franc B. Wilkie and George Rust with the western armies at one time or another. Wilkie's most extensive contribution as a Civil War reporter was made before September, 1863, when he was a correspondent for the *New York Times.* After Storey hired him, Wilkie spent most of his time in Chicago, but in 1864 he returned to the front and sent back accounts of the final campaigns.[96]

Besides exclusive correspondents the *Times* also made generous use of "Telegraphic Dispatches" throughout the war. It was not an idle boast in November, 1863, when Storey asserted "there is not an important point in the country where we do not now maintain one or more special correspondents." The telegraph toll alone was "more than a thousand dollars annually," while special messengers entailed "a heavy outlay."[97]

Thus, while the ill-considered action of General Ambrose Burnside on June 3, 1863, did much to boost the notoriety and readership of the newspaper, it did not, as is frequently stated, "make" the *Chicago Times.* At least one full year prior to Burnside's action, Storey's *Times* was established on its own merits as a source of news from the western armies, and during the entire spring before the suppression anyone who desired the latest on Grant's campaign in Tennessee had to read the newspaper. If any one thing, then, made the *Chicago Times* the widest circulated newspaper west of the Appalachians during the war, it was not the hasty action of a disgruntled military commander but rather the fact that "Wilbur F. Storey, Editor and Publisher" appeared daily on the paper's masthead.

But if the Civil War suppression did not make the *Chicago Times,* it nonetheless was the one event in Storey's life that capped his forty-five year career in midwestern journalism and ensured him lasting immortality of a sort in the history books. For three days, the enigmatic pariah of the Chicago press was the focus of national attention as even the highest ranking officials of the United States Government debated his fate.

The exact charge, as received by Storey at 11:00 A.M. on June 2 read: "On account of the repeated expression of disloyal and

95. Thomas, pp. 56-57; for the best synopsis of the relationship between Cadwallader and Grant see Starr, pp. 280-89.

96. Wilkie, *Pen and Powder, passim.*

97. *Chicago Times,* November 10, 1863.

incendiary statements, the publication of the newspaper known as THE CHICAGO TIMES is hereby suppressed." Storey immediately sought and received a restraining order from Circuit Court Judge Drummond, but to no avail as the military proceeded with "a blow deliberately and directly at the LIBERTY OF THE PRESS. . . . It smites every citizen as severely as it smites us."[98] On June 5, after the direct intervention of President Lincoln, Storey, with an audacity that bordered on blasphemy, compared his ordeal to the "agony of Christ."[99]

The day the suppression was lifted the *Chicago Tribune* decried the cowardice of the Lincoln administration because it gave Storey "free license to belch treason." Storey himself felt "it is to be regretted that the case did not come to a decision by court."[100] If he felt any qualms about his editorial policy as a result of Burnside's action, it was not evident in the newspaper. If anything, the abuse increased. Burnside was hereafter always referred to as "THE BEAST OF FREDERICKSBURG" as a campaign of villification was loosed against the commander of the Department of the Ohio.

On June 24, Burnside was "insane." Two weeks later Storey revealed that the lieutenant Burnside assigned to preside at the trial of Clement L. Vallandigham was "guilty of scandalous offenses against female modesty." According to the *Times* the chairman of the military tribunal, who remained unnamed, proved the depth of Burnside's discernment when he stepped "out of the judicial chair . . . to peep through the keyhole . . . at a disrobing lady." It was through such conduct, Storey concluded, that "decency is outraged and justice defeated."[101]

No epithet was too vile to fling at Burnside. Under the notation "*Quo Deus vuli perdere, prius dementat*" Storey indicted the General because he flung unoffending citizens, without trial and with no warrant but his supreme will, into prison. Burnside also suppressed free speech, and "even carried his insolence and temerity so far as to lay profanely his sacrilegious hand—the hand red with the blood of the Fredericksburg massacre—upon the press."[102] When Burnside spoke in Chicago in March, 1864, the *Times* announced "a ruffian will be on exhibition, in some public place."

98. *Ibid.*, June 3, 1863.
99. *Ibid.*, June 5, 1863.
100. *Chicago Tribune*, as reprinted in *ibid.*, June 6, 1863.
101. *Chicago Times*, July 15, 1863.
102. *Ibid.*, December 19, 1863.

The paper speculated "he will have spectators, as other monstrosities do" and concluded "it must be a singularly morbid mind that will enjoy the repulsive spectacle."[103]

Not a day passed after the suppression without an attack on President Lincoln. He was "a thing, a mean, wily, illiterate, brutal, unprincipled and utterly vulgar creature." Or again, Lincoln was "a blunderer, a charlatan, a temporizer, a man who jokes while a nation mourns, a crude, illiterate, bar-room witling." The entire administration was denounced in a like vein.[104]

As the autumn of 1863 progressed the *Times* seemed more and more dominated by a demonic determination to destroy trust in Abraham Lincoln because his administration "has supplied us with so many things of which we were never possessed before." These things included, by Storey's reckoning, thousands of widows and orphans; streets filled with maimed and broken human beings; military prisons "erected for our accommodation"; a lavish furnishing of military authorities, spies and informers; the blessings of an army of taxgatherers and hungry officials "who consume the subsistence of the people"; and a national capitol aglow with "all the airs and glitter of a court." The administration stood condemned by the teachings of Scripture, of history, of the Fathers of the Republic, of good men of every age, and all the truer and better impulses of the human heart and human judgment. While the nation "groaned" and soldiers "lie bleeding in the field," the President entertained at the White House. "Nearly all the Generals were there," and Mrs. Lincoln "is said to have been lavish in splendid hats and toilettes." The lowest depths reached by Storey occurred on October 9 when he quoted Lincoln to the effect that "I don't amount to pig-tracks in the Army Department." From this day until the President's death, "Pig Tracks" became a *Times* synonym for Abraham Lincoln, with the pseudonym not infrequently appearing as part of a bold-faced headline.[105]

The *Times* Washington correspondent, "who often did his Washington corresponding at home in good old Cook County, Illinois,"[106] was part of the act. "Unimpeachable Washington sources" revealed plans for the President's impeachment on an average of five times a month. When rumored impeachment grew stale, "Spirit-Rapping" stepped in to fill the void:

103. *Ibid.*, March 19 and 21, 1864.
104. *Ibid.*, July 1, 1863.
105. *Ibid.*, August 15, September 19, 21, October 21, 22, and 9, 1863.
106. Sandburg, II, p. 128.

ANOTHER SPIRITUAL SOIREE
AT THE WHITE HOUSE.
How the President Manages
When Ill.
Disgraceful Culpability.

President Lincoln's illness and his arduous labor in the preparation of his message having left him, mentally and physically, in a somewhat exhausted condition, he summoned his spiritual medium a few mornings ago, and requested him to convoke, then and there, the spirits of our most eminent deceased statesmen. . . .

Communication being established, in a few minutes there appeared, at short intervals, vague outlines of forms that gradually assumed sufficient distinctiveness to recall to the President the features they had worn when they "tabernacled among us in the flesh." As soon as the medium ascertained that all were present who were likely to appear, Mr. Lincoln addressed the assemblage as follows:

"Gentlemen: As I have reason to know through my medium, you are cognizant of the events now transpiring in the Union formed and governed by your services and 'dedicated to the proposition that white men are equal to negroes.' It does not necessarily follow from this proposition that negroes are equal to white men. A may be equal to B, but B is not equal to A. Your proposition, therefore, went but half far enough. It should have asserted the equality of both races. From this defect in the government created by you has arisen the present Civil War and the horrors now desolating the country. . . . As you got us into this difficulty, it is only fair that you should get us out. We *cannot* get ourselves out, for 'I don't amount to pig tracks in the War Department,' or indeed, in any of the departments, and if I did, it is not probable that I could improve much the present wretched management. . . . I ask your help."[107]

This story, which appeared on page one, went on to describe how the entire roll call of America's heroes, starting with George Washington, fell into such violent disagreement with Lincoln that confusion resulted and the medium was forced to dismiss the spirits lest they completely wreck the poor old man.

When the Gettysburg address was delivered, Storey accused Lincoln of introducing partisan politics into a funeral oration, and

107. *Chicago Times*, December 21, 1863.

he asked "Is Mr. Lincoln less refined than a savage?" The speech itself manifested "ignorant rudeness" and was "an insult to the memories of the dead." More than that, it was "a perversion of history so flagrant that the most extended charity cannot regard it otherwise than willful."[108] Storey's capacity for vituperation seemed limitless. His city editor, Mort L. Hopkins, recalled that as the war progressed Storey acted "as a man possessed." When writing upon a subject that stirred his ire, "his clearness and force of utterance was something fearful in its intensity. The scathing invective came like a torrent from a heart that for the moment knew only the passions that attend upon consuming, absorbing wrath."[109]

If the government refused to move against the *Times* decisively, some private citizens felt otherwise. It was said that every loyal citizen in Chicago planned "to take a poke" at editor Storey, and many Union soldiers on furlough vowed "to stop long enough in Chicago to clean out that damned secesh sheet, the Times." Against such a contingency, muskets, pistols and ball cartridges were kept in the building and the pipes were connected with the steam boilers of the chest, "an ingenious arrangement whereby, in case of attack, the rooms on the lower floor could be instantly filled with scalding steam." No force ever attacked, however, and Franc Wilkie said "it was well for their skin, their hair, their flesh and their bones" that no one attacked the "secesh sheet."[110]

Storey did not escape completely unscathed. In March, 1864, a corporal and three privates, "brimming full of lofty patriotism and poor whiskey," staggered into the office. Shortly thereafter, Storey strolled in. The corporal lurched into the editor, muttering "Who you a pushin', you damned old secesh s.o.b."

As quick as a flash Storey turned, seized the corporal by the throat and pushed him backward "until they reached the window, through which the patriot went, head and shoulders, carrying a considerable portion of the sash and glass with him into the street." This done, Storey, without a glance at the others "who were rapidly falling back to the sidewalk," went to his room, not having uttered a word during the occurrence.[111]

In June, 1864, George Trussell, a Republican and "a notorious

108. *Ibid.*, November 23, 1863.

109. Hopkins, *Proceedings of Michigan Press Association*, 44.

110. J. W. Abbot, "Chicago Newspapers and Their Makers," *Review of Reviews*, XI (June, 1895), 651; Wilkie, *Reminiscences*, p. 115.

111. Wilkie, *Reminiscences*, p. 116; *Chicago Times*, March 8, 1864.

professional gambler," knocked Storey cold with a cement paving block in front of the *Times* office. Storey pulled a Derringer and fired before the blow was struck, but "the ball missed the scoundrel," a lack of marksmanship for which Storey apologized to his readers the following day.[112]

There was some truth to Storey's charge that his assailant on this occasion was a "professional gambler," and Trussell's assault upon the editor led to a campaign by the *Times* against "gambling dens." The final chapter in the story was written with heart-rending pathos. In September, 1866, the newspaper announced a "SHOCKING TRAGEDY" that occurred in a saloon on Randolph Street, directly opposite the front entrance of the *Times* office. It was a shooting affray in which the aim was truer than Storey's had been in June, 1864:

A GAMBLER SHOT DEAD
BY HIS MISTRESS.

The Victim Receives Three Bullets
From a Revolver and is Instantly
Killed.

The Beautiful Murderess Seduced by
the Deceased.

She Becomes the Keeper of a House of
Ill-Fame—He Grows Rich by Gambling.

Details of the Terrible Affair—The
Woman Arrested and Torn from the
Body of Her Victim.

> . . . Just before the tragic occurrence the victim of his own unrighteous passions was in Seneca Wright's saloon. . . . Molly Trussell entered . . . and advancing to the corner where the men were standing, and grasping George by the coat, she exclaimed: "Come here George, I want you." He followed her . . . and Molly stood between the door and Trussell. Drawing a concealed pistol from her dress, without a word of exclamation or warning, she fired at him. . . . The wounded man staggered, exclaimed "I am shot" . . . and expired. The woman threw herself upon the prostrate body of her victim and cried "Oh George, I would not have shot you if you had not hated me so."[113]

112. *Chicago Times*, June 16, 1864.
113. *Ibid.*, September 5, 1866.

In view of Storey's excesses in his campaign against Lincoln and the war effort after September, 1862, it was easy to understand how many citizens, in the words of Franc Wilkie, "believed they had a God-given right to attack Storey and kill him if they could."[114] Besides the attitude of the newspaper, certain of its employees were notorious for their open boasts of support to the Confederate cause. Frederick Cook stated that "undisguised disunion avowal" was particularly conspicuous in the *Times* composing room, where many of the printers were either southern-born or prided themselves in being members of the Knights of the Golden Circle. "In most northern communities," Cook claimed, "the majority of the compositors . . . would have been denounced as rebel sympathizers." But Cook concluded it was a pity that "their Copperhead pudding was never subjected to the test of eating by a Southern invasion of the North." Had this occurred, Cook was confident "not one in a score" would have failed to help repulse the rebels.[115]

Despite Cook's opinion, a few historians have purported to find evidence that some *Times* employees carried their opposition further than mere boasts of disunion sentiment. Addicted to the theory that a web of conspiratorial and subversive secret societies flourished throughout the North, they have not hesitated to indict Storey and the *Times* on charges of treason. At the time of the Northwest, or Camp Douglas, conspiracy in October, 1864, for example, the charge is that several of Storey's compositors and two or three reporters conspired with the Sons of Liberty to foment an armed uprising in Cook County, free the Confederate prisoners at Camp Douglas, and possibly lead the Northwest out of the Union.[116] Subsequent scholarship has proved, to the satisfaction of this writer, that the so-called "camp Douglas conspiracy" was in reality hatched in the brains of Illinois Republicans to discredit Democrats prior to the 1864 elections. Aided by the *Chicago Tribune*, which conveniently exposed the "plot" on election eve, this Republican "secret society scarecrow" did succeed in stigmatizing the opposition party.[117] Unfortunately, this proved to be a "scarecrow" whose work did not end once the ballots were counted in November, 1864. Myths about Copperhead secret societies, "a

114. Wilkie, *Reminiscences*, p. 116.
115. Cook, pp. 74-75.
116. Milton, pp. 253-54.
117. Klement, pp. 199-205.

political apparition which appeared on the eve of elections," have been used ever since by historians intent on proving the existence of a gigantic ring of treason that operated throughout the North and in the activities of which Storey and the *Times* played prominent roles.

What was the attitude of the editor of the *Times* toward secret plots to overthrow the Lincoln government? The evidence suggests he not only consistently refused to co-operate with such movements, but took positive steps to expose and denounce them. When Phineas C. Wright, Supreme Commander of the Order of American Knights, sought the use of a metropolitan paper to propagandize the society's activities, Storey turned him down cold.[118] During the entire period of the war, moreover, Storey denounced all secret societies in his columns despite the various shifts and nuances of his attitude toward the Lincoln administration. As early as December, 1861, when the rumor first flourished that the Knights of the Golden Circle posed a formidable threat, the *Times* stated its belief that if such an organization really were operating in the North then every patriot was bound to help expose and eradicate it. "We hope that an energetic effort will be made . . . to ascertain whether lodges . . . exist in this State," Storey said, "and if they do exist, to bring their members to trial before the Federal courts."[119]

In September, 1862, in a reiteration of a stand against secret political organizations which he first articulated in the *Detroit Free Press* against the Know-Nothing movement, Storey asked the public authorities to "spare no exertion" to sift out the guilty parties, disperse them, and bring them to punishment. "Their treason is more odious and dangerous than the southern treason, for the latter is open, bold, and may be met in open day, while the former is covert, sneaking, and assassin-like," the *Times* stated. While it was possible that some good men might see "fancied benefits" in a secret association, Storey felt nothing could be more unwise because "when personal liberty in this country can only be protected by the intervention of secret organizations, it may as well be surrendered altogether." Rather than play with secret societies, Storey felt that he and other Democrats should support the Democratic party "with all our might, and be exceedingly

118. Milton, p. 241.
119. *Chicago Times*, December 10, 1861.

watchful that individually we do nothing to make it obnoxious to the support of any loyal man."[120]

Even after the editorial denunciations of Lincoln turned violent after the Emancipation, the newspaper remained consistently opposed to secret plots. In March, 1863, it stated "No defence can be made of secret political organizations at any time, and at the present time they ought to be absolutely forbidden by law." Secret societies existed for no good purpose Storey asserted, and they "will almost certainly become engines of disorder, bloodshed and violence."[121]

In 1864 Storey refused to support or co-operate with the Northwest conspiracy. "It works in secret and is plotting the destruction of the present government," Storey noted. If the conspiracy succeeded "the country must lapse into barbarism. We've nothing to do with the motives of the 'Ancient Order of American Knights.' "[122]

At no time during the war did Storey deny the existence of secret organizations in the North. Rather, he denounced their activities and asserted, with a good deal of justification, that their importance was vastly exaggerated by Republicans. His general attitude was summarized in an editorial printed during the trial of the Camp Douglas conspirators in February, 1865:

> We do not mean that a few fools calling themselves "Sons of Liberty," . . . did not hold mysterious conclaves in mysterious places, and spout preposterous nonsense and utter direful threats which they were about as likely to execute as they were a military assault on the moon. It is probable that there were some such conclaves, one of which, according to the testimony, consisted of two persons, while there were present four detectives! Four detectives leading on two fools![123]

Wilbur F. Storey had too much innate patriotism to associate himself with any secret plots for armed overthrow of the American government. His crime, if crime it was, consisted in his incendiary pronouncements that so readily might induce the gullible and less balanced to busy themselves with such activities. With his policy of vituperation against Lincoln, of course, it was an easy matter for those who differed with Storey to charge the editor affiliated

120. *Ibid.*, September 2, 1862.
121. *Ibid.*, March 6, 1863.
122. *Ibid.*, July 30, 1864.
123. *Ibid.*, February 20, 1865.

with one or more treasonable organizations. Detective William Taylor, sent by the War Department to investigate the Northwest conspiracy in 1864, admitted he could find no evidence linking the editor of the *Times* with the plot. The detective nonetheless concluded that Storey was involved "but he stands so high, and is naturally so very high, as to be unapproachable to the common members."[124]

The faulty conjecture of a government detective surely is not sufficient to convict Storey. Felix G. Stidger, chief witness at the Indianapolis treason trials in October, 1864, wrote a lengthy *Treason History of the Order of the Sons of Liberty.* A self-styled "Spy Complete," Stidger offered elaborate proofs of a vast Copperhead plot for armed insurrection. But even the hostile Stidger exonerated the editor completely. "In no case," Stidger stated, "was there any direct or convincing evidence found which would tend to prove Storey guilty of any such connection [with secret political activities]."[125]

In the first month of 1864 Storey warmed up for the upcoming presidential election with a sagacious notation of a truism he saw but never applied to himself. "Every individual is not at liberty to decide upon the intrinsic importance of matters presented for consideration solely by his own judgment," he observed. "To do so is an arrogance insulting to public opinion in its estimate of values."[126]

1864 represented, in the mind of the editor of the *Chicago Times*, the last year of hope for American liberty. Only a Democratic victory in the national election could accomplish salvation, a truth Storey felt the Republican party itself recognized. "If but a tithe of the charges made by the Chaseites and the Lincolnites is true, they are the most shamefully corrupt and hypocritical parties which ever plundered a people under a pretense of patrio-

124. William Taylor to Colonel J. P. Sanderson, July 12, 1864, in *The Official Records*, Ser. 2, VII, 747.

125. Felix G. Stidger, *Treason History of the Order of the Sons of Liberty* (Chicago: 1903), p. 117; see also Donald B. Sanger, "The Chicago *Times* and the *Civil War*," *Mississippi Valley Historical Review*, XVII (March, 1931), 575-77. Sanger, whose article is the most extensive study yet published of the *Times* during the war, went so far as to state "a careful examination of the *Times* fails to reveal any active support of secret societies or any statement that could be considered treasonable." While the latter half of this statement might be questioned, the assertion that the newspaper gave no support to secret societies stands.

126. *Chicago Times*, January 25, 1864.

tism."[127] Convinced of the righteousness of his self-appointed role as watchdog of American liberty, Storey proceeded with relish to reach depths unequaled even by the *Times* prior to January, 1864.

He began on New Year's Day with the observation that "President Lincoln and his administration are convicted of having betrayed, willfully, the trust confided to them by the American people." As the year progressed, the abuse increased and one attack in March was especially noteworthy. The paper recounted a funeral joke attributed to Lincoln and noted "the question of the re-election of Mr. Lincoln very naturally suggests 'funeral thoughts.' Should he not be elected, he goes to his political funeral when he leaves the White House, and should he have another term, there will be a national funeral." Two weeks later, logic dictated "the extermination of the residents of New England, the hanging of [Horace] Greeley . . . and the expatriation of the whole tribe of Washington officials, from Old Abe down to his doorkeeper."[128]

The report from Washington on March 2 bristled with levity and blasphemy. It told of how the Republican party, by renominating Lincoln, would put forth a candidate whose chief claim to support, by his own admission, rested in the fact "that he is a clown." But "Abe's smutty stories, his jokes and witticisms" did not take with the soldiers, as proved by two prayers the boys offered regularly on the field of battle:

I.

"THE ABRAHAM LAUDAMUS."

We praise thee, O Abe. We acknowledge thee to be sound on the goose.
All Yankee land doth worship thee, everlasting old joker.
To thee all office-seekers cry aloud, "Flunkeydom and all power therein."
To thee Stanton and Welles continually do cry, "Bully, bully, bully, boy with the glass eye."
Washington and Illinois are full of the majesty of thy glory.
The glorious company of political generals praise thee.
O Abe, save thy people, and bless thy parasites. Govern them and increase their salaries forever.
Day by day we puff thee.
And we exhalt thy name ever in the daily papers.

127. *Ibid.*, February 23, 1864.
128. *Ibid.*, March 2 and 18, 1864.

Vouchsafe, O Abe, to keep this day without a change of Generals.
O Abe, have mercy on the army of the Potomac.
O Abe, let thy mercy be upon us, as our trust is not in Stanton.
O Abe, for thee have I voted, let me never be redrafted.

II.

Our Father who art in Washington, Uncle Abraham be thy name; thy victory won; thy will be done at the South as at the North; give us this day our daily rations of crackers and pork; and forgive us our shortcomings as we forgive our quartermasters; for thine is the power, the soldiers and the negroes, for the space of three years, Amen.[129]

The "news" columns and editorials were supported by derogatory filler matter. An idea of its constancy and tone is conveyed by a random sampling from April through election eve:

A Liverpool, England paper says "The tallest man in the United Kingdom serves behind the bar of a public house in Liverpool." It is of such men, who have engaged in a similar occupation, that miscegens make Presidents in the United States.[130]

Mr. Lincoln is abstemious. He eats little but talks a great deal, and seems to feed upon his own words more than the dishes which are placed before him. Medical men say this accounts for his emaciation.[131]

Shakespeare excelled as much in painting as in poetry. His portraits, like his plays, will not only live for all time, but from their "infinite variety," may be selected the "counterfeit presentments" of all who have been, are, or will be. Substitute thimblerigger for fortune teller, and who will fail to recognize the following: "A hungry, lean villain, a mere anatomy, a mountebank, a thread-bare juggler, and a fortune teller; a beady, hallow-eyed, sharp looking wretch, a living dead man."[132]

Have we become worse than slaves, that an uncouth backwoodsman shall spend our treasure and squander the lives

129. *Ibid.*, March 2, 1864.
130. *Ibid.*, April 5, 1864.
131. *Ibid.*, May 10, 1864.
132. *Ibid.*, May 25, 1864.

> of our people, and as an offset, gives us only disaster and disgrace?[133]

> All "accepted recruits" who hereafter are received at Springfield, Ill., will, in accordance with orders from Washington, be branded with the letter "I" in the small of the back. This is Lincoln's "I", and with Lincoln's eye at the small of the soldier's back, his lips will be about where they ought to be—especially if the soldier be a nigger.[134]

By summer Storey's editorials almost advocated violence to get rid of Lincoln. In June he noted the necessity to "ourselves and to posterity to relieve the nation *in some way* of a most intolerable weight of tyranny [emphasis added]." The ballot box was "the first legitimate resort for relief," but should that fail "then the next step is plain and inevitable. We leave its character to the development of the future."[135] This statement was as close as Storey came to a direct advocation of illegal means to remove Lincoln from office. The Chicago editor did not go as far as Marcus ("Brick") Pomeroy of the La Crosse, Wisconsin, *Democrat,* who on August 29, 1864 published his hope that, should Lincoln win re-election, "some bold hand will pierce his heart with dagger point for the public good." But although Storey never did directly advocate the assassination of Lincoln, the very nature of many of his attacks could not help but convince the demented that any resort would be justified to save the nation from the clutches of the "uncouth backwoodsman" in Washington.

For instance, the *Times* celebrated "OUR ANNIVERSARY" on July 4 with the observation that the holiday was crowred with eighty years of glory, and loaded with three years of crime and shame. Lincoln lived and ruled reckless of the people's lives and liberties. His despotism had been built "upon the graves and the bleached and unburied bones" of the Union dead. "From constitutional liberty under Washington to unlimited submission to Lincoln is a fall second only to that of Satan's, when, plunging from Paradise to Hell, he fell 'from morn till noon, from noon till dewey eve.'"[136]

On other occasions the *Times* spoke of Lincoln's "heartless jocularity amid scenes of suffering and death." The President had also "degraded white soldiers" by placing "negroes on an equality with

133. *Ibid.*, July 14, 1864.
134. *Ibid.*, September 15, 1864.
135. *Ibid.*, June 7, 1864.
136. *Ibid.*, July 4, 1864.

them." On election day, Storey advised voters to "vote for Lincoln, imbecillic and unfaithful," if they wished a continuation of "the carnage." Otherwise, Americans should "vote the Democratic ticket." Notice, it was not General George B. McClellan, but "the Democratic ticket" that Storey supported. Throughout the campaign he gave only cursory notice to McClellan. He did oppose the move to nominate Clement L. Vallandigham before the Democratic convention in August. But none of the rabid support he had given James Buchanan in 1856 and Stephen A. Douglas in 1860 was apparent for McClellan in 1864. Rather, Storey seemed obsessed with the necessity of retiring Lincoln, and it did not appear to matter who might replace him. On the day after Lincoln's reelection, a long editorial asked "IS OUR GOVERNMENT A FAILURE?" In it, Storey said "we doubt not that the result of the election will lead . . . impartial and intelligent observers . . . to a conviction that our republican system is a failure."[137]

Beginning late in November the *Times* stopped its more virulent denunciations of Lincoln and the war effort. The dire predictions of the Washington reporter also ceased. During this time, as it became apparent the Confederacy was in fact whipped, Storey confined himself to "speculative" pieces such as one headed "POSTERITY" which appeared in early December and bordered on pacifism. In it, Storey depicted posterity as "unconscious but unhappy. Slumbering calmly in the depths of futurity," it would awaken to "a wretchedness whose endurance is beyond the capacity of human nature." A debt of four billion dollars ensured that it "will come naked into the world, and it bids fair that it will pass through life in the same condition, and finally make its exit in a like manner." But worse than the debt which plundered posterity was the murder of untold millions who "must now slumber eternally" because of the war. "Does not every man know," Storey asked, "that the bullet which stills the heart of a fellow being . . . consigns to nothingness unnumbered members [because it] inflicts eternal quiescence upon unborn millions?"[138]

In February, 1865, the *Times* published its first kind word for Abraham Lincoln since September, 1862. It was occasioned by the President's speech of February 1 in which Lincoln stated that Emancipation "aided only those who came into our lines, and it was inoperative as to those [slaves] who did not give themselves

137. *Ibid.*, September 21, November 8, and 11, 1864.
138. *Ibid.*, December 2, 1864.

up." Storey remained wary of the President's intentions, but hoped "Mr. Lincoln has at last screwed up his courage."[139]

With the second inauguration Storey returned to his usual form with an editorial that overflowed with personal hatred and malice. The fact that it was published just five weeks before the assassination makes it appear additionally distasteful in retrospect. It was headed "LINCOLN," and began by stating "We shall speak plainly, and if, in speaking plainly, we employ terms which should rarely be used in speaking of a man occupying an honorable station [it is because] the truth cannot be expressed in more courteous language." The editor then pointed out that the people of Chicago recognized Lincoln as "a noisome stench thrust under the nostrils of the community." The President was respectable neither as a man nor a magistrate. His honesty was "as flax before the fire." He was a liar, and a catalogue of contradictions and inconsistencies. A partially honest coward transformed into an unblushingly corrupt bully, Lincoln had shown in his first term that he was consistent in his contempt for the Constitution, consistent in disregarding the rights of political opponents, consistent in protecting the corruption of his appointees, and consistent in preserving the repulsive qualities of his character. Storey ended with a flourish of hate:

> "Loyal" men of Chicago, in defiance of law and right, his grasp is upon your lives today. Can you tell how you will shake it off? Dare you try to shake it off? Were it to save your souls from "the gnawings of the worm that never dies" you cannot, and for a less reason, you dare not.[140]

"We shall speak plainly!" Throughout the Civil War Storey did exactly this. His conception of the proper dimensions of "plain talk" included a steady barrage of the most scurrilous and vulgar epithets known to the English language. He had proved in Detroit that he had few equals in the art of invective. The major difference that the war years presented was in the fact that his polemical ravings were now directed against the President of the United States in the midst of the greatest crisis his nation had faced.

Storey was not alone among northern editors in conduct of this sort. Lincoln's own partisan newspapers reached almost as low before Emancipation was proclaimed. On the Democratic side, in addition to Samuel Medary there were Manton Marble of the *New*

139. *Ibid.*, February 4, 1865.
140. *Ibid.*, March 4, 1865.

York World; Fernando Wood of the *New York Daily News*; and Marcus ("Brick") Pomeroy of the La Crosse, Wisconsin, *Democrat*, plus many less well-known editors. All were engaged in a constant campaign against Lincoln and the "nigger war"; and all were likewise, at one point or another, physically assaulted for their policies. Most enjoyed the added distinction of provoking official government action against their concerns.

Medary was indicted by a Federal Grand Jury in Cincinnati in May, 1864, on a charge of conspiracy against the government. His death the evening before Lincoln's re-election prevented a trial on the charge. Fernando Wood, who advocated the secession of New York city from the Union in April, 1861, saw his paper closed down by Federal troops on two occasions during the war. And Marcus Pomeroy, who almost equalled Storey although he spoke to a much narrower constituency from his La Crosse base, barely escaped with his life from a lynch mob during the 1864 election campaign.[141]

Storey remained absolutely consistent right up to the assassination of the President. In the last weeks of Lincoln's life there were even slight indications of a change of attitude in the *Times*. When hostilities ended, and the President's moderate stand on Reconstruction became apparent to Storey, he saw it as a concession to state rights and was pleased.

With this sentiment to his credit, Storey joined the nation in mourning on April 16, 1865, when his black-bordered columns said: "There are not on this day mourners more sincere than the democracy of the northern States." He pointed to "indications in the last few days of Mr. Lincoln's life that he might command support in the close of the war, as he did at the beginning. The democracy may well mourn the death of Abraham Lincoln."[142]

It would be hasty to accuse Storey of hypocrisy in this stand, because throughout his career he remained true to *his* principles as *he* saw them. Lincoln's crime, in the editor's eyes, had been the President's betrayal of state rights and conversion of the Civil War into an antislavery crusade. Once it became manifest that Lincoln did not plan a military dictatorship and the destruction of southern states, Storey moved once more to support the President. At precisely that moment, Abraham Lincoln was cut down by an assassin's

141. A good survey of newspaper attitudes during the Civil War is Robert S. Harper, *Lincoln and the Press* (New York: McGraw, Hill & Co., 1951).
142. *Chicago Times*, April 16, 1865.

bullet. Storey joined his countrymen in decrying the deed and mourning the President.

The extent of the editor's regret is difficult to measure. In more than forty years of journalism, he never once apologized in print for anything his newspapers said regarding any politician. The only hint that Storey might have had a partial change of heart was an editorial the *Times* ran on the fourth anniversary of the assassination in 1869. "As the years roll away, and the assassination sinks deeper into the past," respect for the Civil War President, "is increasing and strengthening among the people who, in his life, were among his firmist political enemies."[143]

Be that as it may, Wilbur Storey's place in American history as the most outrageous of Abraham Lincoln's detractors is secure. From September 22, 1862, until one week before Lincoln's death, the *Chicago Times* daily castigated "the uncouth backwoodsman" with a rancor that knew no bounds. At the time of the second inaugural Storey went so far as to ask the people of Chicago "how will you shake off" the "noisome stench" who possessed "whatsoever in human nature is false, treacherous, weak and cowardly." Five weeks later John Wilkes Booth answered the editor's query. What portion of the blame Storey might merit cannot be measured. If only a minuscule of his charges, made in language deliberately designed to inflame public passions with hatred and contempt for the Chief Executive, were true, then an assassin, deranged with a sense of the theatric, might well justify to himself an act to rid the world of such a depraved, power-mad creature.

History's verdict has been that Wilbur F. Storey was guilty of treason for his Civil War conduct. Actually, he was not. Rather, Storey was no more than an exceedingly unpleasant human being who filled Civil War Chicago news and editorial comment with a phosphorescent and fascinating malice. Fascinating is the correct adjective, because Storey exerted a demonic fascination throughout the twenty-four years that he operated the *Chicago Times*. The Civil War was only the opening chapter, the introduction as it were, to a career unmatched in the history of the Chicago press.

Captain William James, Provost Marshall of the First District of Illinois during the Civil War, in his official report to the War Department in August, 1865, discussed the role of "the wicked, reckless and debauched newspaper press of the State." Captain James manifested surprise at the "persistent fiendishness and trucu-

143. *Ibid.*, April 15, 1869.

lent hatred" of the Illinois Democratic press. He reserved some special remarks for the *Chicago Times* as "chief among these instigators of insurrection and treason, the foul and damnable reservoir which supplied the lesser sewers with political filth, falsehood and treason. The pestilent influence of that paper in this State has been simply incalculable."

Today, a century later, a careful study of Storey's newspaper for the war years will convince the most cautious that the *Times*' "pestilent influence" really was "simply incalculable." While overt treason was avoided, it is impossible to digest the steady diet of daily columns replete with attacks upon the Negro, diatribes against the President, and slanted reports against the northern war effort, and not conclude, with Captain James, that

> In my opinion, without desiring in the least to abridge the regulated liberty of the press, it is as much the duty of the government to suppress such newspapers in time of public danger and war as it is to storm the fortresses, sink the navies and destroy the armies of the common enemy.[144]

144. "Historical Report of the Operations of the Office of Acting Assistant-Provost-Marshal-General, Illinois," Captain William James to Brigadier General James B. Fry, August 9, 1865, in *Official Records*, Ser. 3, V, 837-38.

CHAPTER VIII

CHICAGO: A Hell's Broth in the Times' Cauldrons!

Insolent, audacious, defiant as [Storey] was in war matters, his paper became equally noted for another quality in its post-war existence. This feature was its glaring indecency . . . which reeked, seethed like a hell's broth in the *Times* cauldrons and made a stench in the nostrils of decent people.

—Franc B. Wilkie, *Reminiscences,* p. 130.

THE CIVIL WAR WROUGHT A REVOLUTIONARY CHANGE IN THE AMERICAN newspaper, as it did in American life generally. By 1865 the circulation of the larger metropolitan dailies had soared to a point not dreamed of four years earlier. Political partisanship, the hallmark of the daily newspaper during the passionate decade preceding the conflict, was effectively severed by the general rending asunder of national life that the war produced. The most noticeable journalistic phenomena in the war's aftermath were "the growth of independence from party bonds, the growth of feature material in the place of long political disquisitions, and the accelerated expansion . . . of midwestern journalism."[1]

In the Middle West from 1865 to 1884, the *Chicago Times* made its mark. Its editor, unscrupulous but fearless, debauched but brilliant, held forth for twenty years as the undisputed leader of the western press. A journalistic Robespierre, he guillotined private reputations and characters with an indiscrimination that knew no propriety or logic. Feared, though despised, patronized and pandered to even by those whom he attacked, Storey terrorized Cook County during the lusty period of transition for Chicago from frontier outpost to modern, industrialized, urban complex. Following the fire of 1871, when the city undertook that phenomenal growth which by 1890 made it the hub of a continent bound together by bands of steel, Storey went progressively insane. For almost a decade, the largest and most influential newspaper in the most rapidly growing city in the United States was presided over by a madman.

Debauchery and sensationalism, however, represented only one side of the *Chicago Times*. That its management intended to make it the greatest disseminator of news in Chicago was proved during the Civil War. The paper's editorial utterances might be at variance with the prevailing public sentiment and its vigorous onslaughts against private citizens might cause widespread consternation. But, "as a collector and purveyor of news, it distanced all competitors." Its war news, its political accounts, and its local reports were gathered with the greatest care and attention to detail, and "those who could find nothing but sentiments obnoxious to them in its editorial columns found an antidote in the excellence of the news columns."[2]

Storey made his newspaper well-known in the Middle West because he, more than any other editor in the region, mastered the divergent possibilities that the war opened for American journalism. To keep the wartime circulation gains, some newspapers resorted to exaggerating the available news with a melodramatic flair under headlines intended to keep the attention of the sensation-fed public of the war years. Others broadened the scope of news

1. Frank Luther Mott, *American Journalism: A History, 1690-1960* (New York: Macmillan & Co., 1962), p. 388.
2. "Wilbur F. Storey," in *Encyclopedia of Biography of Illinois* (Chicago: Century Publishing and Engraving Co., 1894), II, 124.

matter, and added variety, human appeal and general readability.[3] Wilbur Storey did both of these things, and he did each better than any competitor. In fact, this dichotomy, "this mingling of the good and the bad," was "the worst feature of Mr. Storey's paper. While he prostituted the moral life of the city and attacked the private lives of men who stood above reproach, he also attacked various public abuses, and above all printed the news."[4]

From the moment that Andrew Johnson succeeded to the Presidency, the *Chicago Times* became an "independent" journal. Of course, "independence" had marked the pronouncements of Storey throughout the 1850s as he insisted that his viewpoint alone constituted proper Democratic doctrine. In the late 1860s, party labels ceased to have further meaning for Storey as he moved "independently" to deliver equal abuse and castigation upon all politicians regardless of affiliation or prominence.

During the 1868 election Storey refused unequivocal support to the Democratic platform. He did not support Ulysses S. Grant, and his endorsement of Democrat Horatio Seymour was lukewarm; but his vehemence against the "soft money" plank of the Democrats was so pronounced that state leaders invited him to Springfield for a personal chastisement. Storey went, "and sat silently for several hours . . . listening to speeches . . . censuring the Times." When the meeting was over, the state party threatened Storey with official censure unless the *Times* changed. Storey arose, took up his hat, and stated, "Gentlemen, I thought that I owned the Times! I think so still. Goodnight gentlemen."[5] The career of Wilbur F. Storey in partisan journalism was ended.

The burning passion that characterized Storey's attachment to the Democratic party from his earliest days with the *La Porte Herald* was now channeled into the service of journalism. The so-called "new journalism" which Frank L. Mott attributed to a formula for the metropolitan daily first devised by Joseph Pulitzer for the *New York World* in the 1880s and 1890s, had six characteristics: "Good news coverage, peppered with sensationalism, stunts

3. Havilah Babcock, "The Press and the Civil War," *Journalism Quarterly*, VI (March, 1929), 3.

4. Eugene Seeger, *Chicago, The Wonder City* (Chicago: George Gregory Printing Co., 1893), pp. 332-33.

5. This episode is recounted in the *Chicago Times*, October 29, 1884. See also Ethan A. Snively, "James M. Davidson, 1828-1894," *Journal of the Illinois State Historical Society*, IX (Springfield, 1916), 191. Davidson was sent to Storey by the state party at this time, "but he could not prevail upon Mr. Storey to accept his views."

and crusades, editorials of high character, size, illustration, and promotion."[6] Substitute debauchery for illustration and licentiousness for promotion, and one has the exact formula that made Storey a millionaire publisher by 1875.

Storey's innovations were most pronounced in the columns of the *Chicago Sunday Times.* Since his first experiment with a Sunday newspaper in Detroit, Storey had shown a keen awareness that ordinary fare would never do for a Sabbath edition. From the very beginning, in Storey's eyes, the publication of a Sunday newspaper called for "something special" in contrast to the regular daily issue. And the "something special" that Storey conceived for the *Times* led to the introduction of the first Sunday newspaper in the Middle West devoted exclusively to "entertainment" journalism. The predominantly "feature story" touch was pioneered by Storey on February 11, 1866, long before comic strips or Sunday supplements had been thought of. Every Sabbath after this date Chicagoans were assured the *Sunday Times* would supply wonderous discourses on "SCIENTIFIC MYSTERIES," "THE SOCIAL SCENE," "WALKS ABOUT CHICAGO," or "POISON."

The definitive authority on the development of the American newspaper, Frank L. Mott, credits Joseph Pulitzer's *World* as the first newspaper "which demonstrated what could be done with Sunday editions." Since Pulitzer was not established in New York until 1883, it would appear that Storey was at least a decade ahead of any other American newspaper publisher in being the first to exploit the possibilities inherent in a Sunday newspaper. If the Sunday features of the *Detroit Free Press* of the 1850s are added, it is apparent that the genesis of the modern Sunday newspaper can be traced back to Storey at an even earlier point in his career. Either way, Wilbur F. Storey deserves important consideration in the history of American journalism as the pioneer of the Sunday newspaper.[7]

By 1873, sixteen-page Sunday editions were standard. On Sunday, May 4, of that year, a full three-and-one-half pages were given over to a detailed exposition on "CHICAGO AND HER SUBURBS." This article, the longest feature story published in a Chicago newspaper up to that date, was written on a special commission from the *Times* by Everett Chamberlin, who the following

6. Mott, p. 439.
7. See Chapter VI, pp. 138-39; and Mott, pp. 480-82.

year published a book-length exposition on the subject.[8] In the early 1880s, a four-page feature section entitled "THE SUNDAY TIMES MAGAZINE" made its appearance. On April 16, 1881, a full five-page story on "AMERICA'S ACRES" described "The Home Which the Great Republic Offers to Europe's Sinewy Masses." The account included a one-half page map of the United States as of 1881, "drawn especially for the Sunday Times by the Rand McNally Company of Chicago."[9]

In 1881 Storey's Sunday edition grew to twenty-four pages, and to accommodate the reader in sifting through the added bulk, a "Table of Contents for the Sunday Times" appeared beginning on April 24. On Sunday, May 22, "fulfilling the law where it is written in substance that all nations should have the gospel brought to them," the *Times* published the entire revised version of the New Testament. In an editorial preface, the paper noted "There is no reason why New York should be served first and this city afterward. Chicago shall not be served after any other city if the Times can prevent it. And the Times can generally." The version was released in New York on Saturday, and in order that the *Times* might lay the revision "before the people of Chicago as early as the New York papers lay [it] before their readers," Storey ordered 118,000 words of the Four Gospels, the Acts, and the Epistles to the Romans telegraphed from New York. It ran from page eight through page nineteen and constituted what the editor felt was "by many fold the largest special dispatch ever sent over the wires."[10]

Under Storey's direction the *Chicago Times* was also the first newspaper in the area to throw out the crammed, four-page, eight- or nine-column edition in favor of an eight-page, wide six-column format. Its layout was a model of typographical perfection, with evenly balanced headlines frequently running a half-column deep, promising "STARTLING DEVELOPMENTS" to all who perused its pages.

The first issue under the new format, on September 22, 1866, presaged the kind of daily newspaper Storey offered until his death. Page one was given over entirely to news, well headed and handsomely displayed. Page two chronicled "THE CONSERVATIVE

8. Everett Chamberlin, *Chicago and Its Suburbs* (Chicago: T. A. Hungerford & Co., 1874), p. 268; *Chicago Sunday Times*, May 4, 1873.

9. *Chicago Sunday Times*, April 16, 1881.

10. *Ibid.*, April 24 and May 22, 1881.

MEETING AT NEW YORK," which included a verbatim account of Confederate General Nathan Bedford Forest's speech, "A Soldier's Pledge of Fidelity to the Government." "THE RINDERPEST," which told of the outbreak of "The Cattle Plague in Kentucky" rounded out the second page. Page three consisted of advertisements and such staples as "NAPOLEON'S MISSION" or "LEW WALLACE IN MEXICO." Page four was the editorial page, filled out by one column on "Chicago Amusements" and sprightly filler items.

Page five, "THE CITY," presented the day's sensation:

MURDER IN THE NORTH DIVISION.

A Man Killed in Front of His Own Door by Three Ruffians.

The Real Murderers Captured in Bed at Three O'Clock in the Morning.

Page six offered additional "Local Intelligence," while page seven was surrendered to "Financial Intelligence." Page eight contained advertisements and details of a Democratic political rally at Rockford on September 20.

Such was the newspaper that, beginning in the autumn of 1866, Wilbur F. Storey offered six days a week to the city of Chicago.

After the Chicago fire, Storey expanded his enterprise until the *Times* "invaded every field of current events and gathered news from all quarters of the globe." News agents of the *Times* were "at every point of consequence on the continent" and beyond. During the Russo-Turkish war Franc Wilkie took up residence in London as director of a *Times* foreign news bureau, thereby making the *Times* the first newspaper west of the Appalachians with its own foreign correspondent. Under Wilkie's direction paid correspondents were sent directly to the front so that "not infrequently the Times had better reports of the battles and other important events of the war than the London newspapers of the same date."[11] In February, 1881, at Wilkie's behest, the newspaper commenced the publication of birth announcements. In announcing the new service it claimed to be the first newspaper in the United States to observe this custom, although it was regularly "observed in England, and it is a very fitting one."[12]

11. "Wilbur F. Storey," in *Encyclopedia of Biography of Illinois*, II, 124; and Franc B. Wilkie, *Personal Reminiscences of Thirty-five Years of Journalism* (Chicago: F. J. Schulte & Co., 1891), pp. 242-56.

12. *Chicago Times*, February 19, 1881.

During the Plains wars of the 1870s, Storey dispatched John F. Finerty, "that reckless Hibernian [who] came tearing over pencil in hand, eager for items," to the front. Finerty established himself as one of the best of the correspondents who covered the Indians' last stand. When Storey hired him in May, 1876, he ordered Finerty to go with General George Crook because Crook "knows more about Indians [than Custer] and is likely to do the hard work." Storey's final instructions, on Saturday morning, May 6, enjoined Finerty "to spare no expense and use the wires freely, whenever practicable." For the next three years, Storey's *Times* filled its columns with Finerty's eyewitness accounts from the front as the Irishman hewed literally to the command of his editor.[13]

It was by such enterprise that for almost twenty years the *Chicago Times* outdistanced area rivals in news gathering and circulation. There is no doubt that the *Times* enjoyed the largest daily circulation in Chicago. In 1878 *Pettengill's Newspaper Directory* credited the *Times* with a daily figure of 32,023, "fully equal to the actual daily circulation of all the other Chicago English morning papers combined." The *Directory* added "no other daily paper in Chicago ever gives its circulation in the form of an affidavit." Advertisers were invited to verify the claim by a personal inspection, with the assurance that the *Times* would afford "every facility to make their examination thorough and satisfactory. It is the only daily paper in Chicago which states and proves its actual circulation to the public."[14]

But spectacular and inventive as the *Chicago Times* was after 1865, it remained dominated in every department by the spirit of its proprietor. Storey's closest *Times* associate, Franc B. Wilkie, noted how "glaring indecency" became the paper's most dominant trait at this time. In corroboration of the opinion of the overwhelming majority of reporters and printers associated with Storey in either Detroit or Chicago, Wilkie opined "Wilbur Storey was a Bacchus, a Satyr, a Minotaur, all in one."[15]

It was true of Wilbur F. Storey as of few other human beings

13. John F. Finerty, *War-Path and Bivouac* (Chicago: Unity Building Press, 1890), pp. 3-5; see also Milo M. Quaife, ed., Lakeside Classics edition (Chicago: R. R. Donnelley & Co., 1955), Introduction; and Oliver Knight, *Following the Indian Wars* (Norman: University of Oklahoma Press, 1960), pp. 159-89.

14. *Pettengill's Newspaper Directory and Advertiser's Handbook* (New York: S. M. Pettengill & Co., 1878), p. 121.

15. Wilkie, p. 131.

that he was dominated by a supreme contempt for mankind. Shy in his personal dealings to the point of eccentricity, there is no record of his ever having addressed a public assembly of any sort after 1850. He was so sensitive about his conversational powers that he usually communicated with his staff by correspondence. *Times* reporter Frederick Cook recalled how his employer could never be persuaded "to overcome his habitual reserve and exhibit himself," although Cook added the certification that had Storey done so "he no doubt would have cast all the rest in the shade." But the editor never did overcome what appeared to be a congenital shyness, and he lamented in his late years that "I never had, when I was young, an opportunity to meet men and women and become accustomed to society." And so it was that he was a perpetual pariah, isolated and inaccessible, a man who compensated for his social deficiencies by playing the part of God with his newspaper. "Exceedingly vindictive in nature and possessed of no consideration for the feelings of others, he fancied himself infallible," Wilkie concluded.[16]

Beginning sometime in 1863 Storey entered a period in his personal life "in which his brute nature dominated." The pressure of the Civil War suppression and the increased sense of helplessness in the face of events he was powerless to influence combined to drive him to the refuge of "debased women, and whiskey, and occasionally a boon companion or two." His wife Maria refused him a divorce although she would not live with him. And so he turned to private vice as his rooms in the Portland Hotel, on Dearborn Street between Madison and the first alley north, "became famous for their infamous practices. Night after night, they were the theater of disgusting orgies."[17]

It was at this time that the editor contracted paresis, a brain disease caused by syphilis of the central nervous system and characterized by mental and emotional instability and paralytic attacks. Dr. Henry M. Lyman, who attended Storey in his final illness, testified that "full development is preceded by a period of evolution as we call it, which reaches over a number of years, sometimes ten or twelve, or a longer period, it is a slow process."[18] Thus it was

16. Frederick Francis Cook, *Bygone Days in Chicago: Recollections of the "Garden City" of the Sixties* (Chicago: A. C. McClurg & Co., 1910), p. 81; and Wilkie, pp. 143 and 150.

17. Wilkie, pp. 142-43.

18. Testimony of Dr. Henry M. Lyman in "Storey Sanity Hearing," *Chicago Times*, August 29, 1884.

that Storey spent almost the last fifteen years of his life in ironclad control of the largest newspaper in Chicago as he daily became more mad. The progression of the disease was mirrored in the newspaper, as each issue reached lower levels of sensationalism. The climactic year was 1875, although both before and after that date the unique combination of journalistic greatness and syphilitic madness was apparent.

In November, 1865, the *Chicago Times* published a comprehensive evaluation of "JOURNALISM EAST AND WEST." In it, Storey discoursed on the impact of his paper on Chicago journalism and discussed future plans. In Storey's view, the Chicago press was unequaled in North America. But this did not suffice for Storey, who foresaw "still greater excellence. . . . THE TIMES has made the press of Chicago the best on the continent; and it will continue its labors until it has made it the best in the world."[19]

So it was that Storey overthrew "the old regime" in Chicago journalism by leading a revolution that "lighted up the northwest with perfect distinctness." His announced goal was to make the Chicago press "the best in the world," and if he failed in this it was primarily because his newspaper's crass sensationalism consistently obscured the contributions a more balanced coupling of genius and journalist might have made apparent. From a technical and typographical standpoint, the *Times* of the late 1870s and early 1880s stood unmatched on the North American continent. But the newspaper's inner soul, reflecting the moral and mental shortcomings of its master spirit, was such that it repelled most clientele.

Storey's postwar enterprise was temporarily halted, as was the enterprise of the city he served, by the terrible conflagration of October 8, 1871. Like the city, however, the *Times* recovered to reach its greatest heights. But the "Great Chicago Fire" served as the natural dividing line for Storey's postwar career.

It was between 1865 and 1871 that Storey introduced the *Sunday Times*, revolutionized and expanded the paper's format, and built his circulation to the highest of any journal in the West. Proof that once he was established he had no peer was indicated by the fact that one of New York city's greatest postwar journalist, Charles A. Dana of the *Sun*, was driven out of Chicago in 1867 because he could not meet and withstand Storey's competition.

Dana came to Chicago at the invitation of moderate Republican

19. *Chicago Times*, November 13, 1865.

elements who wished "to extirpate Joseph Medill and the *Chicago Tribune.*" He arrived in 1866 and launched the *Chicago Republican* "with great expectations of a permanent residence." He found that Medill and Storey "reigned supreme in the Chicago alleys." Dana measured himself against them, raided both of their papers for talent, and then after fourteen months he returned to New York "dissatisfied with his prospects in the western city." In 1868 he purchased the *New York Sun* and within three years he made it the most widely circulated newspaper in that city.[20]

From the day Wilbur Storey purchased the *Chicago Times* until the end of the Civil War, the events of that conflict and the campaign against Abraham Lincoln absorbed most of the editor's attention. Even during the war years, though, Storey's potential as a slick seller of sex, sadism and scandal was apparent. Much of the material of this sort that the newspaper ran during the war was directed at discrediting the Negro or against the Union army.

But the newspaper also blew up civilian Caucasion vice on occasion. The trial of the Reverend Elijah W. Hager, Rector of the Church of the Holy Commission, on several charges of immoral conduct with a twenty-three year old war widow, sizzled on the front page throughout April of 1863. The edition of April 28 featuring this story approached a treatment that would not become standard until Hearst and Pulitzer discovered the possibilities of photographic support in the 1890s. Two multicolumned engraved sketches depicted the Reverend Hager and widow Sarah E. White. The headline read:

THE CLERICAL IMBROGLIO
SKETCH OF ITS HISTORY ANTECEDENT TO
THE TRIAL.
PORTRAIT AND BIOGRAPHY OF MR. HAGER.
MRS. WHITE—HER FIGURE, HISTORY
AND CHARACTER.
AN AWKWARD DILEMMA.[21]

"THE CITY," column one on page three, was the special place for accounts of "The Ruin of A Young Girl 'Under the Willow'" or, in January, 1863 " THE ADVENTURES OF A LOTHARIO" which told

20. Elmer Gertz, "Charles A. Dana and the Chicago Republican," *Journal of the Illinois State Historical Society*, XLV (Springfield, 1952), 124-27; and Mott, p. 374.
21. *Chicago Times*, April 28, 1863.

of "Love, Dissertion and Double Suicide in A Disreputable House."[22]

All of this was as Sunday school fare, however, when compared with the paper's treatment of city scandal by the end of 1865. As Storey could turn full attention to matters closer to home, the *Times* became a veritable sinkhole of the seamier side of Chicago life. Beginning in January, 1866, a daily column headed "NYMPHS DU PAVE" highlighted the doings of Chicago prostitutes. Sprightly, suggestive fillers, such as the following, separated the lead items on the editorial page:

> The Mormons have resolved on commercial non-intercourse with the Gentiles. A resolve to have less intercourse among themselves would be a wiser one.[23]

But it was the divorce case involving sexual irregularities or aberrations that most consistently furnished the *Times* with sustained "hot" copy insuring a continuous circulation growth in the late 1860s. The Stewart divorce case of late 1866 and early 1867, in which the husband stood accused of adultery, ran as a daily feature for almost four months. On January 10, 1867, seven columns of solid minion type were devoted to "ASTOUNDING REVELATIONS" which included the "Visits of Mr. Stewart to Houses of Ill-Repute" where "He Sings Vulgar Songs and Contracts Diseases."[24]

By far the most lurid case exploited by the *Times* in the late 1860s was the Ticknor divorce, with litigation spread from November, 1867, through March, 1868. Column after column of details was spread before *Times* readers, including an account of how the thirteen-year-old Ticknor daughter was seduced by her fourteen-year-old cousin. Of special significance in the Ticknor case was the fact that *Times* staffers Franc B. Wilkie and Mort L. Hopkins were principal witnesses who testified for Mr. Ticknor against his wife because the latter was "a woman of easy virtue and naughty reputation."[25] Both Wilkie and Hopkins offered expert opinions, and their personal involvement in this and similar scandals the paper promoted did much to indicate how it was possible for the *Times* so consistently to satisfy prurience. For neither Storey nor any other single human being could have succeeded alone in making the *Times* the foremost sludge-sheet in the United States.

22. *Ibid.*, January 9, 1863.
23. *Ibid.*, October 22, 1868.
24. *Ibid.*, January 10, 1867.
25. *Ibid.*, December, 1867, *passim.*

"Phlegmatic, cynical, severe in invective, and well informed on political economy." Franc B. Wilkie, Storey's chief assistant between 1863 and 1884; this photograph was taken in the 1880's. Courtesy Chicago Historical Society.

"Guilty of neglect in the administration of wild and dangerous medicines, instead of dispensing soothing remedies." Doctor Hosmer A. Johnson, the principal object of Storey's sustained attack on the medical profession in 1873. Courtesy Chicago Historical Society.

"With a dignity like that which one associates with the patricians of the senate in Rome's palmiest days." Photograph of Wilbur F. Storey taken about 1877.

"A large limbed, beefy specimen of a heavy class of British barmaids." Lydia Thompson, the burlesque dancer who horsewhipped Storey on a Chicago street corner in 1870. Courtesy Chicago Historical Society.

"Phlegmatic, cynical, severe in invective, and well informed on political economy." Franc B. Wilkie, Storey's chief assistant between 1863 and 1884; this photograph was taken in the 1880's. Courtesy Chicago Historical Society.

"Guilty of neglect in the administration of wild and dangerous medicines, instead of dispensing soothing remedies." Doctor Hosmer A. Johnson, the principal object of Storey's sustained attack on the medical profession in 1873. Courtesy Chicago Historical Society.

"With a dignity like that which one associates with the patricians of the senate in Rome's palmiest days." Photograph of Wilbur F. Storey taken about 1877.

"A large limbed, beefy specimen of a heavy class of British barmaids." Lydia Thompson, the burlesque dancer who horsewhipped Storey on a Chicago street corner in 1870. Courtesy Chicago Historical Society.

Agreed to perform "certain duties of a wifely nature for Wilbur F. Storey" in return for a yearly income of $10,000. Mrs. Wilbur F. (Eureka C.) Storey. She was Storey's third wife, and the person responsible for tying up his estate until there was almost nothing left. Photograph taken between 1875 and 1880. Courtesy Chicago Historical Society.

"On the northwest corner of Washington and Fifth Avenue, the most commodious and convenient newspaper building." Chicago Times Building, between 1875 and 1879, when the plant was universally recognized as the foremost newspaper building in the West. Courtesy Chicago Historical Society.

The crew that Storey assembled in the late 1860s was one admirably suited to achieve his aims, "lieutenants selected because of their capacity for the work which he planned. They acted under orders and obeyed implicitly."[26] Chief assistant from 1863 until Storey's death was Franc B. Wilkie, one of the most remarkable newspapermen in Chicago between 1865 and 1890. In addition to being a city reporter and feature writer, Wilkie frequently undertook assignments for Storey to investigate plaintiffs suing the publisher for libel. In 1877 he became the first foreign correspondent representing a midwestern newspaper when he established the *Times* London bureau. He was with Storey in Lucerne, Switzerland, in June, 1878, when the editor suffered the paralytic stroke that led to his final impairment. In 1880 Wilkie took the lead in forming the Chicago Press Club, and he served as president of that organization until January, 1881, when he returned to London to re-establish the *Times* foreign bureau.[27]

This man, the only employee who ever succeeded in serving Storey "in a confidential relation," was remembered by one associate as "phlegmatic, cynical, severe in invective, and well informed on political economy."[28] For twenty years he rendered dedicated service to his employer, only to end his days "carried away in his zeal to blacken the character of [Storey] against whom he felt a bitter personal enmity."[29] There can be no doubt that Wilkie grew to hate Storey as his 1891 book of reminiscences is written with unrestrained venom. According to Wilkie, Storey promised him an eventual partnership, a promise that spurred Wilkie on to extraordinary efforts on Storey's behalf. But while Storey reiterated the promise, he never took action and after 1878 the editor was too broken in mind and body to do so.[30] Hence Wilkie's resentment. It should be noted, however, that with respect to facts Wilkie proved an absolutely reliable witness for without exception his material is verified in the columns of the *Chicago Times.*

26. "Wilbur F. Storey," in *Encyclopedia of Biography of Illinois*, II, pp. 124-25.

27. F. C. Bennett (compiler), *History of the Press Club of Chicago . . . From January, 1880, to September, 1888* (Chicago: H. O. Shepard & Co., 1888), pp. 3-7.

28. Benjamin P. Thomas, ed., *Three Years With Grant As Recalled by War Correspondent Sylvannus Cadwallader* (New York: Alfred A. Knopf & Co., 1955), p. 99.

29. Cook, p. 334.

30. Wilkie, pp. 125-26.

Next to Wilkie in importance on the postwar *Times* was Mort L. Hopkins, editorial writer and specialist on political affairs. Hopkins, an "out and out believer in state rights," joined Storey at Detroit in 1859. He remained with him until the late 1870s, and following the fire in 1871 it was Hopkins who directed the paper's reactionary editorial policy as his employer surrendered himself to bizarre crusades favoring spiritualism and venomous assaults on personal enemies.[31]

The city staff in the late 1860s consisted of men calculated to revel in the particular type of muck that became a *Times* trademark. The city editor was Alexander C. Botkin, intelligent, energetic and capable, a man who once remarked "I'd like to walk into Storey's office and tell him 'You damned old scoundrel, you can go to hell with your paper.'" He evaluated his city staff in 1868 as "a great force. . . . Two of my men are ex-convicts, ten are divorced husbands, and not a single one of them is living with his own wife." Such was the city editor's opinion of the force that provided the daily fare for the local page of the *Times*, a fare described by Wilkie as "fitted only for the tastes and appetites of vultures and carrion-loving vermin."[32]

Many who got their first experience on the city staff of the *Times* became first-rate newspapermen. Those who did tended either to glory in their early exploits in sensationalism or to justify such reporting as a necessary component of newspaper work. Prominent among these was Frederick F. Cook whose assignments were limited to the police run and court scandals from the time he joined the paper in 1862 until after the fire in 1871. In his reminiscences Cook recalled with relish an 1866 assignment that exposed Roger Plant's bawdy house, "one of the most talked about, if not actually one of the wickedest places on the continent." Since Storey was "through and through a *news*paperman" for whom news "included the shoddy side of life," Cook felt such reporting justified. In the 1870s Cook became a Sunday feature writer. "Shortly after the fire," he stated, "I felt moved to go about among the older settlers to revive and preserve their impressions of early days." Cook's series of historical sketches, published under the

31. Mort L. Hopkins, "Reminiscences of Story [*sic*] and the Chicago Times," *Proceedings of the Michigan Press Association* (22nd Annual Meeting, Grand Rapids, July 9-11, 1889), pp. 41-46; Wilkie, p. 188.

32. Wilkie, pp. 165 and 131.

headline "BYGONE DAYS IN CHICAGO," ran as a continuing Sunday feature from September 26, 1875 until November 23, 1878.[33]

Colonel Charles Sanford Diehl, later assistant general manager of the Associated Press, also began his journalistic career in the city department of the *Chicago Times.* He referred to his years of service, from 1872 to 1883, as "a complete apprenticeship." As Diehl reviewed "the tutelage and inspiration I received from Mr. Storey and his chief men" he concluded that it was invaluable in preparing him to succeed with his Associated Press venture. "Wilbur F. Storey was one of the first to recognize that the news could be handled more efficiently through departments," Diehl stated. "He put a man having some knowledge or training for the differing news fields in charge of each department. Gradually, even the departments began to split up."[34]

There were other men on the city staff in the late 1860s who never did rise above "the nasty, the lecherous, the slums and their contents." One such individual was "Shang" Andrews who gained some notoriety as a *Times* reporter in 1869-70 before he was overcome by alcohol and dope addiction.[35]

Wilbur F. Storey, in addition to guiding every detail of his vast enterprise, also wrote editorials at regular intervals justifying the *Times* policy as a service rendered to the public. Typical was an apology headed "THE LICENTIOUSNESS IN OUR MIDST" which ran in July, 1865. It was the business of a newspaper, Storey said, to furnish an abstract and brief chronicle of the time. If in doing this its reports "pain the moral and shock the fastidious," readers must remember that society was responsible for its sins, not a reporter pursuing his business of gathering events of a public character and printing them. "It is only by bringing immorality and crime to the public gaze that society may know of their existence and take the proper methods to insure against them," he concluded.[36] And so Storey became a specialist in serving society by "bringing immorality and crime to the public gaze." He was unmatched in this specialty until *fin de siècle* "yellow journalism" cast its squalid shadow over the American newspaper.

33. Cook, pp. 352-53 and 333, Introduction, xiii; and *Chicago Sunday Times*, September 26, 1875, to November 23, 1878.

34. Charles Sanford Diehl, *The Staff Correspondent: How the News of the World Is Collected and Dispatched by a Body of Trained Writers* (San Antonio: Clegg & Co., 1931), pp. 154-55 and 75-76.

35. Wilkie, pp. 187-88.

36. *Chicago Times*, July 8, 1865.

An event in late September, 1866, offered a glimpse of "that great journalistic captain, Wilbur F. Storey, at the laboring oar." Frederick Cook was the night reporter covering the Old Armory Police Station. It was after midnight, but Cook hung around past "the limit fixed for going to press." About 1:00 A.M. the police brought in a prisoner who had murdered his brother "under rather blood-curdling circumstances."

Cook possessed himself of the outlines of the tragedy and "made a sprint for the office, something over half-a-mile away." Upon arrival, he rushed to the composing room "and to my inexpressable joy" found both Storey and reporter Charles Wright "busy with belated forms." In those days, Storey always remained in the office until, in his own expressive phrase, "the last dog was hanged." Cook presented his material, and recalled "Charlie Wright was instantly on fire." But "the Tycoon—as we were wont to call Mr. Storey when he wasn't listening—remained provokingly unmoved." As Cook stopped to catch his breath, Storey turned to the clock, permitted a half-amused, semi-sardonic smile "to light up his chiselled, enigmatic features—an unmistakeable sign of inward satisfaction," turned quietly and stated "You can have twenty minutes. Cut your cloth accordingly." Then he ordered the foreman to hold what men were left and as Cook and Wright rushed for the local room he called "I'll see to the heading." Then, "stick in hand, he composed a corker for crisp, epigrammatic English." Within the prescribed twenty minutes "a half-column (leaded minion) of as choice a collection as ever warmed the cockles of a ghoul" was put together. The next morning Cook's sensation, under Storey's head, held "the place of honor, first column, first page."[37]

The headlines of the *Chicago Times,* frequently composed by Storey himself, were the paper's most intriguing feature. A typical sample from 1866 might include

SOCIAL CRIME.

An Adulterous Couple For a Year
Inmates of A Respectable
Boarding House.
A Husband Discovers His Wife in the
Embrace of a Paramour.

He Seeks Redress, and Receives A
Beating.[38]

37. Cook, pp. 252-55.
38. *Chicago Times*, May 28, 1866.

By 1869, particularly lurid local sensations rated particularly special headline treatment. One on "POISON" ran three-fourths of a column deep under "City News" on page five. The final deck promised

Sickening Details—The Stomachs
of Deceased to be Admitted to
Analysis.[39]

It must be emphasized that at the time the newspaper grew increasingly bolder with shock and sensation, it pioneered in news and features that made it one of the most advanced journals of its day. Beginning in July, 1867, Franc B. Wilkie began a two year series for the *Sunday Times* on "Walks About Chicago." Written under the pen name *Poliuto* (Martyr), Wilkie's series of sketches was published in book form in 1869, and constituted as entertaining and reliable a set of descriptions and impressions of the "Garden City" of the 1860s as could be found. "SOCIETY GOSSIP" providing "Fashionable Intelligence of Chicago and Elsewhere" made its debut in 1868. "A Soiree Musicale," and "Weddings, Social Clubs and Festivities" were among other types of articles provided to attract the following of Chicago's social elite.

Still another outstanding feature of the *Chicago Times* during the late 1860s was the editorial page. Since the beginning of Storey's career in 1838 this page had remained the almost exclusive preserve of the editor in his newspapers. By 1866, however, he opened the editorial columns more and more to trusted subordinates. Mort L. Hopkins became chief writer on national affairs, while Franc B. Wilkie, Everett Chamberlin and others wrote on state and local topics. The paper remained staunchly opposed to radical Republicanism and supported Andrew Johnson during the impeachment trial.

Storey's hand was by no means completely absent. He frequently wrote editorials opposing the unfair treatment of Indians by the Federal government. One of these, in which Storey described Indian policy as "shameless, cruel and indefensible," complained that whereas Negroes received "school marms, freedmen's bureaus and unlimited rations" Indians received "swindling traders, outrageous exactions and bullets."[40] The most surprising change in

39. *Ibid.*, March 10, 1869.
40. *Ibid.*, May 17, 1866; see also "Application of Great Moral Ideas," *Chicago Sunday Times*, October 11, 1868.

Times editorial policy was reflected in its treatment of the Negro question. By July, 1867, Storey's attitude had modified to the extent that he allowed a series of editorials advocating the enfranchisement of qualified Negroes. One of these, headed "PHASES OF THE INEVITABLE," uttered sentiments that would have been unthinkable in the newspaper two years earlier. It held that the Negro who paid taxes, obeyed the law and understood political principles should be allowed to vote.[41]

Storey's light touch as an essayist also appeared occasionally on the editorial page. When renegade Democrat John Wentworth stood for re-election to Congress in 1866, he hired Crosby's Opera House for a political rally. This innovation so struck the editor of the *Times* that he was moved to review the entire history of political campaigning in America. He concluded that the political concert was better than earlier forms of campaigning because "it furnishes a medium . . . for sublime thought which words are too feeble to express." To the laborious argument on Reconstruction it "adds the magnificence of Mozart and the grandeur of Beethoven." A concert combined amusement with instruction, the beautiful with the useful, and the esthetical with the practical and substantial. "We cannot recommend its general adoption too earnestly."[42]

While Wilbur Storey had some success with his appeals to the upper echelons of the community, the fact remained that the paper's primary appeal was geared toward the essentially unlettered masses who clustered together in "the patch" district of the South Division, and provided the sinewy muscle behind the city's gigantic growth. It was this element that waited anxiously for each new day's sensation in sufficient numbers to insure that advertising revenue remained high. And in the late 1860s, the "Kilgubbin Irish" represented the largest single ethnic group in the South Division. It was because of this fact that the tragedy of extermination nearly befell the *Chicago Times* in August, 1865, when the newspaper published a column and one-half exposé of "SQUATTER SETTLEMENTS" with details on "Shanty Life in Chicago." The story included graphic, derogatory descriptions of the "shanties, the filth of the streets, the crime, brawls and drunkenness of the Irish in our midst."[43]

41. *Chicago Times*, July 7, 1867.
42. *Ibid.*, August 13, 1866.
43. *Ibid.*, August 7, 1865.

The story burst as a bombshell amidst the largest and most faithful element of the *Times* clientele. The editor moved immediately to make amends, and for the only time in the forty-five year career of Wilbur F. Storey, his newspaper published an apology. The story "would not have appeared had the manuscript passed through the hands of the responsible editor," he explained. He hoped, therefore, that "the *Times* will be judged by its general course, rather than by an isolated article."[44]

And well might Storey express such a hope, because from the day he began with a daily newspaper in Detroit, it had been a primary policy to court Irish Catholic support. Not only did the Irish vote the right ticket; they also constituted the dominant working class element in both Detroit and Chicago during the years Storey published newspapers in those cities. Their good graces were thus essential to his success. To keep Irish patronage, the Catholic Church was always defended, as was the foreign immigrant and "the laboring masses." In both cities Storey's newspapers were also the only ones that offered complete and glowing accounts of St. Patrick's Day festivities, including a run-down of toasts.[45]

But all of this was as straw in a hurricane when Chicago's Irish read the August 7 issue of the *Times* in 1865. The Fenian Brotherhood, at a meeting called especially to consider "the Times question," declared the article was the "contemptible work of English adventurers" and the newspaper itself "a journal unfit for introduction into our families." Undoubtedly the unkindest cut for Storey personally was the charge that "the paper's editor is in the secret employ of the British Empire," because there were few other Anglophobes in the history of American journalism who so consistently and vigorously denounced Her Majesty's government for the edification of Irish readers.[46]

Storey's pleas for understanding fell on deaf ears as both past policy and reason failed to placate Hibernia. Subscriptions fell rapidly as Irishmen boycotted the *Times* and Storey was reduced to entreat for "A truce to all this. We have been happy and proud to know THE TIMES possessed the friendship and confidence of the Irish people, and the friendship and confidence have been reciprocated." Six days after the original story appeared, the *Times*, as

44. *Ibid.*, August 8, 1865.
45. See for example *Detroit Free Press*, March 19, 1854.
46. *Chicago Times*, August 10, 1865.

the first move in the Kilgubbin aftermath, began a series of elaborate displays aimed at regaining Irish patronage.[47] Such tactics as these eventually proved irresistible, and by November the *Chicago Times* was once again "fit for introduction" into Irish families. Circulation was back to normal, but for once in his life, at least, Storey had been forced to beat an editorial retreat.

The level of attack that politicians running for city or state office could expect from the "independent" *Chicago Times* was vicious. After the assassination of Abraham Lincoln, Storey paid little attention to candidates for national office beyond a steady policy of attacking them regardless of party affiliation. But on the local level, he took relish in publishing the grossest libels against candidates. John "Dirty Work" Logan, a Chicago Democrat who joined the Republican party in 1861, was a favorite target. When he ran for the state legislature in 1866, Storey printed an editorial headed "A POLITICAL COURTESAN" comparing Logan, "formerly a comparatively decent man," to a Chicago streetwalker. "We would gladly have selected some other illustration to portray properly the commencement of Logan's career as a political harlot, but there is no other one that will as correctly photograph it."[48] The treatment afforded Robert Smith, Republican candidate for Recorder's Court in 1868, typified the headlines Chicago politicians could expect:

"BOB SMITH."

Who He Is, and What He is.
His History and Antecedents.

His Exploits as a Know-Nothing.
His Exploits as a "Wide-Awake."

His Exploits as a Whiskey-Consumer
As a Maine-Lawite, and as a Temperance
Fanatic.

His Wonderful Career as a Legislator.
His Complete Failure as a Soldier.

His Sentiments Concerning the "D---d
Dutch" and the "Mickey Irish"--- He
Holds that Irishmen Ought to be Slaves.

47. *Ibid.*, August 14, 1865.
48. *Ibid.*, August 16, 1866.

He Hopes to be Eternally G-d D---d if He
Ever Votes for a Catholic for any Office.

His Horrible Blasphemy, Immorality,
Criminality, Ignorance, Incapacity.
&c., &c., &c.[49]

Another area of innovation in news coverage in which the *Chicago Times* pioneered was in the extensive reporting of religious news. Every Monday morning a full page was devoted to the sermons preached in Chicago churches on the previous Sabbath, and since the *Times* only cost five cents, this service represented "a more economical method of getting under the gospel dispensation than by going to church. For thus cheapening the gospel the Times is a great moral benefactor."[50] Another advantage was offered by the *Times* position as "an independent religious and political newspaper" which enabled it "to take a much more candid and dispassionate view of the theological views which vex the country than newspapers which are controlled by denomination interests or prejudices."[51]

The *Times* barrage against Chicago pulpits was without surcease between 1866 and 1871. Churches, in the *Times* view, were "places of entertainment" for "those desirous of instruction and amusement." Bitter essays on "THE PREACHER OF THE PERIOD" and "RELIGIOUS CONTROVERSIALISTS" ran with a regularity that suggested demonic possession.[52] In reply to pulpit denunciations of the *Times* "religious" policy Storey wrote of the moral force of newspapers in a manner that did not respect even the memory of Abraham Lincoln:

> One great cause for regret [of Abraham Lincoln's] untimely death is that he did not live long enough to enjoy the pleasure and instruction which the perusal of the SUNDAY TIMES would have given him. One picture of him which is frequently seen in our print shops . . . represents that great and good man as reading the Bible to his son on Sunday morning. After such an exercise, with what delight he would

49. *Ibid.*, April 15, 1868.
50. *Ibid.*, November 24, 1868.
51. *Ibid.*, August 18, 1867.
52. *Chicago Sunday Times*, January 10, 1869; see also "A Lecture on the Chicago Times," June 3, 1867, and "The War of the Evangelists on the Press," December 17, 1868.

> have . . . turned to the columns of the SUNDAY TIMES . . . to prepare his mind for the temple and the duties of the day.[53]

In 1873 the *Times* began a two year series entitled "WALKS AMONG THE CHURCHES." It began on January 12 with a visit to the Baptist Chamber of Chicago where reporters learned "The Peculiarities of Shepherds and Flocks" and "How a Certain Bishop Combines Piety and Business in an Eminent Degree." This series, authored by an ex-army captain named John R. Bothwell, specialized in audacious exposures of social abuses in church bodies while seeking to "illumine flagrant iniquities" involving ministers. According to Franc B. Wilkie "there was a frightful commotion created among the Churches whose misdemeanors had already been given, and an anticipatory convulsion among those whose turn was yet to come."[54]

On April 11, 1869, the *Sunday Times* became "A TRIPLE SHEET!"—the first twelve-page newspaper in Chicago. Its format was also revised as Washington and European correspondence moved off of page one to be replaced by elaborate features on "THE STREET AND AVENUE NAMES OF CHICAGO," "PIANOS," or "THE VELOCIPEDE." Page two on this and subsequent Sundays was given over to lengthy "made news" on such items as "PRISONS," a detailed exposition on the history of correctional institutions or "FOUND DEAD," a "chronicle of strange horrors" on unsolved Chicago murders between June, 1856 and January, 1865.[55] The increased size also provided room for greater length and detail in smut and irreligion.

Because of its policy, the *Times* had a libel suit almost constantly in progress. Before 1871, however, the number of verdicts against the newspaper was small. By far the most publicized of Storey's libels before the fire was the famous "Battle of the Blondes," a case in which the witnesses were heard and the sentence carried out, not in a court of law, but on a Chicago street corner.

Periodically, the *Times* unleashed sham crusades in favor of public morality. Such concessions to decency were intended to quiet the furor raised against the newspaper in pulpits of all denominations. When "THE ERA OF BURLESQUE" swept the country

53. *Ibid.*, July 12, 1868.
54. *Ibid.*, January 12, 1873; and Wilkie, p. 127.
55. *Chicago Sunday Times*, April 11, 18 and 25, 1869.

in the late 1860s, Wilbur Storey came out foursquare against it. It was "without artistic merit" and utterly degraded. "Burlesque in its present form is a monster that will feed upon itself and soon vacate the field."[56]

In February, 1870, the Lydia Thompson Burlesque Troupe, "large limbed, beefy specimens of a heavy class of British barmaids," opened at Crosby's Opera House to the enjoyment of the "susceptible masculine elements." Miss Thompson's act, first predecessor of the modern show-girl review, had scored a hit in New York city in 1869, and this was the group's first appearance in Chicago. In the autumn of 1868 Albert Crosby, owner of the Opera House, started a quarrel with Storey over the treatment his productions received in *Times* reviews. When the "Blondes" opened, they disported in a manner most daring for that day, and Storey decided they were a menace to Chicago's purity. Since they were drawing vast crowds into Mr. Crosby's theater, he decided to lessen patronage by a direct attack upon the dancers. For two weeks, flaming editorials graced the *Times* maligning the virtue of the troupe. The morning after opening night the *Times* lamented because "opera has given way to burlesque. Music is routed by padded calves . . . and the glare of cheap tinsel." The audience came to see legs but "the old members of the company, including Lydia, failed to please."[57]

The climax came on February 20 with a full column blast headed "BAWDS AT THE OPERA HOUSE—WHERE'S THE POLICE?" To retaliate, the girls had a circular printed making an appeal "To the Public of Chicago—The Times vs. the Blondes." It read in part:

> A gross and outrageous public insult having been gratuitously offered to the ladies of the Lydia Thompson troupe by the Sunday and daily editions of the Times, we hereby stigmatize W. F. Storey, its proprietor, as *a liar and a coward* for uttering what he knows to be false in attacking defenceless women.[58]

That Storey was "uttering what he knows to be false" is open to question since Pauline Markham, the leading dancer with the act, was mistress to James Gordon Bennett, Jr., playboy heir of the

56. *Chicago Times*, January 18, 1869.
57. *Ibid.*, February 15, 1870.
58. Frederic Hudson, *Journalism in the United States from 1600 to 1872* (New York: Harper Brothers, 1873), p. 205.

Herald, whenever the troupe performed in New York.[59] Whatever the truth, Storey's attacks did not cease. Crosby's Opera House became "A Wells Street Bagnio," and the morning after the circular made the rounds, the *Times* discoursed on "The Blondes in A Nutshell." The editorial described them as an "abandoned crowd," who "made use of broad, low and degrading language, such as men of any self-respect would repudiate even in the absence of ladies." The editorial concluded by saying that the girls must either concede the justice of Storey's charges or change managers. The last sentence alluded to an unnamed protector who "allowed himself to be publicly whipped by a newspaperman whom he had insulted in New York."[60]

The girls decided to settle accounts in their own way, and the last sentence of Storey's February 23 editorial undoubtedly helped to light their path. At five in the afternoon of February 24, the editor and his second wife strolled south on State Street toward their home on Wabash Avenue. At the corner of 12th and Wabash, the couple was confronted by a man who asked "Is this Mr. Storey?" In Storey's own words "I replied yes." The man then stepped back and Lydia Thompson approached with a riding whip in her hands. "She struck me," Storey recalled, "I think on the shoulders. I did not feel the blow." The editor concluded that "it was the intention to have me whipped by a woman, and to avoid it I caught this woman by the throat and took the whip from her."[61]

When Storey repulsed Miss Thompson, Pauline Markham and three other dancers jumped him. Mrs. Storey was horrified. She shrieked "Pull out your pistol, Wilbur!" but offered no direct assistance. Soon a crowd gathered, and the police arrived. Lydia and Pauline, along with their manager, were arrested. Each was fined $100, but Lydia told a *Tribune* reporter, "It was worth it. I could not break future engagements and return to Chicago to sue Mr. Storey for slander. It was worth it."[62]

In the days that followed, the *Times* version of the episode expanded. On February 26, Dr. B. P. Reynolds, an eyewitness to "THE RAID OF THE PROSTITUTES," testified "Mrs. Storey was crying, as Mr. Storey was in a bush with a tall man and beat him by taking his cowhide." When the police asked Storey to

59. Richard O'Connor, *The Scandalous Mr. Bennett* (New York: Doubleday & Co., Inc., 1962), pp. 134-35.

60. *Chicago Times*, February 23, 1870.

61. *Ibid.*, February 25, 1870.

62. *Chicago Tribune*, February 25, 1870.

ride to the Armory police station in the same hack with those arrested, Storey replied "Me ride to the armory with that crowd? I wouldn't ride with that god damned crowd. I would not be seen on the same avenue with them."[63] The *Chicago Tribune*, in an editorial headed "THE VINDICATION OF VIRTUE," felt the whole episode "a clear case of the pot calling the kettle black." It recommended that instead of attacking the dancers Storey should have emulated "the modest demeanor of persons described in the New Testament as sitting in judgment upon an erring woman and who, when they received the verdict 'let him that is without sin among you cast the first stone' appreciated the delicacy of the situation, and retired without throwing any stone whatever."[64]

Throughout the next ten years Storey kept after the Thompson troupe. Almost a decade after the events of that February afternoon in 1870, Pauline Markham noted publicly that Storey endeavored "with a persistence unworthy the editor of a prominent newspaper, to injure not only my reputation, but my business." Miss Markham made this statement in May, 1879, at a time when her adversary was crippled by a paralytic stroke but had not yet completely lost his mental facilities. The dancer, described by a kinder critic than Storey as "supple, dark eyed and regally statuesque," was back in Chicago and the *Tribune* opened a full column for "Pauline to Wilbur F., Greetings!" Miss Markham took advantage of the *Tribune*'s generosity to call public attention "to the opinions of a citizen of Chicago as regards this pharisee who continues his brutal attacks against me." She then quoted the description of Storey that a certain Mr. Adair had offered to the Chicago Typographical Union:

> That gentleman is an old man, standing with one foot on the earth and the other in perdition. He is covered from head to foot with all the vices, putrefactions and sores that are known to immorality. . . . In all his journalistic career, I have failed to find that he ever attempted to direct the mind of the human family in a proper course.[65]

Storey was immersed in his last war with the printers at this time, while devoting his leisure hours to the pursuit of "spirits in another world." Hence he took no notice of Pauline's "Greetings," and thus

63. *Chicago Times*, February 26, 1870.
64. *Chicago Tribune*, February 26, 1870.
65. *Ibid.*, Miss Markham's letter, May 22, 1879; Mr. Adair's remarks, May 19, 1879.

it was that in the ten-year battle between the *Chicago Times* and the Thompson Burlesque Troupe, one of the Blondes had the final word.

The campaign of the *Times* against the Union shop was bitter and uncompromising. Just as in Detroit, Storey determined no Union printer would remain in his employ, and the extraordinary firmness of his fight is proved by the fact that organized labor never gained entry at the *Times* while Storey lived. He called printers "vermin" and through as spectacular a series of stratagems as ever marked management's fight against the Typographical Union, Storey kept publishing with the help of "literary" employees and such "rat" printers as he could pick up until non-Union compositors were obtained from other cities.[66]

The first strike against the *Times* occurred in April, 1864. Storey was enraged, but after a few days he became "the picture of gentility, and Union men concluded he was reconciled." Arthur Scott White, who became a *Times* compositor in 1862, described what Storey was actually up to on this occasion. The editor decided to make no concessions, stating "I would rather go out of business than yield." He purchased an empty building "on Randolph Street, at the river bank," and quietly installed a complete composing room outfit. "Forty young women were engaged to learn the typographic art," said White. On the morning of September 9, 1864, "Storey marched his girls to the composing room" and locked out the Union.[67]

On the evening of September 10, a "mass" meeting was called to meet in Court House Square by the General Trades Assembly of Chicago. A list of the "depraved sneaks" among the printers who were still working at the *Times* was read, and each name was hissed. Speeches denounced "the publisher of the Copperhead Times" as "a traitor to his country, to his God, and to the workingmen of Chicago." A series of resolutions was presented by the Chicago Typographical Union. One denounced the use of females as "instruments of a base plot . . . to overthrow and crush the manly independence and dignity of labor." Another voiced concern that the labor and habits of compositors "are entirely unsuited to the delicate organizations and constitutions of females." Still another noted that the *Times* was supported by the Democratic

66. Wilkie, pp. 154-56.

67. Arthur Scott White, Letter to the Editor, *Michigan History*, XI (January, 1927), 145.

party in Illinois and asked that state and county party leaders repudiate the newspaper or "stand in danger of losing both prestige and support with the masses of laboring men." Finally, it was resolved to boycott the *Times* "so long as it remains in its present hostile attitude toward the Printer's Union."[68]

On September 12, in an editorial headed "AN INTERNAL CHANGE," Storey stated a twofold purpose in hiring and training lady typographers. "First, to emancipate ourselves from an obnoxious despotism; second, to furnish employment . . . to a class of people . . . deserving of consideration in every labor movement—we mean young women." He closed with a pledge never to submit to the Union. "If the only alternative to submission is the destruction of our business, we will accept destruction. But there are other alternatives."[69]

Despite the resolutions and censure by the Union, Storey's "girls" prevailed until outside male printers were secured. The attempted boycott also failed to achieve the end the printers desired, and in April, 1867, the *Times* was struck again. This time women were not hired as replacements, and an editorial on "WOMEN'S WORK AND WAGES" suggested why. In no place where female printers had been "fairly tried" did they show themselves as valuable as men. Few or none looked upon typesetting as more than "a temporary occupation. There was always a husband in the future." Also, the ladies did not possess the strength or diligence of men; they could not stand "the exhausting labor attending" all night work. "In fine," Storey concluded, "they proved themselves every way inferior to male typesetters."[70] So instead of hiring ladies, the *Times* limped along in 1867 for almost three weeks at reduced size until sufficient outside printers were obtained. In a series of editorials against the Union, Storey argued management's case. One, which asked "SHALL MOBS RULE CHICAGO?" concluded "it were better a thousand times that they should be swept out of existence by a discharge of artillery." Another, headed "WHY TRADE ORGANIZATIONS SHOULD BE ABOLISHED" stated "let Capitalists at once assert their independence" by breaking the entire labor movement.[71]

Storey's campaign against organized labor was more than simply

68. Bessie Louise Pierce, *A History of Chicago* (New York: Alfred A. Knopf & Co., 1940), II, pp. 162-64 and 500-503.
69. *Chicago Times*, September 12, 1864.
70. *Ibid.*, December 14, 1868.
71. *Ibid.*, May 4 and 8, 1867.

another chapter in the history of reaction against progress. It was rather one more proof that the man who edited and published the *Chicago Times* would go to any lengths to annihilate those who enjoined his displeasure. Even organized labor recognized that Storey represented an exceptional case, as a resolution adopted by the Chicago Typographical Union in 1879 attested:

> *Whereas,* the action of Storey is made more galling by the fact that he is not even a decent representative of the capitalistic class to which by his wealth he claims affiliation, being (on account of his indecent actions in the past) socially ostracized by those who claim to be the aristocracy of our city; therefore be it
>
> *Resolved,* that we will use our utmost energy to impress upon our friends the meanness of the action of the said Wilbur F. Storey, and will oppose, and counsel others to oppose, the *Times* and its proprietor until such time as the Lord in His mercy may see fit to remove this indecent and cruel old rascal from the face of the earth.[72]

The furor in 1879 was caused by Wilbur Storey's final campaign against the Union shop. In April the *Times* compositors made another effort to organize, and Storey's response was an order to his composing room foreman that forbade the employment of any Union men in the plant. But this did not suffice for Storey, and in the first week of May he prepared a "Test Oath" that he forced every man in his employ to swear to "with *no mental reservation whatsoever.*"[73]

By 1871 the *Chicago Times* was recognized throughout the Middle West as the foremost newspaper of the region. It occupied a new plant on Dearborn Street, near Madison, in September, 1866. It led the way in Chicago with an eight-page daily edition. By 1869 the *Sunday Times* reached nearly 35,000 circulation, almost unheard of west of the Appalachians at that time.

On October 4, 1871, the paper decried the fact that "the carnival of fires still continues. Already this month there have been fifteen alarms sounded, of which only two were false."[74] On Sunday, October 8, the twelve-page Sabbath edition offered the usual. Highlighted on this day was "AN INSANE ASYLUM" which told "How Nervous and Depressed People Become Raving Maniacs."

72. *Chicago Tribune,* May 19, 1879.
73. *Ibid.*
74. *Chicago Times,* October 4, 1871.

On page three appeared a prophetic piece for this, the last issue of the paper until October 18:

FIRE.
Terrible Conflagration in This
City on Last Night.
Fearful Ravages of the Fire Demon
Among the Fuel.

The story chronicled a Saturday night fire in a west side lumber district.[75]

On Sunday evening an even more "Terrible Conflagration" broke out in the rear yard of a house on the corner of DeKoven and Jefferson Streets. "It was about nine forty-five o'clock on Sunday evening, when the bell sounded the alarm from Box 342," and by sunrise Monday morning most of Chicago lay a smoking ruin.

It was undoubtedly the most fearful night that any Chicagoan of that era experienced. At the *Times* building, a five-story brick front structure with the press in the basement, the entire reportorial and editorial staff worked on a special fire edition. Storey, showing the public consciousness of which he was capable, composed an editorial suggesting the stricken city would need help from sister cities. As the flames drew nearer the Dearborn Street office, all staff members with families left the building. At 2:00 A.M., with the presses working, a final bulletin was set:

> THE VERY LATEST—The entire business portion of the city is burning up, and the TIMES building appears doomed.

By this time the flames were leaping along and over Madison Street, and all hopes of issuing a paper vanished. Between 2:45 and 3:00 A.M. the building caught fire, and within half an hour it was gone. Except for a few back files which the last departing employees managed to save, nothing was left of the *Chicago Times*.[76]

Wilbur F. Storey was but fifty-one years old when the calamity of 1871 struck him down. Never one to bow before adversity, his reaction on this occasion indicated the toll that years of unremitting toil had exerted. The Storey home on Michigan Avenue had escaped destruction, and it was here that Franc Wilkie found the editor about 10:00 A.M. on October 9. He was sitting on his front

75. *Ibid.*, October 8, 1871.

76. *Ibid.*, October 18, 1871. The most carefully documented and entertaining account of this terrible night is found in Robert Cromie, *The Great Chicago Fire* (New York: McGraw, Hill & Co., 1958).

steps, "his head bowed beneath his two hands," staring semi-consciously over the smoldering ruins. Finally, with a halting gesture, he acknowledged Wilkie's presence by suggesting that the top newspaperman on his staff "make a deal as best you can. I shall not resume publication of the *Times*."

Storey, almost alone amongst Chicago businessmen, seemed beaten by the fire. "The city is destroyed. Everything is played out. I am an old man." These were the sentiments he expressed as Wilkie tried to convince him that the name and reputation of the *Times* by themselves were worth enough to get the paper running again. But Storey remained peculiarly unmovable, even when his two hated rivals, the *Tribune* and the *Journal*, re-appeared on October 10 with one sheet numbers. As the debris was cleared, however, his mind sharpened and he remembered an old font of type stored in the loft of a barn at the rear of his residence. It was the last remnant of the 1864 "female seminary of typography," and with this for a start, a shack was rented at 105 West Randolph Street, between Jefferson Avenue and Des Plaines.[77]

On October 18, eight days later than its competitors, the *Times* reappeared with a four page issue in the paper's pre-1866 format. The entire paper was surrendered to a detailed account of "The Great Calamity," that included a description of Mrs. O'Leary, "an old hag . . . whose very appearance indicated great poverty." The paper described her as being about seventy years old, "bent double with the weight of many years of toil," and asserted she had been on the relief rolls "for years." The account was written by Franc Wilkie, who with a bland disregard for facts asserted the woman had sworn revenge on a city that would deny her "a bit of wood or a pound of bacon." It was not known how well she had kept her word, although "there are those who insist the woman set the barn and thus inaugurated the most terrible calamity in the history of the nations." Wilkie's account ended by quoting Mrs. O'Leary to the effect that she had gone to the barn about 9:30 Sunday night, and her cow kicked over the lamp.[78]

It was not until December 8, 1871, that the newspaper appeared "as handsome as ever" in its pre-fire format. In the interim, its characterization of Mrs. O'Leary changed as she was transformed from a "hag" of seventy into "a tall, stout, Irish woman with no

77. White, *Michigan History*, XI, 145.
78. *Chicago Times*, October 18, 1871.

intelligence," who had an infant which "kicked its bare legs around and drew nourishment from mammoth reservoirs."[79]

Five days after resuming publication, the *Times* had an exclusive for page one:

A STARTLING STORY!
The Société Internationale and
The Chicago Fire.
A Diabolical Plot for the Destruction of the City.
How the Plot was Matured and Carried Out.
Fiendish Work of the Communist Incendiaries.[80]

There was now no doubt that Wilbur F. Storey was back in the newspaper business.

79. *Ibid.*, December 3 and 8, 1871.
80. *Ibid.*, October 23, 1871.

CHAPTER IX

CHICAGO: A Reputation for Evil!

There is no man in the city of Chicago that has had a grander opportunity to do something for the interests of humanity than Wilbur F. Storey. . . . He has failed. [Instead] this man has built himself up and established his reputation—and it is a reputation for evil—upon your support [because] your baser passions have prompted you to buy his newspaper.

—Remarks of Mr. Adair to the Chicago Typographical Union as reported in the *Chicago Tribune*, May 19, 1879.

THE TEN YEARS BETWEEN 1871 AND 1881 MARKED THE WILDEST period in the stormy career of Wilbur F. Storey in American journalism. Coincidentally, these same years saw the unfolding of an almost unbelievable chapter in the history of major metropolitan journalism during the nineteenth century. For it was during that decade that the *Chicago Times* established a tyranny throughout

Cook County and beyond, crucifying politicians, the medical profession, the law and judicial system, and private reputations with total abandon. The man behind this was insane, as many tyrants have been, and the community at large stood as one with the Typographical Union, helpless "until such time as the Lord, in His mercy, may see fit to remove this indecent and cruel old rascal from the face of the earth."

In personal appearance, Storey caricatured an Old Testament patriarch, with fierce face and flowing beard. But at first glance he appeared both venerable and respectable, with "a dignity like that which one associates with the patricians of the senate in Rome's palmiest days."[1] Franc Wilkie remembered him in his prime, at age forty-five, with a face "especially noble, dignified and aristocratic. His forehead was deep, full massive, beautifully rounded; his nose strong and characteristic of vast willpower; his mouth artistically carved, and his eyes—one of his finest features—were a deep hazel, large, clear and wonderfully expressive."[2]

The 1871 fire was only the first in a series of personal misfortunes that overtook Storey in the 1870s. In December, 1871, he broke his ankle in a fall from a railroad car. When the cast was removed, his left leg was slightly "out of line" and for the rest of his life Storey walked with a limp. "As Storey was very proud of his figure, the condition of the limb was a frightful mortification."[3]

Of course, the first step in his decline was his residence in the Portland Hotel between 1863 and 1867 "where his life was a continuous debauch." These years sapped his vitality and impaired his mental strength as he entered the first stages of the disease that slowly but surely brought his ruin and death. This malady, when coupled with the completely unexpected death of his second wife began that final impairment of brain and body that led to disaster.

Storey met Harriet ("Bonnie") Dodge in a Chicago boarding house in 1867. He grew so enamored of his new acquaintance that he decided to marry her, and Maria Isham Storey at last consented to a divorce. Mrs. Dodge had come to Chicago in 1866, after her husband was sentenced to a long term in a New York penitentiary.

1. "Wilbur F. Storey," in David Ward Wood, ed., *Chicago and Its Distinguished Citizens* (Chicago: Milton George Co., 1881), p. 298.

2. Franc B. Wilkie, *Personal Reminiscences of Thirty-five Years of Journalism* (Chicago: F. J. Schulte & Co., 1891), p. 111.

3. *Ibid.*, p. 202.

She was not divorced from her husband at the time she met Storey, and Franc Wilkie remembered her as a woman of questionable reputation prior to her second marriage. In 1868, Storey accompanied Mrs. Dodge to New York to secure her divorce, and the nuptials took place before they returned to Chicago.

She was twenty-six years old when she married the editor, and by all accounts a beautiful woman "whose outlines suggested a grand voluptuousness." Storey fell deeply in love with her, and she reciprocated by forsaking her former ways to give her husband "devoted attention and affection." For the "first time in his life," Wilkie noted, Storey "was entirely happy."[4]

In December, 1872, Storey and his wife made their usual Christmas pilgrimage to South Bend, Indiana, to visit the only relatives Storey cared about. Horatio Chapin, the husband of Wilbur's sister, Martha, had established a tidy fortune through shrewd dealings in pioneer real estate. When Martha died in 1846, she left two surviving children, a son, Edward Payson, and a daughter, Mary Agnes. These two became favorites of their Uncle Wilbur. Edward even named a son Wilbur Storey Chapin in 1862, but the boy died in 1864. By 1865, the Chapins were firmly entrenched in South Bend's social aristocracy. Mary's marriage to Andrew Anderson, a prominent business attorney in the city, helped further to cement the family's standing.[5] Thus, in addition to the natural ties of family, attachment to the Chapins also gave Wilbur Storey an acceptance in social circles that he could never achieve in Chicago.

A second sister of the editor, Mary Storey Farrand of Jackson, Michigan, moved to South Bend after her husband's death. By the late 1860s, Christmas at the Chapin house was an annual family ritual. Throughout life the attachment to these particular relatives was the only thing approaching a normal human relationship that the editor allowed himself. But the Christmas trip in 1872 was the beginning of a personal tragedy for Storey from which he never recovered. On the return trip to Chicago, "Bonnie" Storey caught a chill that settled into pneumonia. On January 21, 1873, "Bonnie" died. "This blow nearly drove him insane."

Austin L. Patterson, business manager of the *Times*, was the first man to see Storey after his wife's death. He found the editor in the evening sitting in front of the grate before a fire. "The room was dark and cheerless and Mr. Storey was entirely alone,"

4. *Ibid.*, pp. 204-5.
5. Obituary of Edward P. Chapin, *South Bend Tribune*, March 24, 1928.

Patterson said. It seemed to the business manager that his employer had grown many years older. "I expressed regret over his loss," Patterson said, "when he broke into a passionate fit of sobbing, the only time that I ever saw any exhibition of the kind on the part of a man who had always prided himself on being impervious to blows or misfortunes of any description."[6]

The funeral was on January 24 when "a savage snow-storm and a fierce wind drove the snow, blinding the mourners." Despite the ferocity of the weather, which the *Times* described as "the worst tempest seen in Chicago for several years," Wilbur Storey refused to enter the Cathedral of SS. Peter and Paul Episcopal Church while the service was read. Instead, the editor stood oblivious on the sidewalk opposite the church, his blank stare interrupted at intervals by a sob.[7]

Storey remained inconsolable for months. Never a religious man, he could find no solace in an organized church. And so he turned to "A Pernicious Delusion" that as editor of the *Detroit Free Press* he had styled "the Rochester rapping mania." Spiritualism, discovered by the teen-aged Fox sisters in Rochester, New York in 1848, found thousands of enthusiasts in the decade before the Civil War. "There is no knowing the extent of the delusion, the infidelity it has produced, the misery it has occasioned, and the insanity and idiocy attributable to it," Storey asserted. Because he felt this was true, he stated "We throw the weight of" the *Free Press* against "spiritualism because we believe it a monstrous imposture."[8]

The extent to which the mind of Storey deteriorated following the death of his second wife was indicated by the fact that within three months he became the foremost devotee of "spirit-rapping" in the city of Chicago. First he visited mediums, but once "contact" with "Bonnie" was established, he installed a permanent medium in his home at 668 Michigan Avenue. Seances were conducted nightly, and during a "contact" in June, 1873, "Bonnie" revealed to her husband that a prominent Chicago physician, Dr. Hosmer A. Johnson, had caused her death due to his mistreatment. Possessed of this intelligence, Storey at first decided to murder the doctor because "I have a duty to rid Chicago of a butcher like Johnson."[9] But the calmer counsel of Storey's close associates pre-

6. Austin L. Patterson to Franc B. Wilkie, as cited in Wilkie, p. 203.
7. *Chicago Times*, January 25, 1873; and Wilkie, pp. 203-5.
8. *Detroit Free Press*, July 13, 1855, and July 22, 1857.
9. Wilkie, p. 206.

vailed, and the editor decided to avenge his beloved "Bonnie" by a verbal attack through the Sunday editions of the most widely circulated newspaper in Chicago.

The campaign began on July 20, 1873, with a short notice on the editoral page:

> TO THE PUBLIC.
>
> I believe it to be my duty . . . to make a public statement in the interest of human life. I am impressed with the conviction, and have not a particle of doubt, that the death which occurred in my family six months ago came of the gross recklessness, carelessness and neglect of the attending physician, H. A. Johnson. I make this painful revelation, not hastily or without consideration, in the sole desire to guard others against a like sad experience.
>
> W. F. STOREY.[10]

That Storey's mental faculties were not up to par at this time is evident in the notice itself. Its style lacked the crispness, the sureness and the completeness that had become a Storey trademark. On the other hand, Storey retained a "madly rational" consistency until late 1881. The series of attacks on Dr. Johnson, for example, only appeared in Sunday editions because what better day to attack "Satan himself."

The Monday after the notice appeared, the *Chicago Tribune* sent a reporter to interview Dr. Johnson. The story pointed out that the physician had resided in Chicago for twenty-three years, enjoyed a large practice, was a member of the Board of Health, and a man prominently identified with numerous "scientific and literary" societies. With respect to Storey's charges, the doctor explained that the editor had written him several letters expressing dissatisfaction with Johnson's treatment of Mrs. Storey, "but he has assigned no sufficient reason for such dissatisfaction." The *Tribune* story concluded that Johnson would not seek redress in a civil libel suit because he could not be prejudiced "by articles originating in the brain of a man who, by the death of one dear to him, has brooded over her loss to such an extent as to become morbid, or a monomaniac, on the subject."[11]

Joseph Medill refused to let the opportunity to ridicule his most hated rival pass. The *Tribune* began a series of "fillers" such as the following:

10. *Chicago Sunday Times*, July 20, 1873.
11. *Chicago Tribune*, July 21, 1873.

> Dr. H. A. Johnson, for a long time Mr. Storey's medical advisor, professionally pronounces him a "monomaniac"; which Webster defines as one "affected with mania, or a partial derangement of the intellect." Poor old gentleman.[12]

Storey waited until Sunday, July 27, before he published a second notice. It was almost three-fourths of a column long, and attempted a detailed exposition of Johnson's "neglect in the administration of wild and dangerous medicines." Instead of dispensing "soothing remedies" on the night of Mrs. Storey's death, Johnson gave "a *hypo-dermic injection*, and departed." The effect of the injection was "frightful," and Johnson could not be reached again because he was busy with a society meeting "of which society he has been busying himself many months past, to the neglect of his patients and his own legitimate business." The last paragraph broadened the scope of attack to include the entire medical profession.[13]

The next evening, the Chicago Medical Society met to consider the case. By unanimous agreement the meeting concluded that "Wilbur F. Storey is ignorant of medicine, and his cards are full of assumptions." A resolution stated "Dr. Johnson's position in the medical profession, and his high standing in this city, does not require any endorsement as to his capacity on the part of the society."[14]

But Storey refused to be rebuked by the action of "a dozen members of the medical society, most of whom are chiefly distinguished for their obscurity." He repeated his charges in full, and also published a full-column letter signed "M." The letter, "not written anonymously to avoid public responsibility—the author's name may be acquired by a call upon the editor of the Times," was purportedly written by a doctor of medicine with ten years successful practice. It praised Mr. Storey for his courage "in doing so great a sacrifice [in speaking] of so delicate a subject." The writer concluded "Who is to say what the result would have been had the physician not made his call on that January 20, 1873. Let us take the lesson and handle precious lives more carefully in the future."[15]

Storey continued to pillory Johnson for almost four months.

12. *Ibid.*, July 24, 1873.
13. *Chicago Sunday Times*, July 27, 1873.
14. *Chicago Tribune*, July 29, 1873.
15. *Chicago Sunday Times*, August 3, 1873.

Most of the editor's statements were repetitions of the original charges, and Dr. Johnson stood the attack in silence. Then, his patience finally exhausted, the physician published a terrible reply in the *Tribune*. His account reproduced in full his notes on the case of Mrs. Storey. In all, the physician succeeded in refuting Storey's charges in every particular. But Dr. Johnson "was not satisfied with a vindication of his professional conduct in the case." Instead he added full particulars on the syphilitic condition of Storey, and suggested that something other than pneumonia might have caused Mrs. Storey's death. Storey's reply was one last blast at Johnson in which he declared "the world may set me down as a dog if I do not ruin the man who killed my wife."[16]

Beginning in the autumn of 1873 Storey's newspaper became the editorial organ of "SPIRIT INTERCOURSE." The editor busied himself with rambling, at times incoherent "proofs" of his new-found true dispensation. "Men dread annihilation," he wrote. "Strike out spiritualism and there drops a heavy veil between the living and the dead . . . which no human eye can pierce." How much better, Storey asserted, "to hope for a future in which life is divested of its burdens, and there will continue to exist only those burdens which constituted our greatest happiness in this life."[17]

The *Chicago Tribune*, impressed that "this new and startling departure, by a man of Mr. Storey's positive temper and wide notoriety, will create a profound sensation," opened its columns to the *Times* editor for a long discourse on "PSYCHICAL TELEGRAPHY." In it Storey "renounces forever communion with the Episcopal Church," to which he had never belonged, as he spoke of "mystic and invisible communications" that came to him alone. The *Tribune* added only one editorial comment. It hoped that "what is lost to sensational journalism by this extraordinary lapse, will be gained by sensational rope manipulation."[18]

During 1872-73, while much of Wilbur Storey's attention was thus diverted to spiritualism and personal assaults on the medical profession, the *Chicago Times* made a complete recovery from the fire. On March 5, 1873, the new *Times* building on the northwest corner of Washington Street and Fifth Avenue was occupied. For a decade it was recognized as the foremost newspaper plant in

16. Wilkie, pp. 206-7.
17. *Chicago Times*, September 23, 1873.
18. *Chicago Tribune*, January 27, 1874.

the West. The same year the daily edition expanded to twelve pages, and the Sunday to sixteen pages. The paper's news and feature material were unmatched in Chicago. The *Times* stationed exclusive correspondents at Washington, New York, Boston, Philadelphia, and at every state capital and important town in the Middle West. As a special edition celebrating the move into the new plant declared, "News is the pearl above price, to be searched for, regardless of time, trouble and expense."[19]

The growth of the news collection service, which after 1877 even extended to Europe, was indicated by the paper's telegraph tolls between 1872 and 1878:[20]

> 1872–$25,500; 1873–$26,400; 1874–$59,800; 1875–$72,000; 1876–$81,700; 1877–$88,000; 1878–$105,000.

Henry B. Chandler, father-in-law of *Times* reporter Charles S. Diehl and a part owner of the *Times* between 1869 and 1872, remarked of Storey's extravagance in the use of the telegraph that "it took all the ready money the paper could raise to pay the tolls . . . as the telegraph company demanded money in advance for every word received over the line."[21] Henry M. Hugunin, a *Times* reporter in the years following the fire, substantiated that "liberal compensation was always made for special dispatches." It was a rule of the office, said Hugunin, that "any item which would sell ten copies of the paper was always acceptable."[22] It was through such enterprise that within eighteen months of the Chicago fire Storey's *Times* regained its position as pre-eminent newspaper of the West. It did not surrender its ascendancy until after Storey's death.

Late in 1873, Wilbur Storey confided to Franc Wilkie, "I must have a woman about me. I cannot live without one." There were many ladies anxious to become the third Mrs. Storey, since by 1874 he was a millionaire whom many believed to be on the verge of total insanity.

Eureka Pearson Storey was born in Poughkeepsie, New York,

19. *Chicago Times*, March 15, 1873.

20. Obituary of Wilbur F. Storey, see material on "The Times after the Fire," *ibid.*, October 28, 1884.

21. Charles Sanford Diehl, *The Staff Correspondent, How the News of the World Is Collected and Dispatched by a Body of Trained Press Writers* (San Antonio: The Clegg Co., 1931), p. 53.

22. Henry M. Hugunin, "The Late Wilbur Fisk Storey and his Chicago Times," *Autograph Letter Book*, LXVI, pp. 181-84 (MSS in the Chicago Historical Society).

in 1846. She was the daughter of Benjamin Bissell, a Poughkeepsie merchant. In 1872 both her husband and her father died, and the young widow, accompanied by her mother, moved West to begin life anew in Chicago.[23] She met Storey sometime during the summer of 1874. Storey married Eureka on December 2, 1874, but the day prior to the ceremony he demanded that his intended bride sign an "Ante-Nuptial Contract" in which "said Eureka C. Pearson" agreed to perform "certain duties of a wifely nature" while she disowned "any right of dower or inheritance in the estate of the said Wilbur F. Storey." The agreement provided the bride with a yearly income of $10,000. It also stipulated that upon Storey's death, she would continue to receive that amount annually until she remarried.[24] Eureka tried for the next ten years to convince her husband to write a will nullifying the 1874 agreement. Her court actions after the editor's death so complicated a settlement of his estate that the *Chicago Times* was dealt a death blow.

Within eighteen months of his second wife's death, then, the editor of the *Chicago Times* was the laughing stock of Chicago. But Chicago did not laugh for long, for midway through 1874 Storey emerged from the spiritualist doldrums, a half-lucid madman who wreaked a terrible revenge. The "new course" of the *Times* was typified by the headline over a story dealing with a city council meeting in September, 1874:

BASTARD "CITY FATHERS."

Chicago's Prize Rummers Hold
Their Weekly Carnival at the
City Hall.

And As Usual, Disgrace the City
Over Which They Should
Exercise All Care.[25]

It was not long before such "RUPTURED REPUTATIONS" sought legal redress for libel. In the ten months between September, 1874, and May, 1875, no less than six "City Fathers" brought charges against Storey. A whole corps of attorneys was retained

23. Obituary of Mrs. Eureka C. Storey, *Chicago Times-Herald*, May 24, 1896.

24. For the complete text of the antenuptial contract see "Storey Sanity Hearing," *Chicago Times*, August 23, 1884.

25. *Chicago Times*, September 8, 1874.

by the *Times* to employ every dodge in the shyster's book. Franc Wilkie described the process as a "system of demurring and pleading, the deliberate absence of witnesses, the taking of action we knew would not be sustained—anything to delay so as to worry and wear out the plaintiff and sometimes drive him from the field."[26] The tactic was illustrated when Councilman Ned Fairbank sued Storey in December, 1874. Edgar Assay pleaded the *Times* case on the grounds that one of the members of the Grand Jury who handed down the indictment "might have been over 60 years old" and "If that were so, we might have sucklings for grand jurors."[27] Every account of a libel case involving Storey examined by this writer for the post-fire period, included column reams of like pleadings that generally achieved the desired result. Either the charges were dropped, or the weary jury hung, or in case of conviction, infinitesimal damages were awarded. Little wonder that Wilbur F. Storey grew convinced that he was beyond the reach of the law. In point of fact, he was, as the course of the *Times* proved that the libel laws were insufficient to protect either private individuals or the community at large from his unreasoning thrusts.

In the spring of 1875 there were so many libel cases pending against the *Chicago Times* that an exact count cannot be determined. Franc Wilkie gave the figure as twenty-one civil and three criminal indictments. The three criminal indictments grew out of suits brought by attorney Samuel Ashton and City Councilman James McGrath, and a Grand Jury indictment for publication of an obscene newspaper.

The obscene newspaper charge grew out of a January, 1875, story in the *Times* about the "Can-Can Scourge." With respect to the entertainment, the account stated a dancer "exposes herself in a way which is surprising to one who does not believe in total depravity." It also described "striking and indecent attitudes" and "lacivious motions." The report concluded with details on the "particularly vulgar" last scene, and it was on the strength of this paragraph that the indecent publication indictment was returned.[28] Criminal Court Judge Erastus S. Williams stated in court that the article, with special reference to the conclusion, "was so lewd and indecent as to bring a flush of shame to the face of any pure man."

26. Wilkie, p. 232.
27. *Chicago Times*, December 13, 1874.
28. *Ibid.*, January 4, 1875.

Samuel Ashton, a County Commissioner who lost in a re-election bid in November, 1874, based his case upon an article published in the *Times* three weeks after the election that stated Ashton could leave office with the knowledge that there was not one man in the community "who believes that he has ever performed an official act without having been instigated thereto by some mean or other mercenary motive."[29] Councilman McGrath's case grew out of a similar type of abuse, which included references to him as "a jailbird councilman" and a "fifth-rate politician."

When the Cook County Grand Jury returned the indictments in March, 1875, one of the most sensational chapters in the entire history of *the press* v *the bench* began. Storey determined to terrorize the Grand Jury into rescinding the indictments, and he began his assault on Sunday, March 14, with an editorial headed "DISREPUTABLE VENGEANCE." In it Storey charged "this action . . . is not in the interest of justice or decency, but wholly in the interest of the rascally element that controls the city and county."[30]

Two days later the *Times* described the members of the Grand Jury that returned the indictments as

> men who . . . are themselves immaculate. Their social relations are of the highest, and their private lives are the purest. . . . Not one of these gentlemen but has a record of the most lofty character. Not one of them is a "sport" or a bummer. Not one of them has a bastardy case on his hands. Not one of them keeps a one-third interest in a notorious prostitute; not one is a male strumpet; not one of them is a notorious companion of abandoned women and a regular frequenter of brothels.[31]

Such abuse only hardened the opposition against Storey on this occasion. Samuel Ashton was confronted with "Some Earnest and Dispassionate Statements" in the *Times* of March 27 that described him as a lawyer "second to none in the qualities of unreliability, a resort to petty and disreputable tricks and evasions." Storey also complained that one of the members of the Grand Jury which returned the indictments insured the case was stacked against the editor:

> General [William T.] Sherman, prominent among the men composing [the Grand Jury], was overheard to say in the

29. *Ibid.*, November 28, 1874.
30. *Chicago Sunday Times,* March 14, 1875.
31. *Chicago Times*, March 16, 1875.

> Sherman House saloon, that the editor of this newspaper is a "God damned old son of a bitch," and he further exhibited against him a feeling of bitter hatred which he expressed in language too profane and indecent for publication.[32]

The judge of the Cook County Criminal Court in March, 1875, was the Hon. Erastus S. Williams. He had been a Chicago attorney since 1856, and a county judge since 1862. In his long career, he had built a reputation for impartiality and fairness in dispensing justice.[33] On one occasion, ironically, Williams even earned the approbation of the *Chicago Times* for a verdict beneficial to the interests of that journal. That was in 1865, when Storey was involved in his first brawl with a member of the Chicago judiciary.

In August, 1864, a Chicago war widow named Massina McMurray brought suit in Superior Court against Judge Van H. Higgins. Mrs. McMurray charged that Judge Higgins had defrauded her of some property after the death of her husband. Since Higgins was a well-known Republican and a stockholder in the *Chicago Tribune,* the *Times* sided with the widow and played the case for all it was worth.[34]

On August 16, 1864, Judge Higgins sued Storey for $25,000 because Storey charged the judge had "induced" Mr. McMurray to enlist in the army in order that Higgins might defraud Mrs. McMurray. Litigation in the libel case, heard in Cook County Circuit Court, lasted from September 29, 1864, until December 8, 1865. During the trial, Storey's attorneys found sufficient evidence to substantiate the war widow's charges of fraud. With Storey thus placed in the role of protector of the helpless and the downtrodden, Higgins decided against letting the libel case go to the jury and withdrew his charges.[35]

After Higgins' dismissal move, Storey lauded Judge Erastus S. Williams as "an eminent jurist" for his conduct of the case. The editor claimed to have published the original story against Higgins "to make the public aware of his conduct" since he was a judge, and thus connected with the administration of public affairs. In a concluding paragraph, Storey spoke of the power of the press

32. *Ibid.*, March 27, 1875.

33. Joseph and Caroline Kirkland, *The Story of Chicago* (Chicago: Dibble Publishing House, 1894), II, 430.

34. *Chicago Times,* August 15, 1864.

35. *Ibid.*, August 17, 1864, September 29, 1864, October 26, 1864, January 4, 1865, April 2 and April 4, 1865, and November 28 through December 9, 1865.

to crush any individual guilty of a gross wrong. "The power which we wield," Storey pledged, "shall be wielded in the future for the protection and conservation of the public weal, and never for the gratification of a personal malice."[36]

On March 29, 1875, "eminent jurist" Erastus S. Williams, exasperated beyond further toleration, decided to sentence Storey to jail for contempt of court. In announcing his decision, the judge stated "if the present spectacle was never before presented in the history of American jurisprudence, it is because never before in the history of American journalism has such an outrage been committed upon the rights of jurors." In his decision, Judge Williams summarized exactly what Storey did to the city of Chicago.

"I doubt whether any city in the United States has been the scene of such events as have been transpiring in Chicago for the past few weeks," the judge began. This was because a leading public journal had been persistently employed to undermine the public confidence in the officers and juries of the only criminal court existing in the city. "Far better for the cause of justice," said Williams, "that the editor should be privileged to intrude, pistol in hand, into the grand and petit jury rooms, and overawe the jurors with threats of personal violence" than to intrude upon them with "the far more fearful instrument of cruelty to any honorable man, a libelous and abusive press."

Williams added that Storey had no special privilege because he was associated with a widely circulated daily newspaper, but he had infinitely greater power than most men, and he used that power with sinister intent. "Extreme cases deserve extreme remedies," he said. Since the defendant was the only editor in the United States who, "by a series of articles he published in his paper day after day, AND INCREASING IN VENOM, has deliberately, and persistently attempted to destroy the efficiency of a court of justice," a simple fine would not do. Therefore, Storey "will stand committed to the jail of this county for ten days." To insure that Storey would serve the sentence, Williams also denied bail in the case.[37]

Judge Williams' observation that "no other city in the United States has been the scene of such events as have been transpiring in Chicago" would hold true for Storey's entire Chicago career. What other editor in any other American city carved such an in-

36. *Ibid.*, December 9, 1865.
37. *Ibid.*, March 30, 1875.

credibly distinctive record? Who else in the entire history of American journalism could boast a reckoning that included suppression by the United States Army on charges of treason; a public horsewhipping by a burlesque dance troupe; the creation of a special school for female typesetters in order to beat the Typographical Union; an unremitting assault upon a prominent physician who accidentally raised the editor's ire; the conversion of a prominent public journal into an organ of a crank pseudoreligious sect; and finally an attempt to intimidate the legal system of one of the foremost municipalities in the United States? The record is clear. Nowhere in the history of American journalism has such conduct been so persistent, or, it must be added, so successful. Because even on the one occasion that earthly justice caught up with Wilbur F. Storey, he escaped punishment.[38]

Storey spent exactly ten hours in the city jail before a writ of *Supercedeas* was granted by judge W. K. McAllister of the Illinois Supreme Court. The high court issued the writ on the grounds that Judge Williams had erred in citing Storey for contempt of court. According to the high court the publication of a libel on a grand jury, or any member thereof, in relation to any act already done by them which has no tendency to impede, embarrass or obstruct them in the discharge of duties remaining after the publication is made, cannot be summarily punished as contempt of court. The court admitted Storey's publications tended to bring odium upon the administration of law. "That this is a grave offense, deserving of prompt and severe punishment," said Judge Schofield, "might be conceded without in the slightest strengthening the position that it may be treated as contempt of court." In conclusion, the Supreme Court held that Storey had the right to make a defense that could only properly be tried by a jury.[39]

The morning after his release, Storey promised the readers of the *Times* that the newspaper "will undertake to show, . . . how far Judge Williams is qualified to occupy the conspicuous position, which he has just so flagrantly outraged." He began immediately, with a character sketch of the judge:

> A limited intellect grafted to an enormous vanity underlies and animates his judicial actions and permits him to believe

38. *Ibid.*

39. *Wilbur F. Storey* v *the People of the State of Illinois*, in *Reports of Cases At Law and in Chancery, Argued and Determined in the Supreme Court of Illinois*, LXXIX (Springfield, 1876), 45-53. Hereafter cited as *Illinois Reports.*

> he is beyond criticism and beyond contempt. . . . Will this compound of petty tyrant, this vain occupant of the judicial position, succeed in sending the world back to the 16th century? Probably not.[40]

Storey then loosed a barrage against Williams that lasted five weeks. On March 31, three-and-one-half columns of leaded minion, headed "THE MALIGNITY OF A CONTEMPTIBLE JUDGE," proved that the editor was still capable of incredible invective. The reference was no longer to Judge Williams, but to "Mr. E. S. Williams acting in the character of a judge."[41]

On April 1, even the "Mr." was dropped as the judge became simply E. S. Williams. Crude fillers appeared, such as "In estimating Williams, his constant liability to make an ass of himself must always be considered."[42] By April 5 Williams was compared to religious fanatics who used to "roast 'heretics,' crush the bones of old women's hands in the 'thumbkins,' cut out the tongues of Quakers, bore the ears of Ana-Baptists, burn witches, and fill the world with terrorism."[43]

The power of Wilbur F. Storey over the city of Chicago at this time was proved by the fact that not only were Judge Williams and the entire Cook County legal system powerless to stop his ravings in the spring of 1875, but in all three of the cases that caused the original uproar, not one verdict adverse to the editor was reached. Samuel Ashton decided to abandon prosecution without a trial after Franc Wilkie dug up some "derogatory facts about Ashton's early career" and threatened to use them in court if the case came to trial.[44] Alderman McGrath's case, a comic opera revolving around the proper definition of the term "jailbird," was heard in Cook County Criminal Court between April 29 and May 1, 1875. Franc Wilkie testified as a witness for the defense that the term "jailbird" was "just a slang term in common usage in Chicago." As Wilkie understood it, it was especially common "in politics, something like 'barnburner' or words of that kind. This is a local, Chicago meaning." Storey's counsel, Emery A. Storrs was concerned with the literal definition of the word:

> . . . it is not necessary to maintain that [McGrath] is a bird, that he has feathers and wings and a bill, that he goes around

40. *Chicago Times*, March 30, 1875.
41. *Ibid.*, March 31, 1875.
42. *Ibid.*, April 1, 1875.
43. *Ibid.*, April 5, 1875.
44. Wilkie, p. 234.

> chirping among the trees of a pleasant summer morning like any other bird. Now, if we are going to indulge in ornithological metaphors, what kind of a bird would he be? Truly, the most enthusiastic admirers of McGrath would not call him a canary, nor a cuckoo, nor a cock-robbin. . . . Nor is Jimmy McGrath an owl. He has no appearance of that. We would have to come to the conclusion that he was not a bird unless he was a cock of the wall, which hung around the commissioner's office. . . .

In all, Storr's presentation covered a column-and-a-half of type in the *Times,* and represented another advantage that Storey used in libel proceedings since such testimony, as a matter of public record, represented privileged communication. On May 1, the jury failed to agree on a verdict, and the McGrath case ended.[45]

No judge ever decided a case adversely to Storey's interests without feeling the effects of the editor's malice, a malice deep, persistent and unrelenting, which no lapse of time obliterated. "It may seem to forget its victim, seem to slumber," said the *Chicago Tribune,* "yet it does not; its slumber is the logicalness of the adder waiting its opportunity to strike."[46] The *Tribune* was prompted to make these remarks by Storey's last campaign against a Chicago judge when in May, 1879, he set out to prevent the re-election of Henry Booth to the Circuit Court of Cook County. Judge Booth first incurred the editor's wrath when he presided at a libel trial in 1871 which resulted in the heaviest assessment of damages ever rendered against the *Chicago Times.*

The grounds upon which the *Times* attacked Booth was, of all things, that the judge was irreligious and un-Christian because he professed the Unitarian faith. This, said the *Times,* made Booth unfit to sit on the bench. Since it was not in the nature of things that Booth's "arrogance of opinion, narrow prejudice, lack of impartial tolerance and illiberality of mind should be consonant with fitness for judicial office," Storey asked that the citizens retire the judge "to cultivate in private life that philosophy out of which he evolves such bitter intolerance and prejudice."[47]

The *Tribune* manifested unbelief at Storey's audacity. "W. F. Storey, *defender of the faith?*" it asked. "Orthodoxy needs no such

45. *Chicago Times,* Wilkie testimony, April 29, 1875; argument of Emery A. Storrs, April 30, 1875; final verdict, May 3, 1875.
46. *Chicago Tribune,* May 29, 1879.
47. *Chicago Times,* May 27, 1879.

defenders." The paper then offered a sketch of "him by whom the appeal is made" which rather accurately described the editor of the *Times* as "a man who has done more, through the agency of the paper which he publishes, to corrupt and demoralize the community . . . than any other man in it."[48] To the satisfaction of the *Tribune,* and perhaps symptomatic of Storey's declining influence as the ravages of disease began to take their final toll, Henry Booth was decisively victorious on June 7.

The libel case which precipitated Storey's initial displeasure with Judge Booth grew out of a little noticed story that the *Times* published in September, 1868, on its city page. It was headed "OVER-DRINKING" and told how a Canal Street saloon keeper named James Wallace died suddenly while tending his bar. "In 1861 he enlisted, and was absent three years. On his return he was astounded to find an infant child in his wife's arms—progeny which he could not father. He left his wife, and has since that time drank very hard."[49] The story caused no immediate excitement since it was typical of the sort of thing *Times* reporters regularly dug up in coroner's courts.

About two weeks after publication, Mrs. Mary Wallace of Muskegon, Michigan, showed up at the *Times* office and demanded a retraction. She brought with her a signed affidavit from Dr. S. W. Leonard of Muskegon attesting that Mr. Wallace was at home at the proper time previous to the child's birth. An article was then prepared in her presence that stated the original story "did great injustice to a worthy, hard working woman." Mrs. Wallace expressed satisfaction with the retraction and was promised it would be published the following day. The next day was Sunday, and in the Sunday edition, the retraction was published. It was not published or referred to in any subsequent paper.[50]

Mrs. Wallace returned home and "awaited very eagerly for the promised retraction." But the *Sunday Times* did not go to daily subscribers in Muskegon, and believing the retraction had not been published, on September 29, 1868, the widow began libel proceedings against Storey. There were three trials. In the first the jury found for the plaintiff $3,850 for damages, but the court set the amount aside as excessive. In the second case, the jury did

48. *Chicago Tribune,* May 29, 1879.
49. *Chicago Times,* September 8, 1868.
50. *Wilbur F. Storey et al.* v *Mary Wallace,* in *Illinois Reports* (Springfield, 1872), LX, 52-53.

not agree. In the third, the jury again found for the plaintiff a verdict of $2,500, and Judge Henry Booth upheld the verdict.[51]

Storey then appealed the case to the Illinois Supreme Court. The grounds for the appeal were first, that the libelous paragraph was only a statement of evidence given at the coroner's inquest, and hence the publication was privileged; second, that the publication of the retraction was an accord and a satisfaction; and third, that the judgment should be reversed because of excessive damages.

The court found against Storey on all three points. That the plaintiff was guilty of adultery, said the court, was stated as fact on the authority of the newspaper, and not as evidence upon inquest. It was "a monstrous libel," given with all of the weight of the authority of the *Chicago Times*. Equally untenable, said the court, was the contention that publication of the retraction was sufficient to allay damages.

The final argument, that $2,500 was excessive, was held to be likewise untenable. The court concluded that it was a case of cruel libel published merely to make a paragraph. The persons in charge of such publication gave no thought that the retraction should receive the same publicity as the libel, though "the latter had outraged the sensibilities and sullied the character of an innocent and unoffending woman." The jury, the court conjectured, probably meant to show by the verdict that persons thus libeled need not resort to acts of violence for redress. "It would ill become this court to teach a different lesson."[52]

Mary Wallace's award of $2,500 damages represented the largest libel settlement Storey was ever forced to pay. But hers was not the only instance when the *Times* "outraged the sensibilities and sullied the character of an innocent and unoffending woman." For "outraged womanhood" was a constant adversary of Storey in the 1870s, and the instance of the most spectacular libel case in Illinois during that decade.

On May 26, 1874, Storey received two letters from Rockford, Illinois. One was addressed to Storey personally, and signed "J. H. Blodgett, West Side High School." The other was addressed "To the editor of the Times," and signed "Junius." To the second letter was appended a postscript that stated "the occurrence is well-known in the neighborhood of the parties, as Mr. Early let the cat out,

51. *Ibid.*, 53.
52. *Ibid.*, 54-57.

and Mrs. Crawford understood it as her legal lord came tearing home with nothing on but his shirt." The postscript was signed "L. A. Trowbridge, Municipal Bank." Storey glanced at the letters, "read far enough to ascertain that they related to some scandal," and referred them to a city reporter, Charles Atwood, with a request that Atwood write an article embodying the facts revealed in the two letters.[53] The following day, Atwood's article was published in the *Times:*

FORBIDDEN FRUIT.

A Rockford Roué Caught Poaching in the Garden of a well-Known Legislator.

[*Special Correspondence.*]

> Rockford, Ill., May 25— . . . . The *dramatis personae* in the affair are the Honorable R. F. Crawford, . . . an attorney by profession, an old roué by practice, nevertheless occupying a high social position; Alice, the twenty year old daughter of Senator John Early, a plump young miss of great personal attractions, and one who has some notions of her own regarding "forbidden fruit"; . . . and the Senator himself. . . . Just how long the seducer had been plying his wiles, or just how much the frail Alice frowned upon his lecherous advances, is not apparent, but the denouement would indicate that the fruit was ripe for plucking.
>
> During the night the Senator heard a faint scream. . . . Imagining her beset by burglars, he rushed up to her room, reaching it just in time to see the form of his daughter's seducer disappearing through the window.[54]

On May 29, John Early, a Republican state senator, began trespass proceedings against Wilbur F. Storey for publishing falsehoods defaming the character and reputation of his daughter. Storey ascertained that J. H. Blodgett was the principal of West Side High School in Rockford, and L. A. Trowbridge was associated with a bank there. On June 1 he sent reporter Frederick

53. William C. Goudy, Brief for an appeal from the Superior Court of Cook County, *Wilbur F. Storey* v *Alice A. Early*, Supreme Court of Illinois, Northern Grand Division, September Term, 1875 (in Illinois State Historical Library, Springfield).

54. *Chicago Times*, May 27, 1874.

F. Cook to find the authors of the incriminating letters and ascertain the facts in the case.

Cook spent six days in Rockford and established beyond doubt that the letters were forgeries. Cook reported that the whole story "is a base fabrication, conceived in malice and executed with devilish ingenuity by which the Times was innocently made a party." Cook's retraction stated no young lady in Rockford stood higher than Miss Early in the esteem of her neighbors for possessing "all of those winning qualities which are the especial charm of innocent maidenhood." With respect to Mr. Crawford, Cook reported "it is but necessary to look at him" to establish that his participation in such an episode "is absolutely ludicrous."

In a short notice on the editorial page, Storey directed readers to Cook's dispatch and added the whole business was "one of the most outrageous conspiracies on record to defame the characters of two estimable residents." To prove his good faith, the editor offered $1,000 for information leading to the arrest and conviction of the forger.[55] During the next three years the entire resources of the *Chicago Times* were unable to uncover the identity of the mysterious "forger" who mailed the incriminating letters to Storey.

The Alice Early libel case opened in the Superior Court of Cook County in September, 1874. Judge Josiah McRoberts, a close friend of Criminal Court Judge Erastus S. Williams, presided. The case was not given to the jury for a verdict until April, 1875. According to Illinois law at that time, when a defendant in a libel case did not attempt to justify publication, he might mitigate damages in two ways. One, he might establish the general bad character of the plaintiff. Two, he might show circumstances that tended to disprove malice.[56] Since all evidence indicated that Alice Early was indeed a young woman of impeccable character, Storey's counsel, William C. Goudy, built his entire defense upon "circumstances which tended to disprove malice."[57]

During the trial, Storey and other witnesses for the *Times* went to elaborate lengths to establish the purity of Alice Early and to show that Storey had no personal knowledge of either Miss Early or her father prior to the libelous publication. Storey himself testified that "it is customary to publish stories without sending agents

55. *Ibid.*, June 8, 1874.

56. *Wilbur F. Storey* v *Alice A. Early*, in *Illinois Reports* (Springfield, 1878), LXXXVI, 461.

57. Goudy, Brief for an appeal.

to procure verification . . . in advance." At a crucial point in the litigation, Judge McRoberts disallowed the introduction of the forged letters as evidence by the defense because "they might excite a suspicion" that Alice Early had been guilty of fornication.

In his final remarks to the jury, McRoberts instructed them in part as follows:

> If . . . Wilbur F. Storey acted recklessly or wantonly, or without due care . . . then the jury are at liberty to find against the defendant exemplary or vindictive damages.
>
> and
>
> If the jury should find the defendant guilty . . . in determining the amount of the damage, the jury may consider the wealth and standing of the defendant.[58]

On April 29, the jury found for Alice Early to the extent of $25,000 damages. Goudy moved immediately for a new trial, and was informed by Judge McRoberts that no new trial would be allowed unless Storey remitted $10,000 to the court. This Storey did, and on May 8, the motion for a new trial was heard.

These events occurred, it should be remembered, within six weeks of Storey's assault upon Judge Williams and the Grand Jury, and within a week of the dismissal of James McGrath's libel case against the editor. Judge McRoberts, with a jury verdict in his hands against Storey, was the only judge in Cook County in the position to exact revenge for the judiciary. Accordingly, he overruled the motion for a new trial and rendered judgment against Storey, although he did reduce the damages to $15,000. Goudy then initiated an appeal to the state supreme court.[59]

In an editorial a few days after the decision, Storey complained about the verdict. He boasted how the *Times* "rooted out the vile slander" against Alice Early and "published to thousands who never otherwise would have known her, the purity of her name."[60] In the months that followed, Storey pursued a course of "strategic delay" before his appeal was heard by the supreme court. The tact of "circumstances which might disprove malice" did not strike the editor as the most feasible when there was another road to travel. Why not "establish the general bad character" of Alice Early?

58. *Ibid.*
59. *Ibid.*
60. *Chicago Times*, May 12, 1875.

In line with this strategy, Goudy undertook steps to delay the high court hearing as witnesses were "ill," or new evidence "was being gathered," or any of a dozen ruses was invoked. In the meantime, Franc B. Wilkie set out to uncover dirt, by whatever means necessary, about the girl who by the *Times* own admission "possesses all of those winning qualities which are the especial charm of innocent maidenhood." Before the Early litigation ended, Wilkie himself was involved in a separate court case charged with "conspiracy to defame the name and character of Alice A. Early."

On October 1, 1875, Wilkie, in the company of a Rockford resident named Patrick Flynn, visited the business office of a Rockford merchant named John Graham "to talk over the Early matter." In the course of the conversation, Wilkie and Flynn offered Graham a bribe if he would sign an affidavit "in which there would be serious reflections on the character and virtue of Alice Early." But Graham would not "thus defile paper or use his pen for a purpose so vile." Instead, John Graham informed Senator John Early of the matter. When Wilkie subsequently appeared in the Boone County Circuit Court to answer charges of conspiracy, he claimed "I gave birth to no utterance and performed no act" calculated to harm Alice's reputation. Rather, said Wilkie, "there were in existence rumors which tended to shade the character of the said Alice, and I endeavored to get to the bottom of said rumors in order to submit such information to the counsel of W. F. Storey."[61]

After failing to get John Graham to perjure himself, Wilkie and Flynn next discovered a former Rockford resident named Andrew Jepson. On November 1, 1875, in a saloon at 17 South Halstead Street, Chicago, Wilkie and Flynn plied Jepson with whiskey until he signed a statement that "Alice Early visited me at my house in Rockford, Winnebago County, at various times while I lived there." Jepson later claimed in court that he meant nothing incriminating by the statement, and did not know the use which Wilkie and Flynn intended to make of it.[62]

It was on the basis of the Graham and Jepson episodes that Franc Wilkie and Patrick Flynn were sued by John Early for conspiracy. When the trial opened in February, 1876, the defense moved for a continuance, which was granted until September. When the case reopened on September 12, a further continuance was found necessary on the basis of a physician's affidavit that

61. *Ibid.*, February 15 and February 16, 1876.
62. *Ibid.*, February 16, 1875.

"Franc B. Wilkie is sick and cannot appear in court."[63] Finally, after further delaying tactics, the conspiracy charges against Wilkie and Flynn were dismissed in January, 1877.

During the course of these delays, the *Chicago Times* published a series of attacks upon politician John Early who initiated proceedings in the case so that he could use and imperil his daughter's reputation "for the atrocious purpose of securing political and monetary advantages." According to the *Times*, all that "the Early faction" wished was publicity in order to secure votes, "a most reprehensible political ambition."[64]

By 1877, it became apparent that efforts to ruin the reputation of Alice Early would not succeed, and William C. Goudy proceeded with the appeal of the original verdict. Goudy's brief argued that an error was committed by the court in the original trial when Judge McRoberts refused to admit the forged letters as evidence. Judge McRoberts was in further error, said Goudy, in assessing judgment for a sum "not found by an impartial jury." Finally, according to Goudy, Alice Early was not damaged monetarily by the libel. "Not one dollar of actual pecuniary damage was proved by the plaintiff." Therefore, since $15,000, "a large fortune in itself," represented an excessive sum "it needs no argument to convince an unbiased mind that the verdict must have been produced by passion or prejudice."[65]

The Supreme Court of Illinois heard the appeal in the September term, 1877. The court found for Storey with respect to the admissibility of the forged letters in mitigation of his liability. The majority opinion held that Storey's proof that the letters were forgeries furnished a vindication of Miss Early's purity "more complete than could any verdict of a jury."[66]

The court also found that Judge McRoberts' sixth instruction to the jury, that in fixing damages for the plaintiff "the wealth and standing" of the defendant might be properly considered, was improperly given. "It is not perceived," said the court, "how the injury actually done to the plaintiff by the publication of this libel could be affected by Storey's wealth."[67]

On the basis of these two points, Storey won his appeal. It was not a unanimous decision. Justice Scott, with Justice Sheldon

63. *Ibid.*, September 13, 1876.
64. *Ibid.*, February 15 and September 13, 1876.
65. Goudy, Brief for an appeal.
66. *Storey* v *Early, Illinois Reports*, LXXXVI, 464.
67. *Ibid.*, p. 465.

concurring, felt that the publication of the libel was completely unjustified. It was not legitimate news fit for publication, and if Storey wished such scandalous matter to appear in the columns of his paper, "he ought, in justice to the parties accused, to have first ascertained whether it was true or false." Not to do so, said Justice Scott, showed a reckless disregard for the rights and feelings of innocent parties. Therefore, "believing there is no error in the record, the judgment ought to be affirmed."[68]

But the majority decision was three to two for Storey as the earlier judgment of the Superior Court against him was reversed. Despite the fact that John Early died in the summer of 1878, the Early family began the case all over again and in 1879 a verdict for $500 was finally found against Storey. While "the fair Alice" might not have won the judgment the libel deserved, she was witness to nature's retaliation against Storey, a man against whom human laws had proved inadequate. In the retrial, Storey's last performance before a jury of his peers, he was but a pathetic figure representing the ravages of dissipation. Partially paralyzed by a stroke, his speech "a frightful mumbling of incoherent sounds," Storey sat "unknowing and unanswering" as Goudy attempted to elicit the editor's testimony.[69]

In addition to the Mary Wallace and Alice Early libel suits, and the public beating by Lydia Thompson and Pauline Markham, Wilbur F. Storey was party to one other sensational episode in the 1870s involving "outraged womanhood." It concerned Ann Eliza Young, twenty-seventh and last wife of Mormon prophet Brigham Young, and resulted in the near ruination of Mrs. Young's career as a star on the Lyceum circuit.

In the summer of 1873, Ann Eliza Young deserted her husband and sued him for divorce. In November she escaped from Utah and began a cross-country tour with Redpath's Lyceum, lecturing on the subject "A WOMAN'S STORY OF POLYGAMY." She was accompanied in her travels by a close friend and adviser, Major Chauncey Pond. Her subject was a natural to excite curiosity, and Mrs. Young drew capacity audiences. About February 13, 1874, a lecture was scheduled at Bloomington, Illinois. Present in the audience was a "Special Correspondent" of the *Chicago Times*. On February 18, Storey's newspaper had an exclusive, date lined "Bloomington, Ill., Feb. 17."

68. *Ibid.*, p. 466.
69. Wilkie, p. 239.

The article began with a review of Mrs. Young's Bloomington lecture, but after a paragraph the correspondent was ready "to come to the most absorbing interest of our story." This dealt with how Major Pond, "handsome . . . arrayed in the height of fashion and conversing with a fluent and oily tongue," enjoyed "the greatest familiarity" with "the fair lecturess." The night clerk and the chambermaid at the Ashley House Hotel in Bloomington were both quoted to the effect that "the gallant major had remained with the lovely ex-Mormon during the night." But the real proof of fornication was furnished the next evening, when the couple boarded the Jacksonville train to keep Mrs. Young's next lecture appointment. "The conductor of the train . . . saw the parties (the fair Mormon and her Don Juan) enter the sleeping car together . . . and behind the curtains their licentious conduct was clearly proved." The story ended by noting that this revelation was made only to furnish the public "with the plain unvarnished truth" so that the true character of the woman was understood. In that way, "Christian communities" were afforded "protection from imposition by the wonderful stories and immoral conduct of the frail but beautiful Ann Eliza."[70]

The story shocked Ann Eliza and Major Pond. They concluded that "Brigham's money" was behind it, an ironic thought since Wilbur F. Storey would never have knowingly done anything to render aid and comfort to the Mormon prophet. Earlier in his career Storey had been a persistent critic of the Mormons, stating at one point their conduct proved that "no religious delusion can be so absurd that men and women will not embrace it." When President James Buchanan used force to crush the Mormon rebellion in 1857, Storey lauded the action and observed "although the Mormons may consider themselves 'chosen' in a spiritual sense, yet they will find themselves by no means 'elect' in terrestrial concerns."[71] Only one factor explained Wilbur Storey's publication of the Ann Eliza story. The woman had put herself in the public light with a series of lectures on a sensational topic, and the Bloomington correspondent used his vivid imagination to concoct a tale that he knew he could sell to the *Chicago Times.*

On February 19, there was more news for Mrs. Young and Major Pond in the *Chicago Times.* This time it was the Milwaukee correspondent who sent the tidings. In that city, Victoria Wood-

70. *Chicago Times*, February 18, 1874.
71. *Detroit Free Press*, June 14 and December 13, 1857.

hull, the nation's foremost advocate of free love, was interviewed after a lecture on her favorite topic. "I know of the truth of the scandal," Mrs. Woodhull asserted, "because I was in Bloomington at the same time Ann Eliza was lecturing there." Mrs. Woodhull's story was a complete fabrication, since she had been nowhere near Bloomington at the time of Ann Eliza's lecture.[72] But Victoria had no desire to criticize her fellow lecturer for "preaching one thing and practicing another." Quite the contrary! As an advocate of free love Mrs. Woodhull concluded "women should be encouraged to make love with whom they pleased, when they pleased, and where they pleased."[73]

Victoria Woodhull's confirmation of the scandal proved additionally disconcerting to Mrs. Young. Since it was published on the eve of her Boston appearance, she was "greatly distressed lest it should injure my prospects in that city." She recounted later that friends had taught her to consider "Reform and New England" as synonymous. "But after the attack by the Chicago paper, I regarded failure as certain."[74]

Despite the scandal, Mrs. Young was a success in Boston, and she and Major Pond investigated the origins of the story. The evidence indicated that the libel had its origins in a Bloomington barbershop when a customer who had admired Ann Eliza's beauty remarked "that Pond had a good thing of it." The Jacksonville train conductor, present in the shop, assented and added "the porter says Pond slept with her on the train, and I believe it." From here the story reached the ears of a reporter for the Bloomington *Pantagraph,* who wrote it as a feature and sent it to Storey.[75]

The Salt Lake City *Tribune,* the anti-Brigham Young organ in Utah, said the final word about the "lying and libelous" story with an attack on the editor who had printed it: "Storey has been publicly whipped upon the streets as a woman defamer. He is naturally a cynical, atrabilarious, cold-blooded creature; shunned by his race, and repaying this aversion with intense hatred."[76]

If madness can be said to have characterized the assaults of the *Chicago Times* upon prominent and private citizens alike, what is to be said of the news and editorial policy as a whole? A ran-

72. Irving Stone, *The Twenty-seventh Wife* (New York: Simon and Schuster Inc., 1962), p. 282.

73. *Chicago Times*, February 19, 1874.

74. Stone, pp. 283-84.

75. *Ibid.*, p. 290.

76. Salt Lake City *Tribune*, as cited in *ibid.*, p. 291.

dom sampling of the articles printed daily by the newspaper, would have included:

SPOUSE ROASTING.

The Massachusetts Husband Who Cooked His Wife in Kerosene.

A Sample of New England Conjugal Bliss.[77]

This appeared in November, 1871, shortly after the fire. In 1873:

THE ARSENIC FIEND.

Full Confession of Lydia Sherman, The Connecticut Arch-Murderess.

The Deeds of the Bloodthirsty Borgia Thrown into the Shade.

The Remorseless Murder of Three Husbands and Five Children.

A Story of Arsenic, Arsenic, Arsenic.

A Constant, Itching Temptation Which She Was Powerless to Resist.

She Becomes Pious At Last, and Wants to Go to Heaven.[78]

Beginning in 1874 a full page of leaded minion, headed "CRIME," took over page two. Every day, from all over the world, a potpourri of items such as the following was published:

A LECHER.

[*Special Telegram*]

Winona, Minn., Sept. 29.—There has been a great excitement in the town occasioned by a scandal that has recently come to light. A young man who has for some time past been teaching school in the neighborhood, has seduced several young girls, a number of whom are soon to become mothers.[79]

77. *Chicago Times*, November 21, 1871.
78. *Ibid.*, January 16, 1873.
79. *Ibid.*, October 1, 1874.

In 1875, when the famous "JERKED TO JESUS!" headline appeared, "CRIME," no longer sufficed as a general heading for the scandal page. It was replaced by short, alliterative notices such as "DOSES OF DEVILTRY," "DONE BY DEVILS," "THE GATES OF HELL," "THE DEVIL'S DIVERSION," "RAMPANT RAPE," "THE PREVAILING PUTRIDITY," or "SIMPLY DIABOLICAL."[80] There was no relief from the steady montage of gore and sensation, handsomely printed with the greatest magnificence that typographical technology offered in the 1870s. Any number of the newspaper provided its full share:

KNIVED IN A SALOON.

That Was the Manner in Which
Jack Galena Met His Death
Last Night.

In A Dirty Dive, Filled with
Low People, on West Lake St.[81]

The year 1876 brought "BELIAL'S BANQUET," "HADES HORDES," "ROASTED ON THE RAILS," "HORRID HERDS," "BELIAL'S BEASTLY BAND," and "CHOKE FOR CHOKE." Sometimes the decks offered further details:

HOLY HORRORS.

Mr. Buffum, The Connecticut Bible-
Banging Abortionist, Relieved from
Further Ministerial Duties.

The Testimony of His Wife Concerning His
Hideous Seductions, Rapes, and Villainies.

How He Confessed His Sins, How She Condoned
Them, and How He Piously Returned to the
Ways of the Ungodly.[82]

On March 15, 1879, the *Chicago Times* appeared in the last typographical renovation of a newspaper edited and published by Wilbur F. Storey. It became an eight-column, twelve- to sixteen-page sheet, and from a technical standpoint, took on the final mag-

80. *Ibid.*, December 2, December 1, November 30, November 12, November 11, November 29, and December 9, 1875.
81. *Ibid.*, October 27, 1875.
82. *Ibid.*, April 27, 1876.

nificence that marked it until after Storey's death. The new garb, however, did not change the newspaper's inner soul.

When the regular dispatches did not furnish sufficient sensation, the *Times* was not above resorting to "suppositious journalism." In the most flagrant case of news manufacturing to occur in Chicago in the 1870s, a Saturday edition in 1875 devoted four columns of the front page to a blazing fraud about a theater fire in which the audience roasted to death. The last deck of the headline, set in regular newsprint, told the real story:

Description of A Suppositious
Holocaust Likely to Occur Any
Night.[83]

J. H. McVickers, who operated the most popular theater in Chicago at that time, wrote a letter to the newspaper in which he described the bogus fire story as "the 'can-can' of journalism." Storey's *Times* was permitted to exist, said McVickers, only because "we Americans are so proud of the freedom of the press, we would not gag it by law, even from the utterance of falsehood and indecency."[84] McVickers received support from the *Chicago Tribune* which felt that "suppositious journalism, as upheld by the Chicago Times, does not, in the long run, pay."[85]

The *Tribune* may have been correct in its assertion that Storey's journalism hurt the reputation of the *Chicago Times.* But it was a gross overestimation of the journalistic sensibilities of the majority of Chicago newspaper readers to say the policy would not pay. By 1876, Storey was worth more than $1,000,000. As he prospered, his editorial policy became increasingly reactionary. Sandwiched between the personal diatribes that Storey prepared were learned disquisitions denouncing "radicalism." All reform proposals, from a graduated income tax to universal suffrage, were denounced in editorials that were usually the handiwork of Mort L. Hopkins.

As a champion of property and capital, the *Times* became so vigorous that it found itself allied with the *Tribune* and other big Chicago dailies in a unanimous assault upon Democratic presidential nominee Samuel J. Tilden in 1876. Except for a small weekly, the *National Observer*, only the foreign language press in the city supported the Democratic ticket. On October 14, the *National Ob-*

83. *Ibid.*, February 13, 1875.
84. *Ibid.*, February 15, 1875.
85. *Chicago Tribune*, February 15, 1875.

Vol. III. No. 5 CHICAGO, OCT. 14, 1876. Price, 5 Cents.

JUDGMENT DAY!

Tilden and Hendricks combined would be a trade-mark of political dishonesty that all honest citizens would spurn. * * Mr. Tilden being intrusted with a certain sum of money for specific purposes, diverts it from those purposes into his own bank account.—*Chicago Times.* (See page 2—The Truth.) Key to engraving see page 9, "Judgment day."

server published a front page cartoon [see cut] that depicted the party's plight. Captioned "JUDGMENT DAY!" it showed "the immaculate editor of the Chicago *Times*" who "has been instrumental in facilitating Tilden's downward course," as the leader of a band of good angels chasing the bad angels to perdition. The "good angels" led by Storey in the cartoon included "Plumed Knight" James G. Blaine and his oratorical champion, Robert Ingersoll; prominent Chicago Republicans John Wentworth and John Logan; Republican presidential nominee Rutherford B. Hayes; and the leading lights of the Republican press in the city: Joseph Medill of the *Tribune,* Charles Ham of the *Inter-Ocean,* Melville Stone of the *Daily News*, Andrew Shuman of the *Journal*, and William Taylor of the *Post.* Among the devils that this band drove out of paradise were Tilden and his running mate, Thomas A. Hendricks, Tammany's "Boss" Tweed and Chicago Democratic boss John Morrissey.[86]

Beginning sometime in the spring of 1876, Storey began to feel the first symptoms of paretic dementia. He underwent "periodic attacks, or dizziness," which Chicago physicians at first diagnosed as "billious upset." Austin L. Patterson, business manager of the *Times,* noticed the change first. "I thought his judgment was out a good deal at that time," said Patterson. "His idea was that he was worth a great deal of money, and he kept constantly wanting to go into debt . . . and his actions were so different from what they were before." With his newspaper firmly established as the leading morning daily in Chicago, Storey decided to expand his operation. The counsel of his friends and associates proved useless, and on May 31, 1876, a quarter-page advertisement in the *Chicago Tribune* announced "A NEW THING!" intended to gratify "a long suffering want of Chicago—a lively, newsy, sparkling afternoon newspaper."[87]

On June 5, the *Chicago Evening Telegraph* was born. It was published at the *Times* building, six days a week, with editions at 2:30 P.M. and 5:30 P.M. Despite lavish promotion and a spectacular outlay of cash, the *Evening Telegraph* barely survived the sum-

86. *National Observer*, October 14, 1876, as preserved in Joseph Boyd (compiler), "Scrapbook of Illinois and Chicago Politics, 1876," in Chicago Historical Society.

87. Wilbur F. Storey to Austin L. Patterson, March 29, 1878, letter entered as evidence in "Storey Sanity Hearing," *Chicago Times*, August 29, 1884; see also the testimony of Austin L. Patterson at the sanity hearing, *ibid.*; and the testimony of Austin L. Patterson, "The Storey Estate," *ibid.*, November 15, 1884; and *Chicago Tribune*, May 31, 1876.

mer until it died on September 7. A largesse estimated by Patterson at $1,000 a day proved insufficient as Storey's only experiment in chain journalism ended in complete failure.

With the evening field closed to him, Storey soon sought other ways to expand his operation through huge expenditures of cash. In June, 1877, with the Russo-Turkish war raging in Europe, he made arrangements with Franc Wilkie to establish the first foreign office opened by any midwestern newspaper in Europe. In the months that followed, Wilkie kept up a steady flow of dispatches to the *Times* on such subjects as rumors from the front, war sentiment amongst the English, Irish news, and men and manners of London. Wilkie's "forwarding of cable news of an interesting nature, entirely apart from war news," was considered an extraordinary innovation by an American newspaper; and, according to Charles S. Diehl, "that this was by a paper published in the Middle West added to the daring of the venture." In September, 1877, Wilkie was joined by his son, John, and father and son proceeded to supply Chicago readers with eyewitness accounts of such events as the Pan-Presbyterian convention at Edinburg, Scotland, and in May, 1878, the International Exposition in Paris.[88]

It was while the *Times* partially redeemed itself by such spectacular enterprise that Storey learned the exact nature of his ailment and the fate that awaited him. In June, 1877, his sister, Mary Farrand, visited Chicago and was informed by her brother of the diagnosis. According to Mrs. Farrand, Storey asked her "Why have I worked so hard, and accumulated money, and planned, and given all my years to building up a great business, when I know that at any moment I may become a helpless mass?"[89]

In the months that followed, Storey's periodical attacks became more frequent and prolonged, and in March, 1878, the editor visited the health resort at Hot Springs, Arkansas. He was accompanied by his wife, and sought treatment to alleviate his symptoms and a diagnosis more encouraging than that given by Chicago doctors. He received the latter when specialists at Hot Springs informed him the dizziness was prompted by a "cerebral lesion" caused by "an overtaxed brain." As a remedy, Storey was advised "I should not write, read or think for the next six months." If he followed this advice, and coupled it with a vacation "in the Rocky Mountains

88. Wilkie, pp. 242-56; and Diehl, p. 54.

89. Obituary of Wilbur F. Storey, see the statement of Mary E. Farrand, *Chicago Times*, October 28, 1884.

for three or four weeks," Storey was told he could look forward to "fifteen or twenty years of active work." Encouraged by this report, the editor returned to Chicago about April 3 to make preparations for a trip to Colorado.[90]

Once he was back in Chicago, however, Eureka Storey took matters in hand. She convinced her husband that an extended ocean voyage, followed by a tour of western Europe, would prove far more beneficial and relaxing than three weeks in the Rocky Mountains. Despite the objections of friends and associates that he was not physically up to the rigors of such a voyage, in the last week of April the couple sailed for England. In mid-May, after an uneventful crossing, the Storeys checked in at the Westminster Hotel in London. Here Storey's first act was to send a wire to Franc Wilkie that requested the reporter to join him. Wilkie was in Paris to cover the International Exposition, and was surprised by Storey's visit. He came to London at once, and was "painfully astonished" upon seeing his employer.

Wilkie had not seen Storey since the previous June when he left Chicago to open the London bureau. Now, eleven months later, the reporter was appalled by the physical changes that had overcome his employer. The editor showed all of the symptoms of a man on the verge of a paralytic stroke.[91]

Despite her husband's physical deterioration, Eureka Storey insisted that they proceed with their plans. With Wilkie serving as guide, the three set out in late May on a tour that took them on long rides "through the beautiful hedges and farms of England," across the channel to Waterloo, then to Amsterdam, the Zuider Zee, the cathedral at Cologne, and by late June, to Basle and Lucerne in Switzerland. On the entire tour Wilkie felt that Storey actually noticed nothing. "Mr. Storey seemed keenly and unfavorably impressed in a persistent environment of gloom," Wilkie noted. About June 20, as the party was preparing to leave Lucerne for Geneva, Wilbur F. Storey was felled by the first of a series of paralytic strokes.

Since adequate medical attention was not available in Lucerne, Franc Wilkie took the fallen editor to Paris. He stayed in the apartment of Chicago attorney Lambert Tree, an old friend, and Parisian specialist Dr. Brown-Sequand was called in to treat the case. The

90. Storey to Patterson, March 29, 1878, in *Chicago Times*, August 29, 1884.

91. Wilkie, p. 259.

doctor prescribed a moxa treatment for Storey and advised Wilkie to take him back to Chicago immediately. In the first week of August, with Wilkie's assistance, the Storeys arrived home.[92]

Shortly thereafter, Austin Patterson had occasion to consult Storey on a business matter. "I went to his house and saw him there," Patterson stated. He could not walk, and in Patterson's opinion manifested symptoms of lunacy. "It would appear, from what I know, that Storey has probably been insane, going insane, since the time of his second wife's death," Patterson concluded.[93]

Eureka C. Storey now moved to collect the final dividend as the wife of Wilbur F. Storey. Her marriage, of course, had already proved profitable. In 1877 the Storeys moved into a fashionable new house at 1834 South Prairie Avenue. Also, as the wife of Chicago's foremost newspaper publisher, Mrs. Storey was outfitted in a manner befitting a woman of her position. But the antenuptial contract of 1874 remained valid, and so long as it did Eureka was permanently precluded from inheriting Storey's wealth. Specifically, according to the agreement, she consented "to accept the provisions of this contract in lieu of any and all right of dower in and to the real and personal property of the said Wilbur F. Storey, and any part thereof, and of all right of inheritance under and from the said Wilbur F. Storey."[94] With her husband in a permanently enfeebled condition, Eureka began a concerted effort to get him to prepare a will revoking the 1874 contract.

Her first move was made in November, 1878. She effectively severed all contact between the editor and his relatives who lived in South Bend, Indiana. If Storey died intestate, with the 1874 agreement in effect, they stood to split his entire estate. Then, Mrs. Storey called Alfred S. Trude, Storey's attorney, to discuss the matter. She explained to Trude that she was devoted to her husband and provided good care for him, and thought therefore that she was the person most entitled to Storey's estate and property. She informed Trude that she could not live on the amount stipulated in the antenuptial agreement, but needed the home, control of the *Times*, "and enough to live on."[95]

92. *Ibid.*, pp. 260-67.

93. Testimony of Austin L. Patterson, "Storey Sanity Hearing," *Chicago Times*, August 29, 1884; and testimony of Austin L. Patterson, "The Storey Estate," *ibid.*, November 15, 1884.

94. "The Ante-Nuptial Contract," entered as evidence, "Storey Sanity Hearing," *ibid.*, August 23, 1884.

95. Testimony of Alfred S. Trude, "The Storey Estate," *ibid.*, November 15, 1884.

Storey had partially recovered from his first stroke by this time. He was able to converse a little, walk with help, and occasionally he even visited his office at the *Times*. Between November, 1878, and August, 1879, several drafts of a new will were drawn by Trude, all of them favorable to Eureka's interests. "I was drawing wills right along, off and on, for some considerable length of time," Trude testified. Most of these were drawn in the presence of the editor, with the provisions prompted by his wife as she reminded Storey "I love you Wilbur, and have taken good care of you. Remember how sick you were in Paris and Berne? And while you are getting better, and your health is improving, still it is a good idea to make a will in favor of those that love you best."

At one testament-writing session in June, 1879, Trude recalled that Mrs. Storey was called from the room for several minutes. "I ventured to remark to him about his sister Mrs. Farrand," Trude stated. Storey then remembered how Fairchild Farrand had helped him back in 1844 in Jackson, Michigan, and "he spoke of Mary in terms of endearment." When Mrs. Storey returned, the editor refused to consider a new will. Eureka then became angry, and informed Trude "You had better mind your own business and not be calling Mr. Storey's attention to subjects he does not ask for and that I do not suggest."[96]

Finally, on August 16, 1879, Storey signed a document that left his entire estate to his wife, except for $1,000 annually to his sister Mary, a brother Anson, and his niece and nephew, Mary Chapin Anderson and Edward Chapin.[97]

By late 1879, Storey had recovered his health sufficiently to attempt active direction of the *Times* once more. He also ordered construction of a mansion on the corner of Vincennes Avenue and Forty-third Street. Storey's "Marble Monstrosity," which the editor intended as "a permanent memorial" to himself, was described by the *Tribune* as "like a hennery. It is as much out of harmony with the interests of a dwelling-house as the thick walls of a prison for the building of a summer arbor or a floral conservatory." Storey visited the site of his proposed home almost daily in early 1880, and with each visit he changed the construction plans until the building "exhibited all the vagaries of a person laboring under some form of dementia." Ultimately he sank $250,000 into the

96. *Ibid.*

97. Will presented for probate by Eureka C. Storey, November 11, 1884, in *ibid.*, November 12, 1884.

project, which was never completed.[98] Sometime in late spring, 1880, Storey suffered a second stroke, and while recuperating he rediscovered spiritualism. More accurately, instead of recuperating, Wilbur F. Storey entered a period of almost total idiocy.

In June, 1880, Eureka Storey's mother, Mrs. Benjamin Bissell, moved into the Storey household on South Prairie Avenue. This was sure evidence of the editor's incapacitation, because he had forbidden the woman to ever set foot inside his home. Mother and daughter then hired a certain Mrs. Rose and installed her in the house as a permanent medium for the benefit of the master of the house. With Wilbur Storey playing the role of "Great Chief," and Eureka performing as "White Lilly," Mrs. Rose, as "Little Squaw," proceeded to keep the editor in contact with the other world. According to Alfred S. Trude who witnessed several of the sessions, "Whatever the spirits advised, Mr. Storey pliantly assented to." The spirits usually informed "Great Chief" that he should cut off his relatives from all consideration as heirs. "You ought to leave your property to those you love best so that when you go to the other world you will not be a roaming, rambling, troubled spirit, but you will be in a condition of peace," said the spirits. Under these influences, Storey prepared one last "final will and testament," a document that he partially signed in front of Alfred S. Trude and Austin L. Patterson at his *Chicago Times* office on February 1, 1881.[99]

From June, 1880, until May, 1882, Storey existed somewhere between madness and moments of seeming rationality. While his leisure hours were given over entirely to seances, he left the spirit world behind when it came to directing his newspaper. In the summer of 1880, Clinton A. Snowden was hired as *Times* managing editor. Since he had served on the city staff of the *Times* for several years prior to his promotion, Snowden was fully aware of Storey's mental condition. He was a young and ambitious man and determined to make the *Times* "the biggest thing on the continent." Storey's mental balance was unsettled enough that he went along with his new managing editor unquestioningly. With Snowden prompting the editor with delusions of grandeur, the *Chicago Times* entered its final phase of spectacular achievement. By 1882, Storey

98. Wilkie, pp. 269-70.

99. Testimony of Alfred S. Trude, "The Storey Estate," *Chicago Times*, November 15, 1884; will presented for probate on November 8, 1884, in *ibid.*, November 9, 1884.

was spending $625,000 a year, or about $12,000 a week, to produce a newspaper without peer in the Middle West.[100]

The focus was almost entirely on expansion of news services and spectacular feature innovations. With Storey willing to spend money at an unheard-of rate to improve the *Times*, Franc Wilkie suggested that the editor re-establish a European bureau. In January, 1881, the newspaper announced that Wilkie was going abroad to set up the "most completely organized and effective establishment of the sort in existence, maintained by an American newspaper." The bureau "will involve a very large cost, but the *Times* hesitates at no cost which involves the procurement of news," Storey boasted.[101]

Wilkie opened his office in February, 1881, at No. 6 Ogan Street, Strand. Under his direction, correspondents were hired and stationed at Berne, Rome, St. Petersburg, Berlin, Dublin, Paris, Cairo, "and in North Africa." By March, the *Times* was publishing exclusive dispatches from these points, in addition to a steady flow of interesting and informative feature material that Wilkie personally accounted for from London.[102]

At home, the newspaper moved to three morning editions, with the final one, published at 6:00 A.M., frequently containing local news less than two hours old. The front page of the "6 O'Clock A.M. edition" of January 6, 1881, for example, featured a lead story about a 4:00 A.M. fire on East Madison Street that included an interview with one of the survivors. The boldface of the headlines became larger, and the headlines themselves took on a sassy flavor less repellent than those that had characterized the *Times* of the 1870s.

By 1882, Storey was on the verge of total incapacitation. His periods of rationality became shorter and less frequent. He began to hear "angel's voices" and the "roar of heavenly chariots." At an editorial conference in the spring of that year, the editor suddenly stopped the proceedings when he pointed to the ceiling and exclaimed, "Do you hear that music? Do you hear the rumbling of those wheels? Look at it!"[103]

About this same time he created his last sensation for the Chicago press when he published a series of incoherent editorials set

100. Wilkie, p. 291; and *Chicago Times*, May 4, 1881.

101. *Chicago Times*, January 23, 1881.

102. Wilkie, pp. 291-92.

103. Testimony of Alfred S. Trude, "The Storey Estate," *Chicago Times*, November 15, 1884.

in bizarre type patterns. From the depths of a madness that could not completely obscure his typographical genius, Storey strained to find some new combination that would shatter the prevailing standard. Fonts usually reserved for display advertising were indiscriminately mixed with headline boldface and news print as the editor strove to outreach the typographical technology of 1882. Since display ads at this time frequently featured multi-column come-ons, the logical conclusion of Storey's experimentation was some form of multi-column typeset. Perhaps Storey stood on the threshold of breaking the bounds of the one-column rule in which headlines were confined. He did not succeed in the attempt, however, and the multi-column banner was forced to wait until the following decade.[104] But it was his last act as a newspaper editor.

In May, 1882, Storey entered the final phase of his disease when a third stroke left him totally paralyzed. As his death became certain, the editor's relatives moved to deny Eureka Storey control of his estate. In August, 1884, Mary Farrand, Edward Chapin, Mary Chapin Anderson, and Anson L. Storey petitioned the Cook County Probate Court to appoint a conservator with power to manage the *Times.* They claimed the rights of heirs at law. In an intervening petition, Eureka claimed Storey had prepared a will that bequeathed her the bulk of his property. She claimed familiarity with the management of the *Times,* and stated that since her husband was in feeble health, either she or someone suitable to her should be named conservator. The case was heard in August, and a jury found "Wilbur F. Storey mentally incapable of managing his business." Austin L. Patterson was appointed conservator of Storey's estate by the court, with power to manage the newspaper.[105]

Anson L. Storey was the only surviving brother of the editor in 1884. A resident of New York, he arrived in Chicago in July and secured a court order that forced Eureka to allow him to visit Wilbur. "I saw him several times and endeavored to converse with him," Anson testified. But Wilbur was unable to talk and showed no recognition of his brother. Storey's attending physician, Dr. Henry M. Lyman, described the editor in the summer of 1884 as "one in the condition of an automoton, that is giving response to impulses from without in an unintelligent way." Lyman concluded that Storey had no intelligent comprehension of any-

104. *Ibid.,* March and April, 1882, *passim.*
105. "The Storey Sanity Hearing," *ibid.,* August 23 and August 29, 1884.

thing. "There is no prospect whatever of his ever recovering his mind," said Lyman. "He can't live long."[106]

On October 27, 1884, the Storey heirs, upon being informed by Dr. Lyman that the editor's death would occur at any time, received a court order directing Eureka C. Storey to allow Mary Farrand, Edward Chapin, Mary Anderson and Anson Storey to visit her husband in his sickroom.[107] They were admitted to his residence late in the afternoon. At 9:15 P.M., with his family present only by the grace of the Probate Court, Wilbur F. Storey died. The Associated Press obituary the next day noted:

> When he could no longer wield the pen, the only gratification left him was to visit the *Times* office daily. Growing feebler, his appearance there became less frequent, and finally ceased. This to him was his death.[108]

When Storey died, he left an estate of $800,000 in cash and property, and a newspaper evaluated on November 4, 1884, at $1,000,000. In February, 1888, when his estate was finally settled, the entire worth had been reduced to less than $500,000. But at the moment he died, the *Chicago Times* was a great newspaper. Precisely what it meant to the city it served was indicated by a publication that Chicago hotels put out in 1883 as "A Stranger's Guide to the Garden City." The pamphlet noted that in 1860 the *Times* was published by five men, whereas in 1883 there were fifty men in the editorial and business departments alone. In addition there were over 400 telegraphic and special correspondents. The most prominent feature of the newspaper, according to the guide, was the lavish expenditure of money for every improvement facilitating the speedy gathering and printing of the latest news.

Pneumatic tubes connected the editorial rooms directly with the Western Union office, "over a block distant." All night long "brilliant jets" of electric lights "shine out of the editorial rooms upon the slumbering city," while the employees received news from all over the civilized world and set it in type for perusal by thousands the following morning. Promptly at 4:00 A.M. "the great half-cylinder shaped rolls of lead laden with news" were set in place in the eight presses that had a capacity of 10,000 copies per hour, or a combined capacity of 80,000 copies per hour. "As the

106. Testimony of Anson L. Storey and Dr. Henry M. Lyman, "Storey Sanity Hearing," *ibid.*, August 23, 1884.
107. *Ibid.*, October 28, 1884.
108. South Bend (Indiana) *Evening Register*, October 28, 1884.

weary workmen step out of the office, they find the building environed by newsboys, eagerly watching for the first copies from the press." This was "the nightly and daily routine at the great *Times* building," on the northwest corner of Washington and Fifth Avenue.[109]

Such was the achievement produced by forty-five years of unrelieved toil in midwestern journalism that began in March, 1838, at La Porte, Indiana, when an eighteen-year-old printer's devil from Vermont decided "to try my hand at a newspaper" with an investment of $200. When he died, a downstate neighbor, the *Peoria Transcript*, stated "Wilbur F. Storey left an imprint on the journalism of the 19th century left by no other newspaperman."[110]

In a sense, the *Transcript* was correct because no other career in American journalism exactly paralleled Storey's. He pioneered the modern Sunday newspaper. He was the first editor in the Middle West to offer serious competition to the eastern seaboard in the search for news. The imprint he left on journalism, of course, was part of the school that Pulitzer, Hearst, and later, Bernarr MacFadden carried to perfection. Still, and this must be emphasized, the *Chicago Times* with all of its meanness, led the way in the Middle West in blazing untrodden and unexplored paths for news that transformed the daily paper from a mere chronicle of local events into an epitome of the news of the world.

When the *Chicago Times* expanded into an eight-page daily on September 22, 1866, Wilbur Storey boasted that his enterprise was "UNPARALLELED IN WESTERN JOURNALISM." The boast was true, and should serve as his epitaph. Although he was completely broken in mind and body for two years before his death, Storey's unique accomplishment was recognized by his Chicago journalistic colleagues when they met at the Press Club to pay him tribute. Professor Rodney Welch, a former chemistry instructor at the University of Illinois who joined the *Times* as a science specialist in 1881, reminded the newsmen, of the day when the entire press west of New York City "was the laughing stock of the world." Even the few western newspapers of thoughtful opinion counted for nothing beyond the immediate neighborhood where they were published. "All that is changed today," Welch concluded. "It is known to each of us that the distinguished man who

109. *Chicago Illustrated and Descriptive . . . The City As it Appears in 1883* (Chicago: C. D. Relyea & Co., 1883), pp. 68-69.
110. *Peoria Transcript*, as reprinted in *Chicago Times*, October 30, 1884.

now lies dead, whose hand will never be able to write again, has done more than anyone, than perhaps any other man could do, to bring western journalism, especially that of this city, to the front rank."[111]

On October 30, 1884, Storey was buried in "HIS LONG HOME" at Rosehill cemetery. An Episcopal service was read at his home prior to the interment, while "the hand which once wielded a pen which was a terror to the enemies of justice lay like a sculptured marble on the pulseless breast, its life work done."[112] On March 3, 1895, the *Chicago Times* died, never to be resurrected. Eleven years after its moving spirit was gone, the huge plant stood "old and battered, but still the most commodious and convenient newspaper building, empty and dreary on its bustling corner, a dumb memorial to Wilbur F. Storey and a melancholy spectacle to the newspapermen of Chicago."[113]

Ironically, Storey would not have disapproved such a memorial. In a prophetic burst of egotism in 1876 he stated to Franc Wilkie, "I don't wish to perpetuate my newspaper. *I am the paper*! I wish it to die with me so that the world may know I was the *Times*!"[114]

111. Professor Rodney Welch, "Memorial Tribute to Wilbur F. Storey," delivered to the Chicago Press Club, October 29, 1884, as reported in *Chicago Times*, October 30, 1884.

112. "His Long Home," *Chicago Times*, October 31, 1884.

113. J. W. Abbot, "Chicago Newspapers and Their Makers," *Review of Reviews*, XI (June, 1895), 650.

114. Wilkie, p. 272.

CHAPTER X

EPILOGUE: Bring Me the Morning Paper!

IN AUGUST, 1854, WILBUR F. STOREY WROTE AN ESSAY ABOUT MORNING newspapers for the *Detroit Free Press.* It captured, better than anything else the editor wrote, the dual spirit of his career as a journalist. On the one hand, it indicated a passionate attachment to his profession coupled with a keen awareness of exactly what it took "to get up a good newspaper." On the other hand, it also showed an open contempt for the reading public that his life of rigorous toil served.

> "Bring me the morning paper!" How many tonuges called for it—how many eyes read it—how many men laud it—how many damn it? From all the breakfast tables at all the hotels, in all the cities, morning after morning, ever and ever goeth out the order, and ascendeth the cry, "Bring me the morning paper!" Old and young, ugliness and beauty, avarice and prodigality, alike bend over the morning paper.
>
> The greasy old gentleman, with rubescent nasal appendage, pendulous double chin, and prodigious ponderosity of bowels, puts on his glasses, sips his coffee, and phlegmatically rolls himself through the entire contents of the morning paper. Slowly he reads on—that great lazy piece of unsurprisability. "Shocking accidents," "dreadful calamities,"

"horrid catastrophes," "outrageous villainies," he views without one wink of wonder, not one long breath of astonishment. And then he comes to the place where he ought to laugh, right where some poor, worn out "item's man" had been as funny as he could, and pursued his wit under difficulties; but his big, blank, beef face doesn't change a bit; and he looks "over the leader," and the face is the same. What are dreadful accidents, murders and catastrophes to him? Why, they are nothing more than he expected—nothing more than *some newspaper* ought to furnish for his gratification, even if the editorial force had to turn out and kill a few themselves, just to make the paper interesting. How could he eat without his paper? And what would his paper be without a few murders for relishes? What is wit to such superb stupidity? Try to vivify such stolid features into a smile with a pungent pun or a jolly joke? Why you might as well try to stir up the laughter of a rhinocerous, by tickling his pachydermatous majesty under the seventh rib with a goose quill. And as for the "leaders," they are very often beyond endurance and above comprehension—that we'll admit—to all such.

But the gouty fat man is not the only "object of interest" who calls for the morning paper; for we hear at the same table, the faint, feeble voice of dandyism, affecting inquiry after truth, saying "watah, bwing me the mohning papah!" And then you will see a pair of gold quizzicals soar away over a pair of mustaches, and finally light astride of a delicately dyed nose, before a couple of empty looking optics, which seek to learn what the "ahmusements" promise for the night.

And so it goes—"that morning paper"—the world around, flying over railroads, crossing over oceans, and traversing continents. Everybody calls for it, everybody reads it, and all consider the "morning paper" a necessity, an indispensable article of comfort. But not one in a thousand that pores over its columns, as he pours out his coffee, and in easy dressing gown and slippers, takes his morning meal, gives a single thought to the industry and indefatigability that is, year after year, wearing out its hundreds in telling the news, making that same morning paper.

Reader, when you peruse this, just be kind enough to remember that the morning paper which you so indifferently

> order, is the result of some reasonably hard work. And at night, when you retire, just remember that all over the Union, wherever anyone orders his morning paper, there are lots of pale printers pelting types, into sticks as though their arms and fingers were propelled by the same tireless engine which is running the iron press, and keeping awake and busy the devils and Dutchmen, in the cellars below. So this morning, when you read your paper, think of it as the product of sleepless labor, a great part of which has been performed while you were wrapped in quiet slumber, and pleasantly dreaming. And remember that, although there are thousands of types in a single column, each letter, in taking its place, has caused the movement of an arm and a hand; and that thus, oftimes, thirty arms and their one hundred and fifty fingers have each been flitting thousands and thousands of times from stick to case, from case to stick, during the long night before. Remember, that the same ideas that come to you in type-garb, were, perhaps, born of an aching, throbbing brain, and dressed in language by a tired pen and a weary hand. Remember that your morning paper is to editors and printers, the Eurythmic of this labor age—an age in which the twelve labors of Hercules would be regarded as mere sports or pastimes for the youngest advocates of Young America.[1]

From the morning Storey issued his first number of the *Detroit Free Press*, he dedicated his life to "the reasonably hard work" of putting news and ideas in "type-garb." With fanatical devotion, he immersed himself in the task. Until state rights and Negrophobia became lost causes during the Civil War, his "aching, throbbing brain" stood at the forefront of a self-imposed crusade against what he considered the political extremism of the Republican party. After the war, his entire individuality became absorbed in the task of making the *Chicago Times* a great newspaper. He lived, toiled, thought and wrote with one end in view, the improvement of his beloved *Times*. When the ravages of disease upset his mental balance, he published a more sordid sensationalism that any previous American editor had; but at the same time, he created a great western newspaper. Its scope was as wide as the earth, and its technical execution unexcelled for his day. He controlled each aspect of his enterprise so thoroughly that it was truthfully said "Storey alone is the author of every improvement,

1. *Detroit Free Press*, August 20, 1854.

literary, editorial, and mechanical, which made THE CHICAGO TIMES."[2] Beginning on March 15, 1873, the masthead of each issue of his newspaper read

THE TIMES
by W. F. Storey.

This legend was literally true, and appropriately, it was destined to retain its place of distinction for three and one-half years after the editor's death as, ghostlike, while his mortal remains deteriorated in the grave, W. F. Storey presided in a very personal way over the death agony of his newspaper.

On November 5, 1884, Eureka C. Storey presented the will dated February 1, 1881, to the Cook County Probate Court as the last will and testament of her husband. On the same day, in the same court, Anson L. Storey began a separate proceeding with a petition that alleged that his brother died intestate. Control of almost $2,000,000 was at stake, and in a torturous proceeding which involved two separate appeals to the state supreme court, Eureka Storey eventually lost all control over the disposition of the estate. The litigation lasted until April, 1888, and while it was underway the *Chicago Times* deteriorated from a million dollar property to a drab, pathetic sheet worth only $150,000.

It was a spectacular contest, as both Mrs. Storey and the heirs employed the best legal talent available to argue their respective cases. Chief counsel for the widow was Lyman Trumbull, the former Republican senator, who was recognized as one of Chicago's foremost probate lawyers in the 1880s. The heirs employed Alfred S. Trude and William C. Goudy as chief advocates, while Mary Farrand, in a separate proceeding, hired the services of a relative newcomer to Chicago legal practice by the name of John P. Altgeld.

On November 29, 1884, the 1881 will was refused admission to probate because the testimony of subscribing witnesses convinced the court that Wilbur F. Storey was not of sound mind and memory at the time he signed the writing. Both Eureka Storey and Mary Farrand appealed the decision to the Circuit Court. On November 11, Eureka, convinced that the 1881 will would not be admitted, presented the writing of August 16, 1879, for the court's consideration. Under the terms of both wills Mrs. Storey was appointed sole executrix with authority to manage the estate and continue

2. Obituary of Wilbur F. Storey, *Chicago Herald*, October 28, 1884.

publication of the *Times* until she arranged "an advantageous sale thereof." Storey's blood relatives, therefore, could only gain control of the estate if both wills were nullified.

On December 18, Lyman Trumbull presented a motion for Eureka asking that her appeal of the decision regarding the 1881 will be dismissed. It was a move destined to be of decisive importance, as it would eventually cost Mrs. Storey the entire estate. Trumbull intended, of course, to establish the validity of the 1879 writing since it would be easier to prove Wilbur F. Storey's sanity as of the earlier date. Probate Judge Joshua C. Knickerbocker stunted this strategy, however, when he declared on December 23 that he would not consider the 1879 will until the Circuit Court had ruled on Mary Farrand's appeal.

In the course of this early maneuvering, the business affairs of the *Chicago Times* began to waiver as no one had clear legal right to conduct its affairs. On November 18, at the instigation of Storey's heirs at law, Judge Knickerbocker named Austin L. Patterson administrator. The following day Mrs. Storey appealed the appointment on the grounds that "Patterson is prejudiced against me." On November 29, the court honored Eureka's appeal when it dismissed Patterson and named one Horace A. Hurlbut as receiver with instructions to make no change in the management of the paper without the express order of the court.

In January, 1885, Eureka Storey re-entered the appeal to the Circuit Court regarding the 1881 will with a petition that stated that she, as the executrix in the document under consideration, wished a trial of the matter at the court's earliest convenience. Despite the objections of Mrs. Farrand's attorneys that Mrs. Storey could not control the appeal, Mrs. Storey's motion was allowed, and the trial was set for July 6, 1885. Both sides engaged in various legal maneuvers during the course of the trial, and in each instance the Circuit Court upheld the right of Eureka Storey to conduct the appeal as executrix of the estate and the proponent upon whose petition the will had originally been presented in probate. Towards the end of the trial it became apparent that the Circuit Court would reverse the earlier judgment and admit the will. At this point, on January 29, 1886, John P. Altgeld presented a motion for Mary Farrand that the Farrand appeal be dismissed at her cost. The court overruled the motion, and on February 3 found that the will dated February 1, 1881, was the last will and testament of Wilbur F. Storey.

Besides gaining control of Mary Farrand's appeal in 1885, Eureka Storey also petitioned the state supreme court to grant a writ of *mandamus* that would force Judge Knickerbocker to probate the 1879 will. In the petition, Eureka's counsel argued that Mrs. Farrand was pursuing her appeal in bad faith since her real intent was to establish intestacy. The high court, on September 23, 1885, denied the *mandamus* on the grounds that Mrs. Farrand was only exercising her legal right in taking an appeal "and her motive in so doing seems hardly inquirable into."

Throughout 1885, "THE TIMES by W. F. Storey" faltered.

When the Cook County Circuit Court admitted the 1881 will to probate, Anson L. Storey appealed the decision to the First District Appellate Court where, in June, 1886, the judgment of the circuit court was affirmed. Mary Farrand and Anson Storey then made a final appeal to the state supreme court. The latter heard the appeal on March 22, 1887.

John P. Altgeld represented Mrs. Farrand. He argued that Eureka Storey, when she dismissed her appeal from the final order of the Probate Court, lost all standing in the Circuit Court as an appellant or proponent of the will, because the only appeal pending was that of Mary Farrand, who alone had the right to conduct her own appeal. Lyman Trumbull and Wirt Dexter, for Mrs. Storey, argued that on appeal, as in original probate, only the person named as executrix in the writing under consideration was a legal proponent of a will, with the right to conduct the trial. In addition, Trumbull and Dexter claimed it would be an injustice to permit Mrs. Farrand to withdraw her appeal from the Circuit Court after Mrs. Storey had borne the expense and produced evidence that established the validity of the 1881 writing. Such an action, said Trumbull, "would forever defeat the probate of this will and the intention of the testator."

The Illinois Supreme Court decided for Mary Farrand on the grounds that an appellant on appeal may, at any time before judgment, dismiss his appeal, and may do so over the objection of an adversary. To the argument that its decision would forever defeat the probate of a will the validity of which had already been upheld by the Circuit and Appellate Courts, the Supreme Court replied "if such would be the legal consequences, it does not lie in the mouth of Mrs. Storey to complain." The judgment explained that both Mrs. Storey and Mrs. Farrand had the undoubted right to appeal from the decision which originally denied the probate of the 1881 will. This right Mrs. Storey had understood and exercised. The same law likewise gave her the undoubted right to dismiss her appeal, and thereby, "so far as she was concerned, leave in full force the judgment of the probate court." This right also Mrs. Storey had understood and exercised. It was unfortunate for Mrs. Storey that by dismissing her appeal she had "put it in the power of Mrs. Farrand to exercise the same right under the law," but with consequences unfavorable to the widow. But, the court concluded, "we are unable to perceive upon what principle this court . . . can be asked to declare one rule for Mrs. Storey and another for Mrs. Farrand, in the same cause and in respect to the same subject matter." The judgment of both the Appellate and Circuit courts was reversed, and the cause remanded to the Circuit Court with directions to set aside its order probating the 1881 will and sustain the action of Mary Farrand in dismissing her appeal at her costs, as of January 29, 1886.[3] In effect, after thirty months of expensive litigation, the original finding by the Probate Court that Wilbur F. Storey was not of sound mind and memory when he signed the 1881 will was final.

Two and one-half years after his death, the status of the estate of Wilbur F. Storey was exactly where it had been within a month of his demise. But its overall worth had declined considerably as its most valuable component, the *Chicago Times,* continued to falter. Immediately after the Supreme Court judgment, Eureka C. Storey presented the will of August, 1879, for probate. Within a month, it was admitted as the final will and testament of Wilbur F. Storey. Anson L. Storey thereupon appealed the decision to the Circuit Court.

"THE TIMES by W. F. Storey" meanwhile was in serious trouble. With the prospect of still another year of involved litigation, it appeared the newspaper might die completely. Lyman Trumbull, noting that "the Times is running down," attempted to save the property with an invitation to J. Sterling Morton to take over the receivership. If Morton could be persuaded to "take personal charge . . . with the authority to control the establishment in all its departments," Trumbull felt the paper could be revitalized. "By infusing

3. A lengthy summary, with dates, of the various steps in the litigation of the Storey estate is contained in *The people ex rel. Eureka C. Storey* v *Joshua C. Knickerbocker, Probate Judge,* September 23, 1885, *Illinois Reports* (Springfield, 1886), CXIV, 539-50; and *In the matter of probate of the will of Wilbur F. Storey,* March 27, 1887, *Illinois Reports* (Springfield, 1888), CXX, 244-61.

new life . . . and reducing the price under responsible editors, I believe the Times could be made a great success," Trumbull wrote to Morton.[4]

J. Sterling Morton was provisional governor of Nebraska in 1887. He had been a close friend of Wilbur F. Storey since the editor defended young Morton in his argument with university officials at Ann Arbor, Michigan, in 1854. A regular contributor to the *Chicago Times* throughout Storey's years of control, he was even offered a partnership by Storey in the late 1870s. But Morton preferred Nebraska politics to newspaper management, and refused Storey's offer. In 1887, faced with a chance to save the newspaper, he again refused.[5]

In the twelve months between April, 1887 and April, 1888, while the final litigation was heard involving Storey's estate, *The Times* became an almost totally paralyzed enterprise. During the intervening summer, the newspaper nearly escaped Storey's death grasp when Joseph Pulitzer considered buying a controlling interest for $300,000. But Pulitzer's faltering health made him decide against the investment, just as in the previous spring Pulitzer refused a chance to buy a London, England, daily for the same reason. "Obviously," according to W. A. Swanberg, "had his health permitted, [Pulitzer] would have founded a newspaper empire stretching across two continents."[6] Just as obviously, had this been done, the *Chicago Times* would have continued as a leader in midwestern journalism.

In November, 1887, it was established in the Cook County Circuit Court that Wilbur F. Storey had not been of sound mind and memory from at least June, 1878, when he was felled by his first stroke. He therefore died intestate, and his heirs at law were allowed to split what remained of his estate. Eureka C. Storey's motion for an appeal of the decision was denied, and she was forced to settle for $10,000 annually so long as she did not remarry. The property at Vincennes Avenue and Forty-third Street, the residence at 1834 South Prairie Avenue, the newspaper, and the accrued debts were split between Anson L. Storey, Mary Farrand, Edward P. Chapin, and Mary A. Anderson.

But before the heirs could dispose of the *Chicago Times*, one

4. Lyman C. Trumbull to J. Sterling Morton, April 22, 1887, in Sterling Morton papers, Chicago Historical Society.

5. Sterling Morton to Dr. Paul Angle, December 3, 1959, in Sterling Morton papers, Chicago Historical Society.

6. W. A. Swanberg, *Pulitzer* (New York: Charles Scribner's Sons, 1967), p. 158.

final claim against Storey's estate awaited settlement. In December, 1887, Maria Isham Storey filed a bill for dower under the terms of her 1868 divorce settlement. In the trial, Storey's heirs established that since the *Chicago Times* was destroyed by fire in October, 1871, all of the personal property and accumulations left by Storey were acquired by him after his divorce. The Probate Court accepted this reasoning, and in February, 1888, denied Maria Storey any rights of dower in the estate.[7]

On April 18, 1888, the last number of "THE TIMES by W. F. Storey" was published. It was an effeminate, hollow sheet of eight drab, seven-column pages. It was purchased by James J. West for about $150,000, and on April 19, the new management promised readers a speedy return to the heights enjoyed by the paper earlier in the decade. Instead, it continued its downward course, and in 1891, Carter J. Harrison, Sr., purchased the paper.

The elder Harrison intended to be the Democratic candidate for mayor in 1892 in a city without a Democratic newspaper. With John P. Altgeld sitting as governor in Springfield, the party was in need of an organ in the largest city in Illinois. So Harrison paid $265,000 for the property and entrusted his two sons, Carter J. Harrison, Jr., and William P. Harrison with the management on orders to re-establish the *Times* as a Democratic mouthpiece. But a malevolent cloud hovered over the property. In 1892, although Harrison senior won the mayorality, the *Times* lost $165,000. The semi-Populism of the new editors proved unacceptable in the Chicago of the early 1890s, and circulation refused to rise above the 15,000 level. Then, in 1893, Mayor Harrison was assassinated by a deranged political opponent. Although his sons attempted to continue the *Times*, the paper lost an additional $120,000 by 1894. In March, 1895, with the newspaper almost bankrupt, the Harrison brothers sold it to Henry H. Kohlsaat who merged it with his own *Chicago Herald*, and as the *Times-Herald*, it continued a life of sorts until 1901.[8] The last issue as the *Chicago Times* appeared on March 3, 1895. Appropriately, it was a Sunday edition. The following day, all activity in the building on the northwest corner of Washington Street and Fifth Avenue ceased as operations were transferred to the *Herald* office. Wilbur F. Storey's newspaper was no more.[9]

7. *Chicago Times*, February 17, 1888.
8. Carter H. Harrison, *Stormy Years: The Autobiography of Carter Harrison* (Indianapolis: The Bobbs Merrill Co., 1935), pp. 37-60.
9. *Chicago Sunday Times*, March 3, 1895.

The *Times* building stood vacant for several years. Eventually, it was converted into a hotel, and about 1905, it became a general office building. The rear two-thirds of the building, on Washington Street, has been razed. The Wells Street side (formerly Fifth Avenue) still stands. It houses a short-order restaurant, a shoe repair shop, and the offices of the Marian Kane Realty Company, the present owners of the site. All trace that the building once served as the grand entrance to Chicago's foremost daily newspaper has long since disappeared.

Eureka C. Storey died on May 23, 1896. She never remarried, and her remains were interred beside those of her husband at Rosehill cemetery.[10] At the gravesite is Storey's only monument. It is an impressive, thirty-foot cement obelisk, set firmly on a stone table, from whence it reaches majestically skyward. Across the base of the table, sculpted in marble, is the signature "Wilbur F. Storey." There are no dates on the memorial, and no indication that anyone other than the signatory lies at rest underneath. In death, as in life, Wilbur F. Storey stands alone, the sole witness to his own grandeur.

Storey left no descendants. None of his vast correspondence with a host of prominent Americans over a forty year period has come to light. The newspaper he made great followed him to the grave within a dozen years of his own death. James W. Abbot, who was a reporter for the *Times* during its days of glory, stated in 1895 that any who believe a newspaper is greater than its maker "will find a telling argument against their theory in the fact that the greatness of the *Times* began and ended with Storey. Before him, it was nothing. After him, it died."[11]

Today, Storey and his newspapers are all but forgotten. The editor, hated by almost everyone who knew him in life, remains an enigma eighty years after his death. Mort Hopkins, in a memorial address for Storey delivered to the Michigan Press Association in 1889, put it aptly:

> There was a rumor that at an early period of life he belonged to the Methodist Church. If the rumor were true, he must have joined when he was drunk, asleep, or in his rage, or about some act which had no relish of salvation in it, because the man had not the material in him for a Methodist,

10. Obituary of Eureka C. Storey, *Chicago Times-Herald*, May 26, 1896.

11. J. W. Abbot, "Chicago Newspapers and Their Makers," *Review of Reviews*, XI (June, 1895), 650.

nor an atheist, nor an infidel, nor a Christian, nor an agnostic, nor a Democrat, nor a Republican, nor anything but that unique combination of mind and matter which made up Wilbur F. Storey.[12]

12. Mort L. Hopkins, "Reminiscences of Story [*sic*] and the Chicago Times," *Proceedings of the Michigan Press Association* (22nd Annual Meeting, Grand Rapids, July 9-11, 1889), p. 45.

Bibliography

The major sources used in the preparation of this book were the following newspapers:

Chicago Times, June, 1861, through February, 1888.
Chicago Tribune, scattered numbers from June, 1861, through November, 1884.
The Crisis, Columbus, Ohio, January, 1861, through November, 1864.
Detroit Daily Advertiser, July, 1855, through June, 1861.
Detroit Fress Press, February, 1853, through June, 1861.
Detroit Tribune, scattered numbers from February, 1853, through June, 1861.
Goshen (Indiana) *Democrat*, March, 1838, through December, 1840.
Jackson (Michigan) *American Citizen*, October, 1849, through February, 1853.
Jackson (Michigan) *Patriot*, April, 1847, through April, 1849.
South Bend Free Press and St. Joseph County Advertiser, January, 1841, through March, 1842.

In addition to newspapers, the following memoirs and reminiscences by reporters and printers associated with Wilbur F. Storey also served as indispensable sources:

Abbot, J. W. "Chicago Newspapers and Their Makers," *Review of Reviews*, XI (June, 1895), 646-65. Abbot was employed on the *Chicago Times* in the 1870s, and he provided valuable information on Chicago journalists and newspapers for the years that Wilbur F. Storey operated the *Times*.
Cadwallader, Sylvannus. *Three Years With Grant As Recalled by*

War Correspondent Sylvannus Cadwallader, ed. with introduction and notes by Benjamin P. Thomas. New York: Alfred A. Knopf & Co., 1955. Cadwallader was Storey's exclusive correspondent with General Ulysses S. Grant and the Army of the West from October, 1862, until the end of the Civil War. His reminiscences, written in the early 1880s, helped prove how the *Chicago Times* was the foremost newspaper in the United States for news from the Army of the West.

Chamberlin, Everett. *Chicago and Its Suburbs.* Chicago: T. A. Hungerford & Co., 1874. Chamberlin was a feature writer for the *Chicago Times*, and this book grew out of material originally gathered for that newspaper. Included are the author's impressions of Storey as a newspaperman.

Cook, Frederick Francis. *Bygone Days in Chicago, Reflections of the "Garden City" of the Sixties.* Chicago: A. C. McClurg & Co., 1910. Cook was a reporter for almost twenty years on the *Chicago Times*, and his recollections provided valuable information about Storey and the *Times* prior to 1871. Cook's account was especially vital because the author is vociferous in defending Storey as an employer as well as a great newspaperman. The chapter on Wilbur F. Storey was prepared especially to refute the book of *Reminiscences* published by Franc B. Wilkie in 1891. The evidence uncovered by this writer, both in the *Chicago Times* and other sources, tended to substantiate Wilkie rather than Cook. Wilkie's indictment of both Storey and his newspaper is so scathing, however, that it is easy to understand why a man associated with the *Times* for as long a period as Cook was would seek to temper Wilkie with a more favorable apologia.

Diehl, Charles Sanford. *The Staff Correspondent, How the News of the World Is Collected and Dispatched by a Body of Trained Reporters.* San Antonio: Clegg & Co., 1931. Diehl began his journalistic career on the *Chicago Times* in 1871, and he gives Storey credit for training him in the techniques that later proved invaluable when he helped establish the Associated Press.

Drew, John. "Reminiscences of Old Time Printers," *Detroit News-Tribune*, November 7, 1897. Drew was a compositor on the *Detroit Free Press* in the 1850s, and remembered Wilbur F. Storey as a hard-boiled employer, but a first-rate typographer.

Finerty, John F. *War Path and Bivouac or the Conquest of the Sioux.* Chicago: Unity Building Press, 1890. Finerty, one of the foremost correspondents during the Plains' Indian wars of the 1870s, was exclusive correspondent for the *Chicago Times.* This account of his adventures, drawn largely from the dispatches he sent to the *Times*, not only makes exciting reading but also illustrates the enterprise that made the *Times* the most widely read newspaper in the Middle West in the 1870s.

Ham, Moses. *Recollections,* as reprinted in James E. Scripps, "Wilbur F. Storey—Detroit's First Great Journalist—Some Recollections of a Very Remarkable Man," *Detroit Sunday News-Tribune*, September 16, 1900. Ham's *Recollections* constitute the only extensive memoir written by a close Detroit associate of Storey. Ham joined the *Free Press* as a commercial reporter and editorial writer in 1853, and he remained on the staff until 1861. He then moved to Dubuque, Iowa, and in 1863 he became owner and editor of the *Dubuque Herald.*

Hopkins, Mort L. "Reminiscences of Story [*sic*] and the Chicago Times," *Proceedings of the Michigan Press Association* (22nd Annual Meeting, Grand Rapids, July 9-11, 1889), pp. 41-46. Hopkins joined Storey as a reporter for the *Detroit Free Press* in 1859, and remained closely associated with the editor until the late 1870s. His reminiscence, although only five pages in length, is one of the most valuable insights into the character and personality of Wilbur F. Storey to be found.

Hugunin, Henry M. "The Late Wilbur Fisk Storey and his Chicago Times," *Autograph Letter Book,* LXVI, 181-84. Unpublished MSS in Chicago Historical Society. Hugunin was a reporter for the *Times* from about 1872 until after Storey's death.

Quinby, William E. "Reminiscences of Michigan Journalism," *Michigan Pioneer and Historical Collections,* XXX (Lansing, 1906), 507-17. Quinby joined the *Free Press* in 1859 as a legal reporter, and in 1860 became Washington correspondent for the paper. In the 1870s he became sole proprietor, and under his direction it maintained its position as dominant newspaper in the city. His "Reminiscences" were useful for information of Detroit journalists of the 1850s.

Scripps, James E. "Wilbur F. Storey—Detroit's First Great Journalist—Some Recollections of a Very Remarkable Man," *Detroit Sunday News-Tribune,* September 16, 1900. The author, an older brother of the famous E. W. Scripps, began a half-century association with Detroit journalism in 1859 when he joined the staff of the *Detroit Daily Advertiser.* His "Recollections" of Storey were rich in anecdotal material, and Scripps concluded that it was Storey's eight years of toil with the *Free Press,* more than any other single factor, that brought Detroit journalism to maturity.

———————. "Some Other Old Time Journalists," *Detroit Sunday News-Tribune*, September 23, 1900. Scripps' reminiscences of other Detroit editors of the 1850s were particularly valuable for their sketches of Joseph Warren, editor of the *Detroit Tribune* from 1852 to 1856, and Rufus J. Hosmer, corpulent chieftain of the *Detroit Daily Advertiser*, and Storey's number one rival in Detroit.

Seitz, John H. "Interesting Story of An Early Strike—The Peculiarities of An Old Time Editor," *Detroit Journal,* March 10, 1902. Seitz was the founder of the Detroit Typographical Union, and a compositor on the *Free Press* in the 1850s. He told of how the Detroit Union was founded as a result of dissatisfaction with wages and conditions when Storey inaugurated the *Sunday Free Press* in October, 1853.

Stocking, William. "Prominent Newspaper Men in Michigan," *Michigan Pioneer and Historical Collections*, XXXIX (Lansing, 1915), 155-73. Stocking's memoir is filled with information on Storey, Joseph Warren, Rufus J. Hosmer, and especially the Reverend Warren P. Isham, the first father-in-law of Storey and a renowned journalist in his own right.

Tiller, James A. "More About Storey," *Detroit Sunday News-Tribune*, September 23, 1900. Tiller was a *Free Press* compositor in the 1850s, and his remarks offered insight to Storey as a typographer and employer.

White, Arthur Scott. Letter to the Editor, *Michigan History*, XI (January, 1927), 145-47. White joined the *Chicago Times* as a compositor in 1862 and remained with the paper throughout most of Storey's Chicago years. His letter substantiated the details on the school for female typographers that Storey established in 1864 in order to beat the Chicago Typographical Union.

Wilkie, Franc B. *Pen and Powder*. Boston: Little, Brown & Co., 1888. Wilkie's account of his activities as Civil War correspondent in the West for the *New York Times*, and after September, 1863, the *Chicago Times*.

——————. *Personal Reminiscences of Thirty-five Years of Journalism*. Chicago: F. J. Schulte & Co., 1891. Franc B. Wilkie was the closest and most trusted associate of Storey for the last twenty years of the editor's life. He knew Storey better, probably, than any other man ever succeeded in knowing him, and his book devotes almost 200 pages to Storey and the *Times*. The reporter obviously hated his employer, and this reminiscence is written with unrestrained venom. But Wilkie proved absolutely reliable with respect to facts, as without exception this writer found his claims substantiated in the columns of the *Chicago Times*.

Unpublished manuscripts, collections of private papers, and miscellaneous items which proved useful included:

Banta, Richard E. "Senator Ed Hannegan." Unpublished MSS, Wabash College Library, Crawfordsville, Indiana. Hannegan was the first partner of Storey in the newspaper business, since the two joined together to begin the *La Porte Herald* in March, 1838. No accounts of Hannegan's colorful career as Congressman and Senator from Indiana between 1832 and 1848 have been published.

Boyd, Joseph (compiler). "Scrapbook of Illinois and Chicago Politics, 1876." Chicago Historical Society. Boyd's scrapbook was especially useful for its material regarding Storey's break with the Democratic party in the election of 1876.

"General Burnside's Order No. 84, Suppressing the Chicago Times." Chicago: the Chicago Times, 1864. Pamphlet in the Chicago Historical Society.

Clarence M. Burton papers in the Burton Historical Collection, Detroit Public Library. Burton made an extensive effort in the 1920s to trace down materials on Storey, and the Storey file in his private papers provided valuable leads on sources for various aspects of the editor's career.

George B. Catlin papers in the Burton Historical Collection, Detroit Public Library. Catlin is the only student to have attempted a study of Storey's career with the *Detroit Free Press*. His papers contain two unpublished manuscripts on Storey and several notes dealing with Storey's years in Michigan.

Sterling Morton collection, Chicago Historical Society. Sterling Morton's father, J. Sterling Morton, was a life-long friend of Storey, and this collection includes letters dealing with the attempt to get the elder Morton to take over the *Chicago Times* after Storey's death.

Salkeld, E. W. "The Story [*sic*] Family in Vermont." Unpublished MSS in the Vermont Historical Society Library, Montpelier.

[Storey, Wilbur F.] "The Suppression of the Chicago Times." Chicago: the Chicago Times, 1863. Pamphlet in the Chicago Historical Society. Storey published this thirty-two page reprint of "pertinent material" from the columns of the *Times* in July, 1863.

Henry N. Walker papers in the Burton Historical Collection, Detroit Public Library. Walker purchased the *Free Press* from Storey on June 4, 1861, and the "Free Press materials" folder in the Walker papers contains full details of the transaction.

Public documents and records that were useful included:

Brainard, Homer Worthington (compiler). *A Survey of the Ishams in England and America, Eight Hundred and Fifty Years of History and Genealogy.* Rutland, Vermont: the Tuttle Co., 1938. This volume was indispensable for the genealogy of the family of Maria Parsons Isham, first wife of Wilbur F. Storey.

Goudy, William C. "Brief for an Appeal from the Superior Court of Cook County." *Wilbur F. Storey* v *Alice A. Early*, Supreme Court of Illinois, Northern Grand Division, September Term, 1875. Illinois State Historical Library, Springfield.

Journal of the Constitutional Convention of the State of Michigan, 1850. Lansing: R. W. Ingalls, 1850.

Pettengill's Newspaper Directory and Advertiser's Handbook. New York: S. M. Pettengill & Co., 1878.

Report of the Proceedings and Debates of the Convention to Revise the Constitution of the State of Michigan. Lansing: R. W. Ingalls, 1850.

Reports of Cases At Law and in Chancery, Argued and Determined in the Supreme Court of Illinois (*Illinois Reports*). Springfield,

LX, *Wilbur F. Storey et al.* v *Mary Wallace*, 51-58; LXXIX, *Wilbur F. Storey* v *the People of the State of Illinois*, 45-53; LXXXVI, *Wilbur F. Storey* v *Alice A. Early*, 461-67; CXIV, *Eureka C. Storey* v *Joshua C. Knickerbocker, Probate Judge*, 539-50; CXX, *In the matter of probate of the Will of Wilbur F. Storey*, 244-61.

A Stranger's Guide to the Garden City: Chicago Illustrated and Descriptive, The City As It Appears in 1883. Chicago: C. D. Relyea & Co., 1883. This booklet, a city guide provided by Chicago hotels to visitors in 1883, contains the most graphic description of the *Chicago Times* in its prime to be found.

The War of the Rebellion. A Compilation of the Official Records of the Union and Confederate Armies. 128 vols. Washington: the Government Printing Office, 1880-1901.

The following state, county, municipal or organizational histories supplied elementary information about newspapers, politics, and prominent persons connected with Wilbur F. Storey:

Andreas, Alfred T. *History of Chicago From the Earliest Period to the Present Times.* 3 vols. Chicago: A. T. Andreas & Co., 1886.

Bennett, F. C. (compiler). *History of the Press Club of Chicago . . . From January, 1880, to September, 1888.* Chicago: H. O. Shepard & Co., 1888.

Burton, Clarence M. and Agnes. *History of Wayne County and the City of Detroit, Michigan.* 4 vols. Detroit: S. J. Clarke & Co., 1930.

Catlin, George B. *The Story of Detroit.* Detroit: The Detroit News, 1923.

Daniels, Rev. E. D. *A Twentieth Century History and Biographical Record of La Porte County, Indiana.* Chicago: Lewis Publishing Co., 1904. The study of the La Porte career of Storey would have been considerably more restricted without Daniels' volume, since Daniels made extensive use of the *La Porte Herald*, and no known copies of the Herald are extant.

Farmer, Silas. *The History of Detroit and Michigan or the Metropolis Illustrated . . .* 2 vols. Detroit: Silas Farmer & Co., 1889.

Howard, Edward Timothy. *A History of St. Joseph County, Indiana.* 2 vols. Chicago: Lewis Publishing Co., 1907. Howard treated the life and career of South Bend pioneer Horatio Chapin, brother-in-law of Wilbur F. Storey.

History of La Porte County, Indiana, Together With Sketches of Its Cities, Villages, Townships, Educational, Religious, Civil, Military and Political History. Chicago: Charles C. Chapman & Co., 1880. Compiled by the Chapman Co. as a volume in its series of midwestern county histories, this volume made use of the *La Porte Herald* in its treatment of the years 1838 to 1842.

Moses, John, and Joseph Kirkland. *Aboriginal to Metropolitan, A*

History of Chicago, Illinois. 2 vols. Chicago: privately published, 1895.

Oglesbee, Rollo B., and Albert Hale. *History of Michigan City, Indiana.* La Porte: Edward J. Widdell & Co., 1908.

Packard, Jasper. *The History of La Porte County, Indiana* . . . . La Porte: S. E. Taylor & Co., 1876. Packard's work was especially useful because he devoted special attention to early La Porte newspapers, and his volume reproduces several entire editorials from the *Herald* that were written by Storey.

Pierce, Bessie Louise. *A History of Chicago.* 3 vols. New York: Alfred A. Knopf, 1937 to 1950. Pierce's volumes constitute the definitive history of Chicago, and it is impossible to work on any topic dealing with nineteenth-century Chicago history without consulting this work.

Seeger, Eugene. *Chicago, The Wonder City.* Chicago: George Gregory Printing Co., 1893.

Stoll, John B. *An Account of St. Joseph County from Its Organization.* (*History of Indiana from Its Exploration to 1922*, ed. Logan Esarey, Vol. III.) Dayton, Ohio: Dayton Historical Publishing Co., 1923.

White, H. A. *A History of Rutland County, Vermont.* Rutland: privately published, 1889. This work contains valuable genealogical information on the Storey family in Vermont.

Articles that treated Storey's career, Michigan and Illinois history, and developments in nineteenth-century American journalism, included:

Babcock, Havilah. "The Press and the Civil War," *Journalism Quarterly,* VI (March, 1929), 1-6.

Bowen, N. H. "A Fighting Detroit Editor of Seventy-five Years Ago: The Career of Wilbur F. Storey Who Made the Free Press Famous," *Detroit Saturday Night,* May 5, 1928, Sec. 2, p. 1.

Catlin, George B. "Little Journeys in Journalism—Wilbur F. Storey," *Michigan History,* X (October, 1926), 515-33. This article is the only source that has been published dealing extensively with Storey's career in Jackson and Detroit, Michigan. While the treatment is popular, and lacks documentation, it does contain vaulable information on Storey's activities before he moved to Chicago in 1861.

Ellis, E. W. "The Chicago *Times* During the Civil War," *Illinois State Historical Society Transactions for the Year 1932* (Springfield, 1933), pp. 136-81. Mrs. Ellis attempted a thorough analysis of Storey's newspaper for the Civil War years. She wrote without knowledge of his earlier career in Detroit and his subsequent career in Chicago, however, and hence the article lacks sure characterization and exaggerates Storey's motives. There is also an undue emphasis on economic motivation as the sole determinant of Storey's conduct during the war.

Ferry, William M. "Ottawa's Old Settlers," *Michigan Pioneer and Historical Collections*, XXX (Lansing, 1906), 572-82.
Fitch, Rev. W. "Reminiscences of Detroit," *Michigan Pioneer and Historical Collections*, V (Lansing, 1884), 541-42.
Gertz, Elmer. "Charles A. Dana and the Chicago Republican," *Journal of the Illinois State Historical Society*, XIV (Springfield, 1952), 124-35.
Holmes, J. C. "A Sketch of the Michigan Farmer," *Michigan Pioneer and Historical Collections*, VII (Lansing, 1886), 98-103.
Klement, Frank L. "Midwestern Opposition to Lincoln's Emancipation Policy," *Journal of Negro History*, XLIX (July, 1964), 169-83.
Lindsey, David. "Clement L. Vallandigham: Traitor or Martyr?" *Tradition, The Magazine of America's Past*, III (November, 1960), 45-51. Although written for popular consumption, Lindsey's knowledge of Civil War era Ohio politics is thorough, and his treatment of the arrest, trial and banishment of Vallandigham is well documented.
Malin, James. "Three Kansas Democrats in the Civil War," in *On the Nature of History: Essays About History and Dissidence*. Ann Arbor: J. W. Edwards, Inc., 1954, pp. 207-26. One of the three Malin considers is Samuel Medary, who resigned as Territorial Governor of Kansas in December, 1860, to return to his home in Columbus, Ohio, where he founded the weekly *Crisis*, a newspaper that he made one of the leading Copperhead organs of the area.
Perry, Charles M. "The Newspaper Attack on President Tappan," *Michigan History*, X (October, 1926), 497-514. Perry's article is a detailed analysis of the campaign that Storey led against Henry J. Tappan, President of the University of Michigan.
Sanger, Donald B. "The Chicago *Times* and the Civil War," *Mississippi Valley Historical Review*, XVII (March, 1931), 557-80. Sanger's article is the most detailed study of the Civil War *Chicago Times* yet published. Its major weakness is that it lacks the perspective that a study of Storey's entire career gives. The article was useful, however, for its extensive treatment of the relationship between Storey and the activities of secret societies such as the Knights of the Golden Circle and the Sons of Liberty.
Schlesinger, Arthur M., Jr. "The Causes of the Civil War: A Note on Historical Sentimentalism," *Partisan Review*, XVI (October, 1949), 968-81.
Skidmore, Joe. "The Copperhead Press and the Civil War," *Journalism Quarterly*, XVI (December, 1939), 345-55.
Snively, Ethan A. "James M. Davidson, 1828-94," *Journal of the Illinois State Historical Society*, IX (Springfield, 1916), 184-94.
"Wilbur F. Storey," in *Biographical Sketches of the Leading Men of Chicago*. Chicago: Wilson and St. Clair, Inc., 1868, pp. 133-40.
"Wilbur F. Storey," in David Ward Wood, ed. *Chicago and Its Dis-*

tinguished Citizens: The Progress of Fifty Years. Chicago: Milton George Co., 1881, pp. 297-99.

"Wilbur F. Storey," in Vol. II, *Encyclopedia of Biography of Illinois.* 2 vols. Chicago: Century Publishing and Engraving Co., 1894, pp. 121-25.

Finally, in addition to numerous general books on nineteenth-century American history, the following volumes dealing with contemporaries of Storey, journalistic history, or specialized aspects of the Civil War, were used:

Andrews, J. Cutler. *The North Reports the Civil War.* Pittsburgh: University of Pittsburgh Press, 1955. This volume is by far the most comprehensive study of Civil War newspaper reporters. It is extensively documented, well organized, and an indispensable guide for any student of journalism for the war period.

Basler, Roy P., ed. *The Collected Works of Abraham Lincoln.* 9 vols. New Brunswick: Rutgers University Press, 1953.

Billington, Ray Allen. *The Protestant Crusade, 1800-1860: A Study of the Origins of American Nativism.* New York: Rinehart & Co., 1952.

Buley, R. Carlyle. *The Old Northwest, Pioneer Period, 1815 to 1840.* 2 vols. Bloomington: Indiana University Press, 1950.

Carlson, Oliver. *The Man Who Made News: James Gordon Bennett.* New York: Duell, Sloan and Pearce, 1942. The best biography of the elder Bennett, this book was particularly useful for its careful study of Bennett's pioneer work in sensational journalism with the *New York Herald* in the spring of 1836. At that time, the sixteen-year-old Storey was a journeyman apprentice on the New York *Journal of Commerce.*

Cromie, Robert. *The Great Chicago Fire.* New York: McGraw, Hill & Co., 1958. This is the most readable account of "the terrible conflagration" of October 8, 1871. The book is lively, well documented, and includes details of the fire's effects on the *Chicago Times.*

Crozier, Emmett. *Yankee Reporters, 1861-1865.* New York: Oxford University Press, 1956.

Fehrenbacher, Don E. *Chicago Giant, A Biography of "Long John" Wentworth.* Madison, Wisconsin: The State Historical Society Press, 1957. Wentworth was a pioneer of Chicago journalism, a Democrat who turned Republican by 1860, and an implacable foe of Storey.

Gray, Wood. *The Hidden Civil War, The Story of the Copperheads.* New York: The Viking Press, 1942. Gray was harsh on the Copperhead movement, and concluded it constituted a real internal threat to the survival of the United States government during the Civil War. Almost everyone in the North who opposed the Republican party and Abraham Lincoln is included in Gray's indictment, and it should be remembered that the book was published in 1942, within a few months after American entry into World War II.

Harrison, Carter H., Jr. *Stormy Years, the Autobiography of Carter H. Harrison.* Indianapolis: Bobbs, Merrill & Co., 1935. Harrison, Jr., was the last owner and editor of the *Chicago Times* from 1891 to 1895, and he includes a chapter on the newspaper's last years.

Harper, Robert S. *Lincoln and the Press.* New York: McGraw, Hill & Co., 1951. A good, concise study of the newspaper treatment of Abraham Lincoln.

Horan, James D. *Confederate Agent, A Discovery in History.* New York: Crown Publishers, Inc., 1954. Horan sees Civil War Copperheads as precursors of midwestern isolationism and the various native, white, Protestant supremacy movements. He offers little evidence to substantiate his elaborate claims.

Hudson, Frederic. *Journalism in the United States from 1600 to 1872.* New York: Harper Brothers, 1872. One of the first attempts at a comprehensive history of American journalism, Hudson's book was particularly useful for this study because he reproduced much of the documentary material concerning the battle between Storey and the Lydia Thompson Burlesque Troupe.

Hutchinson, William T. *Cyrus Hall McCormick.* 2 vols. New York: Appleton, Century Co., 1930-1935. Storey purchased the *Chicago Times* from Cyrus McCormick in June, 1861, and Hutchinson offers the pertinent details of the transaction.

Johannsen, Robert W., ed. *The Lincoln-Douglas Debates of 1858.* New York: Oxford University Press, 1965.

Kinsley, Philip. *The Chicago Tribune: Its First Hundred Years.* 2 vols. Chicago: The Chicago Tribune, 1943-1945. The only attempt at a comprehensive study of the *Tribune*, Kinsley's volumes are exceptionally poor. They read as an almost random pasting together of clippings from the newspaper's columns. The selections show no understanding of possible significance or importance, and the work is useful only insofar as it enables a researcher to approximate where he is likely to find material in the newspaper.

Klement, Frank L. *The Copperheads in the Middle West.* Chicago: University of Chicago Press, 1960. This recent study of the Copperhead movement is the most dispassionate account available.

Knight, Oliver. *Following the Indian Wars.* Norman: University of Oklahoma Press, 1959. The definitive story of the newspaper reporters who covered the last stand of the American Indians between 1865 and 1890.

Lader, Lawrence. *The Bold Brahmins: New England's War Against Slavery, 1831-1863.* New York: E. P. Dutton & Co., 1961.

Lindsey, David. *"Sunset" Cox: Irrepressible Democrat.* Detroit: Wayne State University Press, 1959. Cox was a leading figure in Democratic politics, first in Ohio, and later in New York, from the mid-1850s until 1890. His career is almost contemporary to that of Storey's, and Lindsey's book proves that Storey was far from alone among northern Democrats in the ideas that the editor propagated.

Milton, George F. *Abraham Lincoln and the Fifth Column.* New York: The Vanguard Press, 1942. Milton is the worst of all offenders in his indiscriminate, unsubstantiated charges against those whom he decided to classify as Copperheads. Of Storey, for example, Milton concludes he must have been engaged in secret, treasonable activities, although Milton admits he could find no evidence to prove such conjecture. It is difficult to read Milton's book and not conclude that it was written in the heat of wartime hysteria in 1942, just as the United States entered World War II.

Monaghan, Jay. *The Great Rascal, The Life and Adventures of Ned Buntline.* Boston: Little, Brown & Co., 1952.

Mott, Frank Luther. *American Journalism: A History, 1690 to 1960.* New York: Macmillan & Co., 1962. This is without doubt the finest one-volume history of American journalism.

Nichols, Roy Franklin. *The Disruption of American Democracy.* New York: Macmillan & Co., 1948.

O'Connor, Richard. *The Scandalous Mr. Bennett.* New York: Doubleday & Co., 1962.

Olson, James C. *J. Sterling Morton.* Lincoln: University of Nebraska Press, 1942.

Rice, Madeleine H. *American Catholic Opinion in the Slavery Controversy.* New York: Columbia University Press, 1944.

Sandburg, Carl. *Abraham Lincoln.* 6 vols. New York: Harcourt, Brace & Co., 1939. The most widely read of Lincoln biographies, this remains the most readable account of the life of the sixteenth President.

Sherwin, Oscar. *Prophet of Liberty, The Life and Times of Wendell Phillips.* New York: Bookman Associates, 1958.

Starr, Louis M. *Bohemian Brigade, Civil War Newsmen in Action.* New York: Collier Press, 1954.

Staudenraus, P. J. *The African Colonization Movement, 1816-1865.* New York: Columbia University Press, 1961.

Stidger, Felix G. *Treason History of the Order of the Sons of Liberty.* Chicago: A. C. McClurg Co., 1903.

Swanburg, A. W. *Pultizer.* New York: Charles Scribners, 1967.

Williams, T. Harry. *Lincoln and the Radicals.* Madison: University of Wisconsin Press, 1941. Still the best study of Republican opposition to Abraham Lincoln.

Index

D

M

N

O

P